FAIRY TAIL
100 YEARS QUEST

6

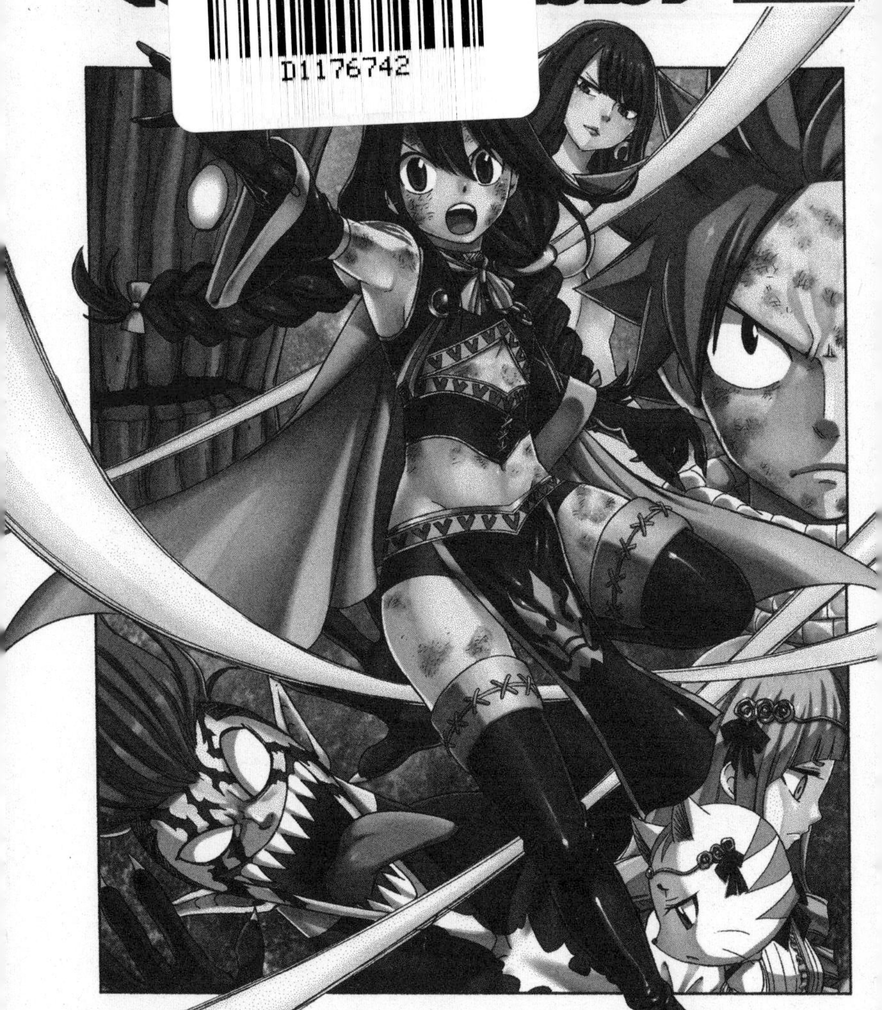

HIRO MASHIMA ATSUO UEDA

CONTENTS

FAIRY TAIL 6
100 YEARS QUEST

CONTENTS

FAIRY TAIL 100 YEARS QUEST

Chapter 46: White Will

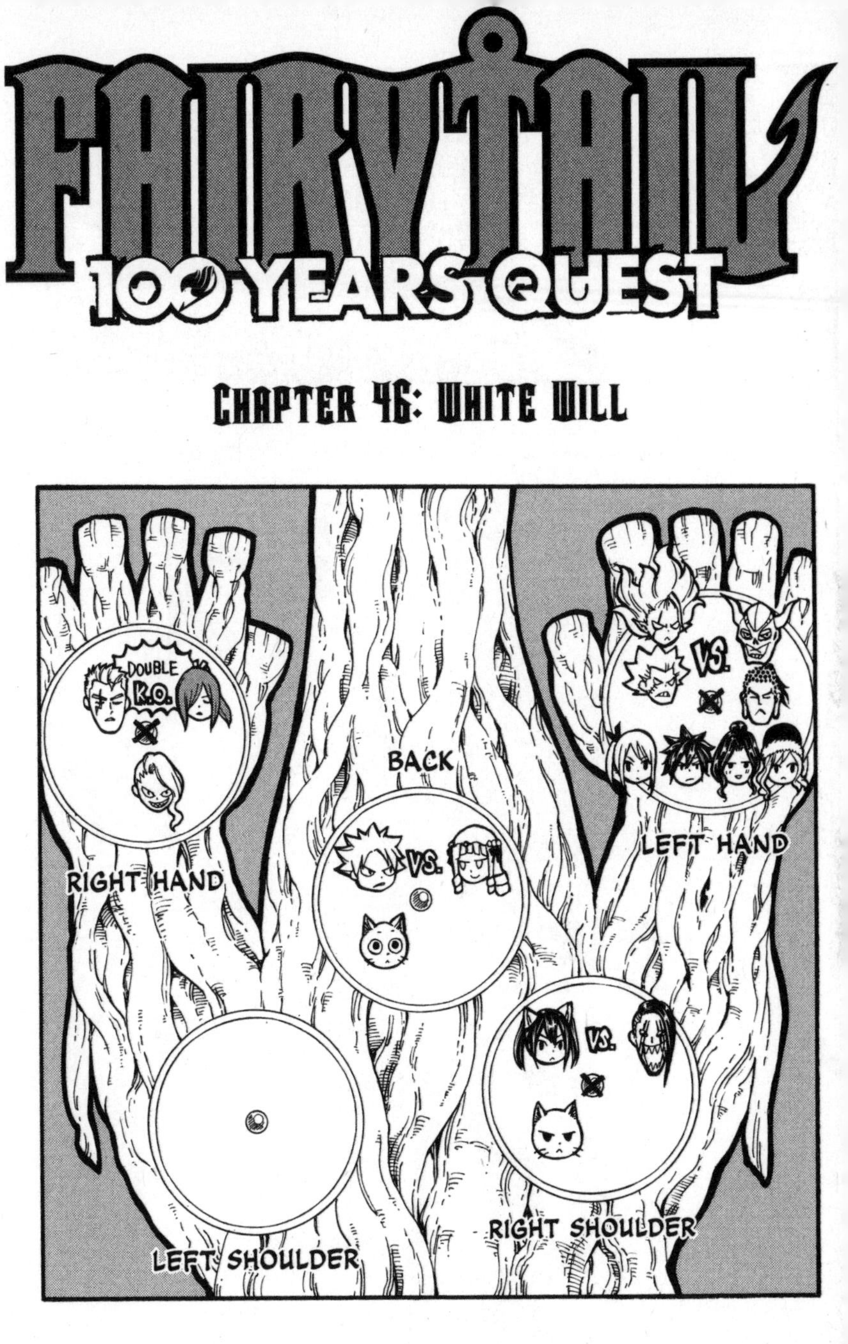
VS.
LEFT HAND
BACK
VS.
DOUBLE K.O.
RIGHT HAND
VS.
RIGHT SHOULDER
LEFT SHOULDER

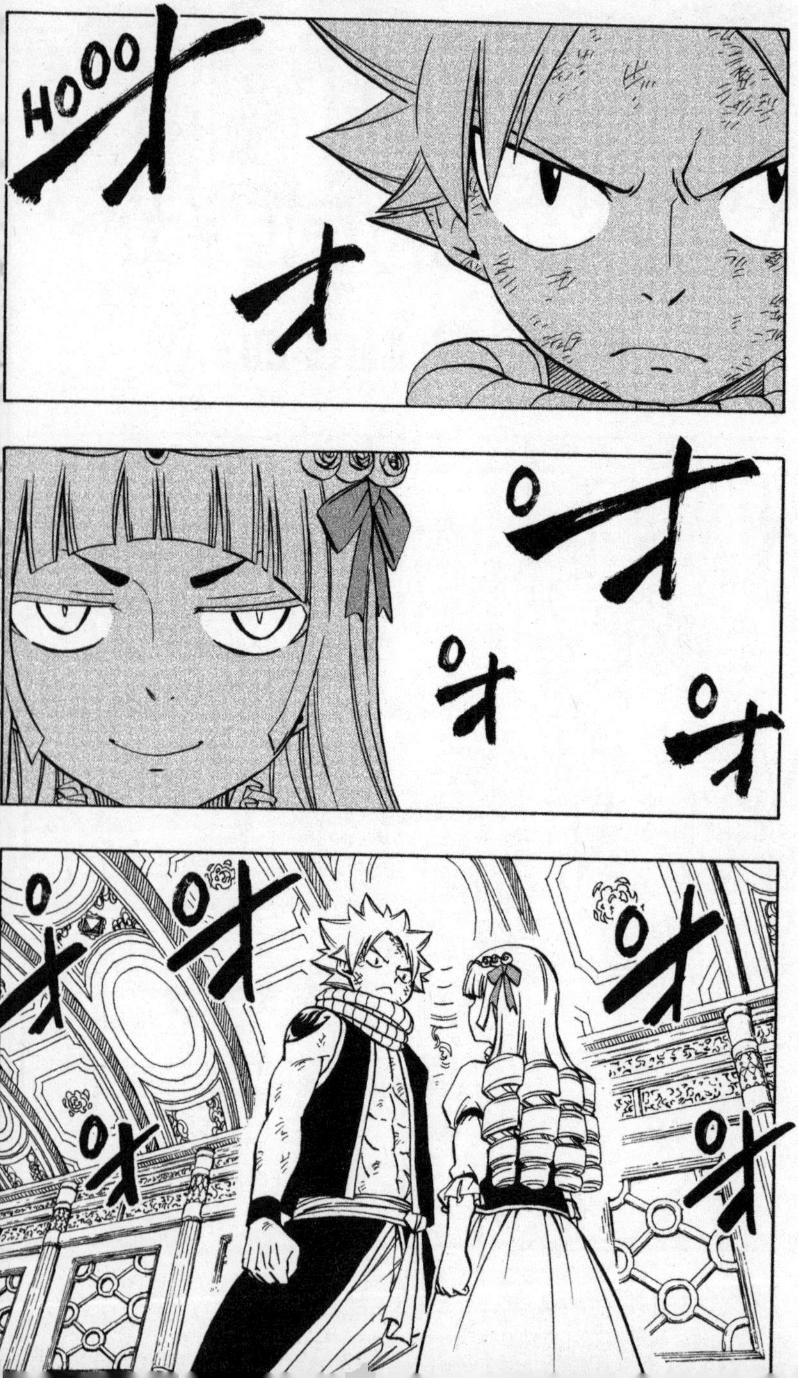
HOOO

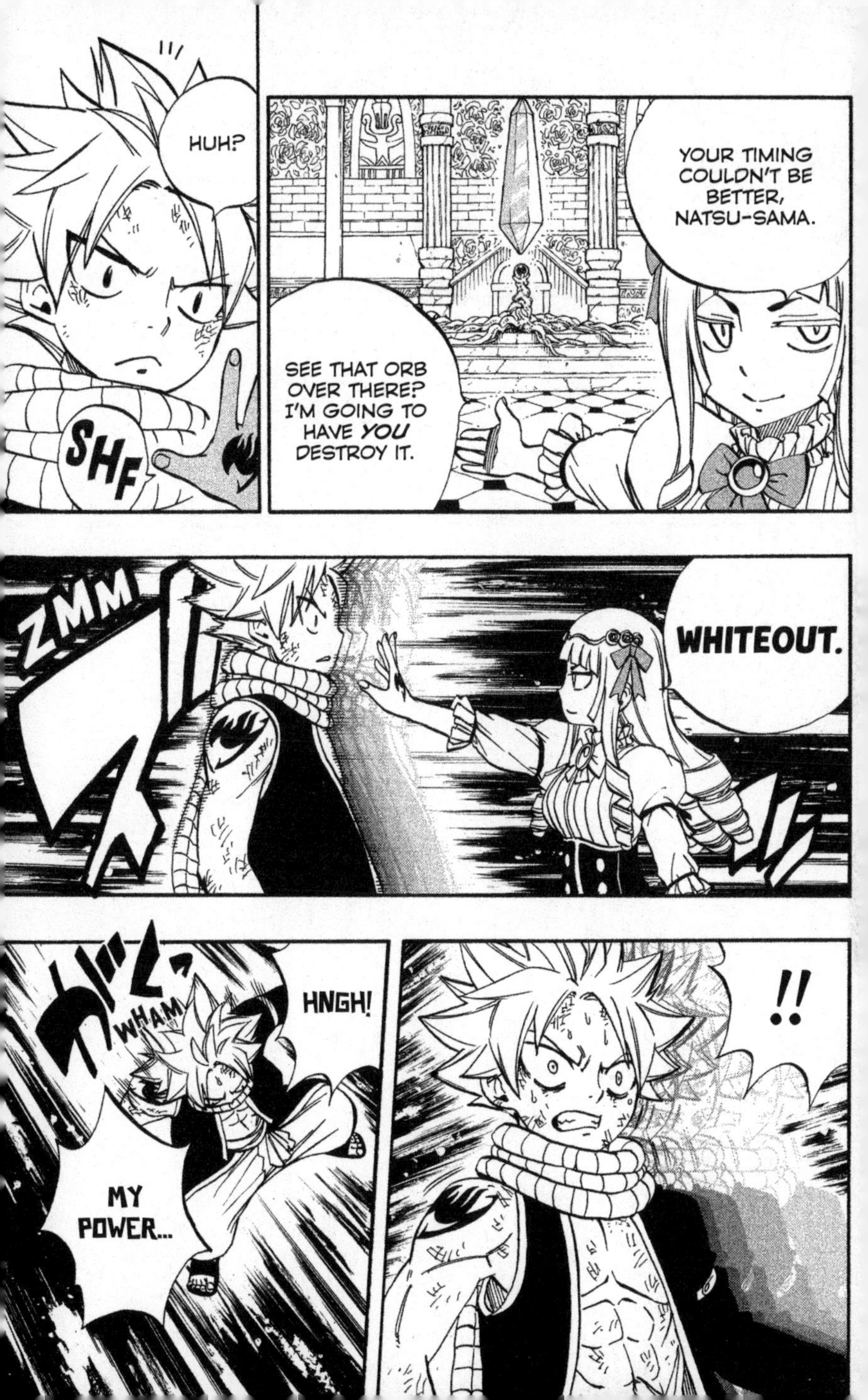
YOUR TIMING COULDN'T BE BETTER, NATSU-SAMA.
SEE THAT ORB OVER THERE? I'M GOING TO HAVE *YOU* DESTROY IT.
HUH?
SHF
WHITEOUT.
ZMM
!!
HNGH!
WHAM
MY POWER...

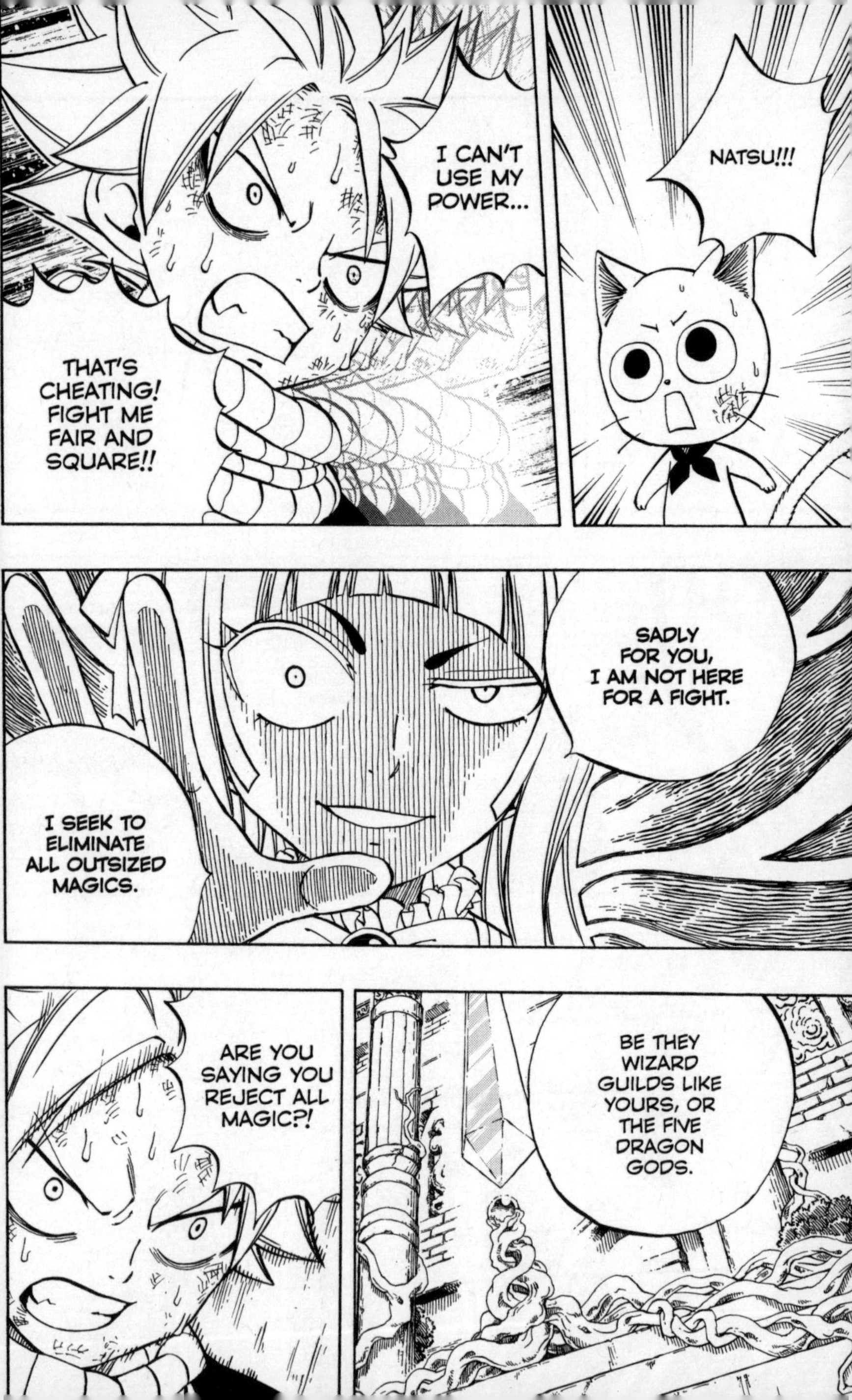
NATSU!!!
I CAN'T USE MY POWER...
THAT'S CHEATING! FIGHT ME FAIR AND SQUARE!!
SADLY FOR YOU, I AM NOT HERE FOR A FIGHT.
I SEEK TO ELIMINATE ALL OUTSIZED MAGICS.
BE THEY WIZARD GUILDS LIKE YOURS, OR THE FIVE DRAGON GODS.
ARE YOU SAYING YOU REJECT ALL MAGIC?!

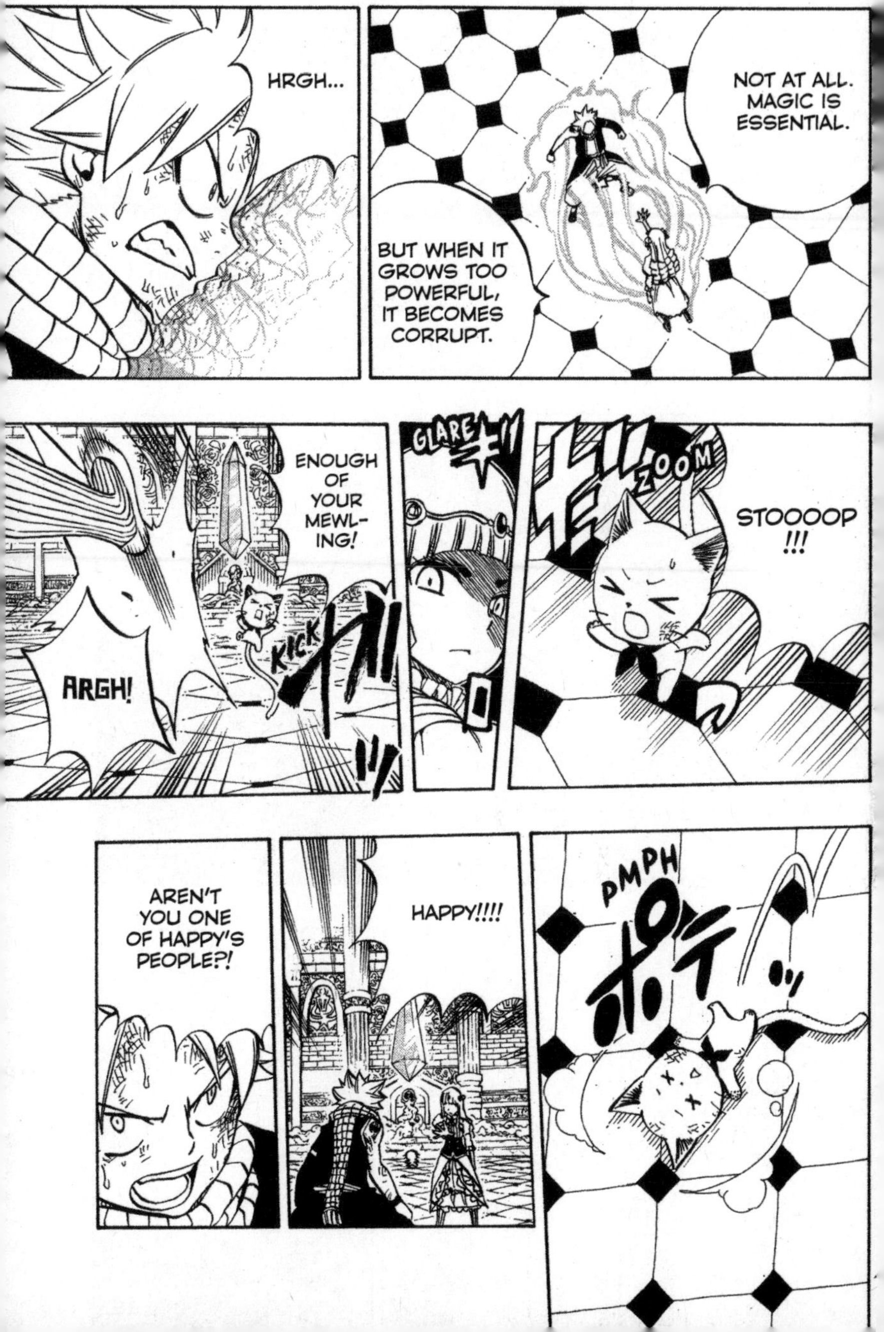
NOT AT ALL. MAGIC IS ESSENTIAL.
BUT WHEN IT GROWS TOO POWERFUL, IT BECOMES CORRUPT.
HRGH...
ZOOM
STOOOOP!!!
GLARE
ENOUGH OF YOUR MEWL-ING!
KICK
ARGH!
PMPH
HAPPY!!!!
AREN'T YOU ONE OF HAPPY'S PEOPLE?!

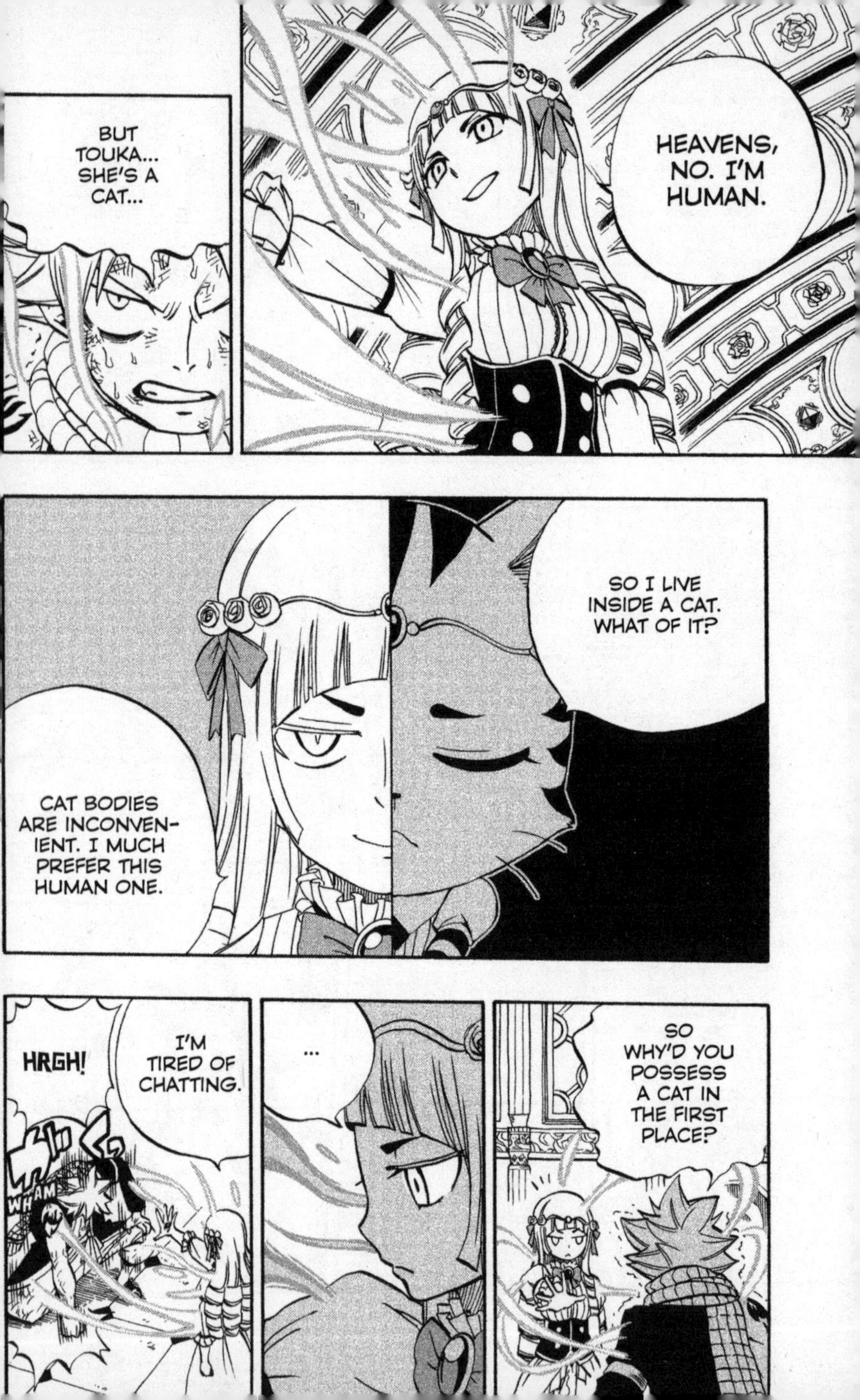
HEAVENS, NO. I'M HUMAN.
BUT TOUKA... SHE'S A CAT...
SO I LIVE INSIDE A CAT. WHAT OF IT?
CAT BODIES ARE INCONVEN-IENT. I MUCH PREFER THIS HUMAN ONE.
SO WHY'D YOU POSSESS A CAT IN THE FIRST PLACE?
...
I'M TIRED OF CHATTING.
HRGH!
WHAM

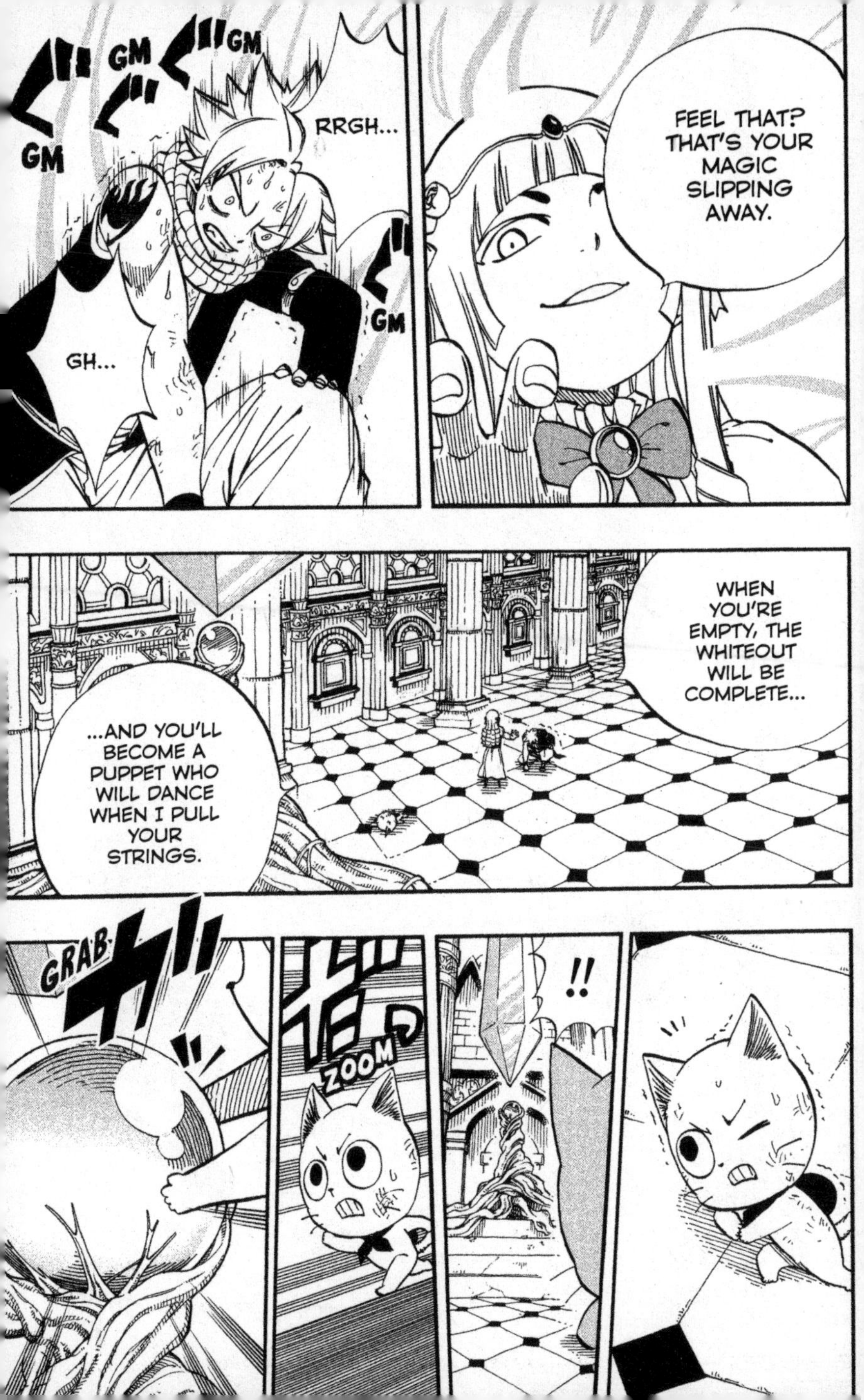
FEEL THAT? THAT'S YOUR MAGIC SLIPPING AWAY.
RRGH...
GM
GM
GM
GM
GH...
WHEN YOU'RE EMPTY, THE WHITEOUT WILL BE COMPLETE...
...AND YOU'LL BECOME A PUPPET WHO WILL DANCE WHEN I PULL YOUR STRINGS.
!!
ZOOM
GRAB

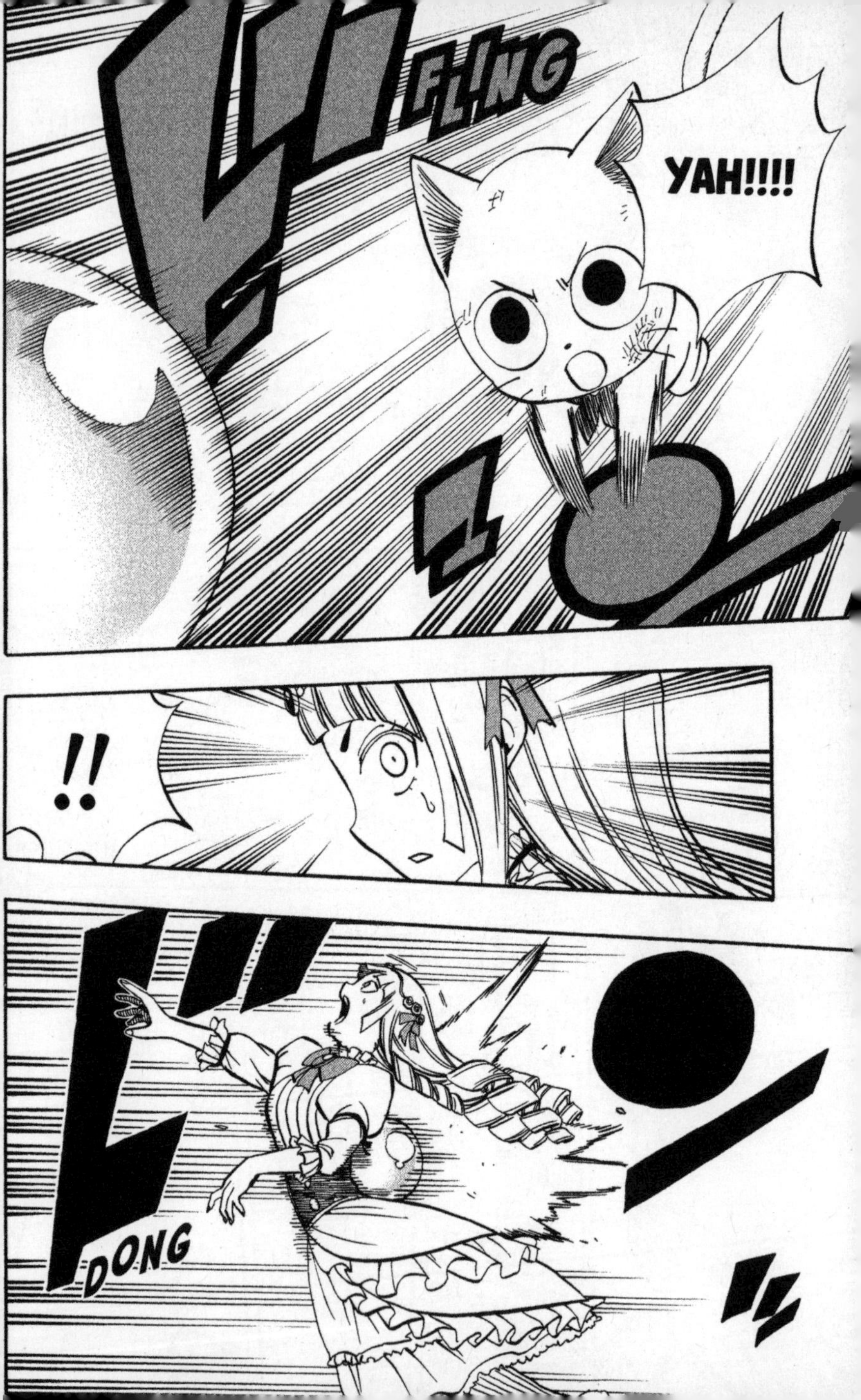
YAH!!!!
FLING
!!
DONG

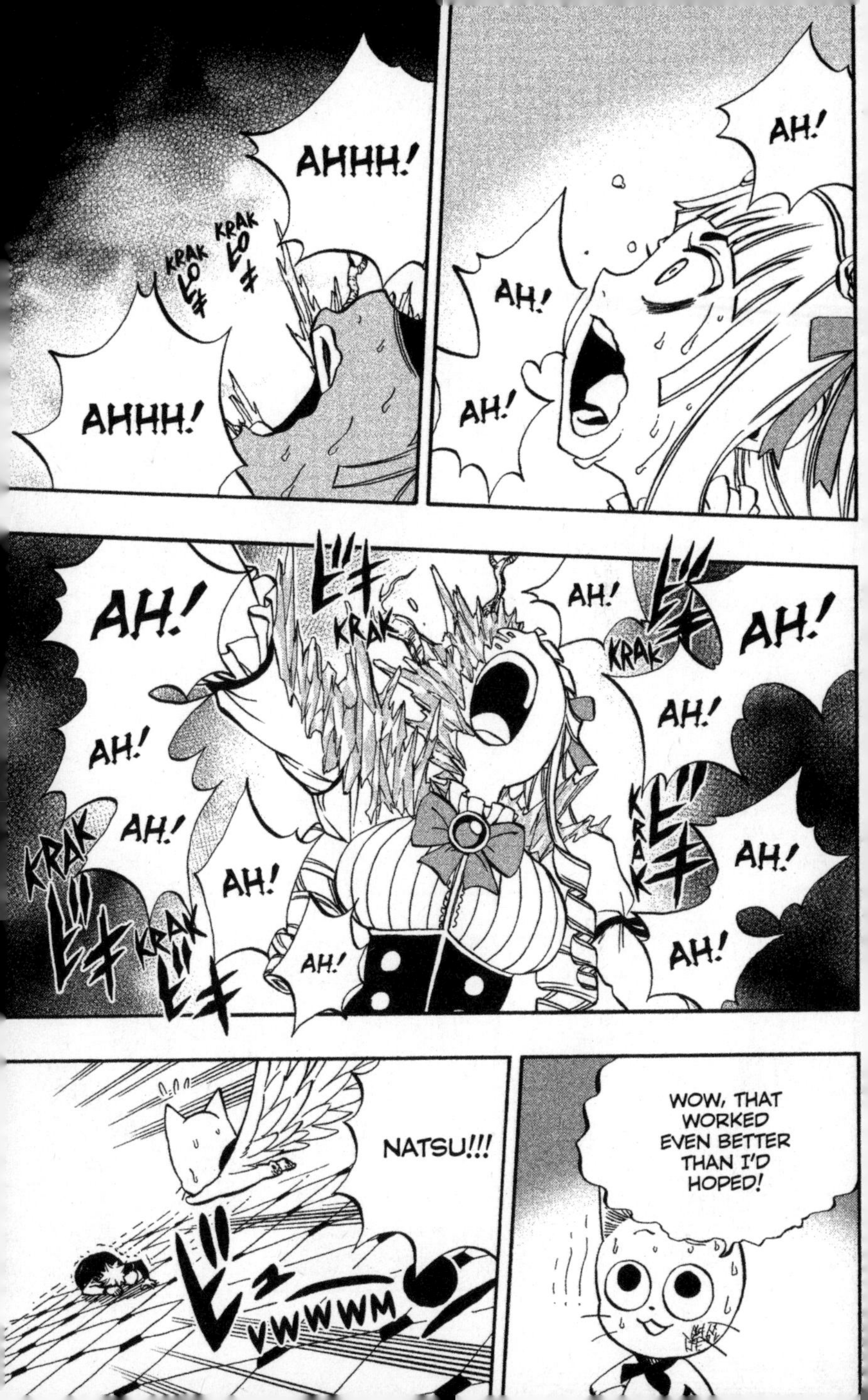
AH!
AH!
AH!
AHHH!
KRAK
KRAK
AHHH!
AH!
AH!
KRAK
AH!
AH!
KRAK
AH!
AH!
KRAK
AH!
AH!
AH!
KRAK
KRAK
AH!
WOW, THAT WORKED EVEN BETTER THAN I'D HOPED!
NATSU!!!
VWWWWM

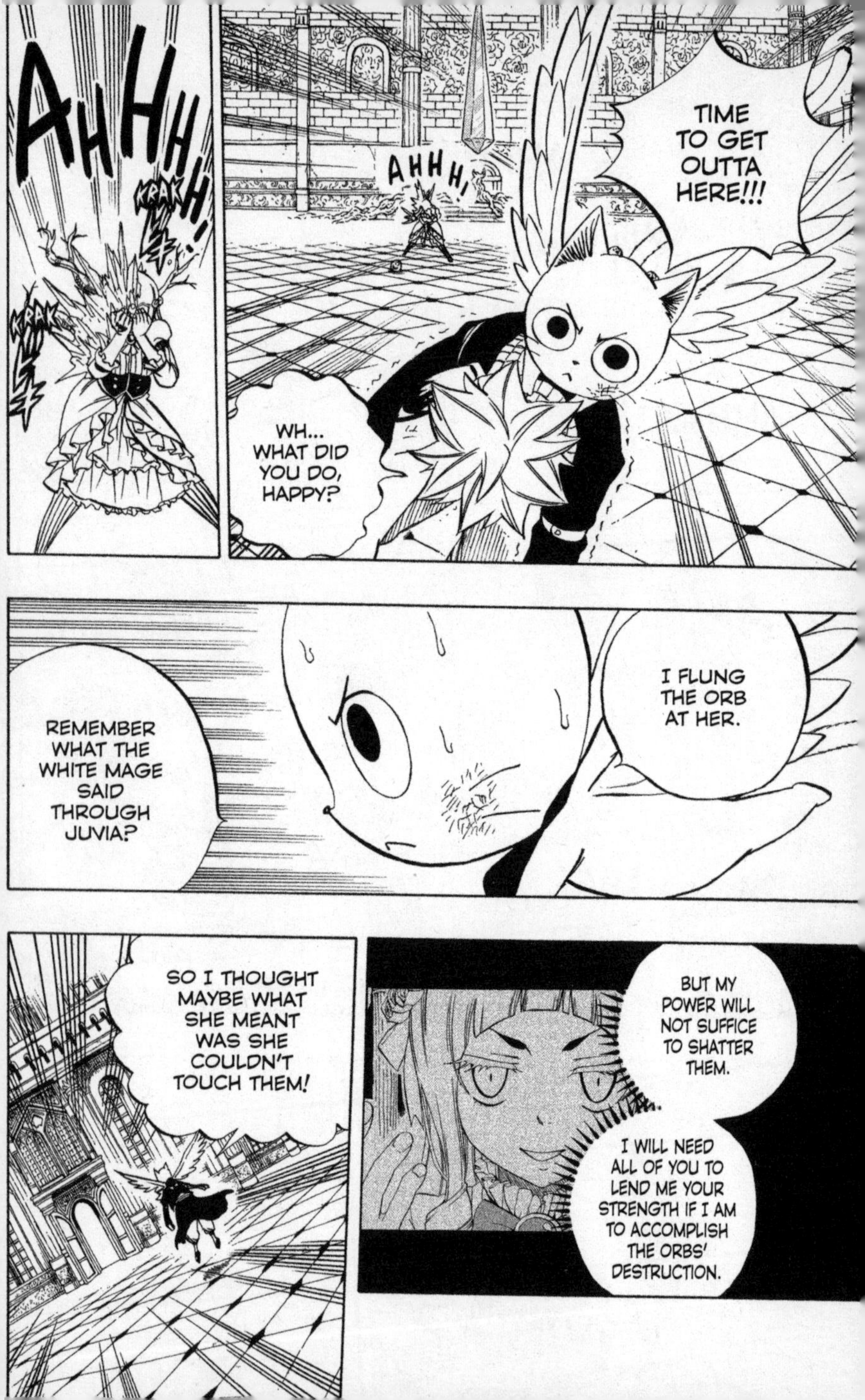
AHHH!
TIME TO GET OUTTA HERE!!!
WH... WHAT DID YOU DO, HAPPY?
AHHHH!
KRAK
KRAK
I FLUNG THE ORB AT HER.
REMEMBER WHAT THE WHITE MAGE SAID THROUGH JUVIA?
BUT MY POWER WILL NOT SUFFICE TO SHATTER THEM.
I WILL NEED ALL OF YOU TO LEND ME YOUR STRENGTH IF I AM TO ACCOMPLISH THE ORBS' DESTRUCTION.
SO I THOUGHT MAYBE WHAT SHE MEANT WAS SHE COULDN'T TOUCH THEM!

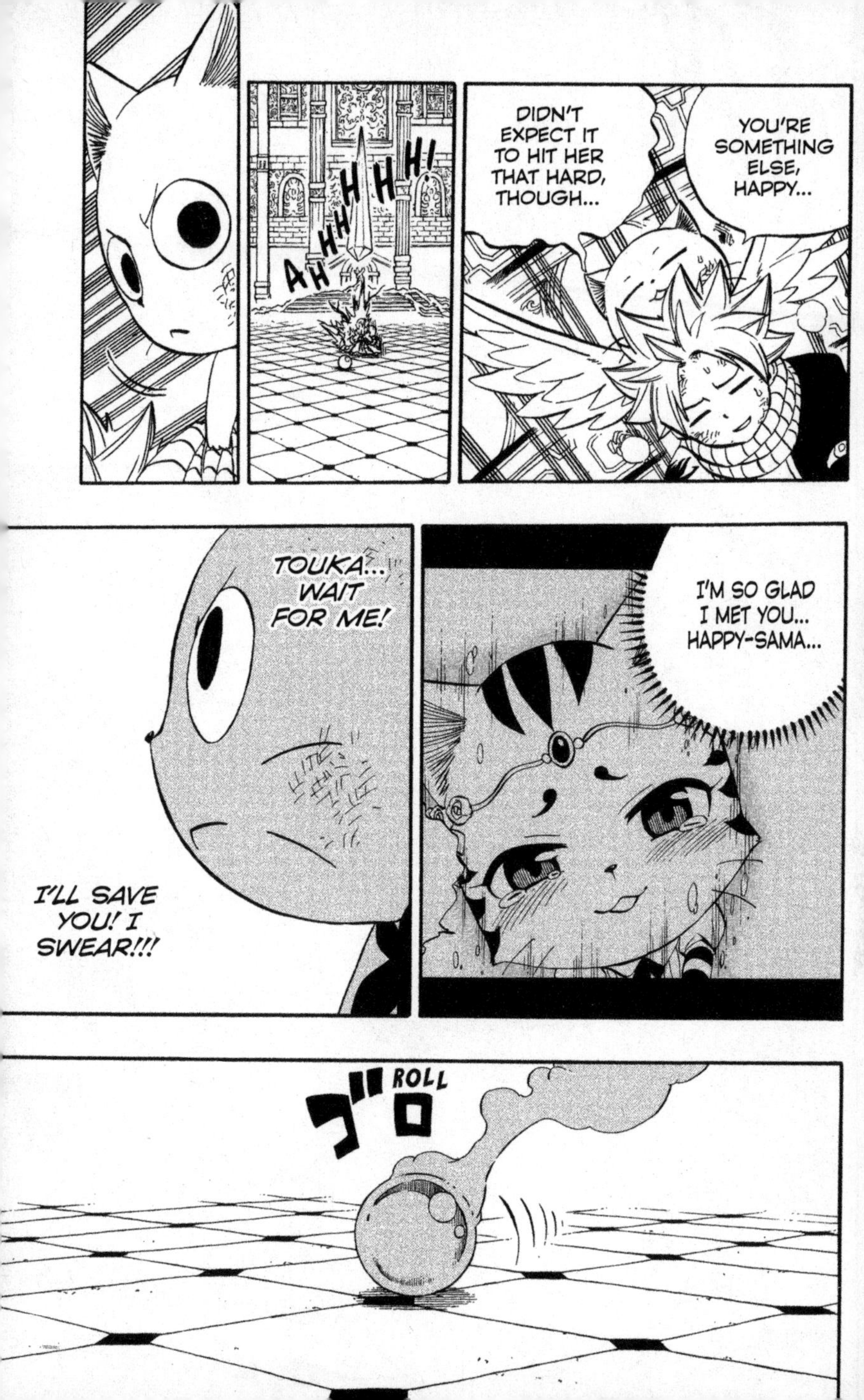
YOU'RE SOMETHING ELSE, HAPPY...
DIDN'T EXPECT IT TO HIT HER THAT HARD, THOUGH...
AHHHHHHHH!
I'M SO GLAD I MET YOU... HAPPY-SAMA...
TOUKA... WAIT FOR ME!
I'LL SAVE YOU! I SWEAR!!!
ROLL

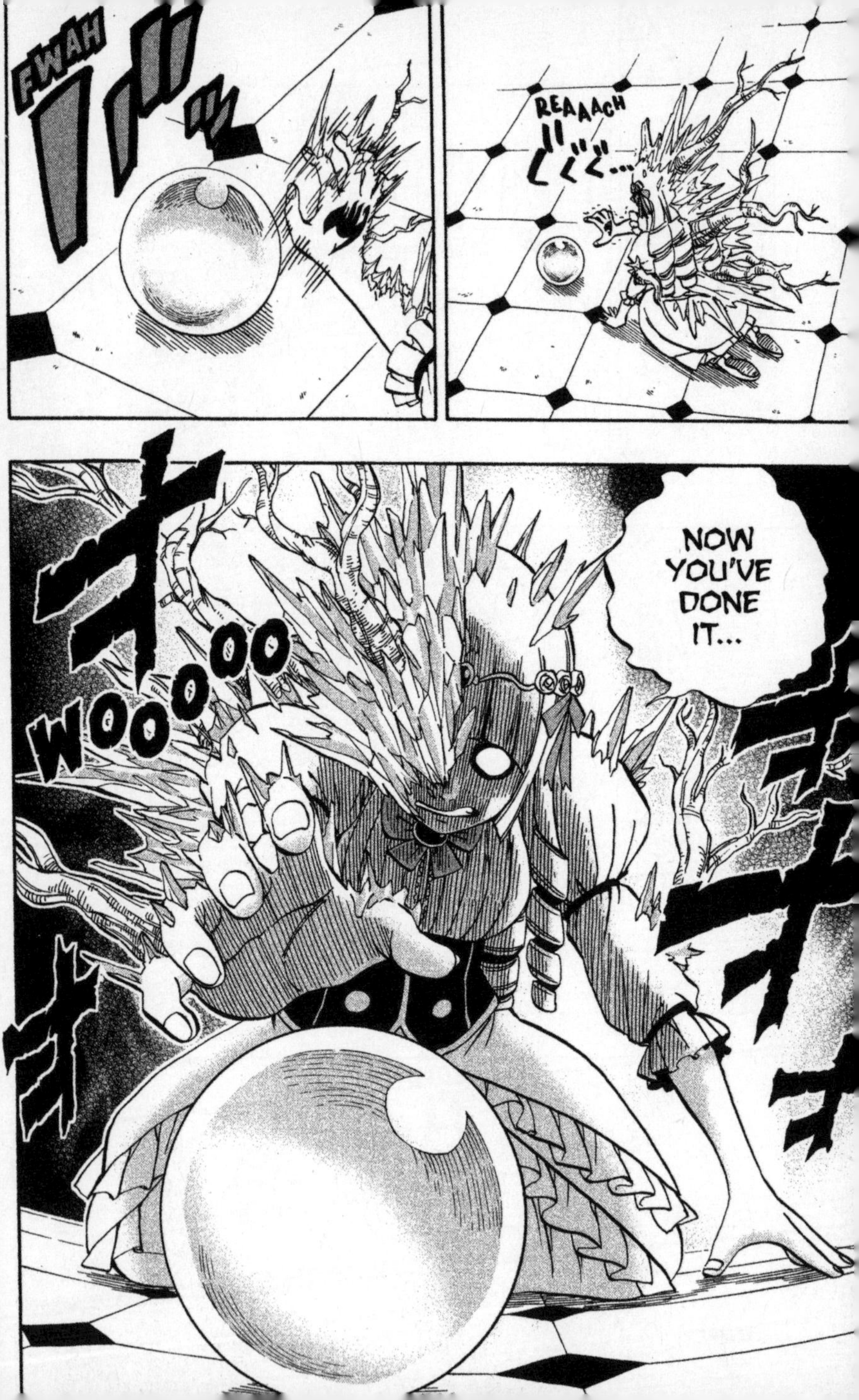
REAAACH
FWAH
NOW YOU'VE DONE IT...
WOOOOO

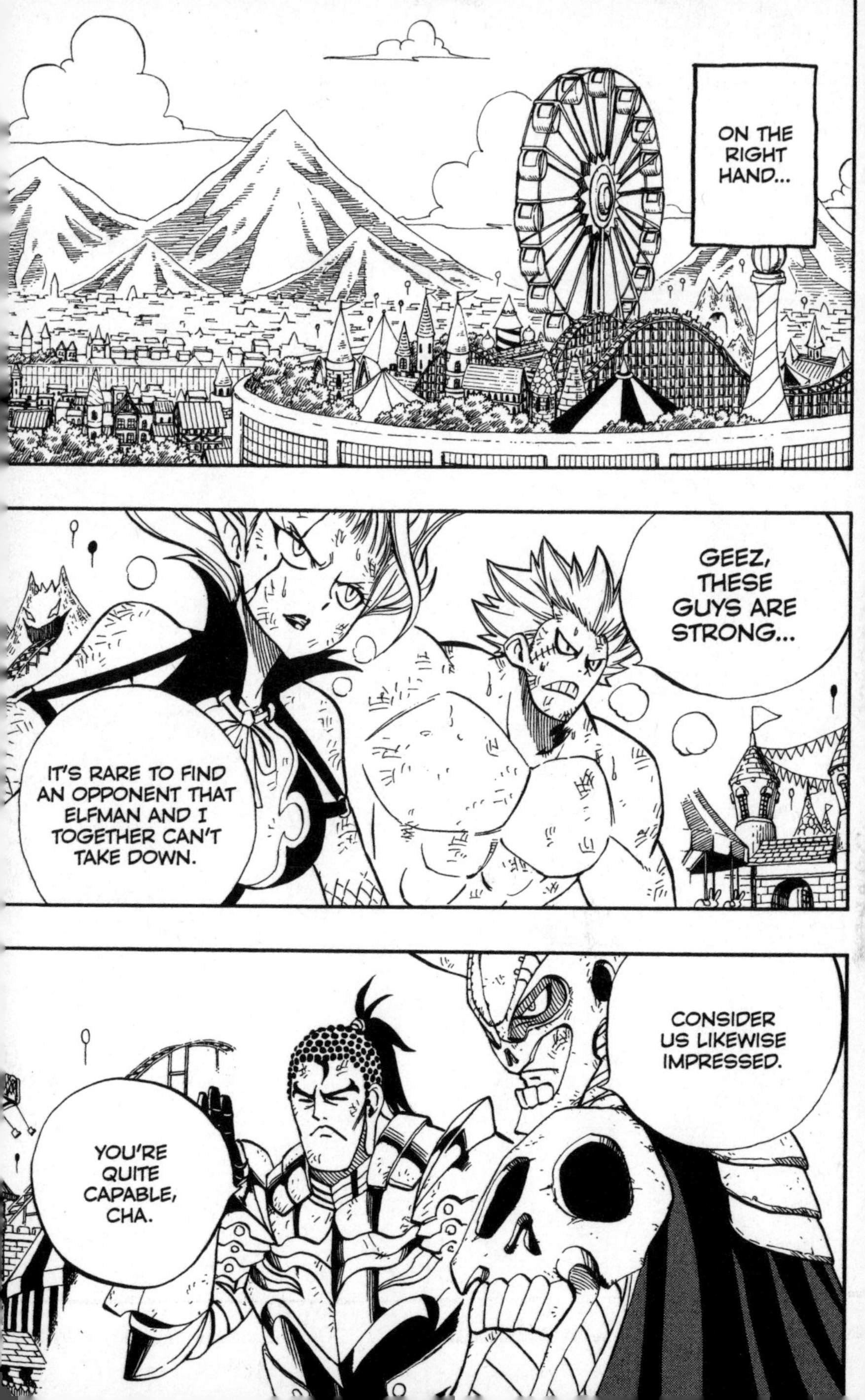
ON THE RIGHT HAND...
GEEZ, THESE GUYS ARE STRONG...
IT'S RARE TO FIND AN OPPONENT THAT ELFMAN AND I TOGETHER CAN'T TAKE DOWN.
CONSIDER US LIKEWISE IMPRESSED.
YOU'RE QUITE CAPABLE, CHA.

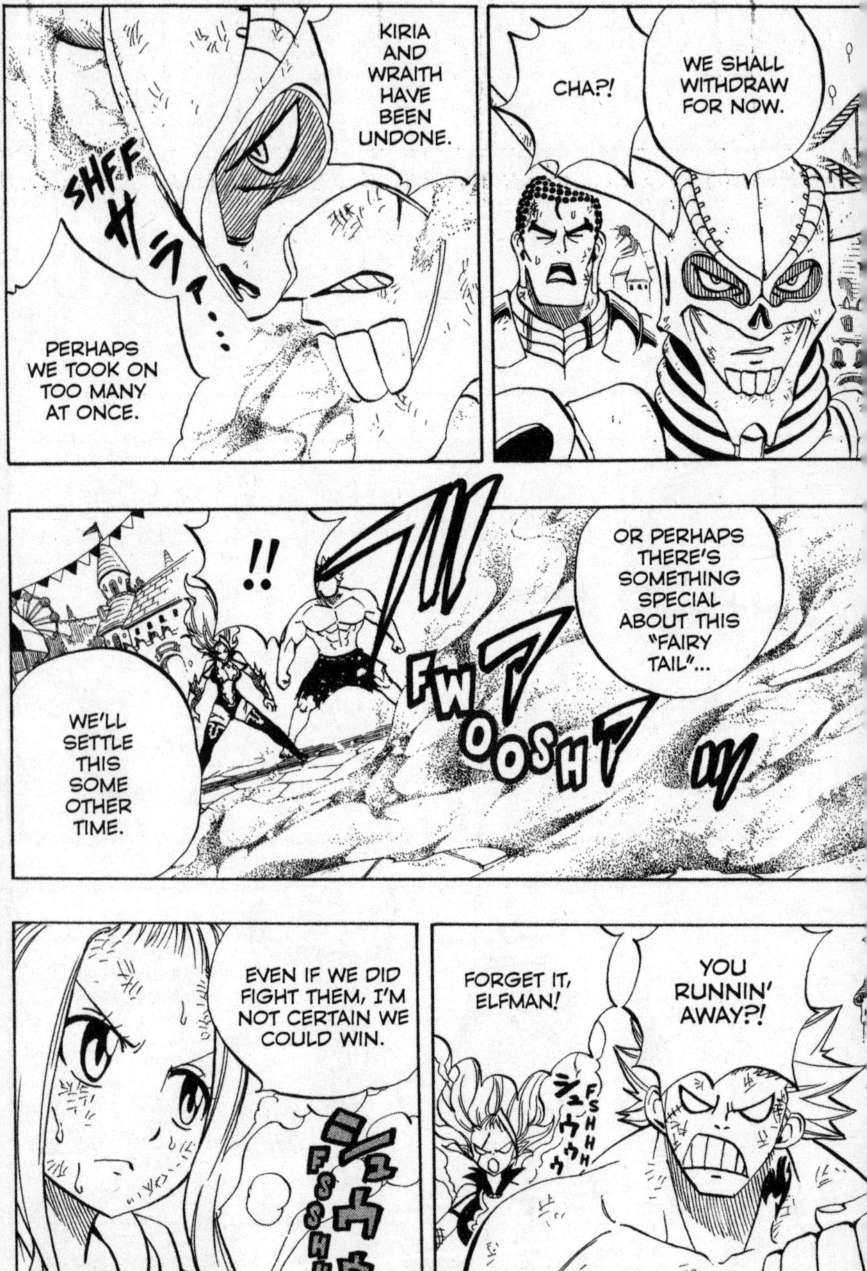
WE SHALL WITHDRAW FOR NOW.
CHA?!
KIRIA AND WRAITH HAVE BEEN UNDONE.
SHFF
PERHAPS WE TOOK ON TOO MANY AT ONCE.
OR PERHAPS THERE'S SOMETHING SPECIAL ABOUT THIS "FAIRY TAIL"...
FWOOSH
!!
WE'LL SETTLE THIS SOME OTHER TIME.
YOU RUNNIN' AWAY?!
FORGET IT, ELFMAN!
FSHHH
EVEN IF WE DID FIGHT THEM, I'M NOT CERTAIN WE COULD WIN.
FSSHH

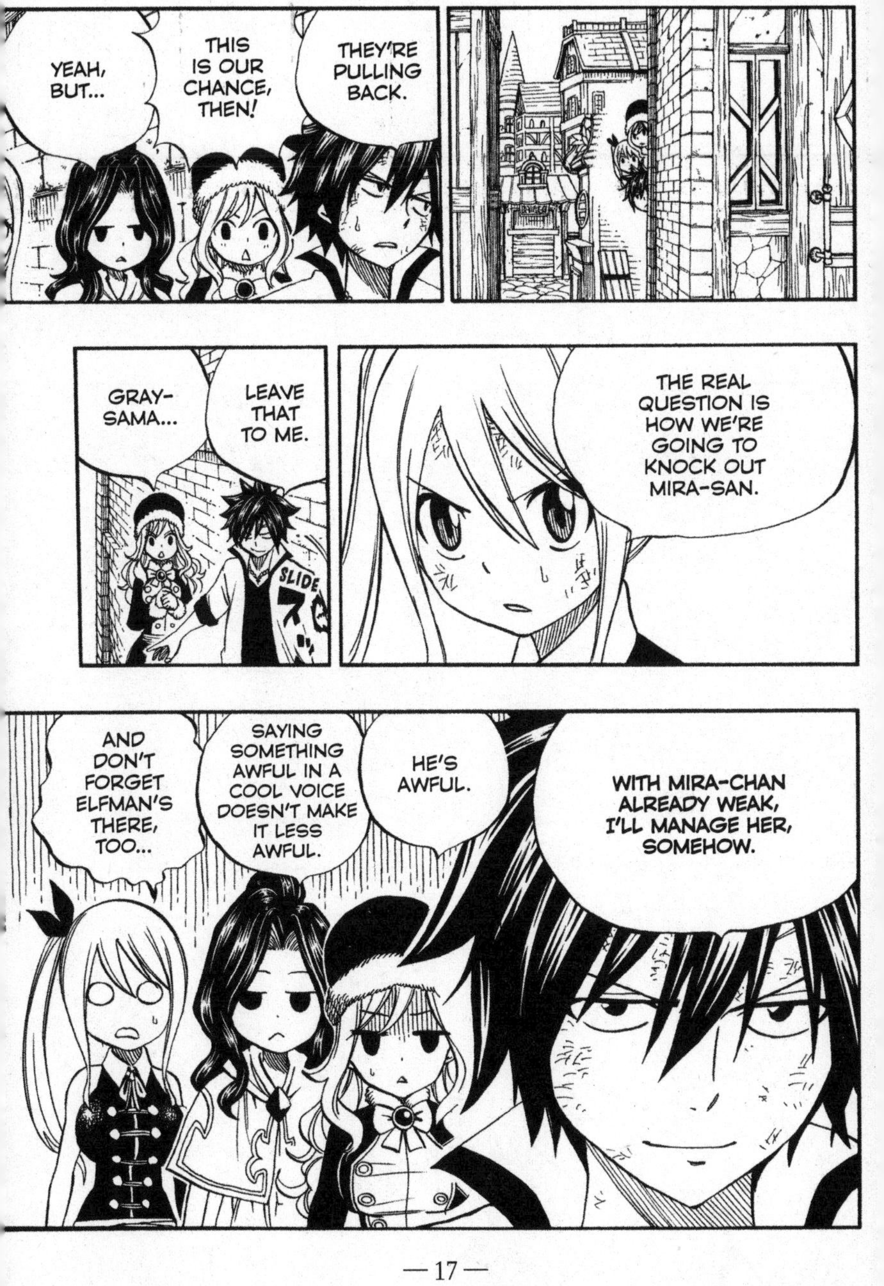
THEY'RE PULLING BACK.
THIS IS OUR CHANCE, THEN!
YEAH, BUT...
THE REAL QUESTION IS HOW WE'RE GOING TO KNOCK OUT MIRA-SAN.
LEAVE THAT TO ME.
GRAY-SAMA...
SLIDE
WITH MIRA-CHAN ALREADY WEAK, I'LL MANAGE HER, SOMEHOW.
HE'S AWFUL.
SAYING SOMETHING AWFUL IN A COOL VOICE DOESN'T MAKE IT LESS AWFUL.
AND DON'T FORGET ELFMAN'S THERE, TOO...

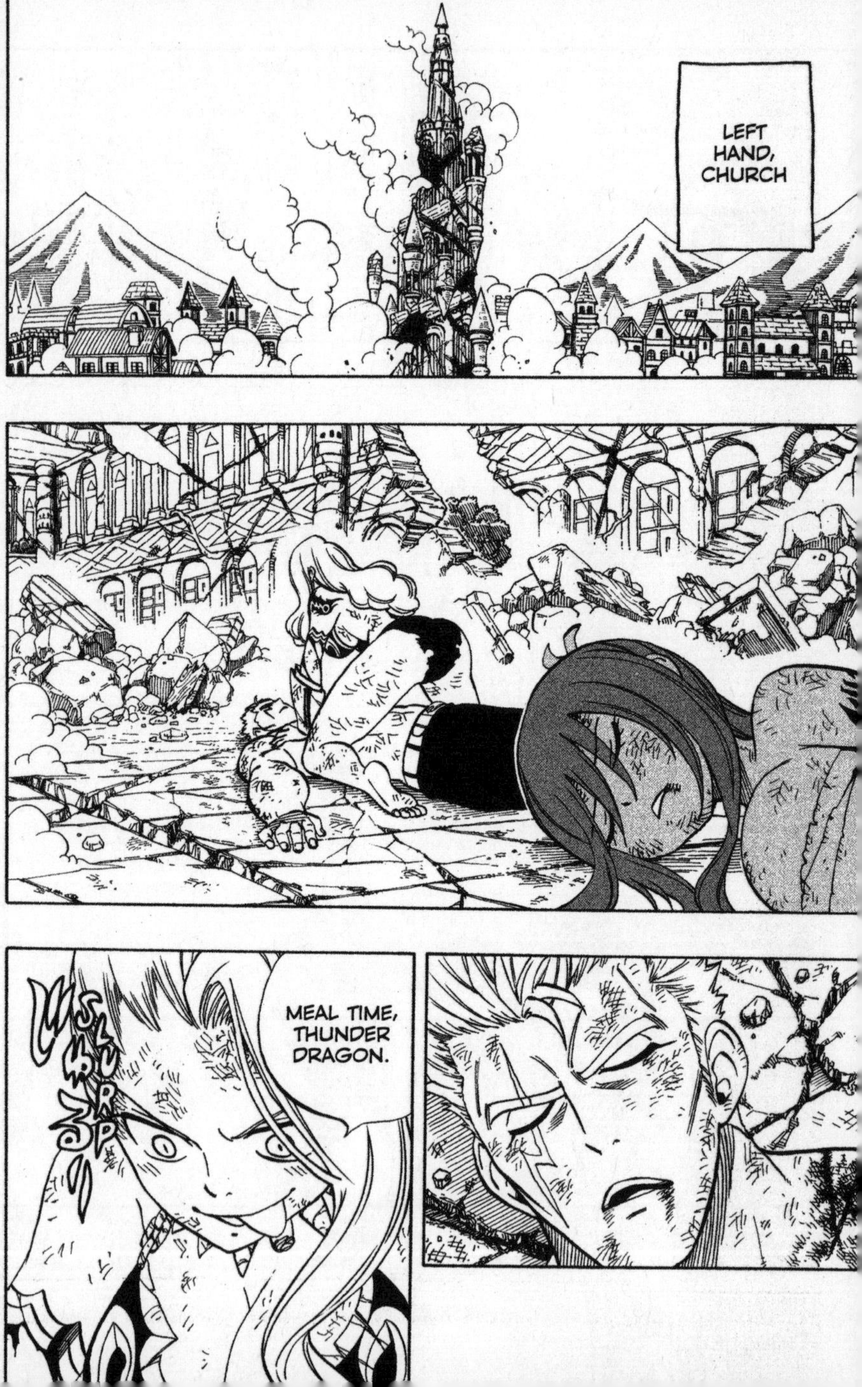
LEFT HAND, CHURCH
MEAL TIME, THUNDER DRAGON.
SLURP

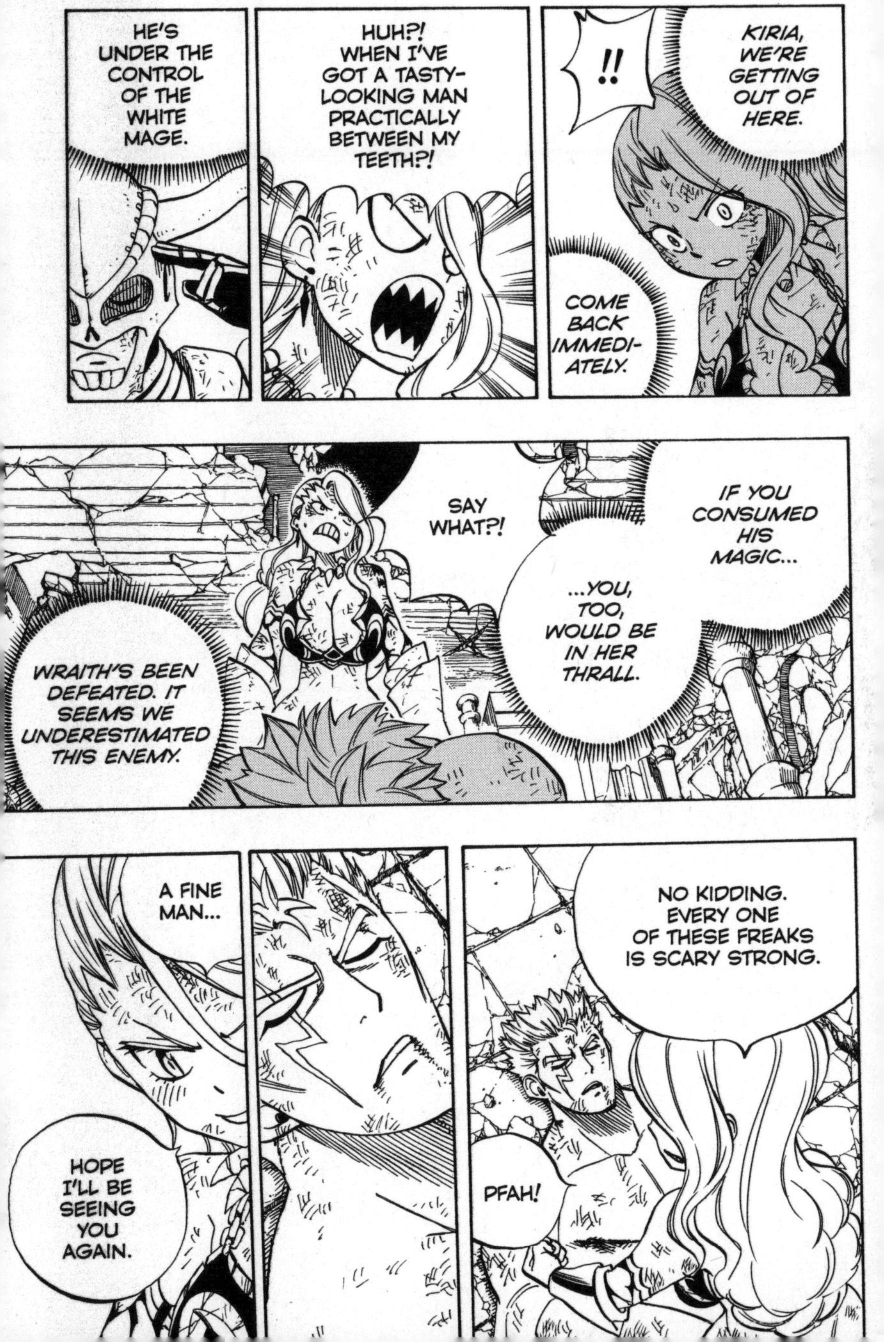
KIRIA, WE'RE GETTING OUT OF HERE.
!!
COME BACK IMMEDI-ATELY.
HUH?! WHEN I'VE GOT A TASTY-LOOKING MAN PRACTICALLY BETWEEN MY TEETH?!
HE'S UNDER THE CONTROL OF THE WHITE MAGE.
IF YOU CONSUMED HIS MAGIC...
...YOU, TOO, WOULD BE IN HER THRALL.
SAY WHAT?!
WRAITH'S BEEN DEFEATED. IT SEEMS WE UNDERESTIMATED THIS ENEMY.
NO KIDDING. EVERY ONE OF THESE FREAKS IS SCARY STRONG.
PFAH!
A FINE MAN...
HOPE I'LL BE SEEING YOU AGAIN.

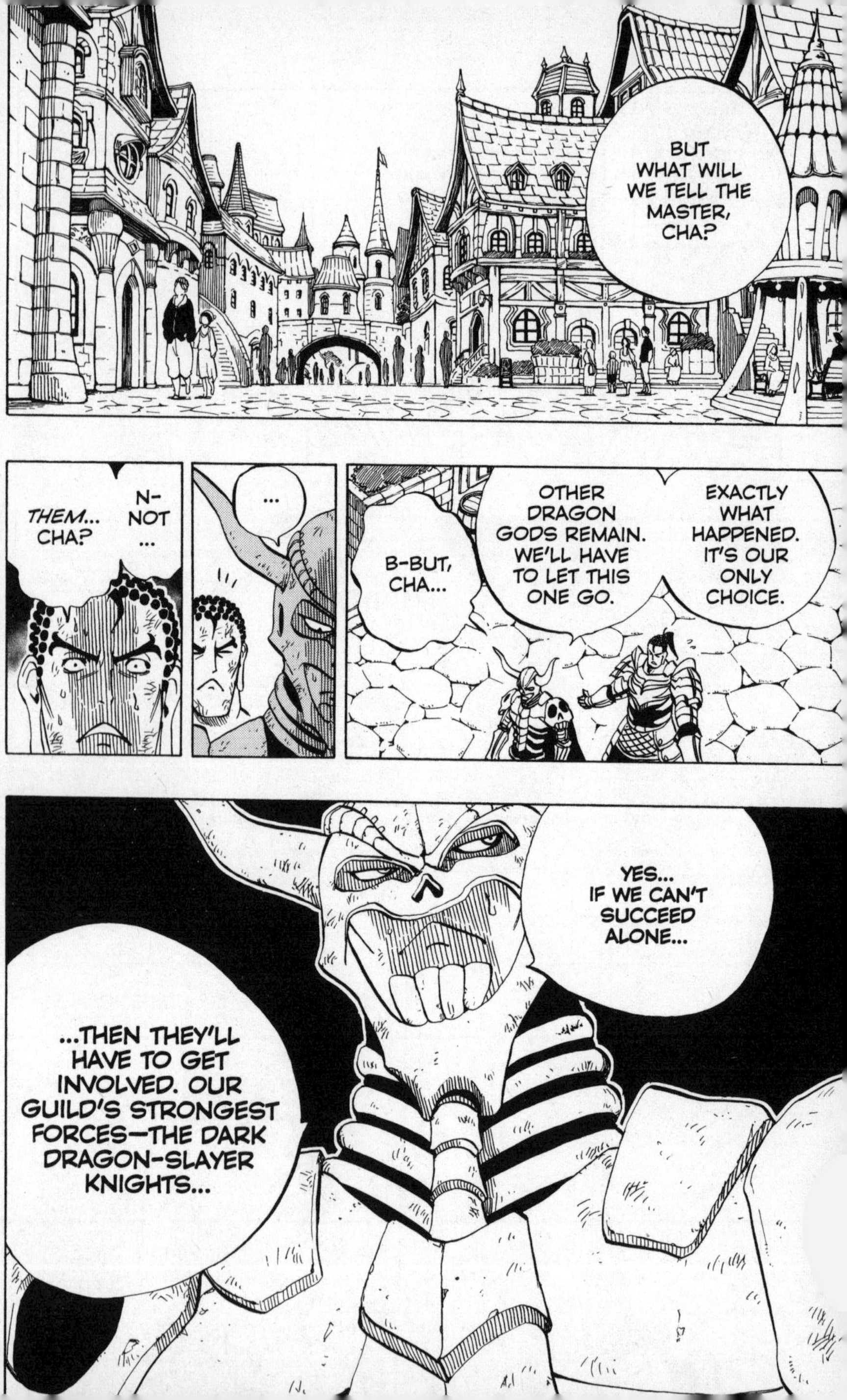
BUT WHAT WILL WE TELL THE MASTER, CHA?
EXACTLY WHAT HAPPENED. IT'S OUR ONLY CHOICE.
OTHER DRAGON GODS REMAIN. WE'LL HAVE TO LET THIS ONE GO.
B-BUT, CHA...
...
N-NOT ...
THEM... CHA?
YES... IF WE CAN'T SUCCEED ALONE...
...THEN THEY'LL HAVE TO GET INVOLVED. OUR GUILD'S STRONGEST FORCES—THE DARK DRAGON-SLAYER KNIGHTS...

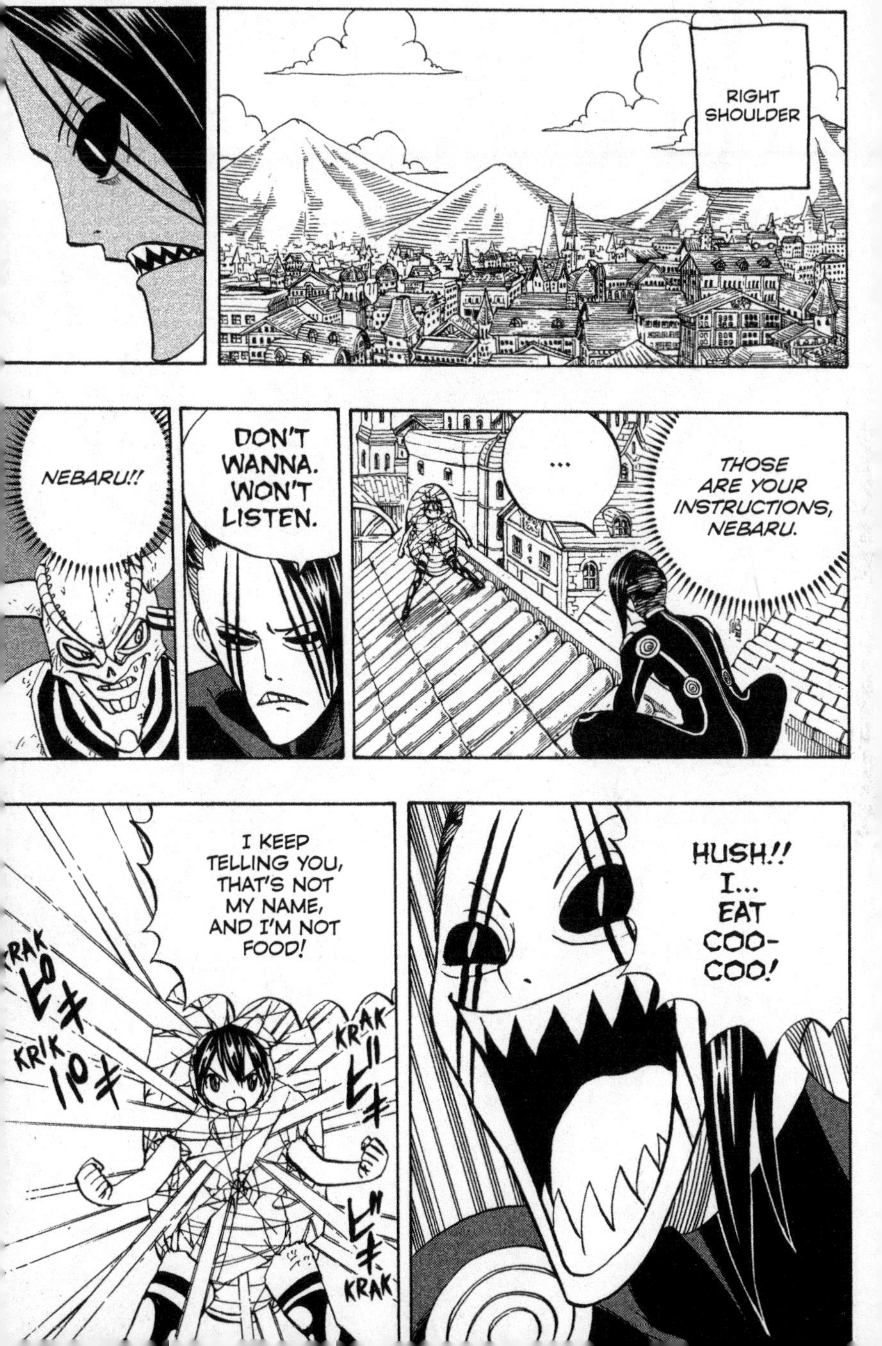
RIGHT SHOULDER
THOSE ARE YOUR INSTRUCTIONS, NEBARU.
...
DON'T WANNA. WON'T LISTEN.
NEBARU!!
HUSH!! I... EAT COO-COO!
I KEEP TELLING YOU, THAT'S NOT MY NAME, AND I'M NOT FOOD!
KRAK
KRAK
KRIK
KRAK

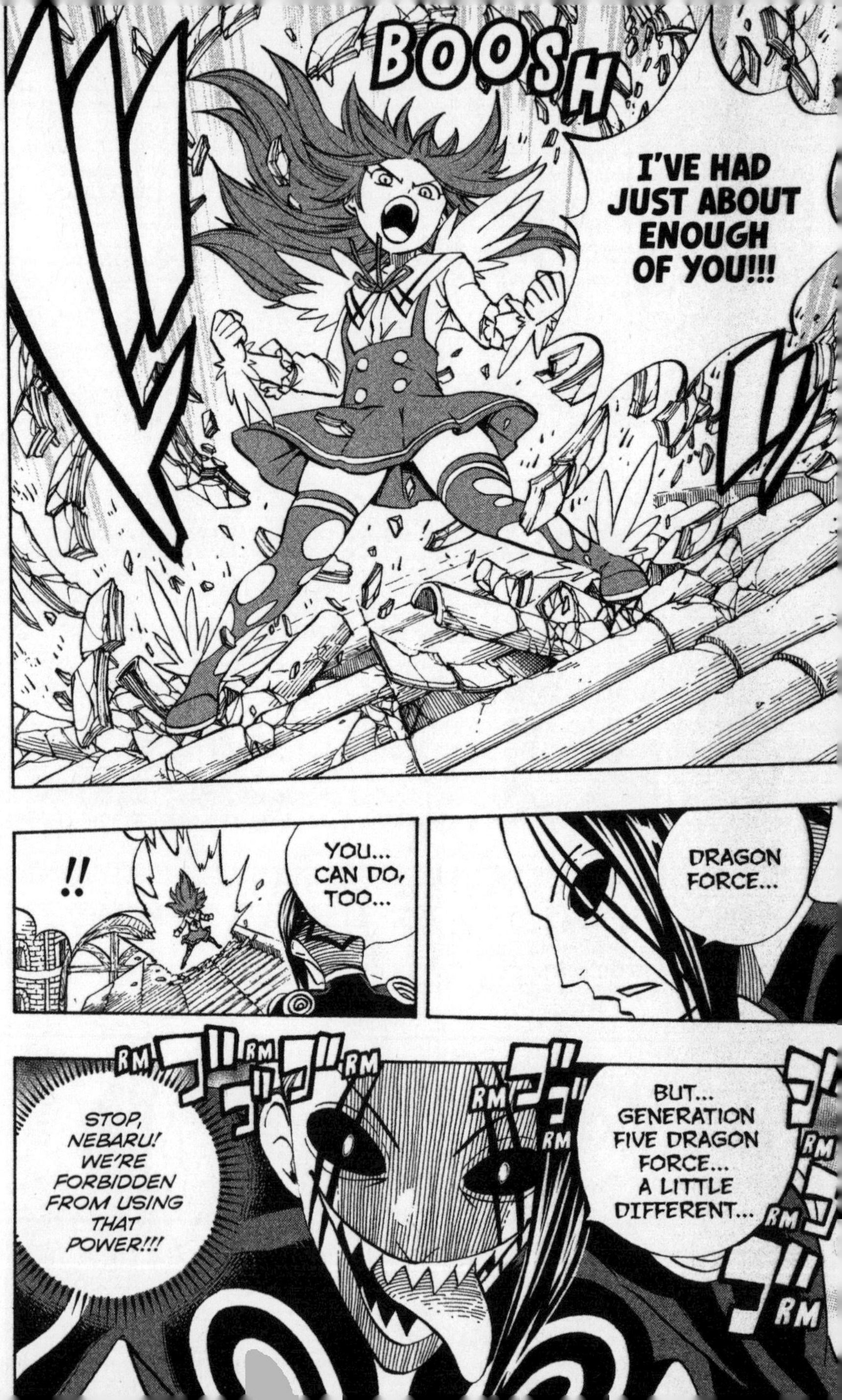
BOOSH
I'VE HAD JUST ABOUT ENOUGH OF YOU!!!
DRAGON FORCE...
YOU... CAN DO, TOO...
!!
RM RM RM RM RM RM RM RM
BUT... GENERATION FIVE DRAGON FORCE... A LITTLE DIFFERENT...
STOP, NEBARU! WE'RE FORBIDDEN FROM USING THAT POWER!!!

FAIRY TAIL 100 YEARS QUEST

Chapter 47: Clinging Dragon Berserk

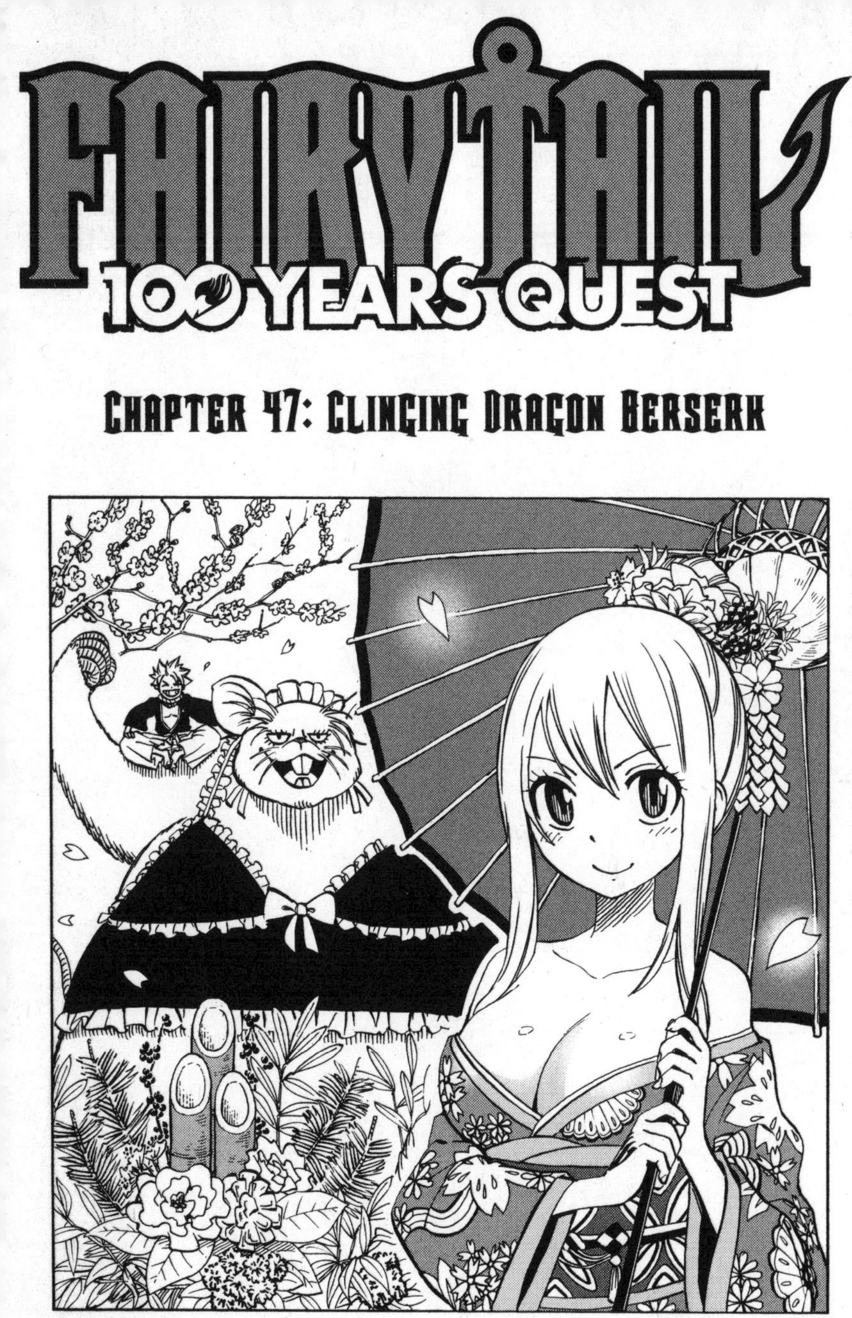

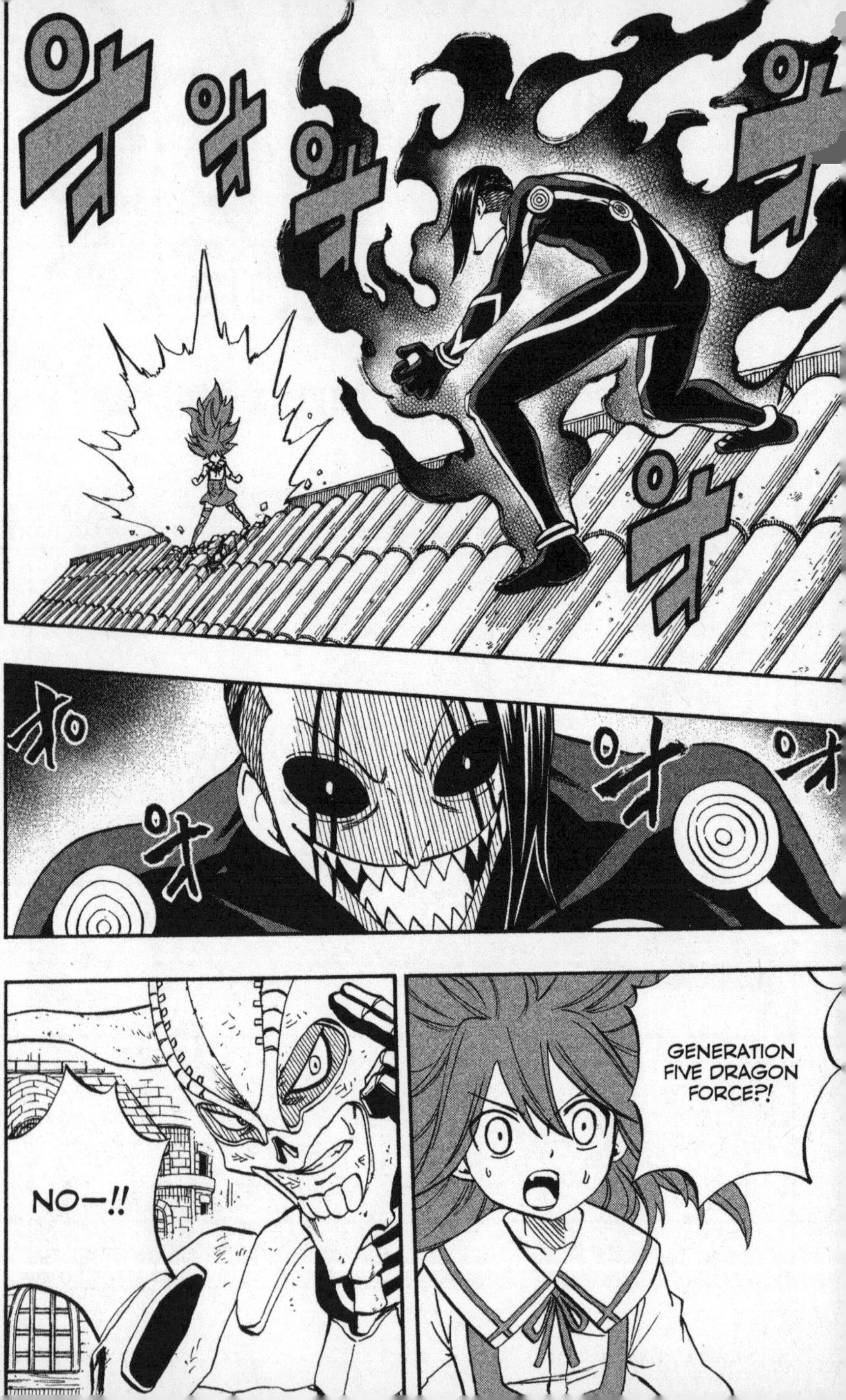
GENERATION FIVE DRAGON FORCE?!
NO—!!

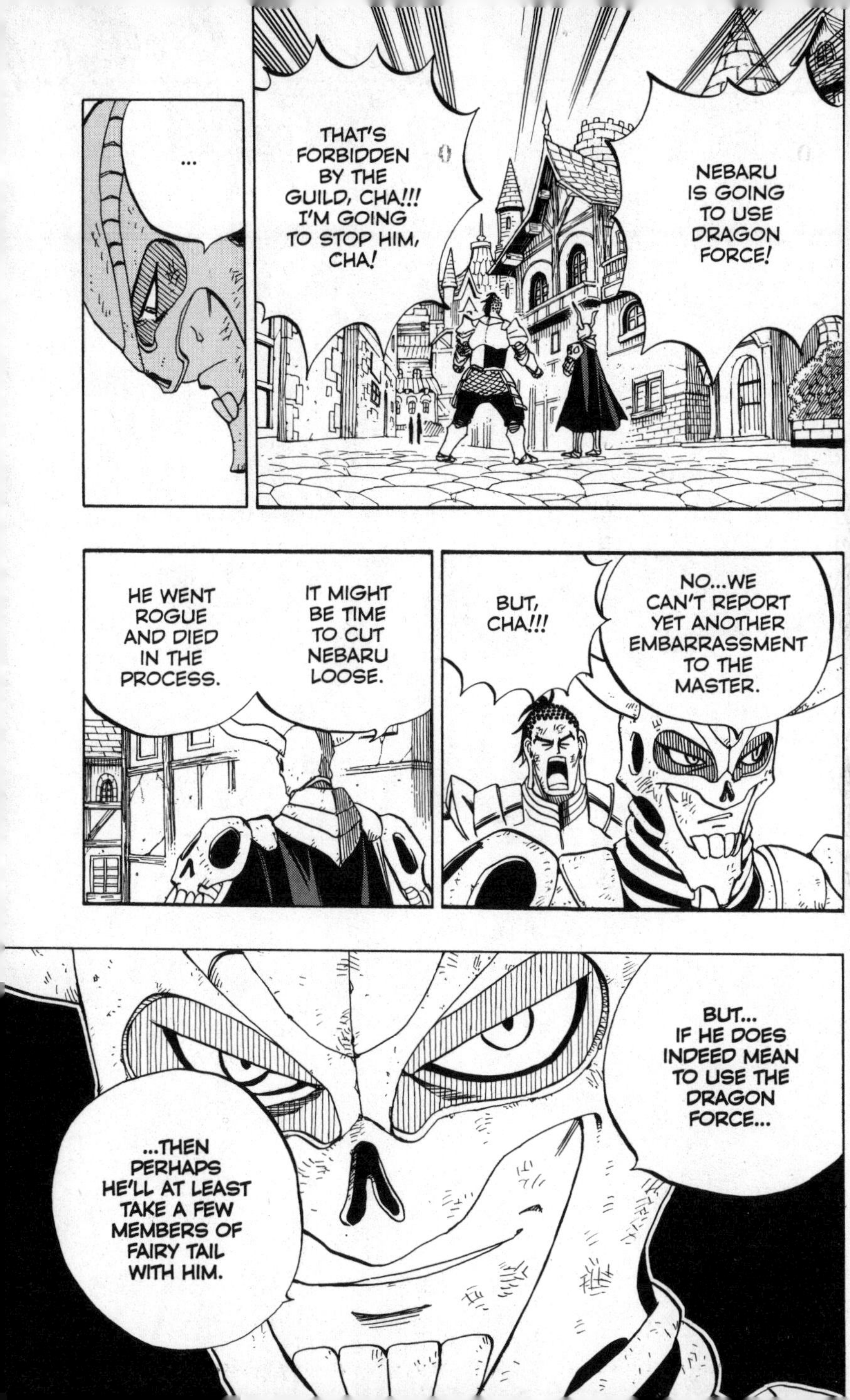
NEBARU IS GOING TO USE DRAGON FORCE!
THAT'S FORBIDDEN BY THE GUILD, CHA!!! I'M GOING TO STOP HIM, CHA!
...
NO...WE CAN'T REPORT YET ANOTHER EMBARRASSMENT TO THE MASTER.
BUT, CHA!!!
IT MIGHT BE TIME TO CUT NEBARU LOOSE.
HE WENT ROGUE AND DIED IN THE PROCESS.
BUT... IF HE DOES INDEED MEAN TO USE THE DRAGON FORCE...
...THEN PERHAPS HE'LL AT LEAST TAKE A FEW MEMBERS OF FAIRY TAIL WITH HIM.

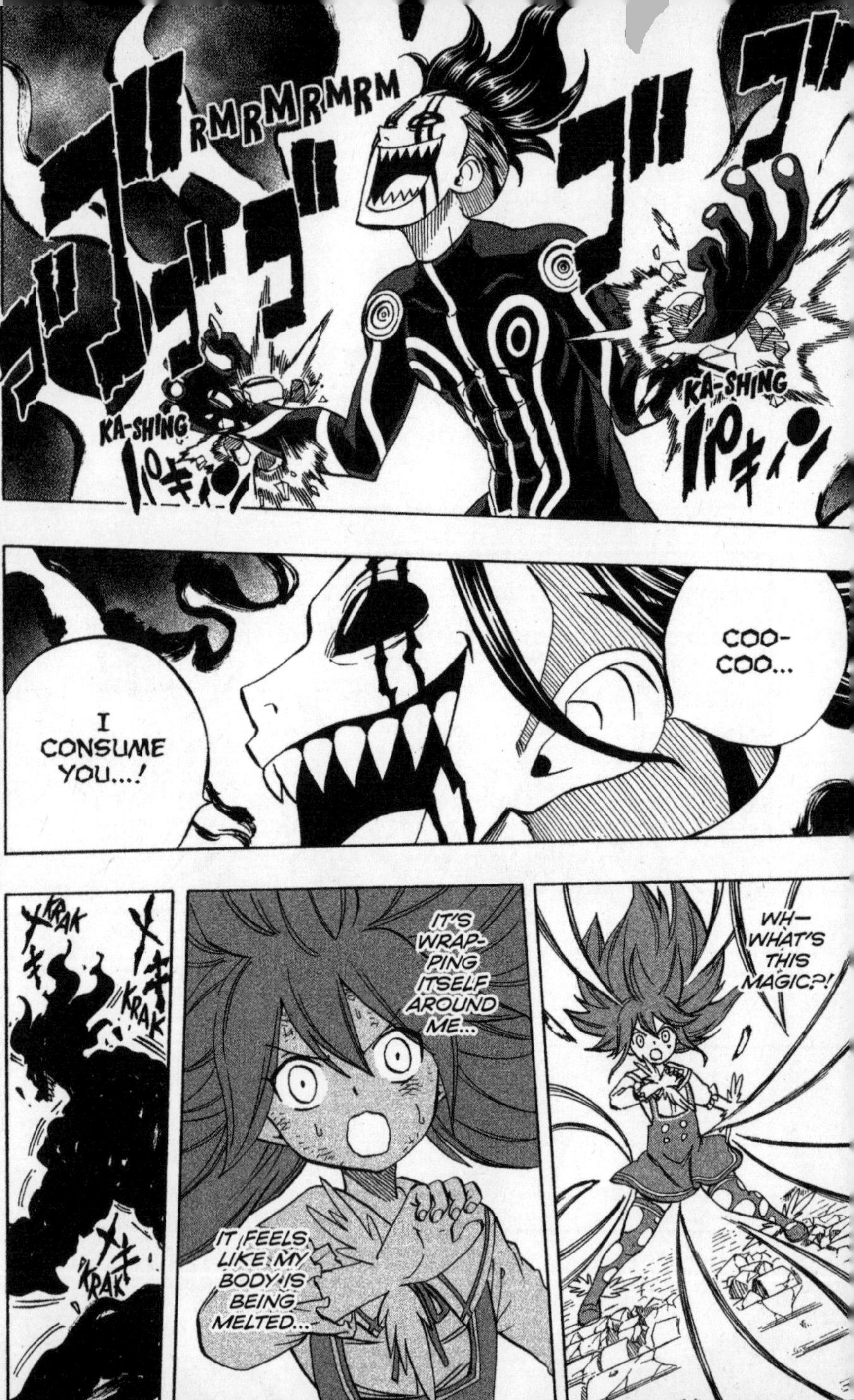
RMRMRMRM
KA-SHING
KA-SHING
COO-COO...
I CONSUME YOU...!
WH— WHAT'S THIS MAGIC?!
IT'S WRAP-PING ITSELF AROUND ME...
IT FEELS LIKE MY BODY IS BEING MELTED...
KRAK
KRAK
KRAK

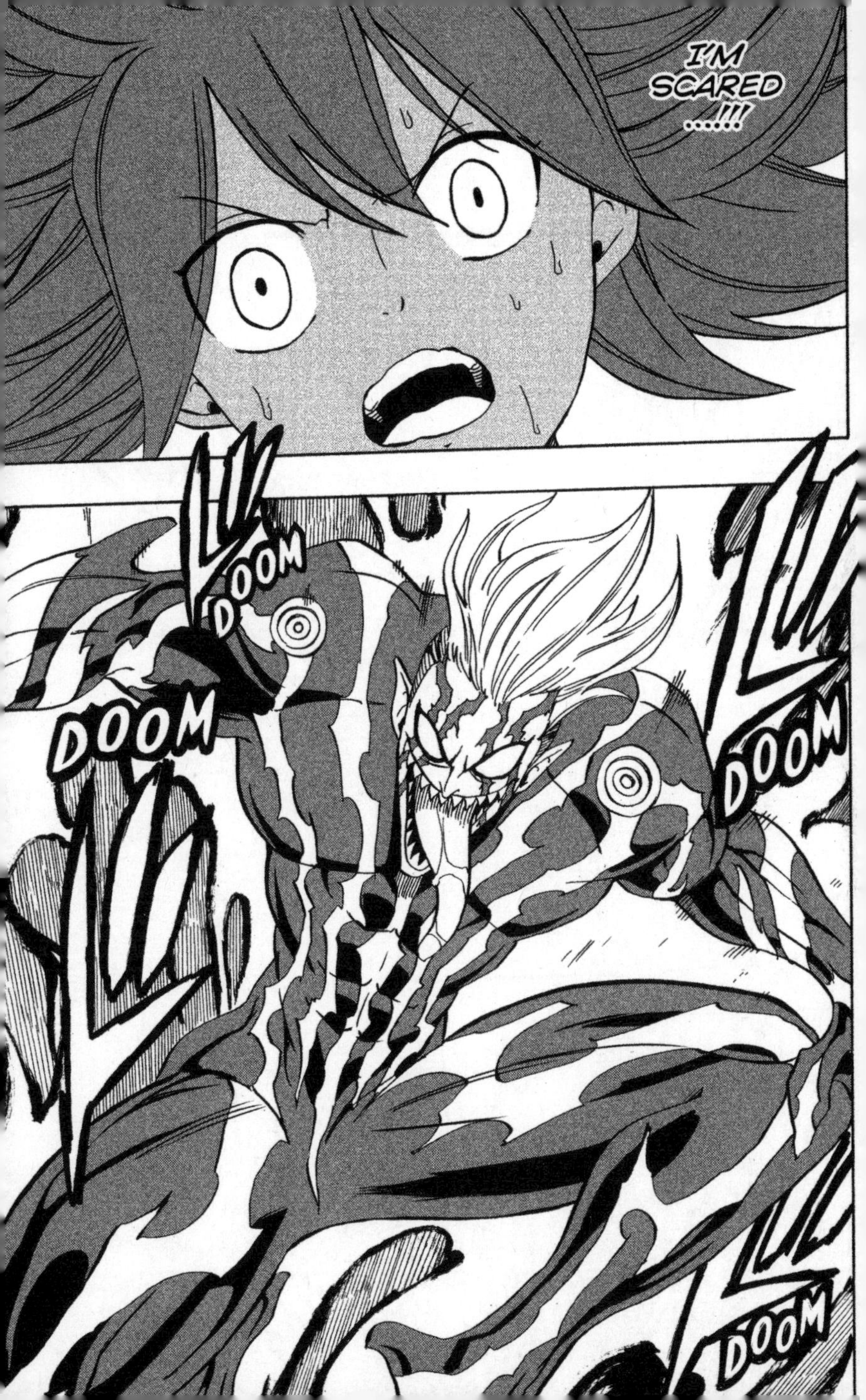
I'M SCARED ......!!!
DOOM
DOOM D
DOOM
DOOM

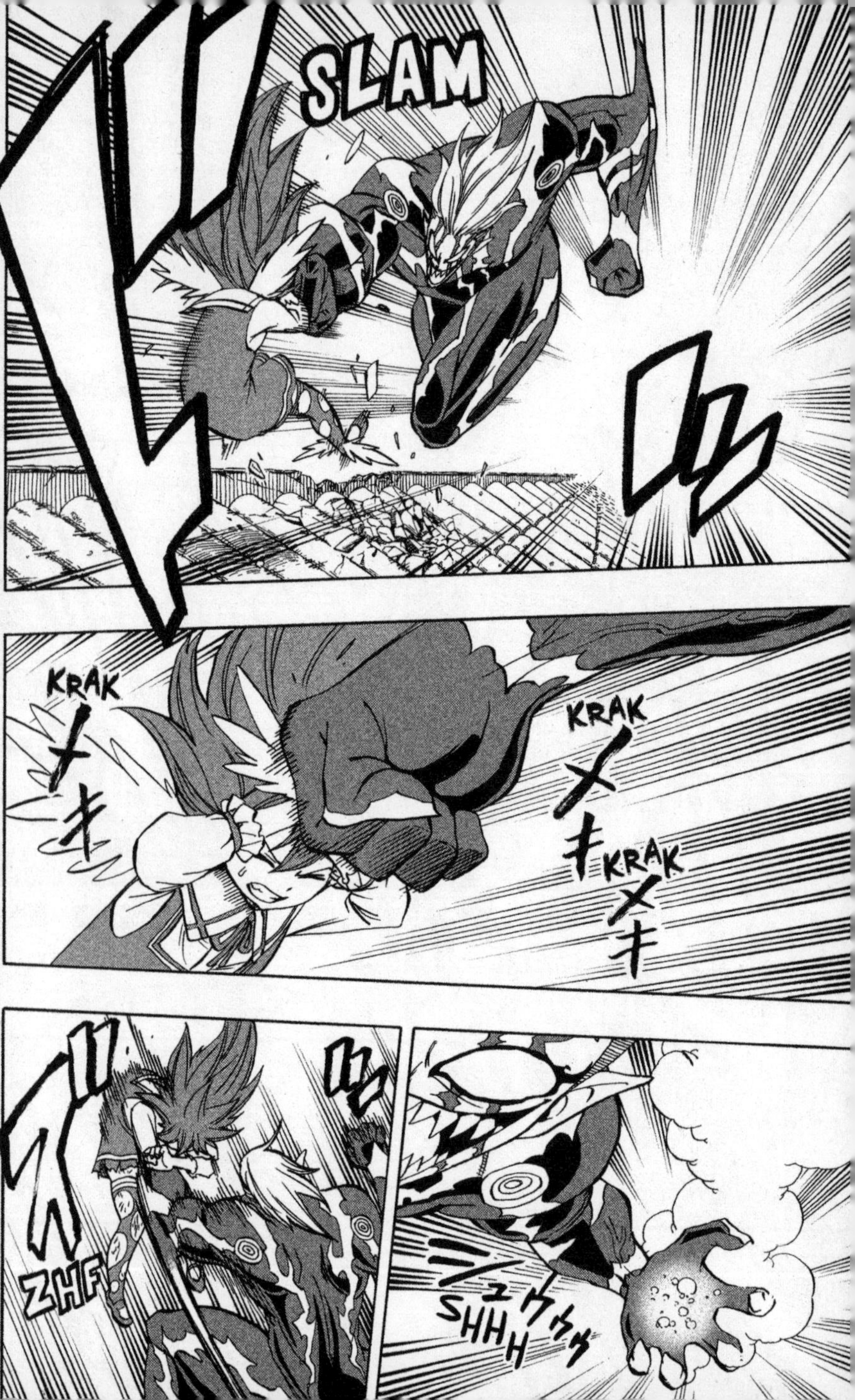
SLAM
KRAK
KRAK
KRAK
SHHH
ZHF

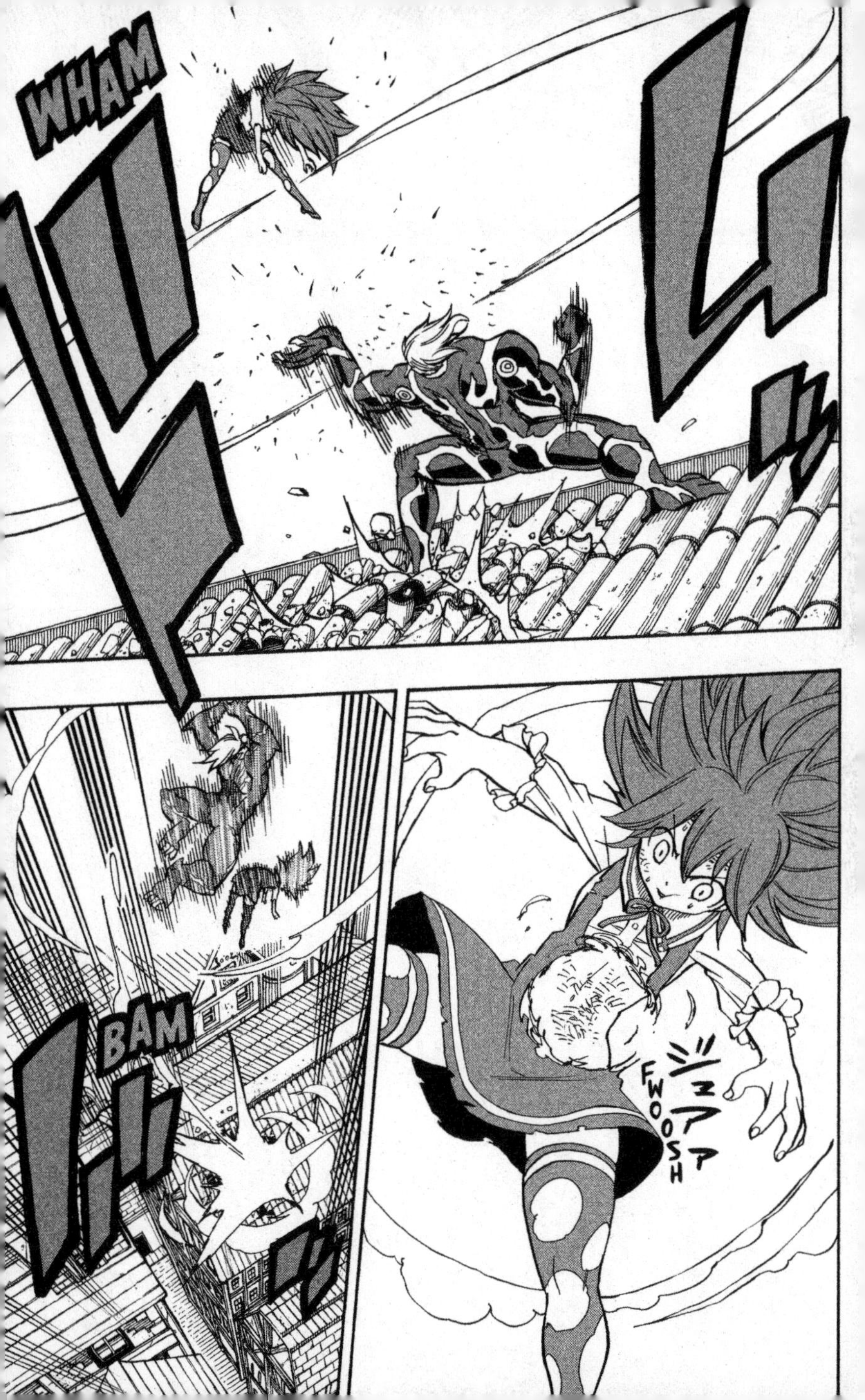
WHAM
FWOOSH
BAM

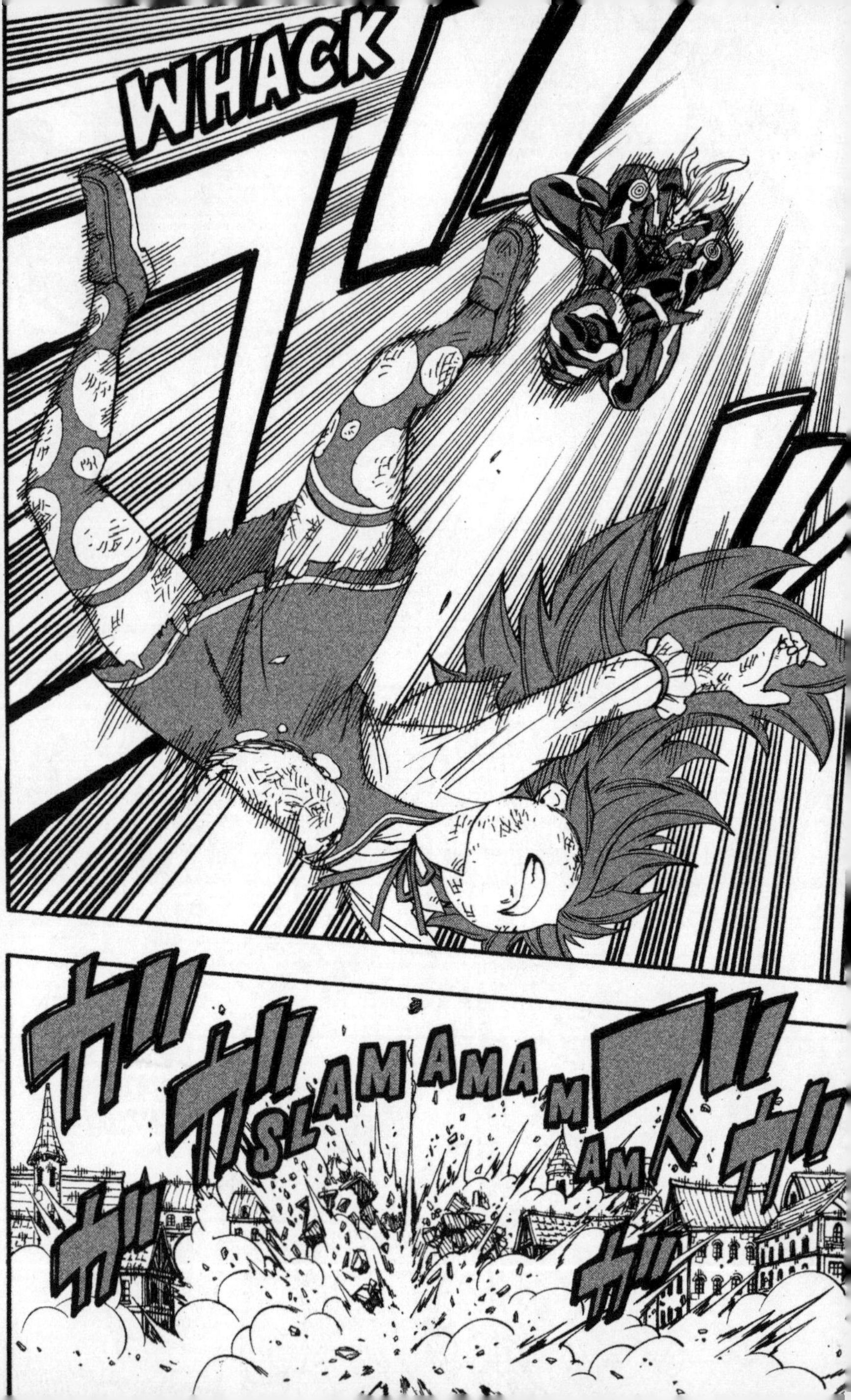
WHACK
SLAMAMAMAM

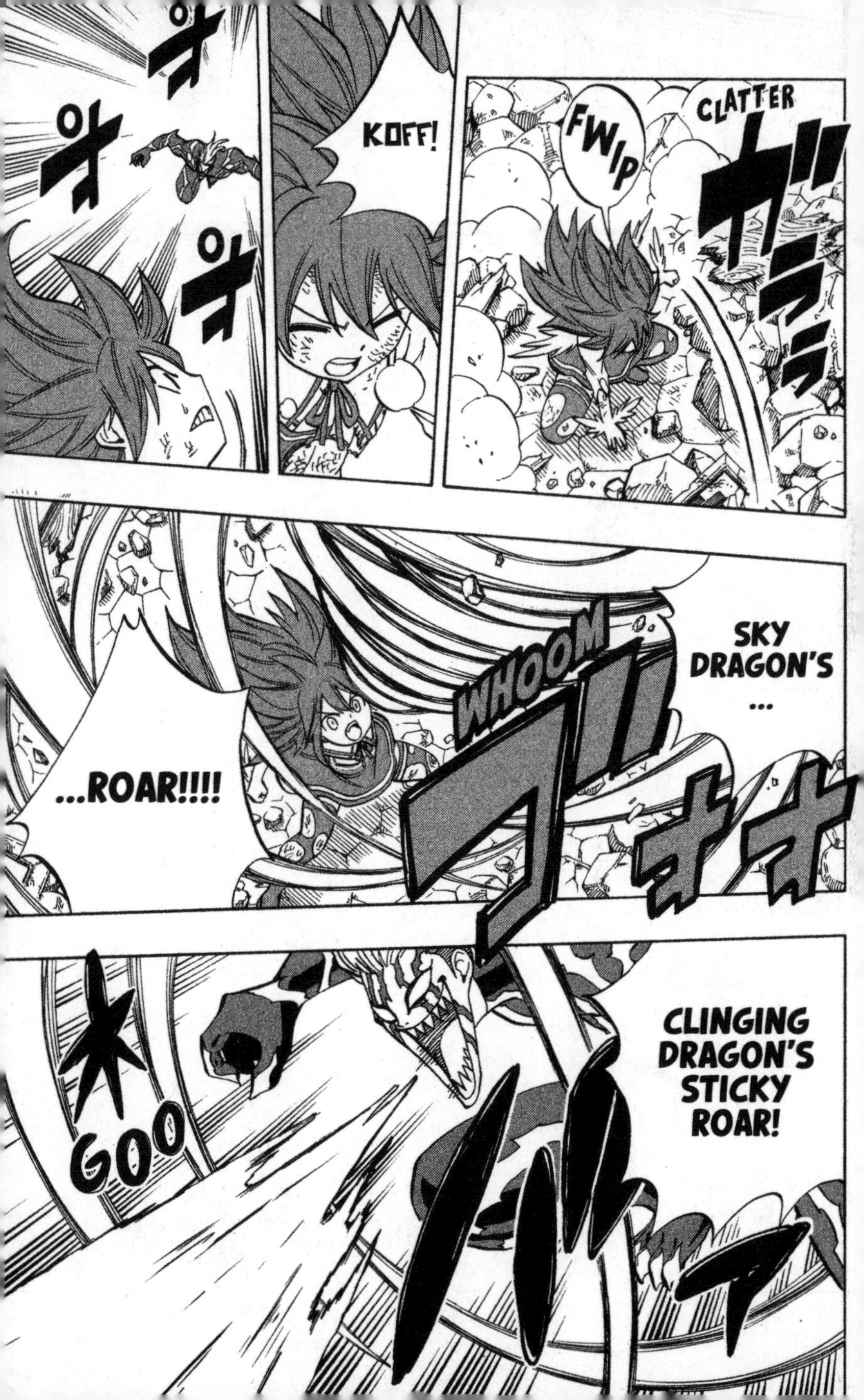
CLATTER
FWIP
KOFF!
SKY DRAGON'S ...
WHOOM
...ROAR!!!!
CLINGING DRAGON'S STICKY ROAR!
GOO

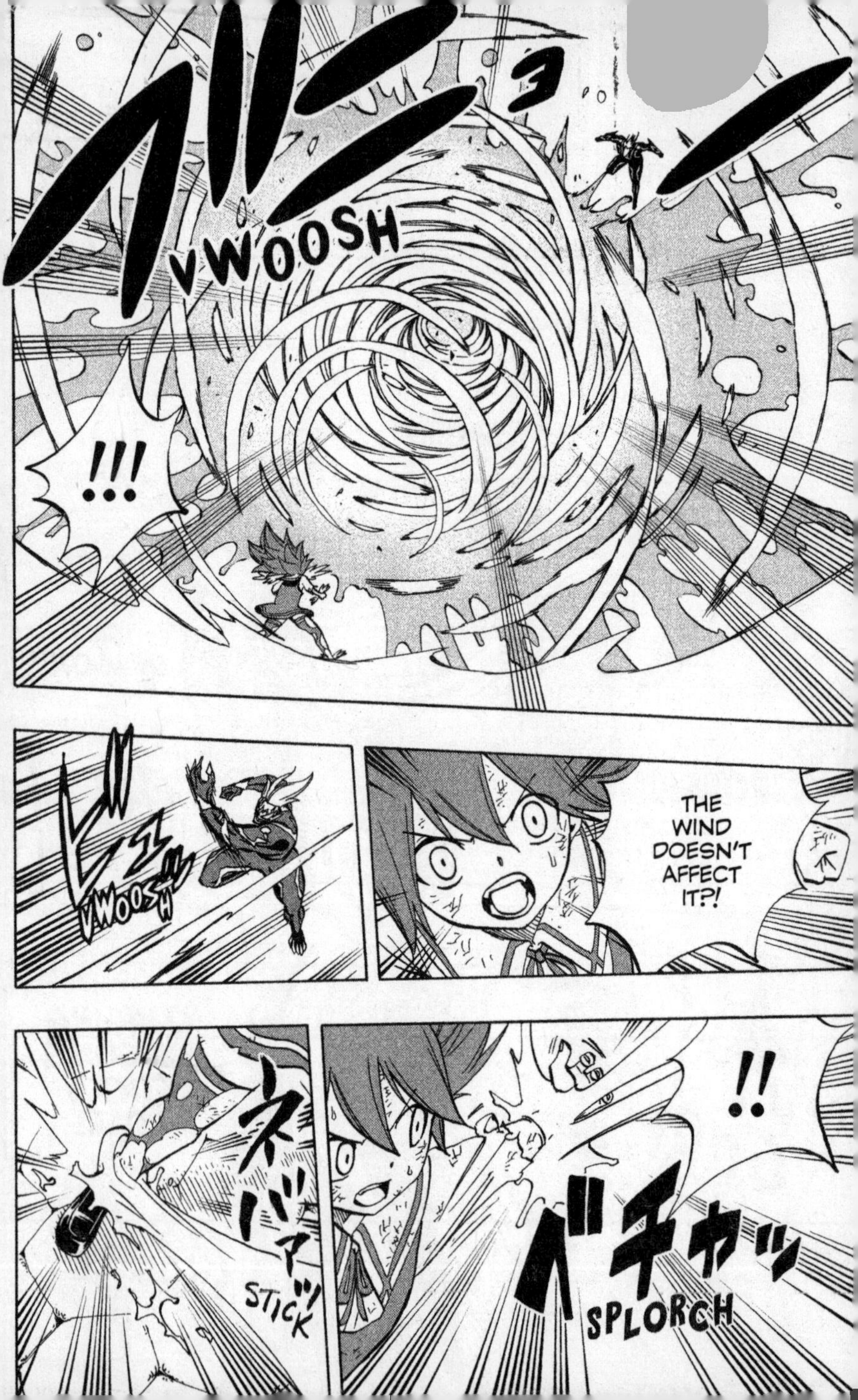
VWOOSH
!!!
THE WIND DOESN'T AFFECT IT?!
VWOOSH
!!
SPLORCH
STICK

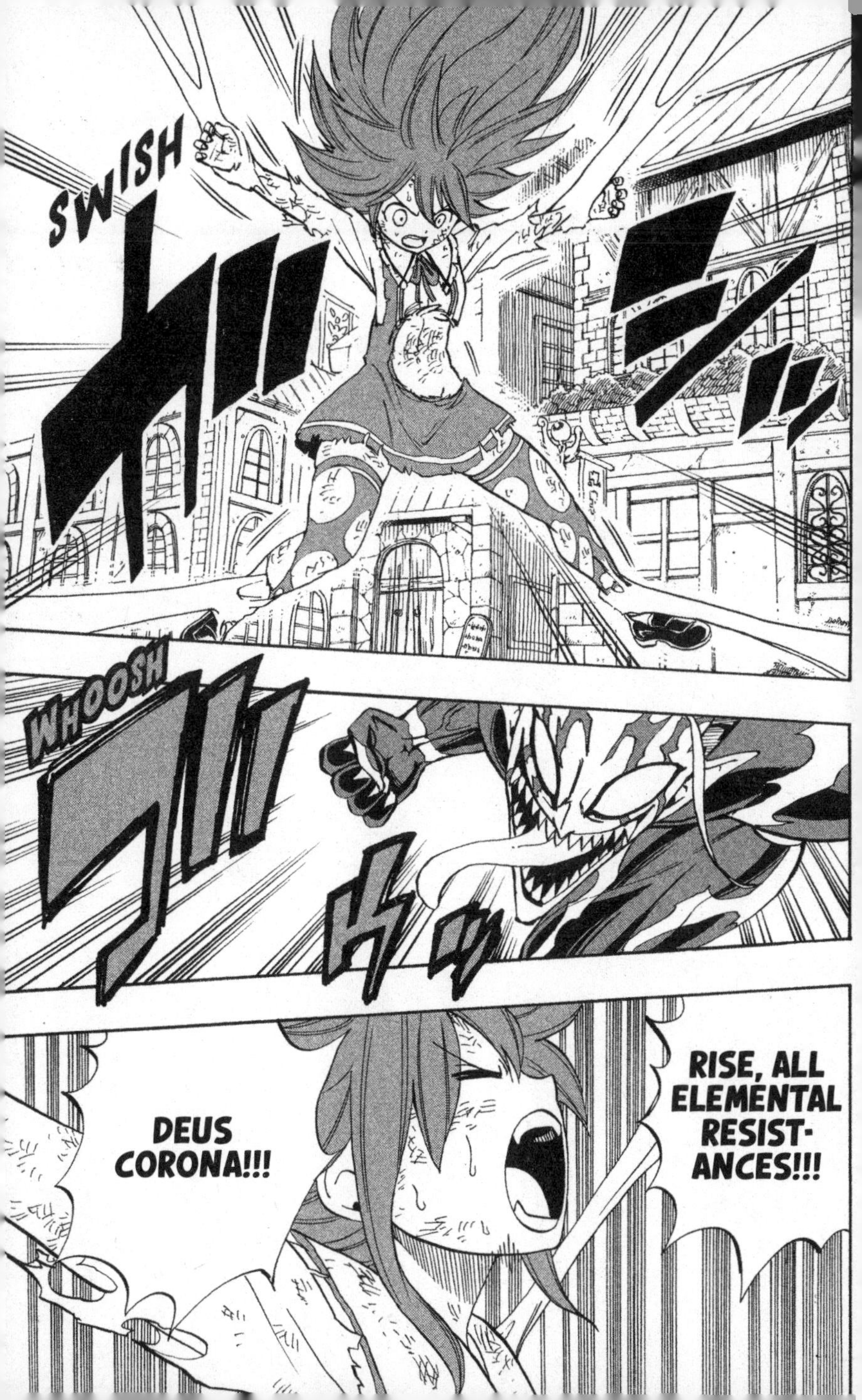
SWISH
WHOOSH
RISE, ALL ELEMENTAL RESIST-ANCES!!!
DEUS CORONA!!!

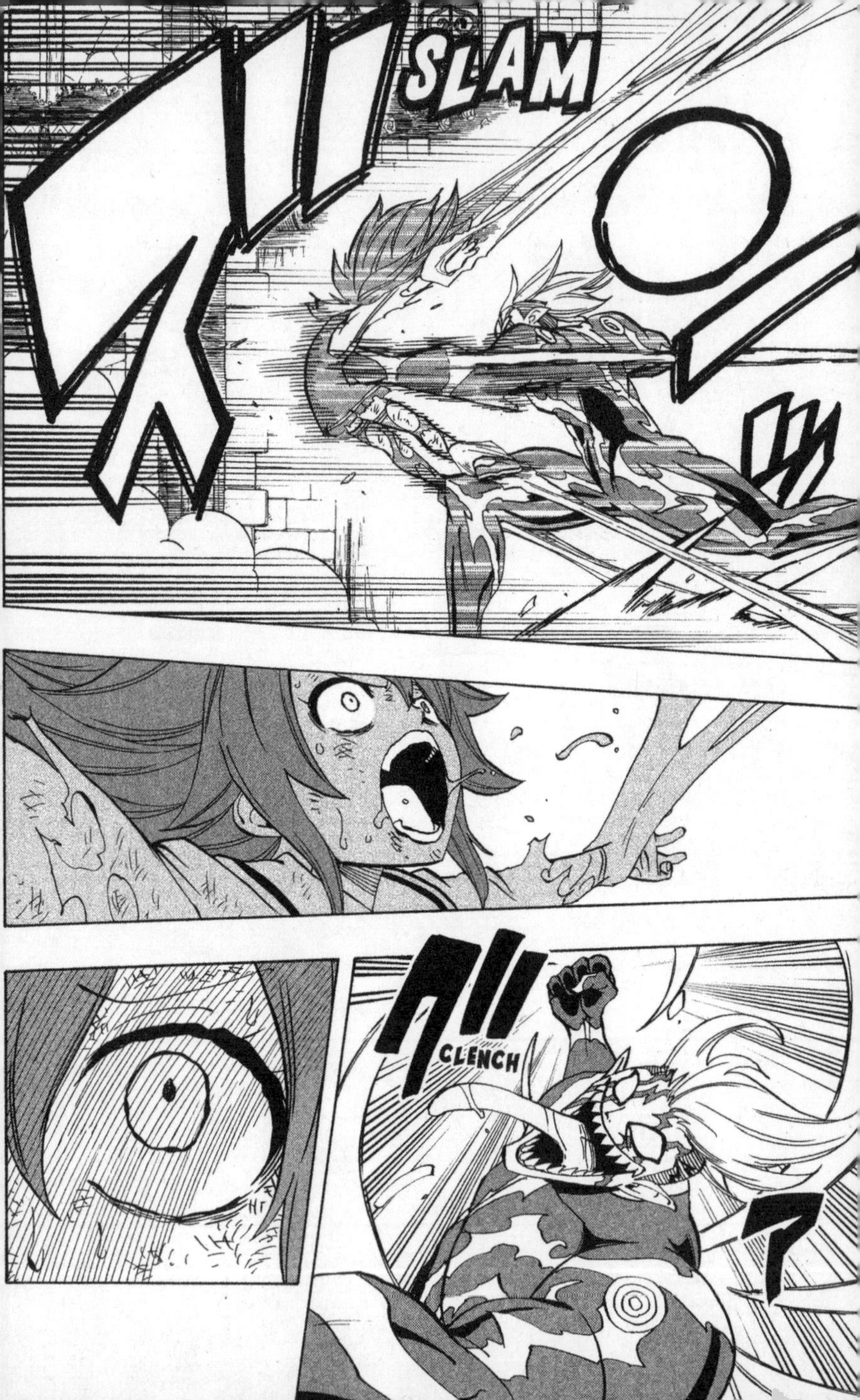
SLAM
CLENCH

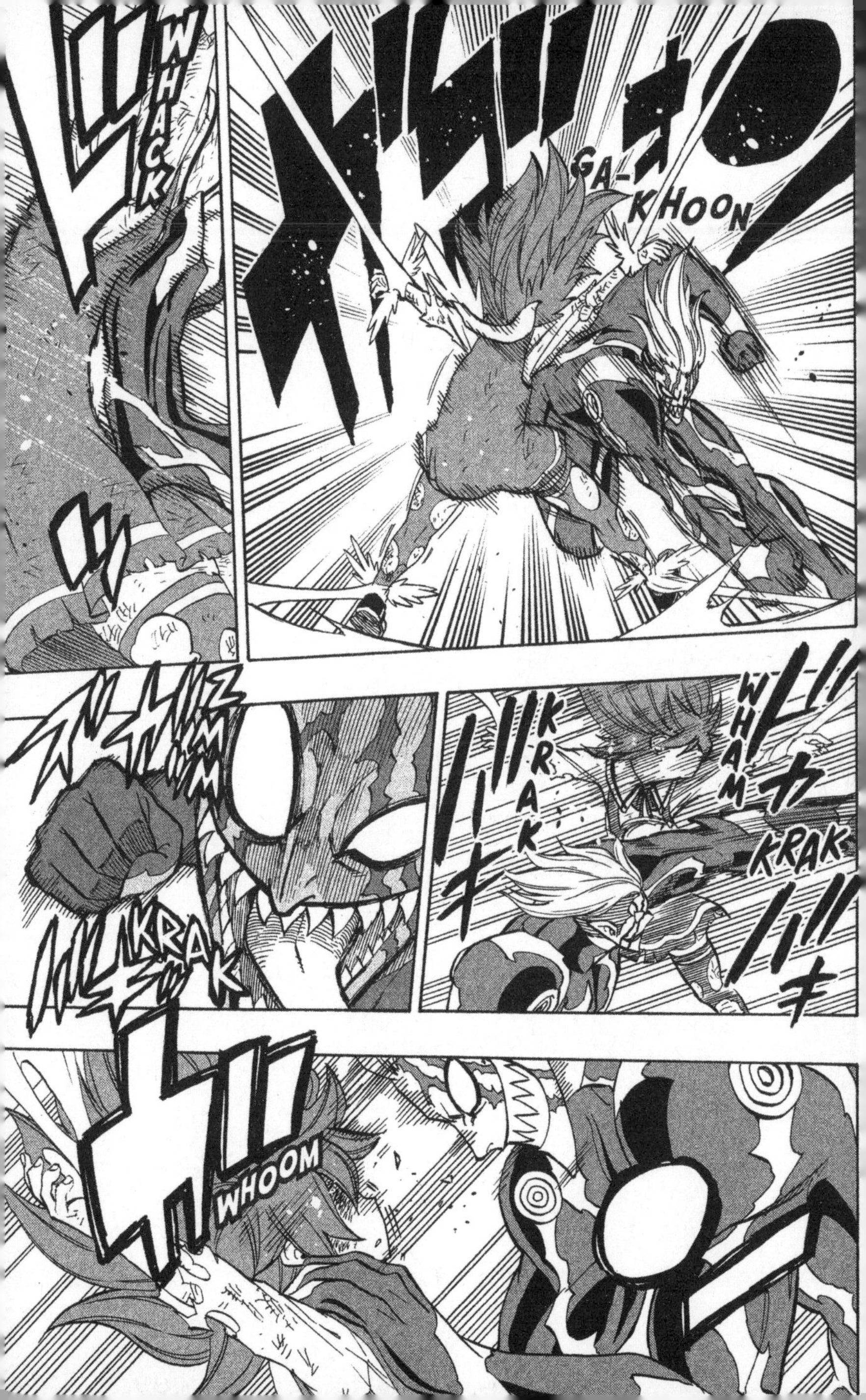
GA-KHOON
WHACK
WHAM
KRAK
KRAK
ZMMM
KRAK
WHOOM

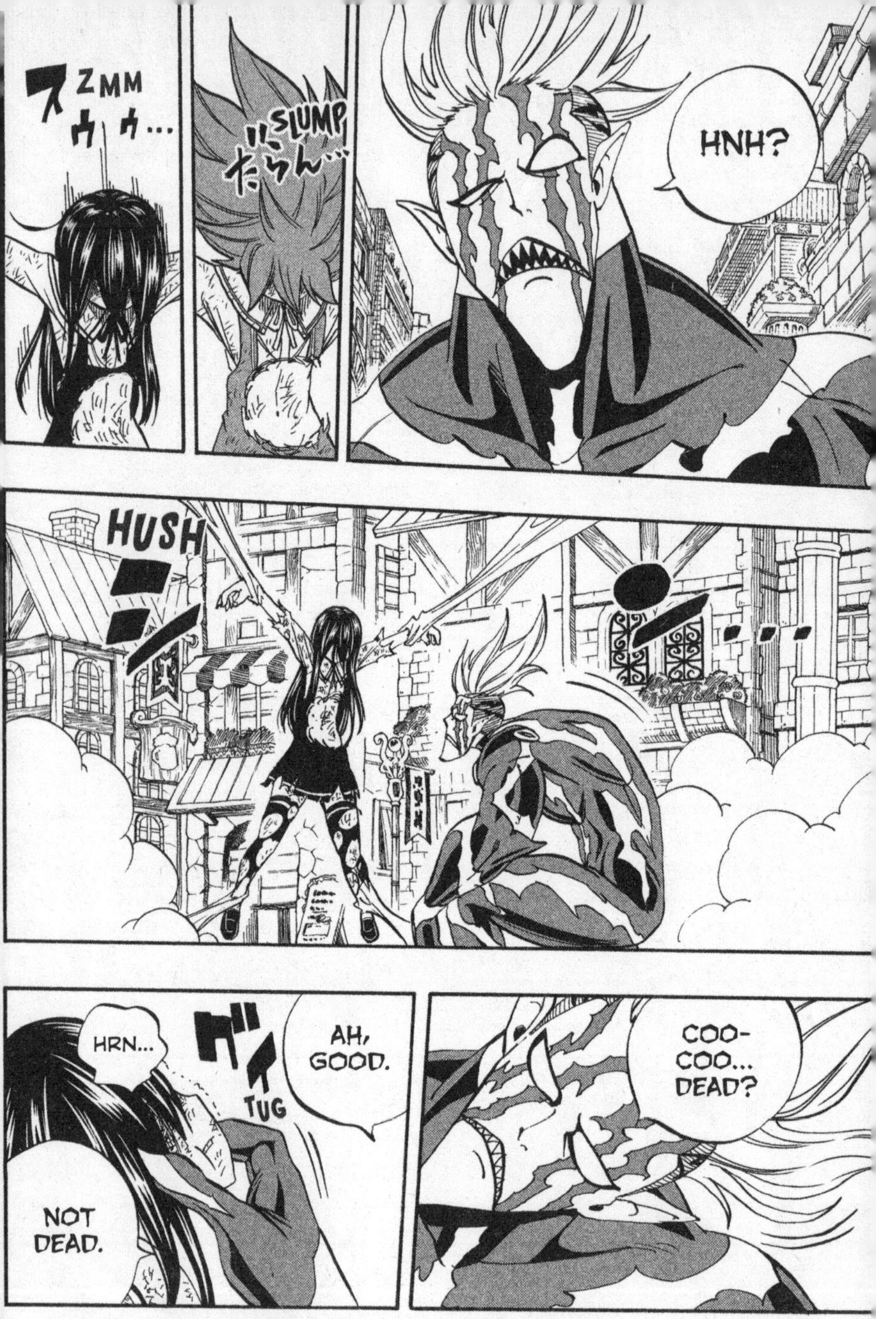
HNH?
SLUMP
だらん…
ZMM
スゥゥ…
HUSH
COO-COO... DEAD?
AH, GOOD.
TUG
HRN...
NOT DEAD.

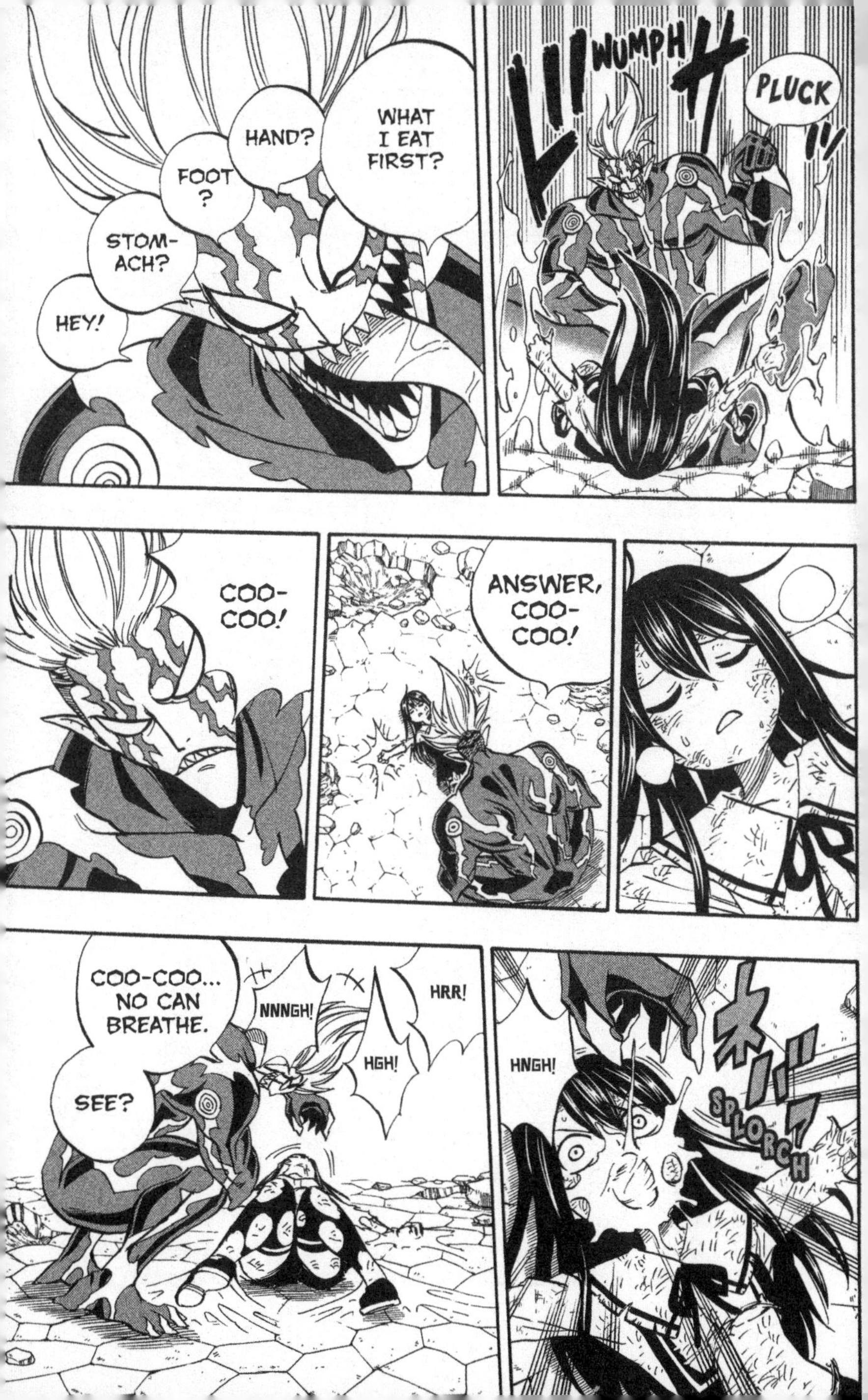
WUMPH
PLUCK
WHAT I EAT FIRST?
HAND?
FOOT?
STOM-
ACH?
HEY!
ANSWER, COO-COO!
COO-COO!
HNGH!
SPLORCH
HRR!
NNNGH!
COO-COO... NO CAN BREATHE.
HGH!
SEE?

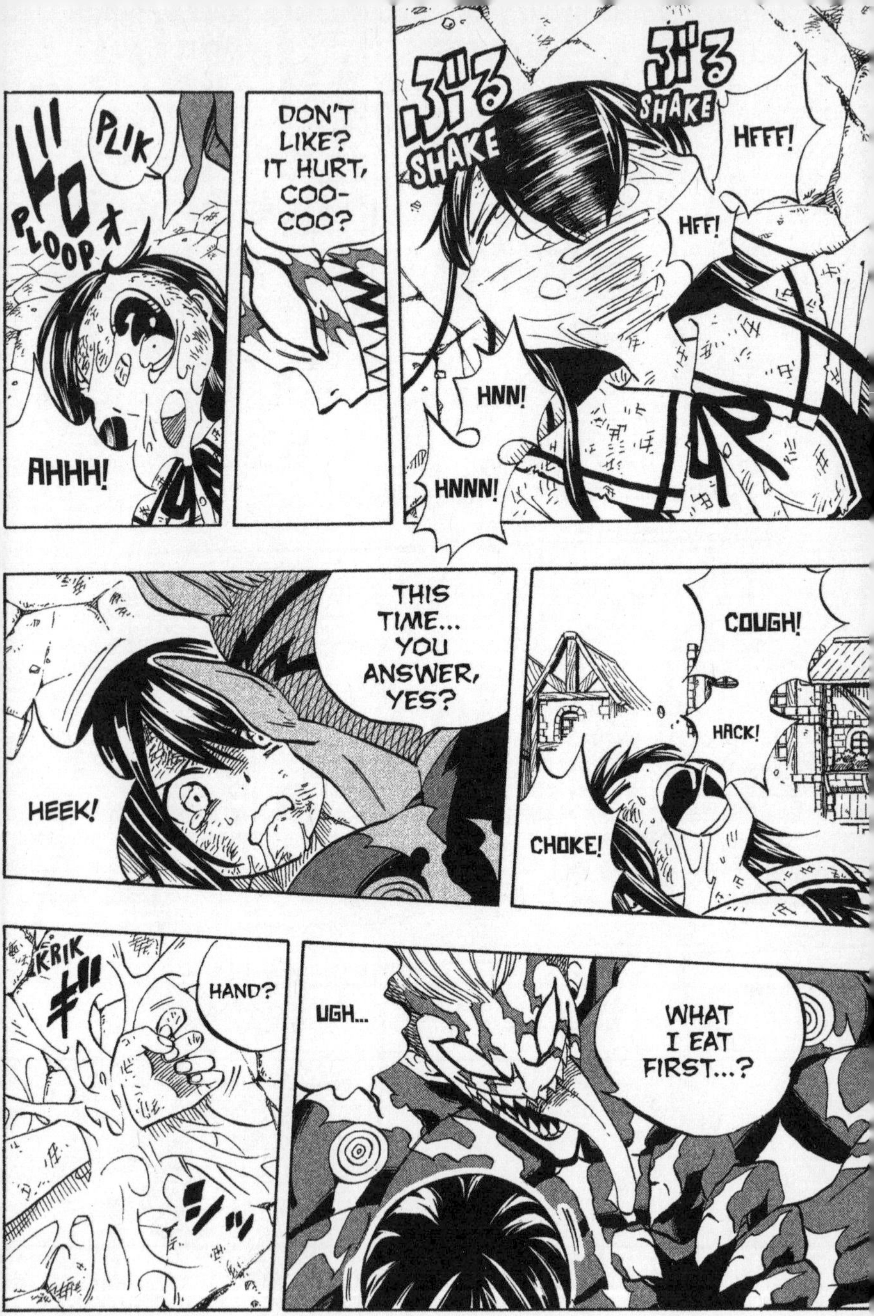
ぶる
SHAKE
HFFF!
ぶる
SHAKE
HFF!
HNN!
HNNN!
DON'T LIKE? IT HURT, COO-COO?
PLIK
PLOOP
AHHH!
COUGH!
HACK!
CHOKE!
THIS TIME... YOU ANSWER, YES?
HEEK!
WHAT I EAT FIRST...?
UGH...
HAND?
KRIK

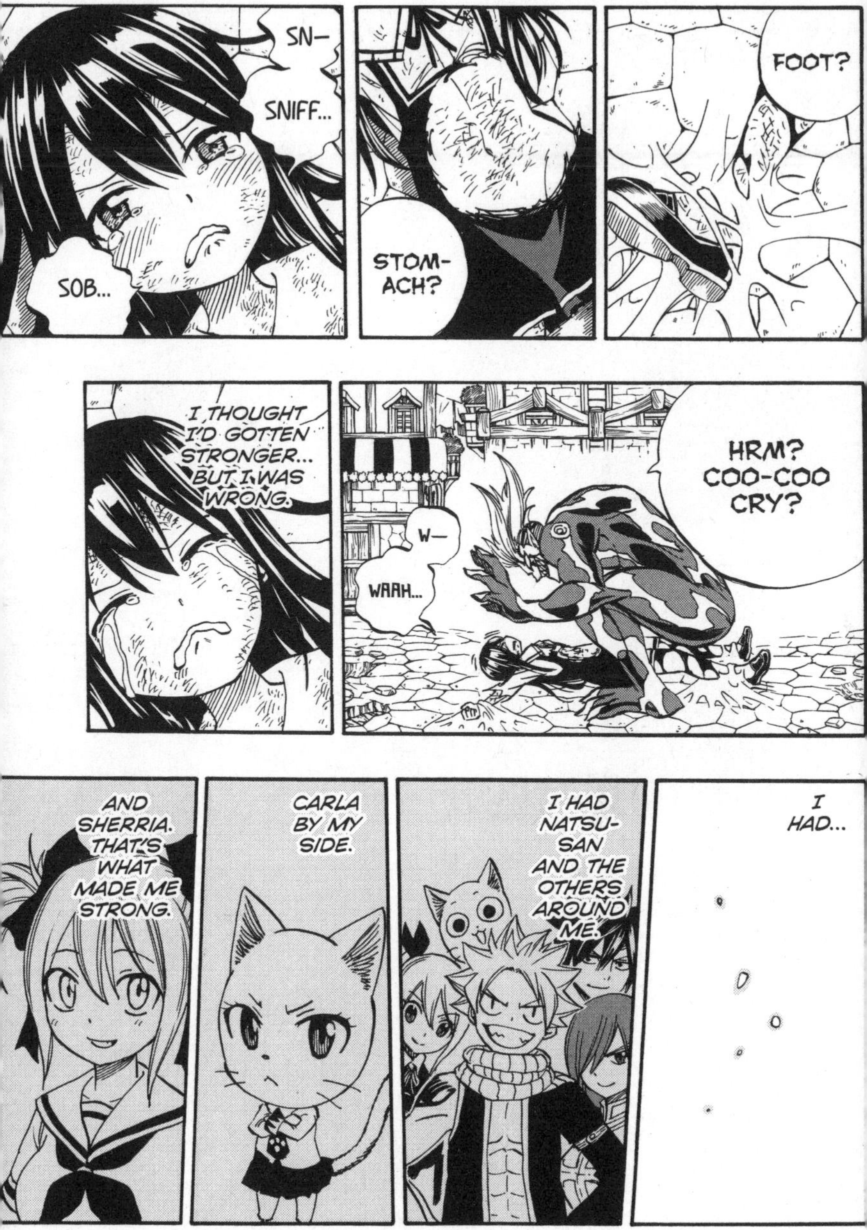
FOOT?
STOM-ACH?
SN—
SNIFF...
SOB...
HRM? COO-COO CRY?
W—
WAAH...
I THOUGHT I'D GOTTEN STRONGER... BUT I WAS WRONG.
I HAD...
I HAD NATSU-SAN AND THE OTHERS AROUND ME.
CARLA BY MY SIDE.
AND SHERRIA. THAT'S WHAT MADE ME STRONG.

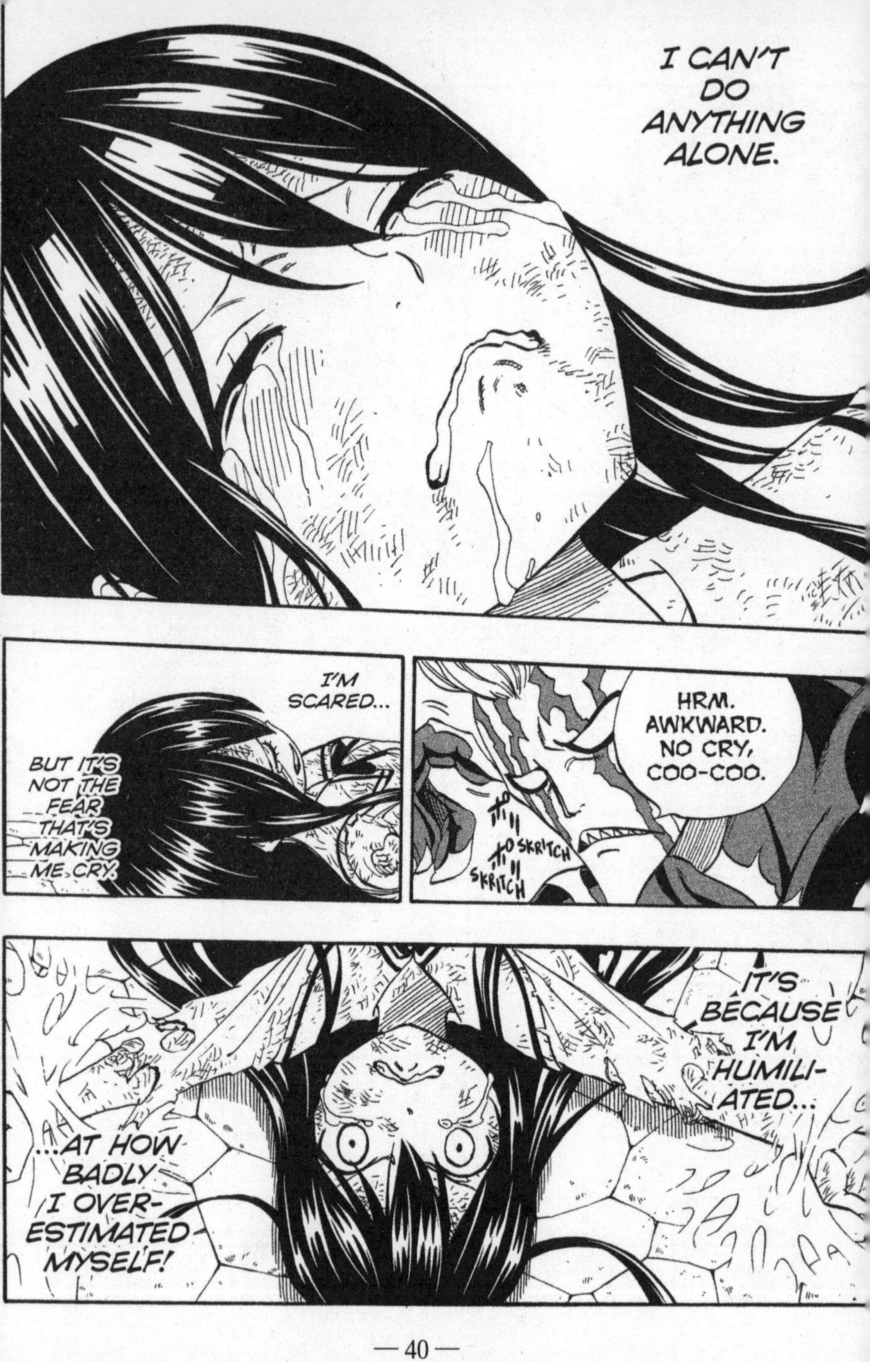
I CAN'T DO ANYTHING ALONE.
HRM. AWKWARD. NO CRY, COO-COO.
SKRITCH
SKRITCH
I'M SCARED...
BUT IT'S NOT THE FEAR THAT'S MAKING ME CRY.
IT'S BECAUSE I'M HUMILI-ATED...
...AT HOW BADLY I OVER-ESTIMATED MYSELF!

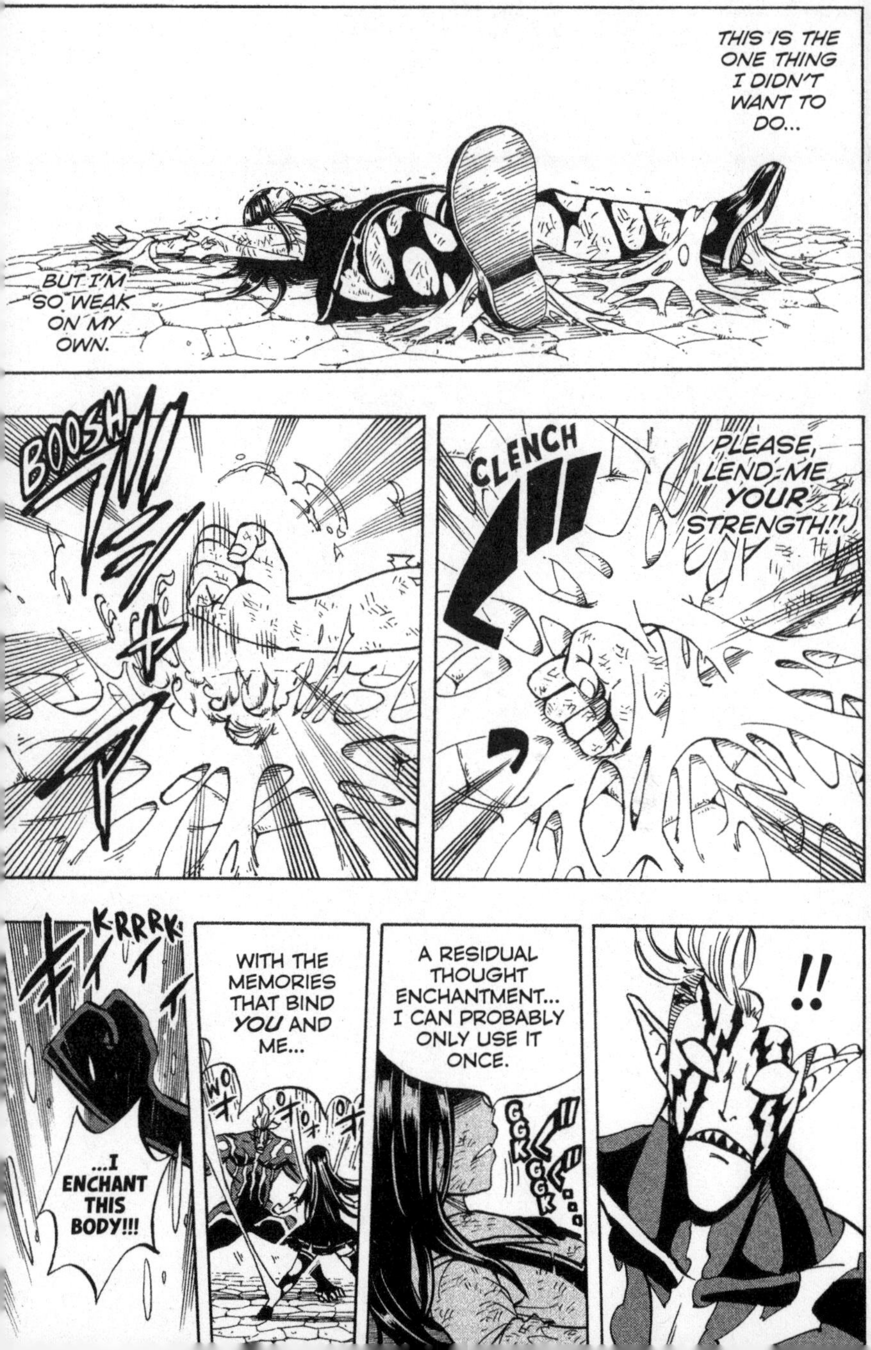
THIS IS THE ONE THING I DIDN'T WANT TO DO...
BUT I'M SO WEAK ON MY OWN.
PLEASE, LEND ME YOUR STRENGTH!!
CLENCH
BOOSH
!!
A RESIDUAL THOUGHT ENCHANTMENT... I CAN PROBABLY ONLY USE IT ONCE.
GGK GGK
WITH THE MEMORIES THAT BIND YOU AND ME...
K-RRRK
...I ENCHANT THIS BODY!!!

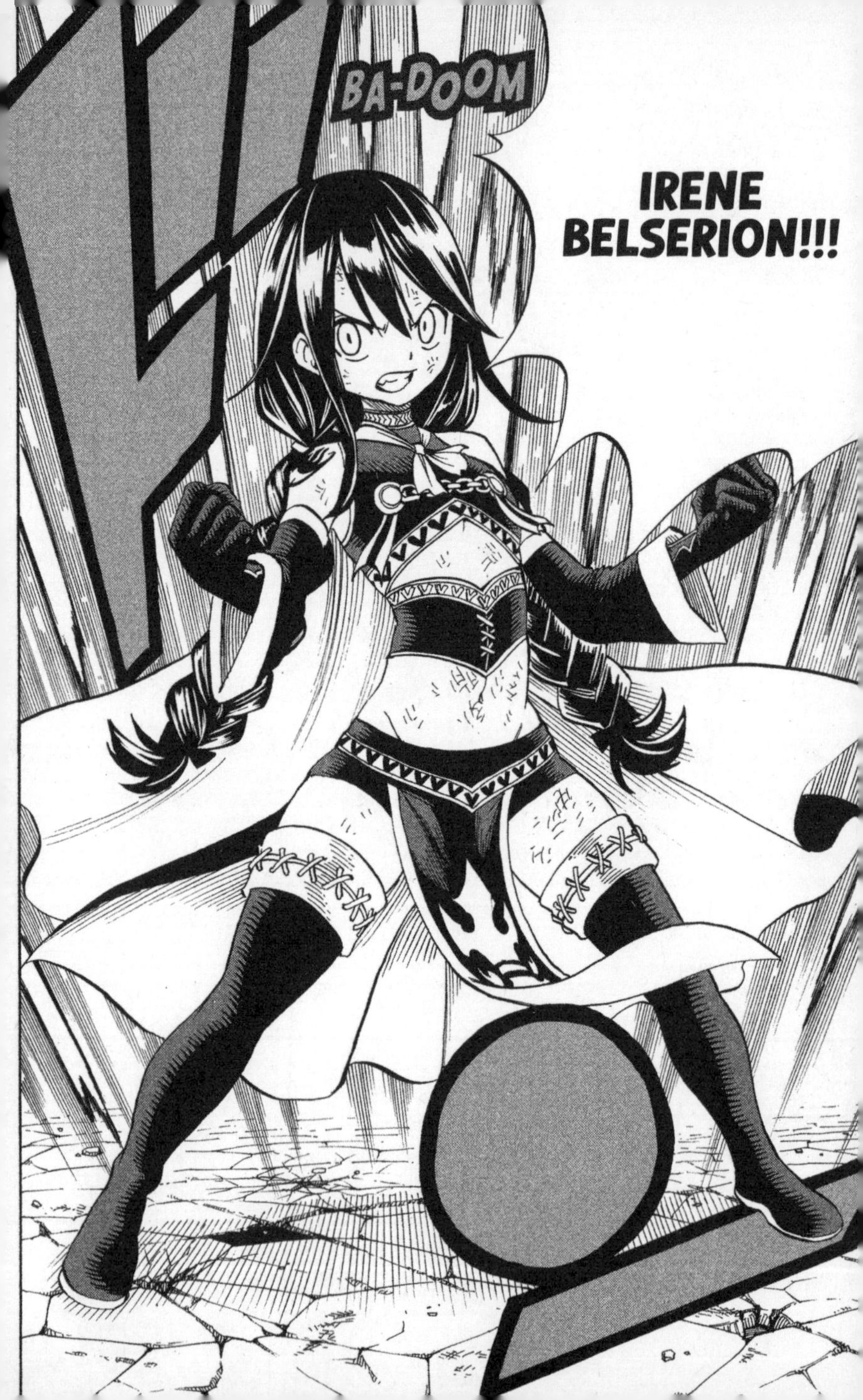
BA-DOOM
IRENE BELSERION!!!

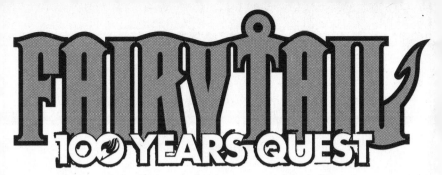

FAIRY TAIL
100 YEARS QUEST

Chapter 48: Fifth-Generation Dragon Force

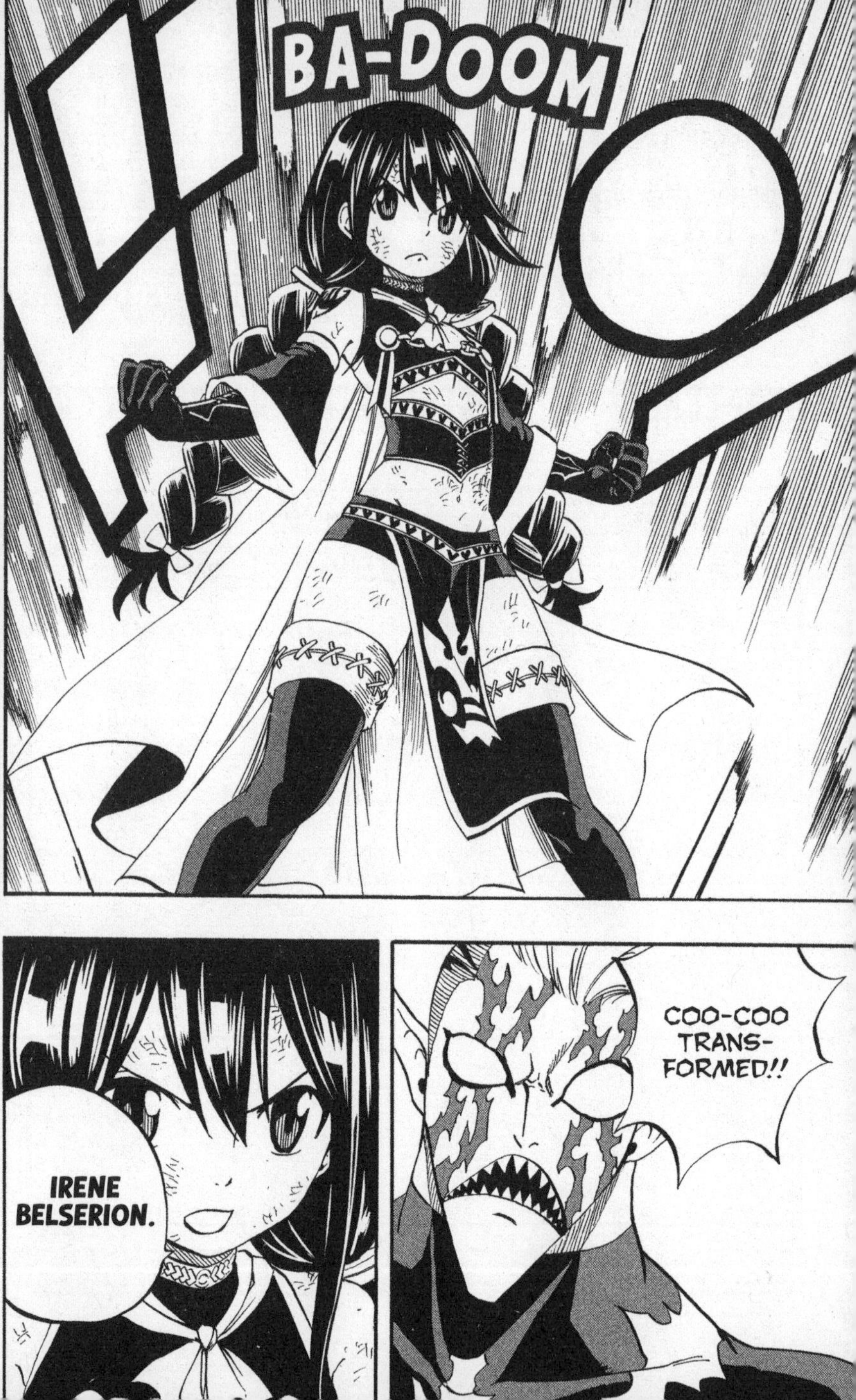
BA-DOOM
COO-COO TRANSFORMED!!
IRENE BELSERION.

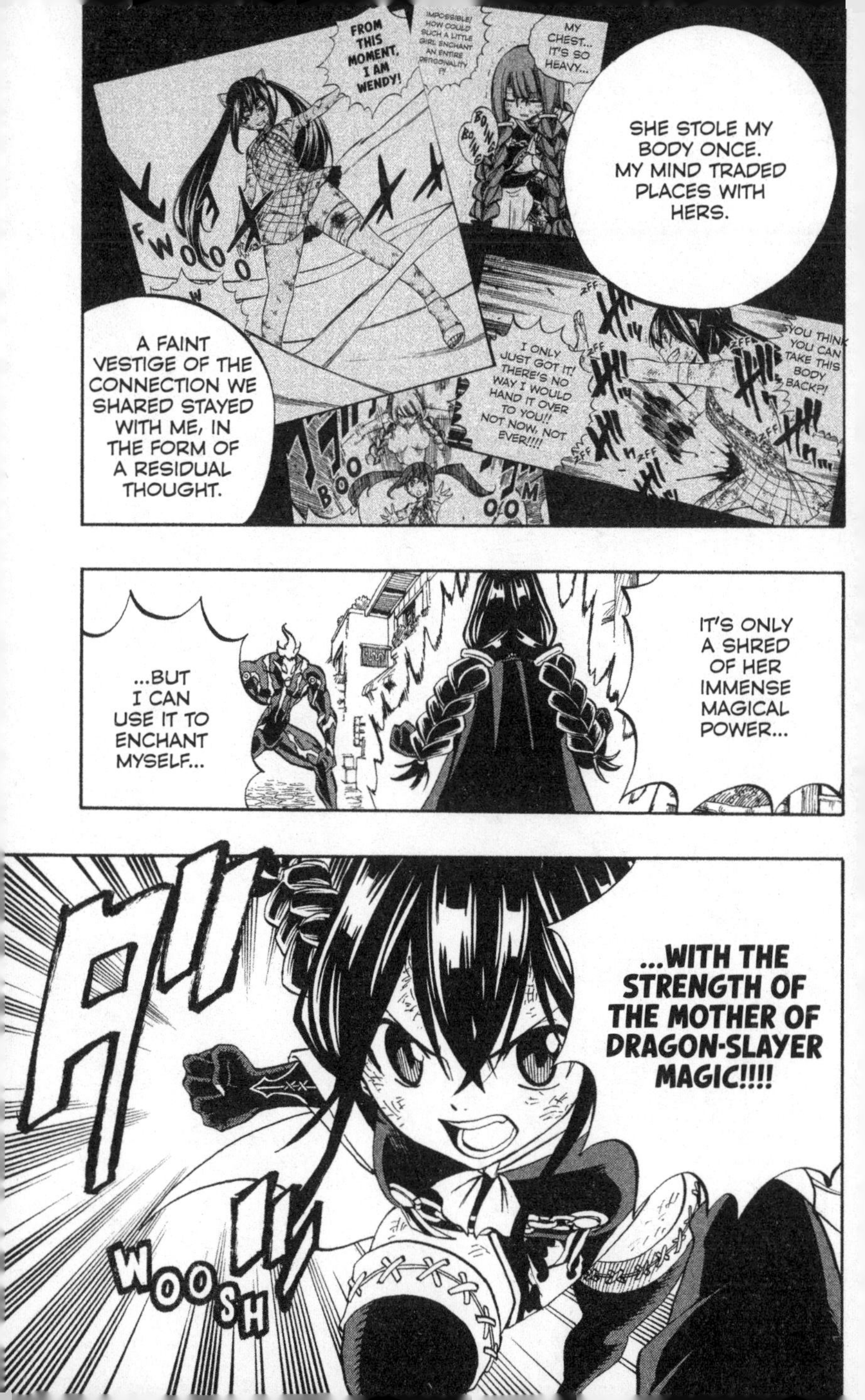
SHE STOLE MY BODY ONCE. MY MIND TRADED PLACES WITH HERS.
MY CHEST... IT'S SO HEAVY...
IMPOSSIBLE! HOW COULD SUCH A LITTLE GIRL ENCHANT AN ENTIRE PERSONALITY?!
FROM THIS MOMENT, I AM WENDY!
BOING BOING
FWOOOO
YOU THINK YOU CAN TAKE THIS BODY BACK?!
I ONLY JUST GOT IT! THERE'S NO WAY I WOULD HAND IT OVER TO YOU!! NOT NOW, NOT EVER!!!!
BOOOM
A FAINT VESTIGE OF THE CONNECTION WE SHARED STAYED WITH ME, IN THE FORM OF A RESIDUAL THOUGHT.
IT'S ONLY A SHRED OF HER IMMENSE MAGICAL POWER...
...BUT I CAN USE IT TO ENCHANT MYSELF...
...WITH THE STRENGTH OF THE MOTHER OF DRAGON-SLAYER MAGIC!!!!
WOOSH

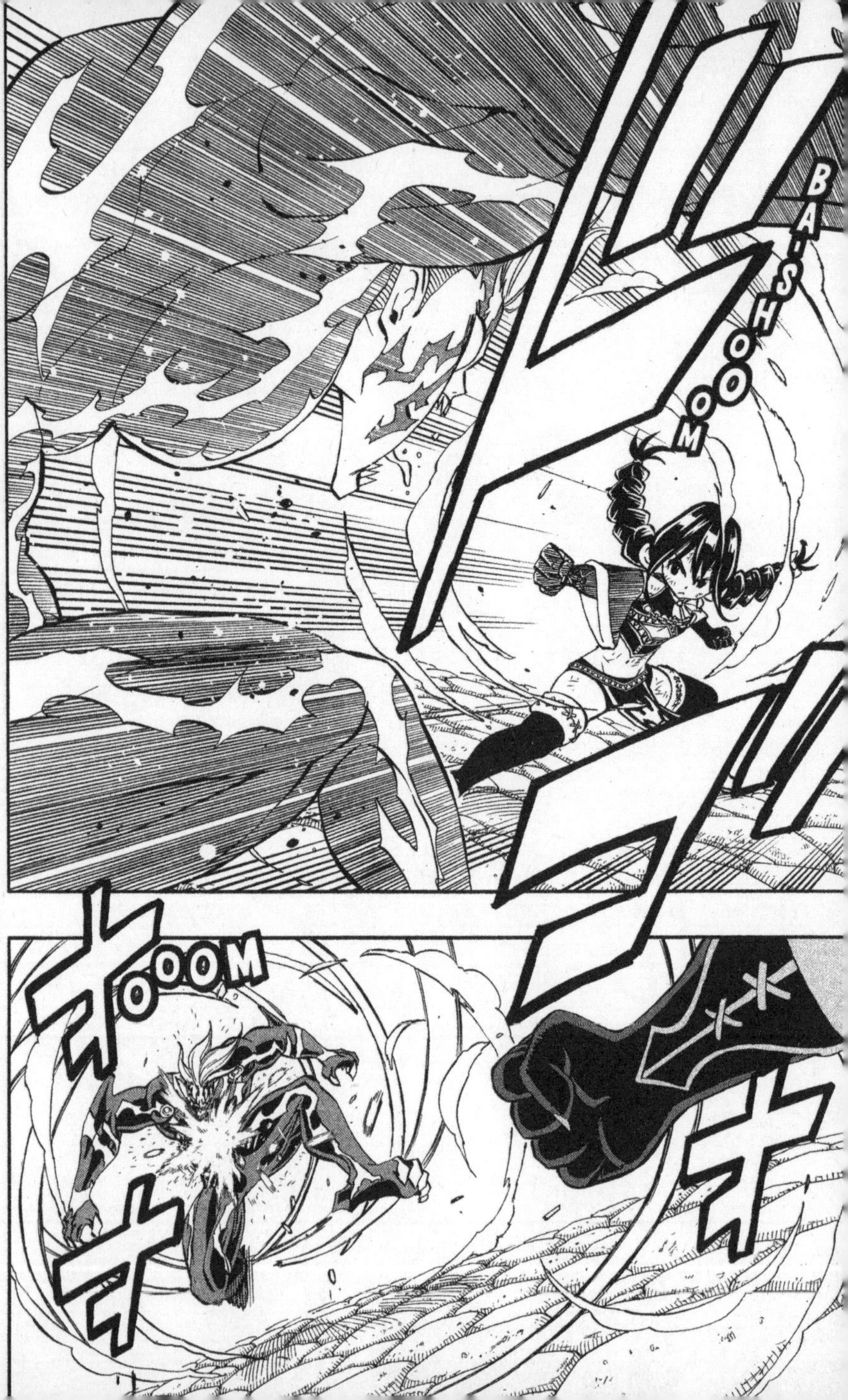
BASHOOOOM
WOOOM

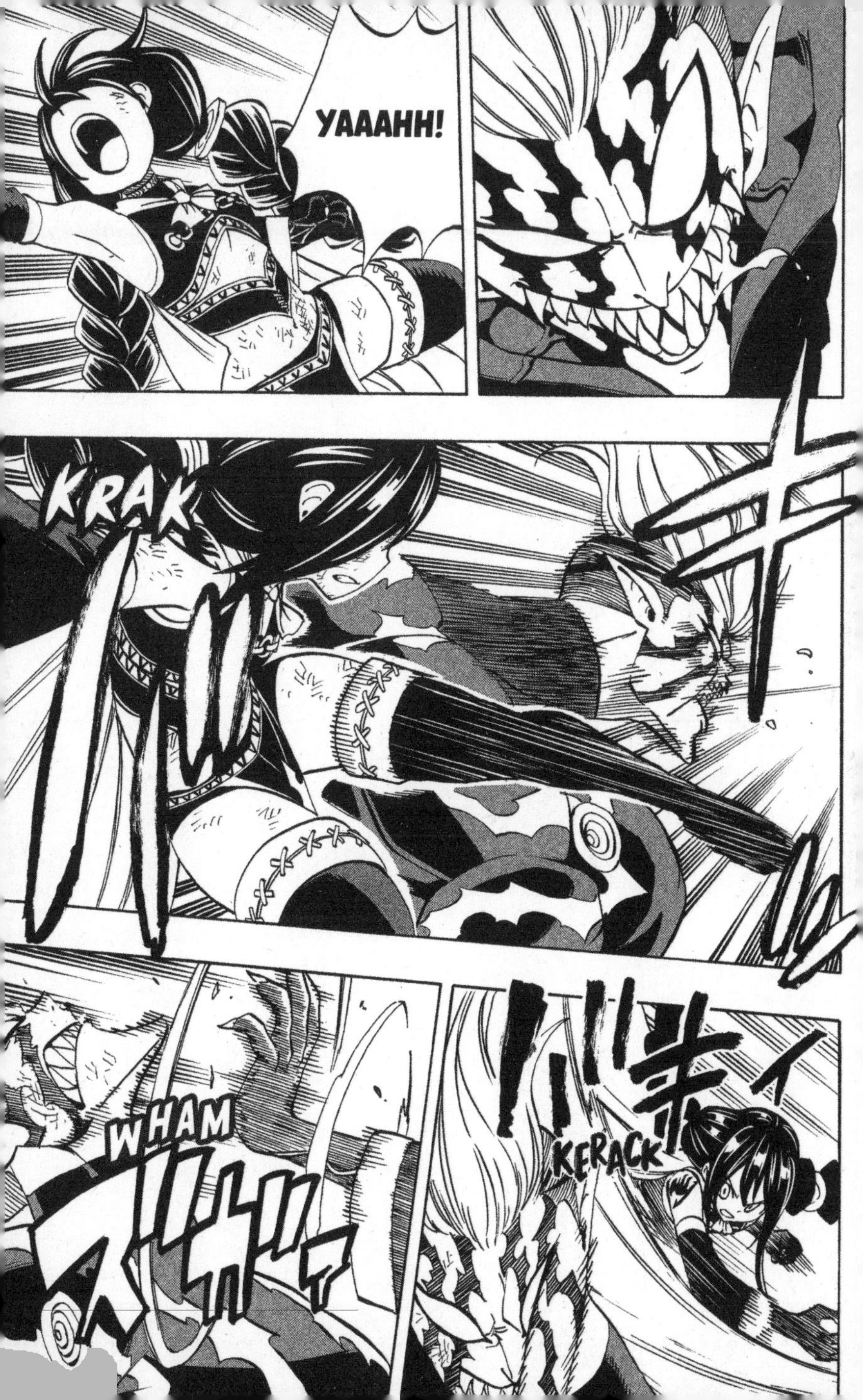
YAAAHH!
KRAK
KERACK
WHAM

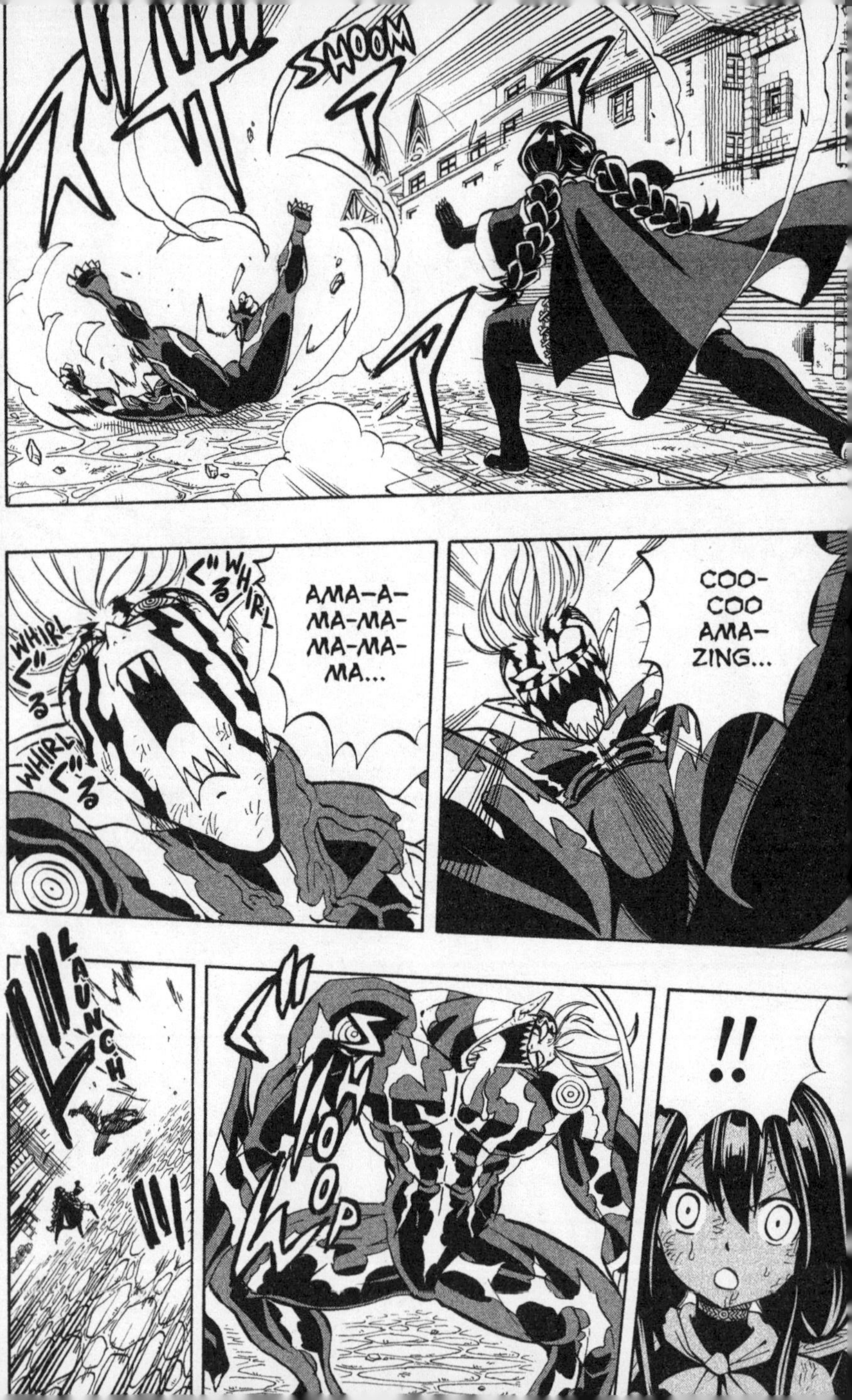
SHOOM
COO-COO AMA-ZING...
WHIRL ぐる
AMA-A-MA-MA-MA-MA-MA-MA...
WHIRL ぐる
WHIRL ぐる
!!
WHOOP
LAUNCH

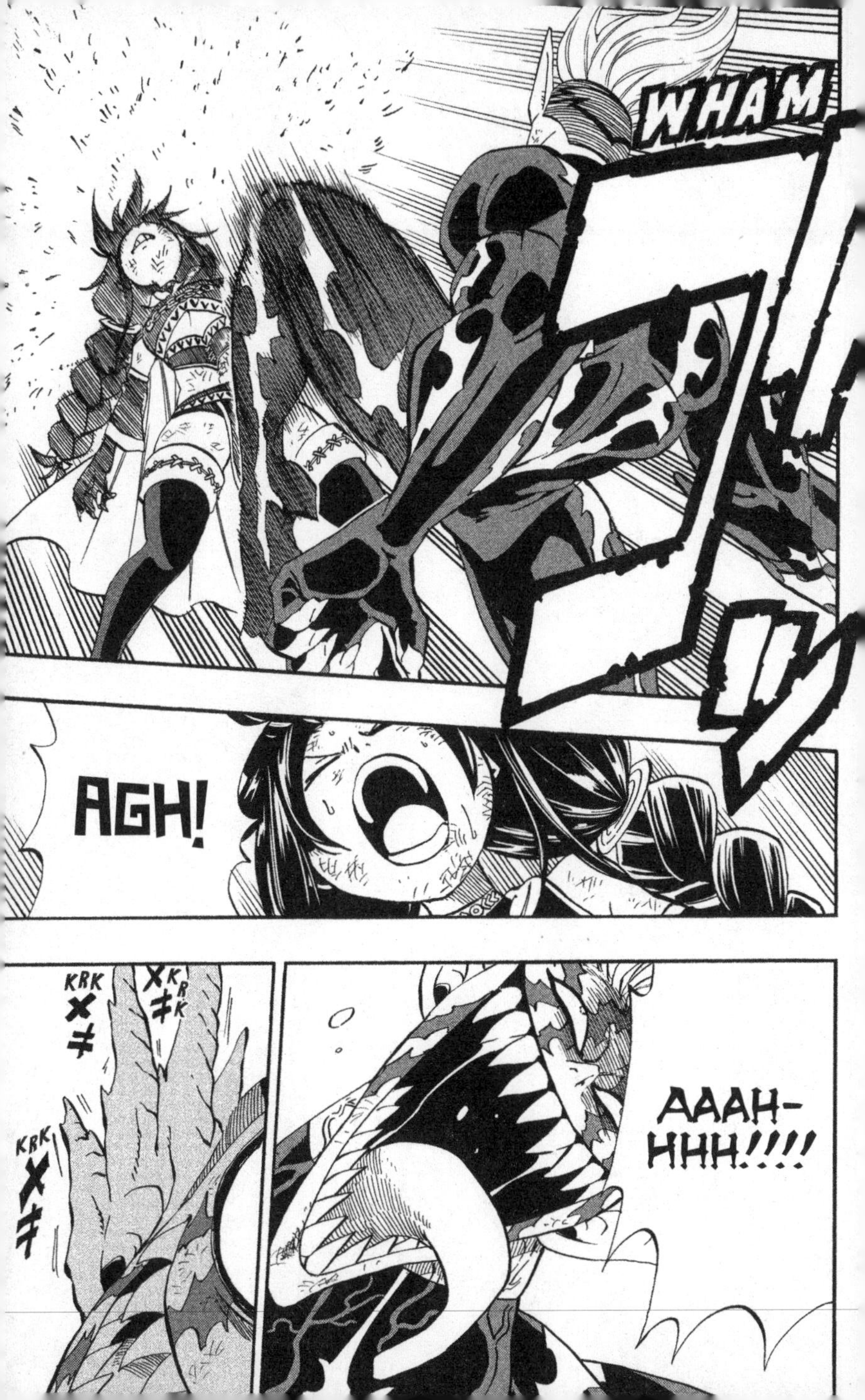
WHAM
AGH!
AAAH-HHH!!!!
KRK メキ
KRK メキ
KRK メキ

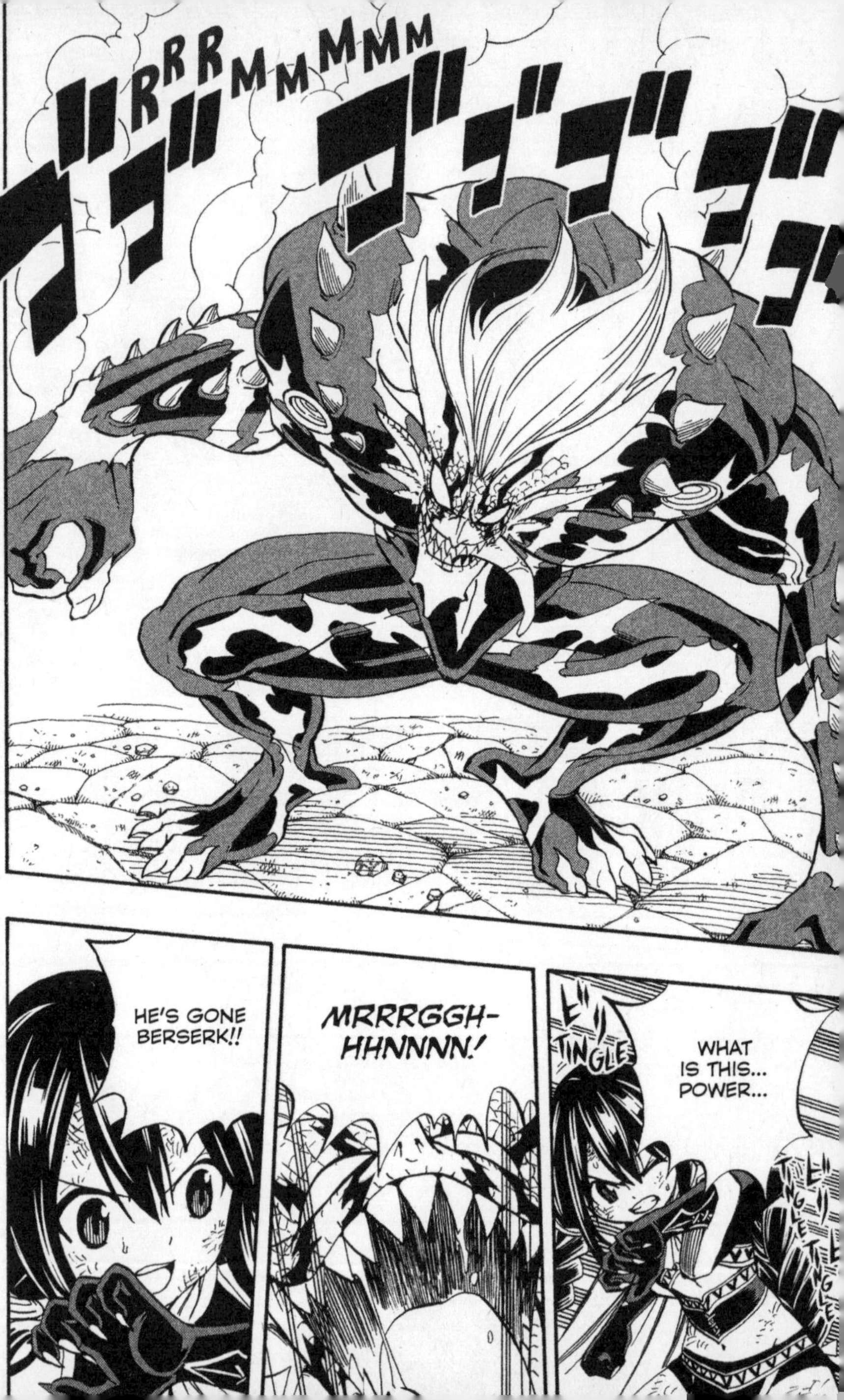
RRRMMMMM
TINGLE
WHAT IS THIS... POWER...
TINGLE TINGLE
MRRRGGH-HHNNNN!
HE'S GONE BERSERK!!

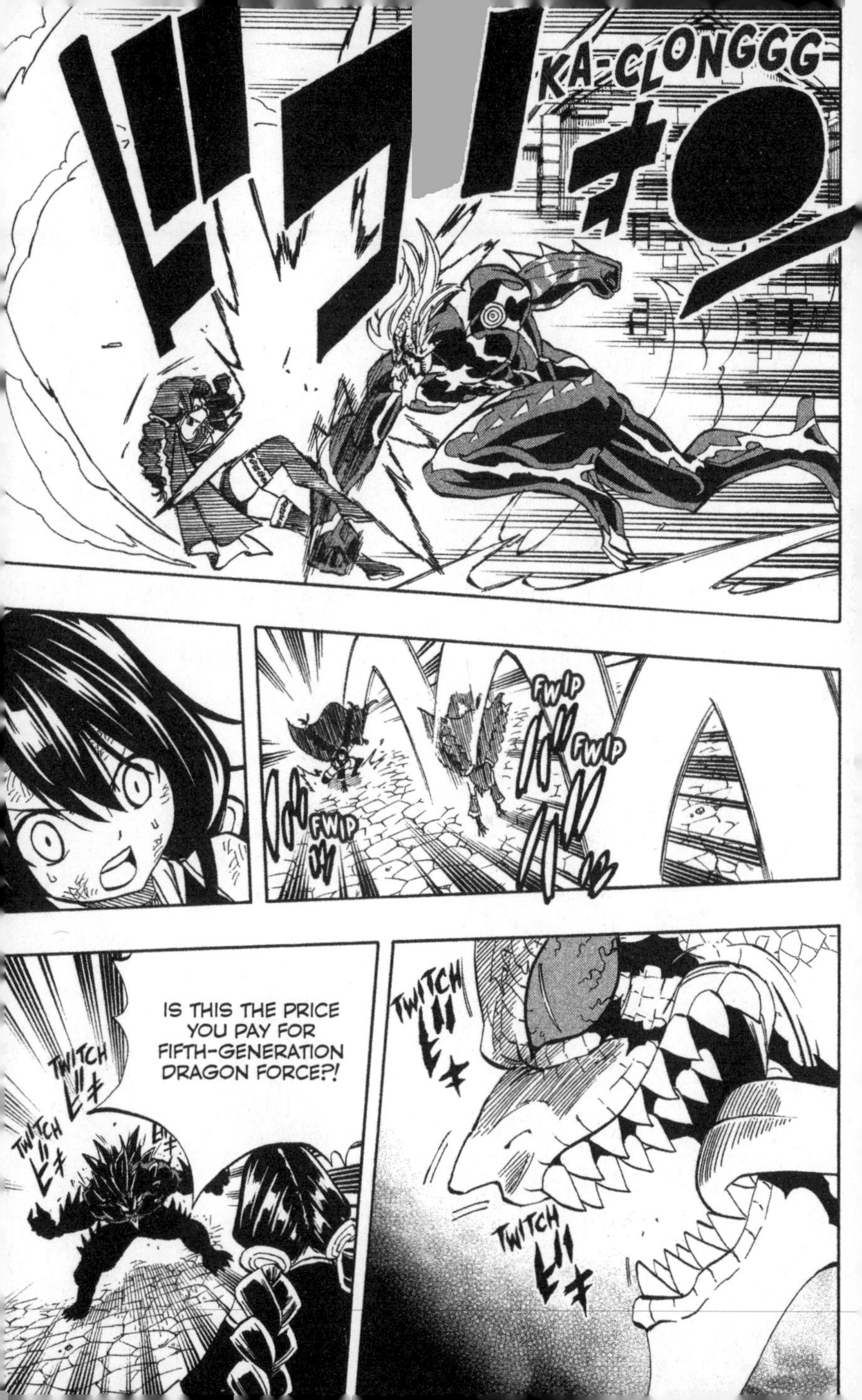
KA-CLONGGG
FWIP
FWIP
FWIP
TWITCH
TWITCH
IS THIS THE PRICE YOU PAY FOR FIFTH-GENERATION DRAGON FORCE?!
TWITCH
TWITCH

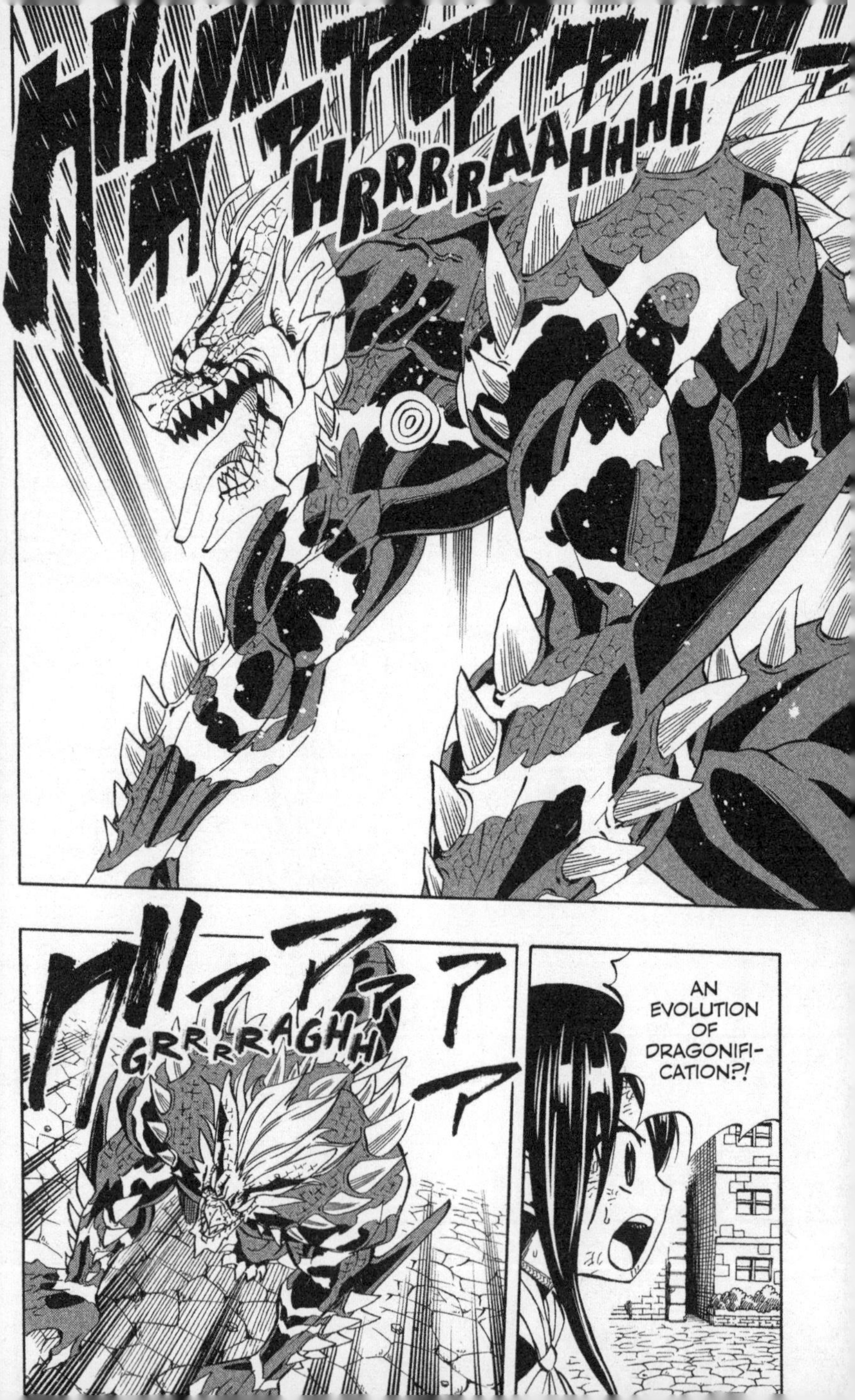
HRRRRAAHHHH
AN EVOLUTION OF DRAGONIFICATION?!
GRRRRAGHH

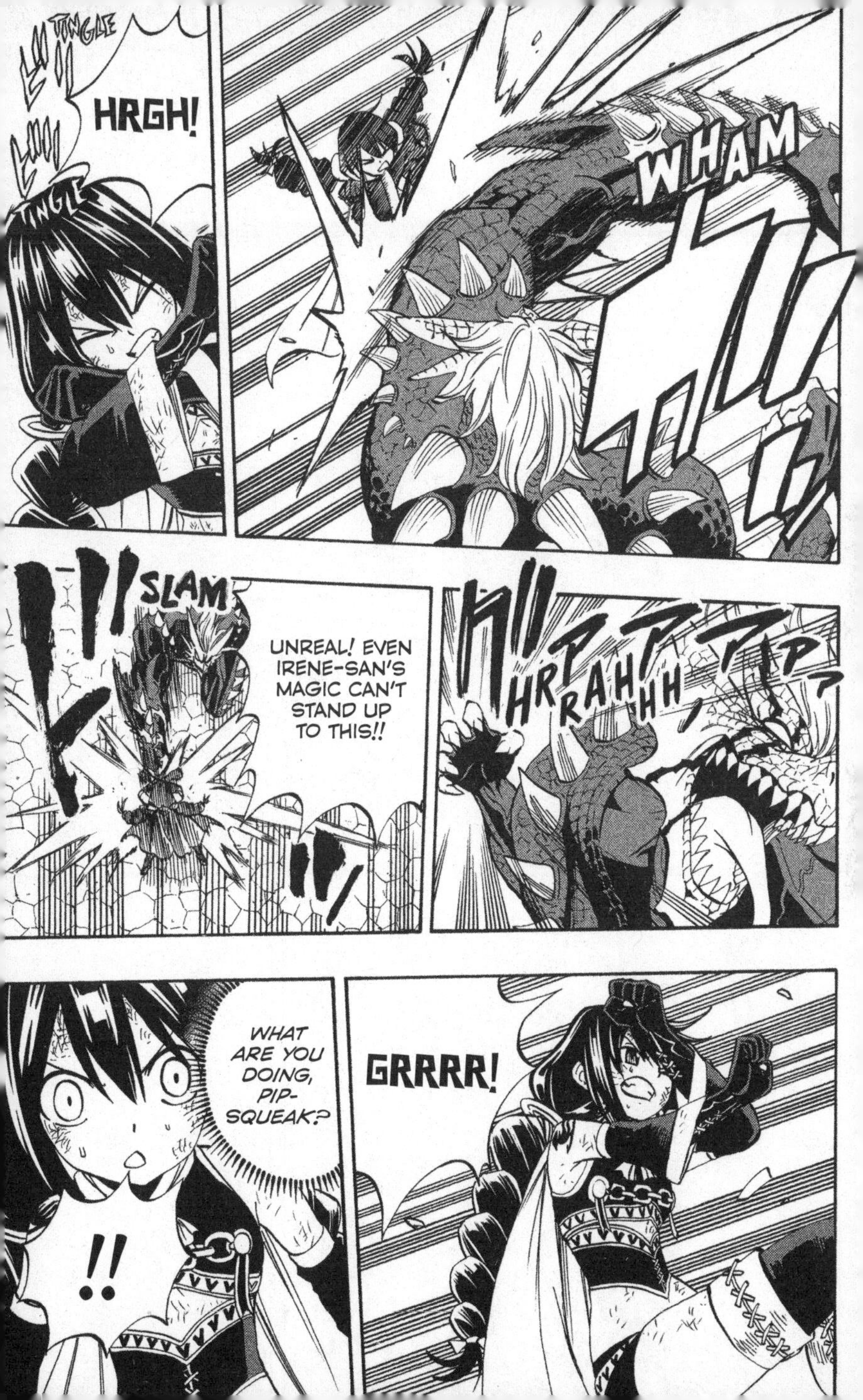
WHAM
TINGLE
HRGH!
TINGLE
HRAHHH
RIP
UNREAL! EVEN IRENE-SAN'S MAGIC CAN'T STAND UP TO THIS!!
SLAM
GRRRR!
WHAT ARE YOU DOING, PIP-SQUEAK?
!!

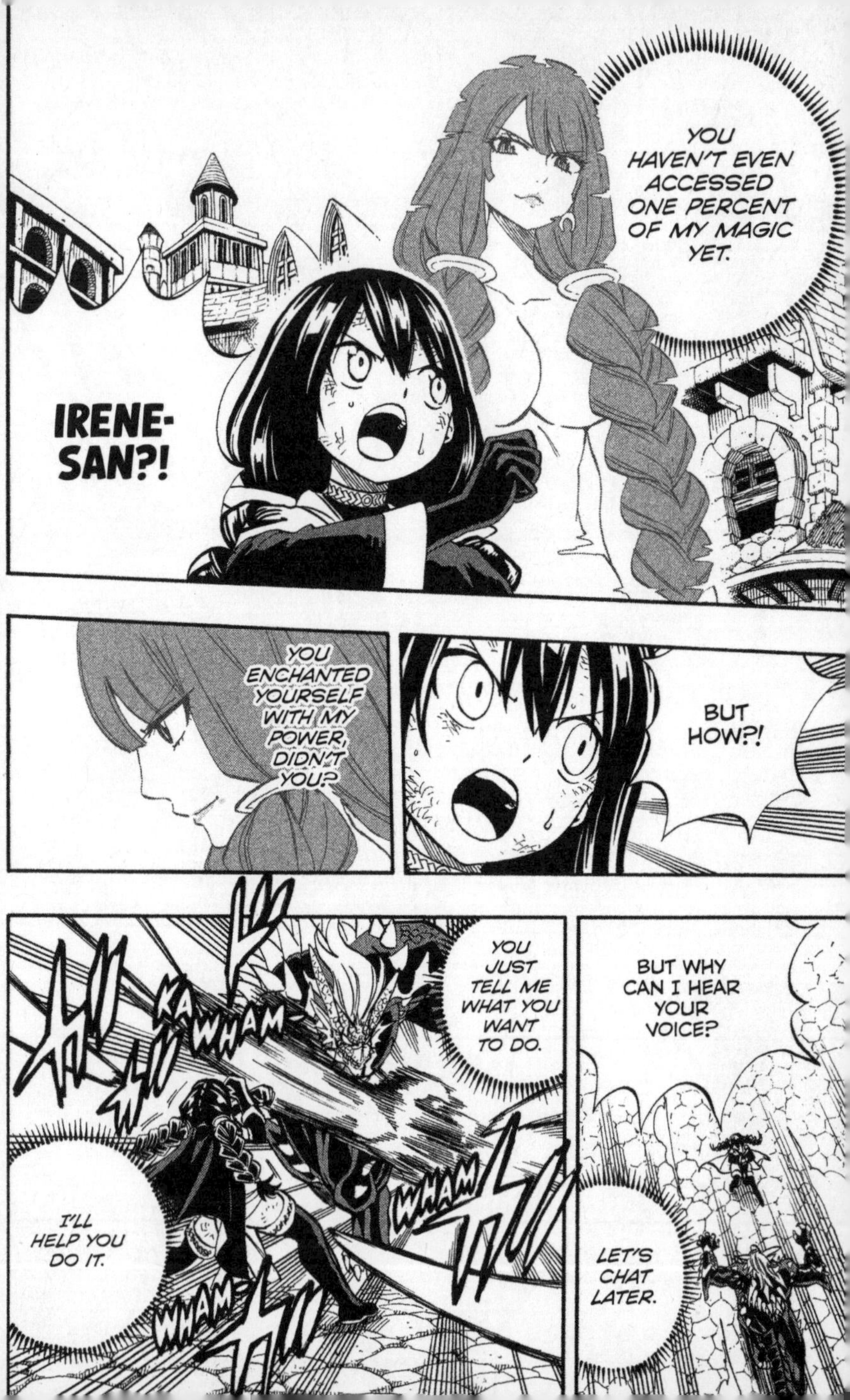
YOU HAVEN'T EVEN ACCESSED ONE PERCENT OF MY MAGIC YET.
IRENE-SAN?!
BUT HOW?!
YOU ENCHANTED YOURSELF WITH MY POWER, DIDN'T YOU?
BUT WHY CAN I HEAR YOUR VOICE?
LET'S CHAT LATER.
YOU JUST TELL ME WHAT YOU WANT TO DO.
KA WHAM
WHAM
I'LL HELP YOU DO IT.
WHAM

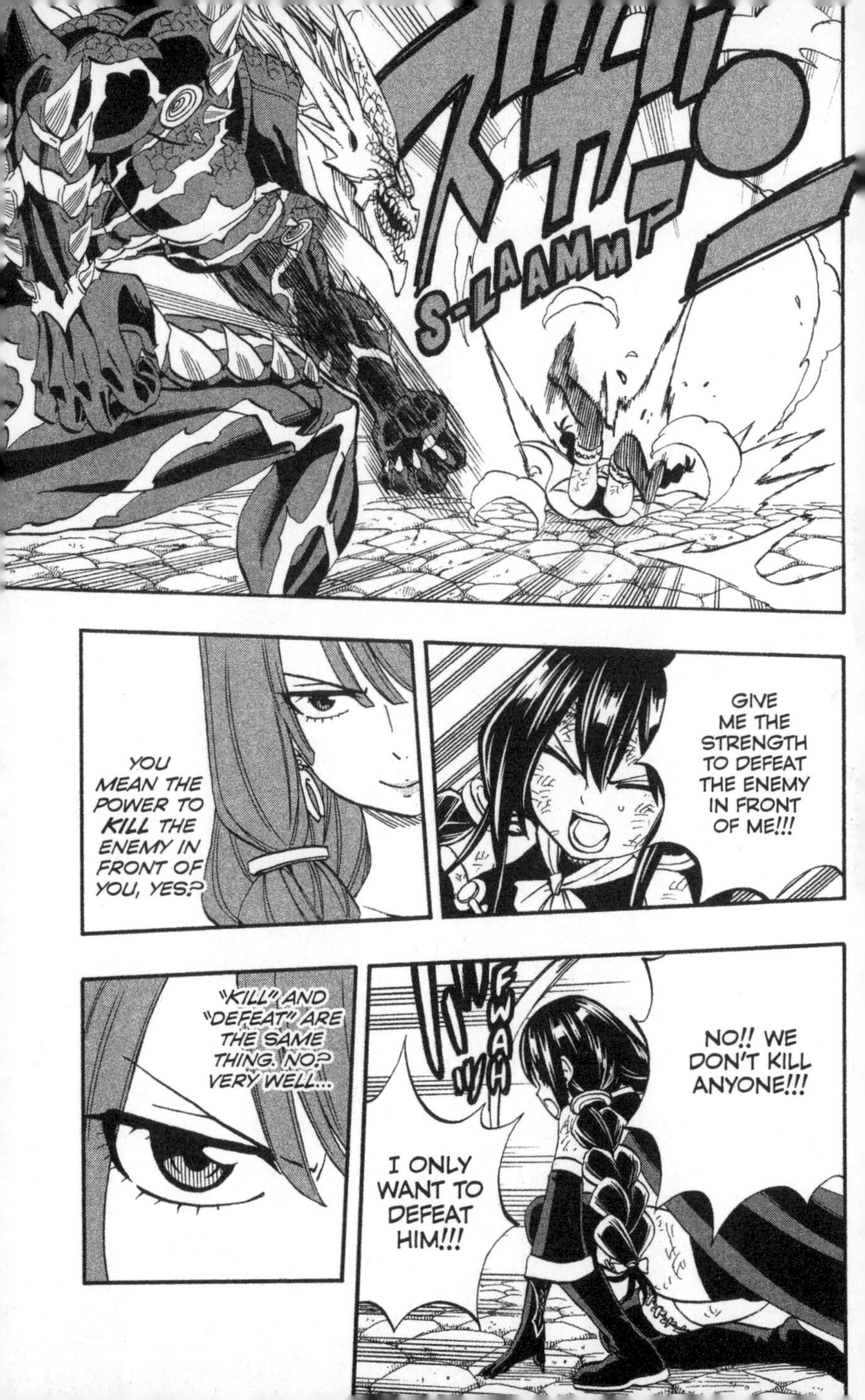
S-LAAMMP
GIVE ME THE STRENGTH TO DEFEAT THE ENEMY IN FRONT OF ME!!!
YOU MEAN THE POWER TO **KILL** THE ENEMY IN FRONT OF YOU, YES?
NO!! WE DON'T KILL ANYONE!!!
FWAH
I ONLY WANT TO DEFEAT HIM!!!
"KILL" AND "DEFEAT" ARE THE SAME THING. NO? VERY WELL...

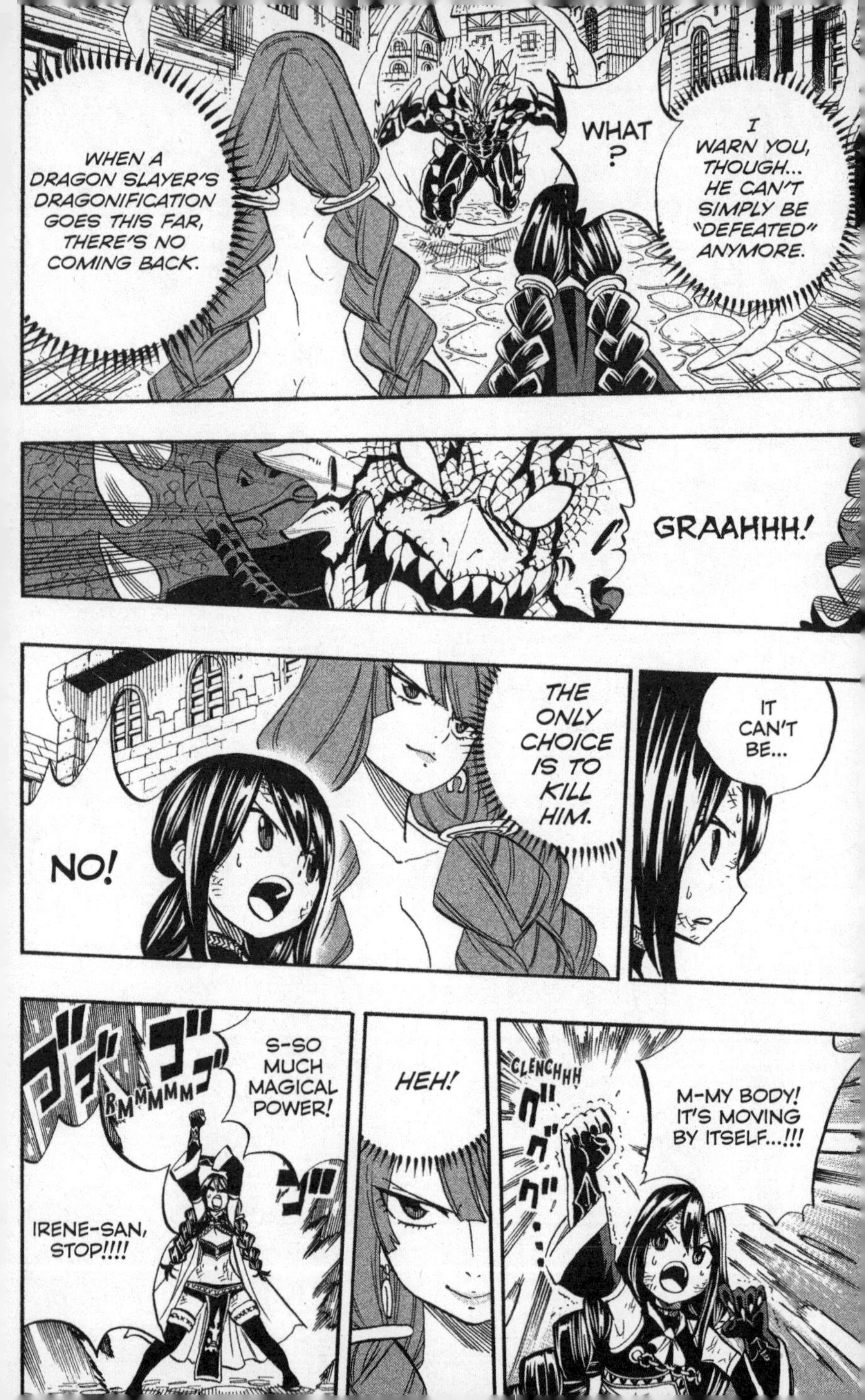
I WARN YOU, THOUGH... HE CAN'T SIMPLY BE "DEFEATED" ANYMORE.
WHAT?
WHEN A DRAGON SLAYER'S DRAGONIFICATION GOES THIS FAR, THERE'S NO COMING BACK.
GRAAHHH!
IT CAN'T BE...
THE ONLY CHOICE IS TO KILL HIM.
NO!
CLENCHHH
M-MY BODY! IT'S MOVING BY ITSELF...!!!
HEH!
S-SO MUCH MAGICAL POWER!
RMMMMM
IRENE-SAN, STOP!!!!

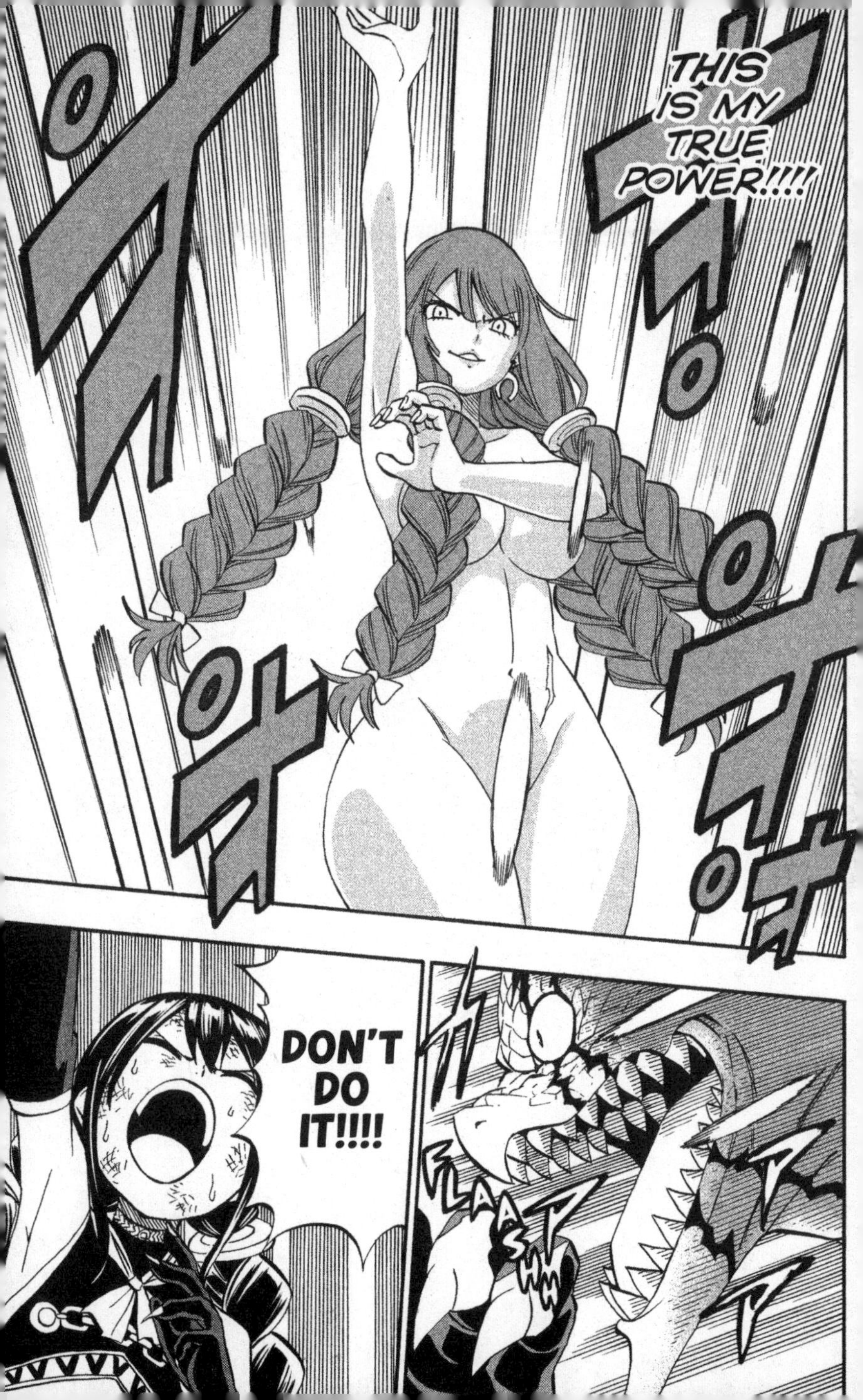
THIS IS MY TRUE POWER!!!!
FLAASHH
DON'T DO IT!!!!

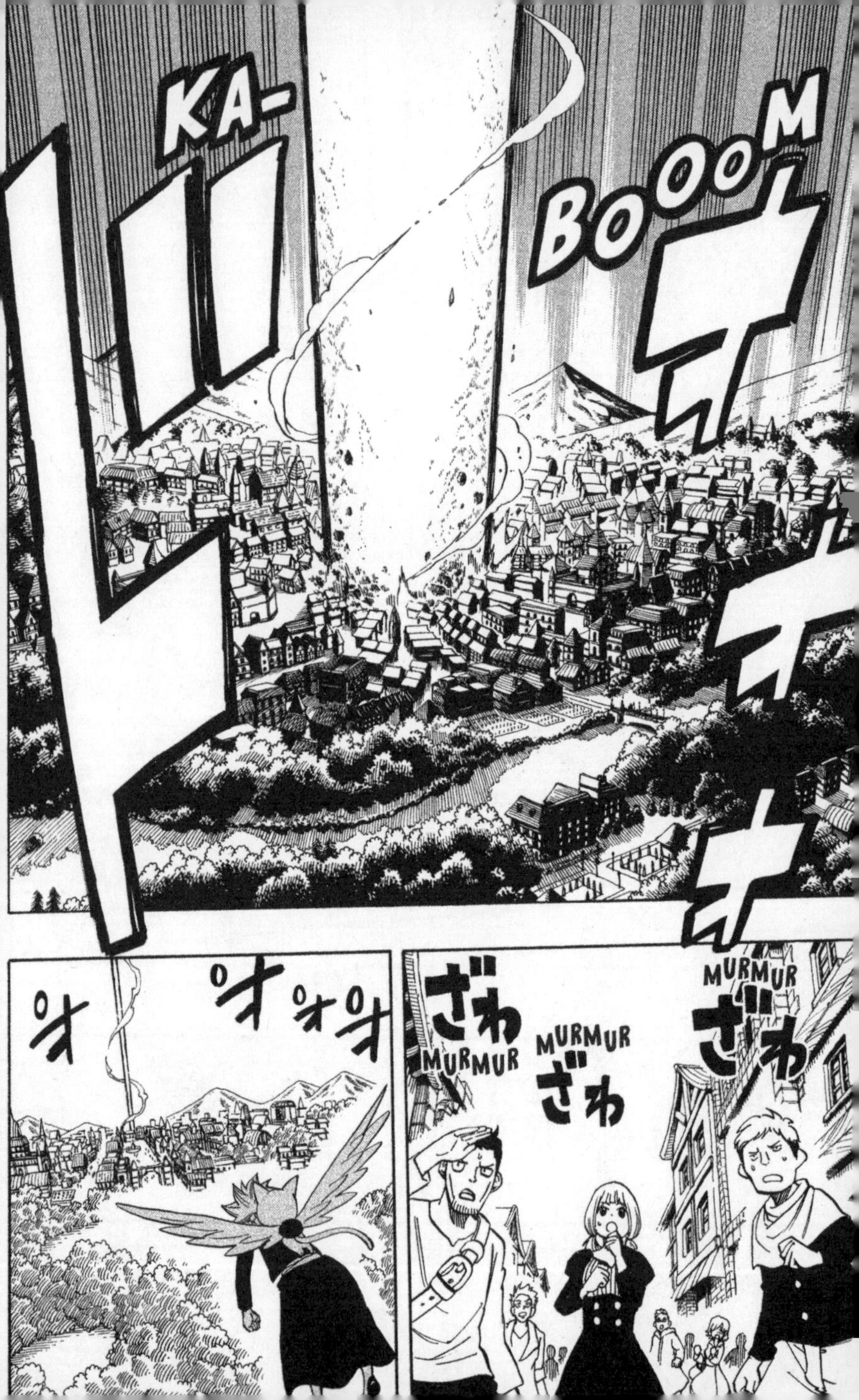
KA-
BOOOOM
MURMUR
ざわ
ざわ
MURMUR
MURMUR
ざわ

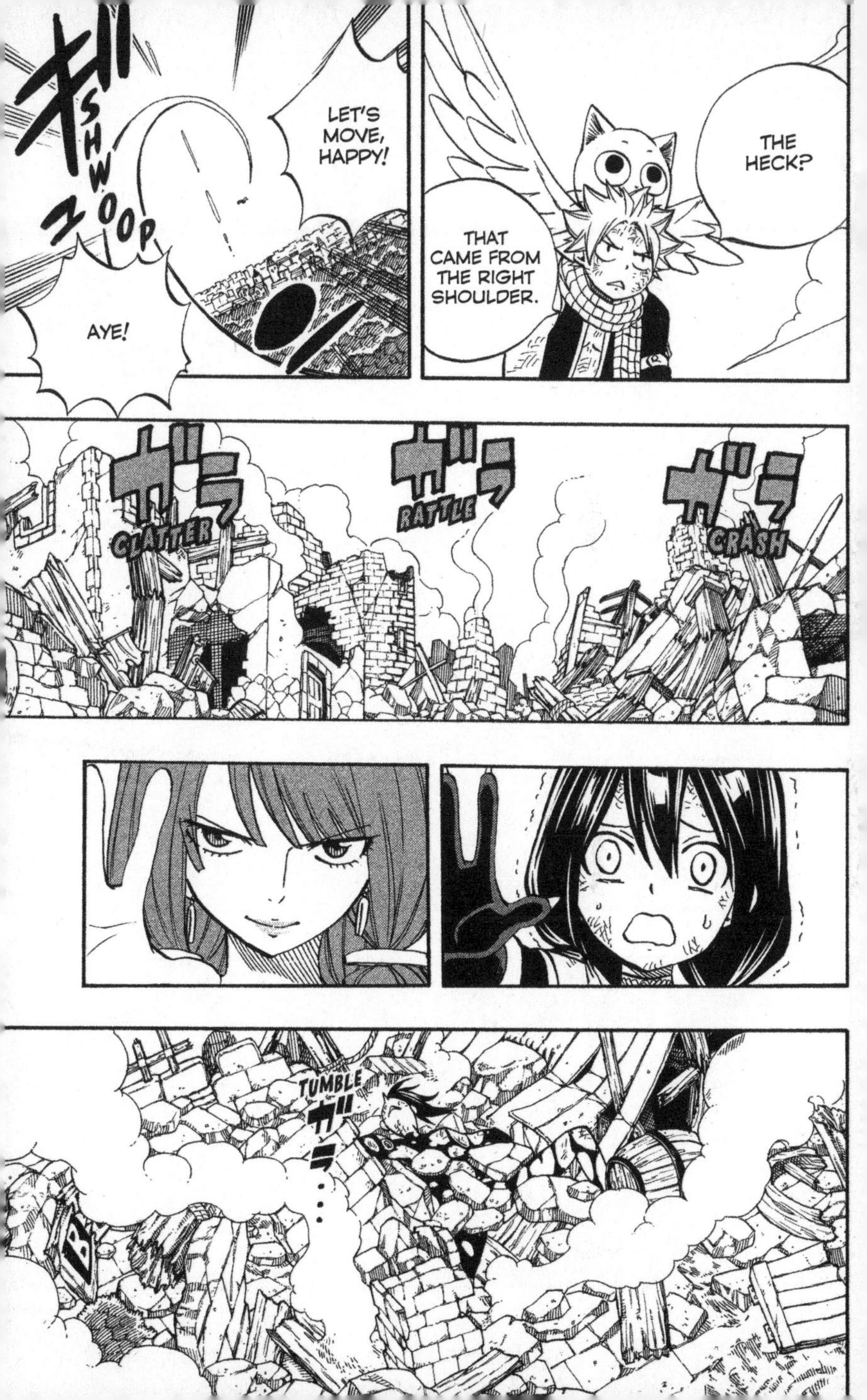
THE HECK?
THAT CAME FROM THE RIGHT SHOULDER.
LET'S MOVE, HAPPY!
SHWOOP
AYE!
CRASH
RATTLE
CLATTER
TUMBLE
...

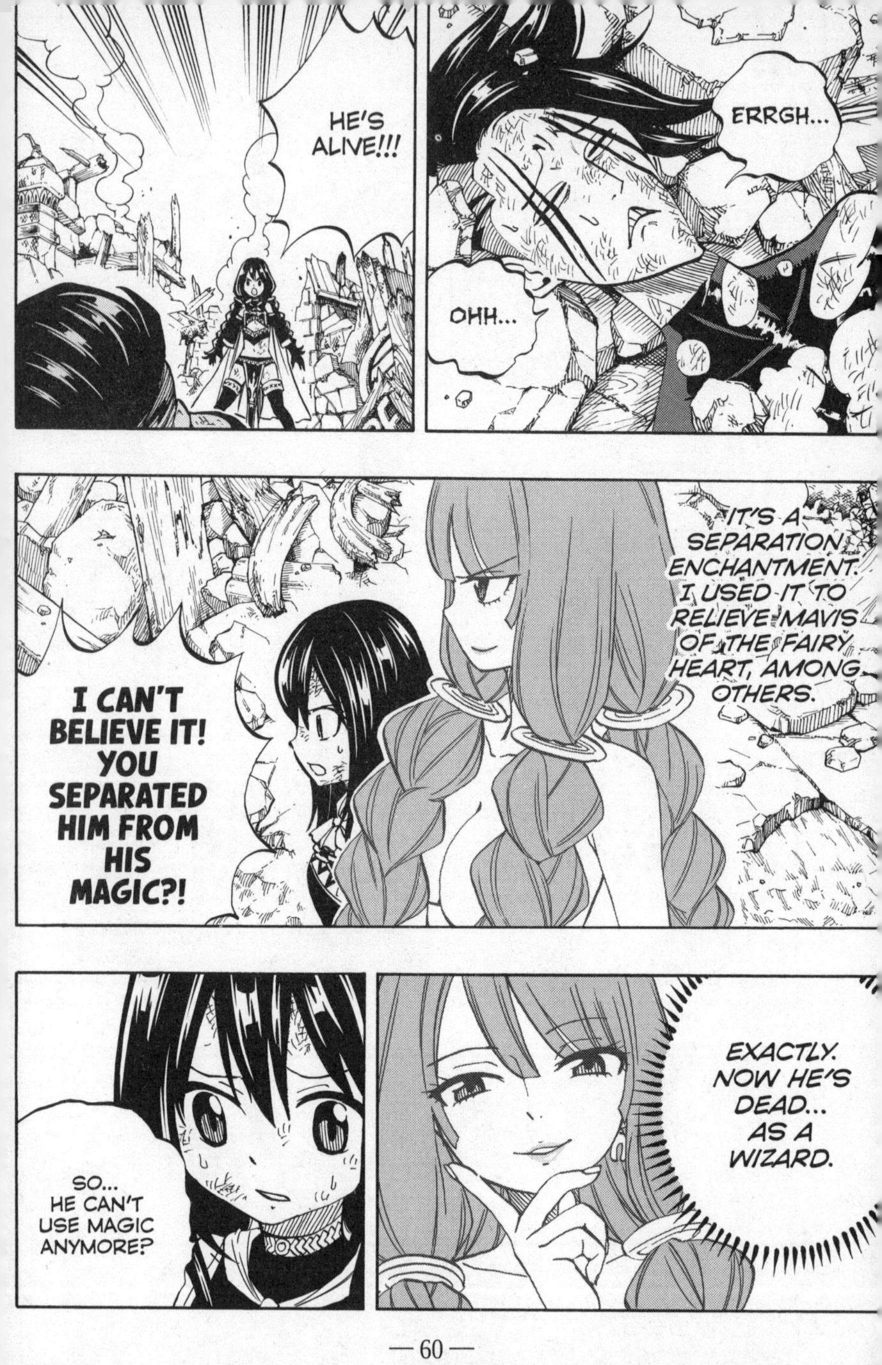

ERRGH...
OHH...
HE'S ALIVE!!!
IT'S A SEPARATION ENCHANTMENT. I USED IT TO RELIEVE MAVIS OF THE FAIRY HEART, AMONG OTHERS.
I CAN'T BELIEVE IT! YOU SEPARATED HIM FROM HIS MAGIC?!
EXACTLY. NOW HE'S DEAD... AS A WIZARD.
SO... HE CAN'T USE MAGIC ANYMORE?

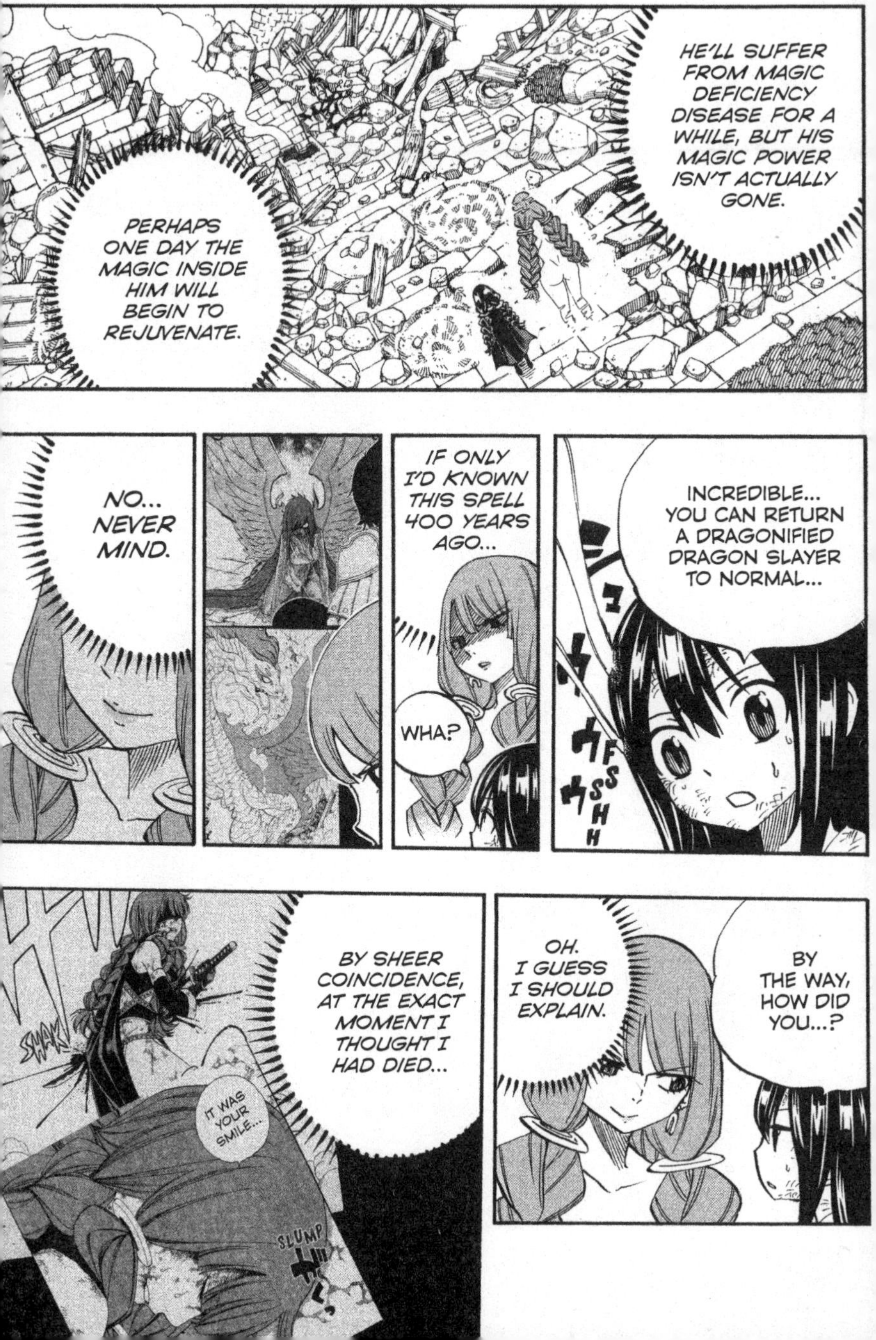
HE'LL SUFFER FROM MAGIC DEFICIENCY DISEASE FOR A WHILE, BUT HIS MAGIC POWER ISN'T ACTUALLY GONE.
PERHAPS ONE DAY THE MAGIC INSIDE HIM WILL BEGIN TO REJUVENATE.
INCREDIBLE... YOU CAN RETURN A DRAGONIFIED DRAGON SLAYER TO NORMAL...
FSSHH
IF ONLY I'D KNOWN THIS SPELL 400 YEARS AGO...
WHA?
NO... NEVER MIND.
BY THE WAY, HOW DID YOU...?
OH. I GUESS I SHOULD EXPLAIN.
BY SHEER COINCIDENCE, AT THE EXACT MOMENT I THOUGHT I HAD DIED...
SWAK
IT WAS YOUR SMILE...
SLUMP

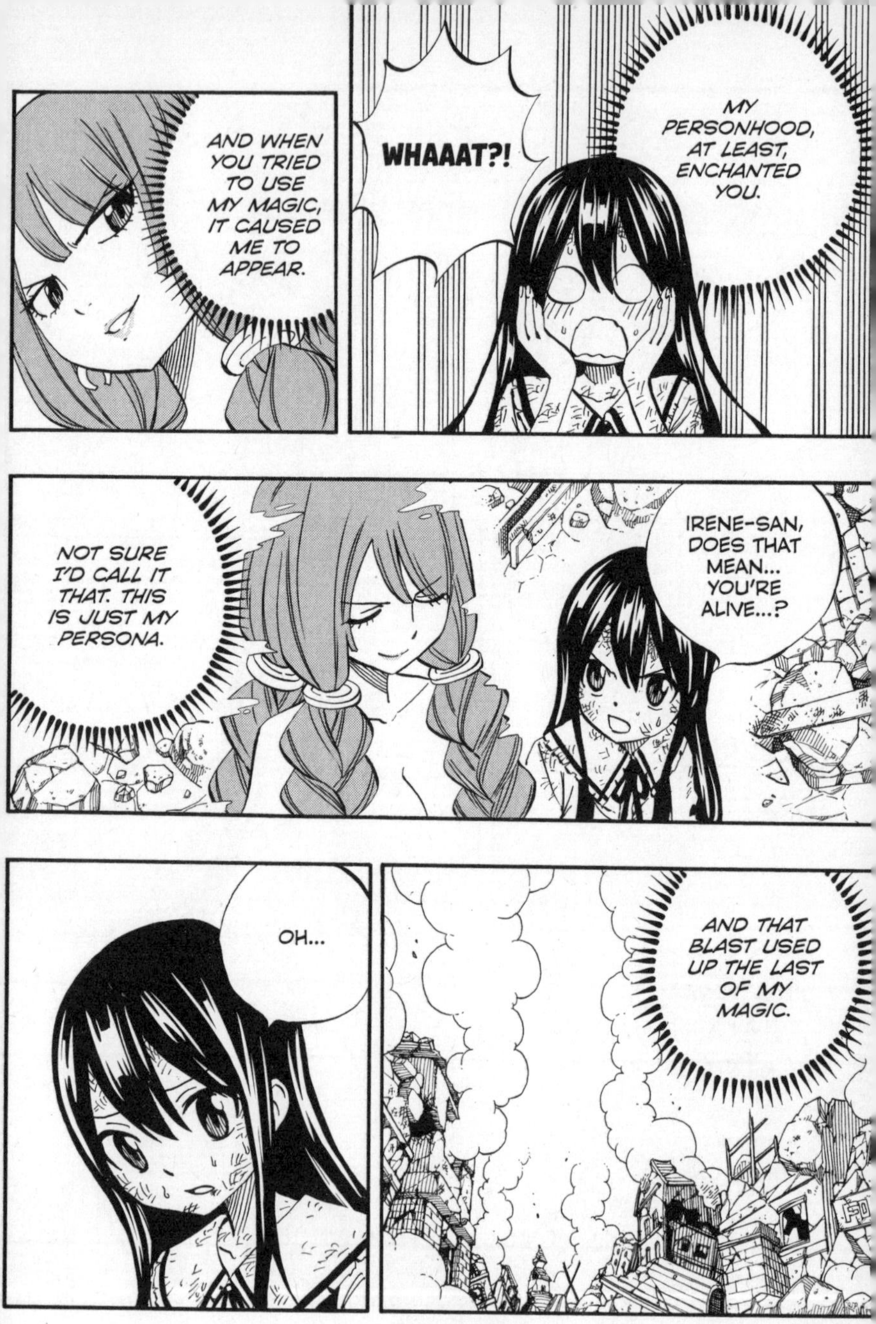
MY PERSONHOOD, AT LEAST, ENCHANTED YOU.
WHAAAT?!
AND WHEN YOU TRIED TO USE MY MAGIC, IT CAUSED ME TO APPEAR.
IRENE-SAN, DOES THAT MEAN... YOU'RE ALIVE...?
NOT SURE I'D CALL IT THAT. THIS IS JUST MY PERSONA.
AND THAT BLAST USED UP THE LAST OF MY MAGIC.
OH...

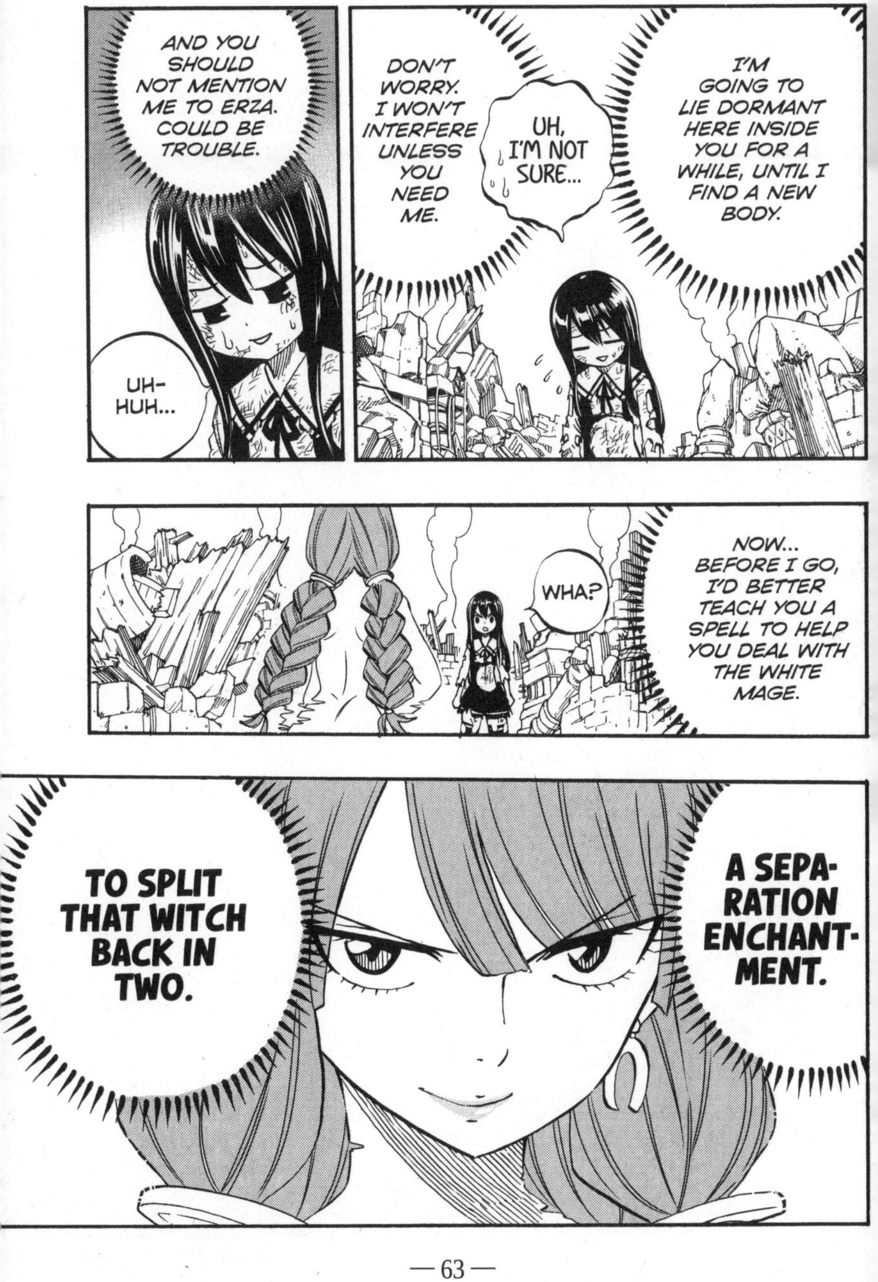
I'M GOING TO LIE DORMANT HERE INSIDE YOU FOR A WHILE, UNTIL I FIND A NEW BODY.
UH, I'M NOT SURE...
DON'T WORRY. I WON'T INTERFERE UNLESS YOU NEED ME.
AND YOU SHOULD NOT MENTION ME TO ERZA. COULD BE TROUBLE.
UH-HUH...
NOW... BEFORE I GO, I'D BETTER TEACH YOU A SPELL TO HELP YOU DEAL WITH THE WHITE MAGE.
WHA?
A SEPARATION ENCHANTMENT.
TO SPLIT THAT WITCH BACK IN TWO.

FAIRY TAIL
100 YEARS QUEST

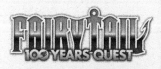

FAIRY TAIL 100 YEARS QUEST

Chapter 49: The Final Orb

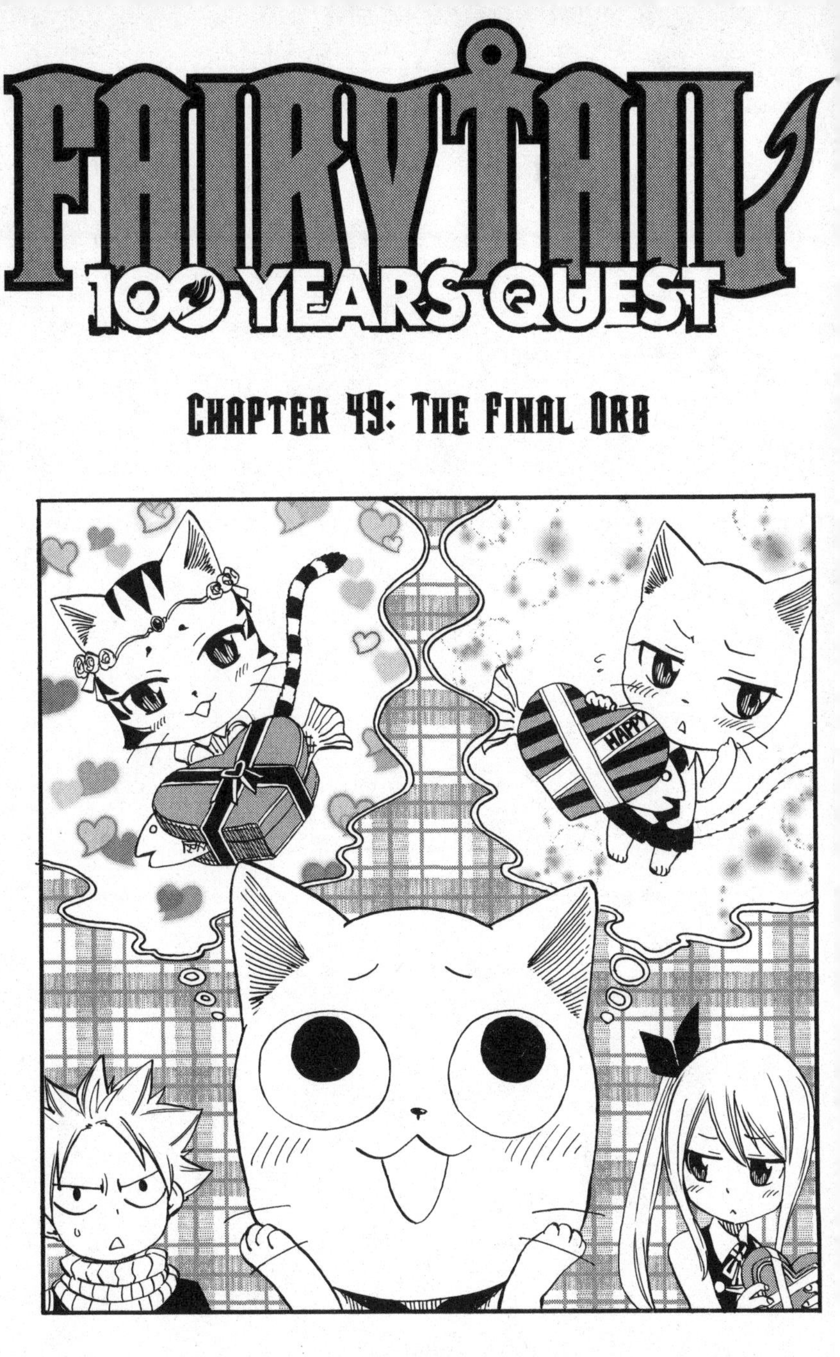
HAPPY

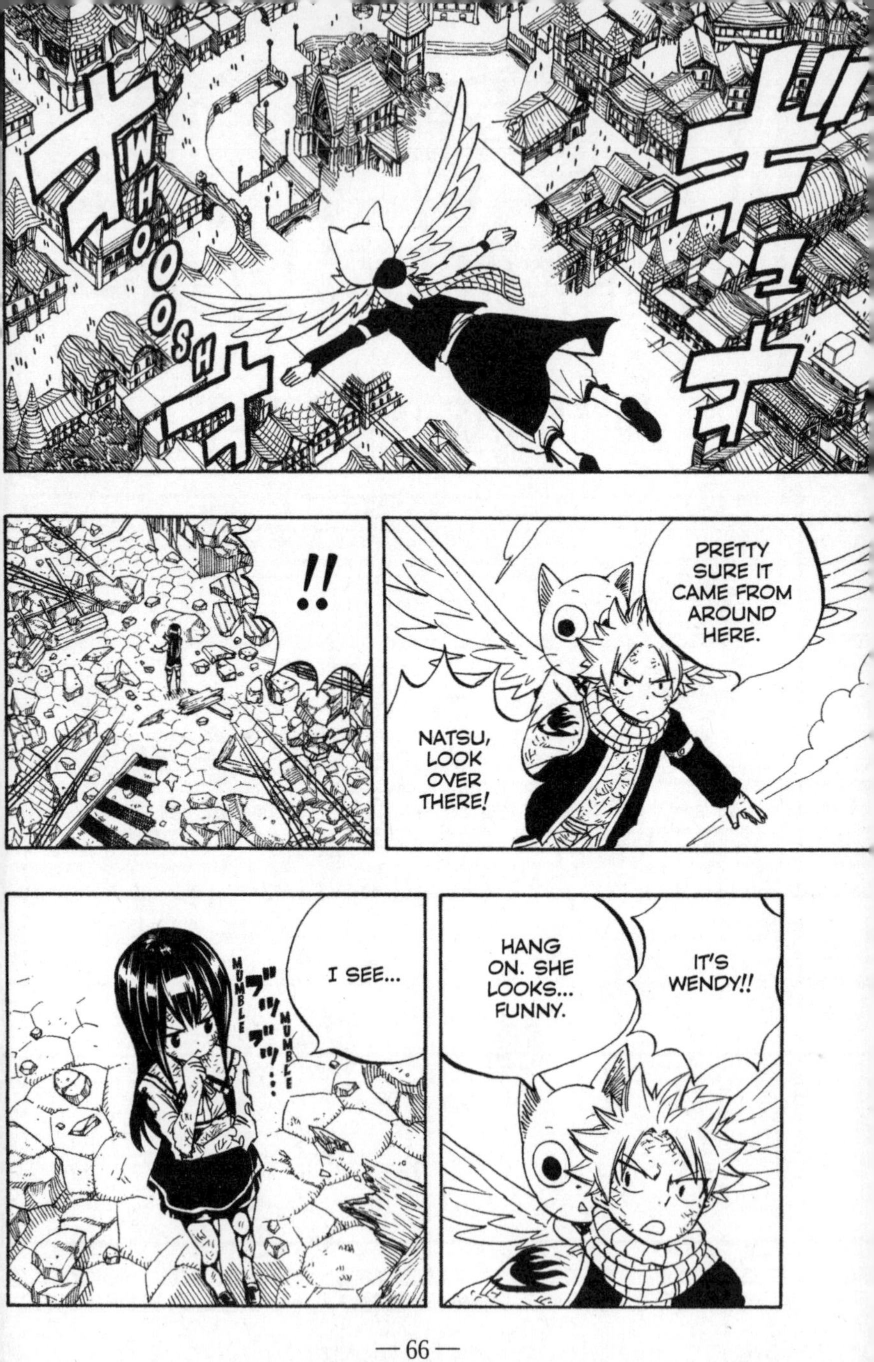
WHOOSH
PRETTY SURE IT CAME FROM AROUND HERE.
NATSU, LOOK OVER THERE!
!!
IT'S WENDY!!
HANG ON. SHE LOOKS... FUNNY.
I SEE...
MUMBLE
MUMBLE

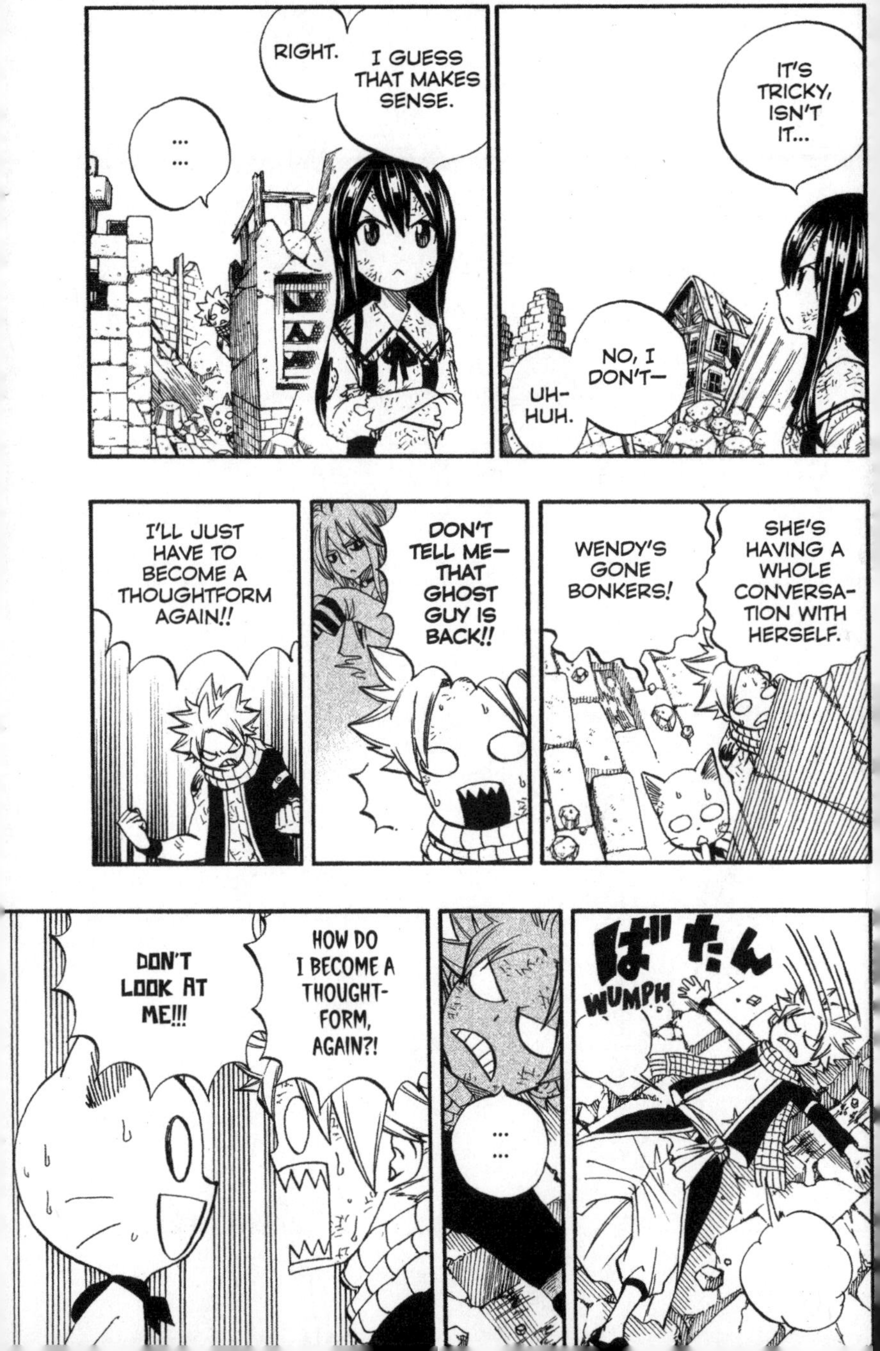
IT'S TRICKY, ISN'T IT...
NO, I DON'T—
UH-HUH.
RIGHT. I GUESS THAT MAKES SENSE.
... ...
SHE'S HAVING A WHOLE CONVERSATION WITH HERSELF.
WENDY'S GONE BONKERS!
DON'T TELL ME— THAT GHOST GUY IS BACK!!
I'LL JUST HAVE TO BECOME A THOUGHTFORM AGAIN!!
ばたん
WUMPH
... ...
HOW DO I BECOME A THOUGHT-FORM, AGAIN?!
DON'T LOOK AT ME!!!

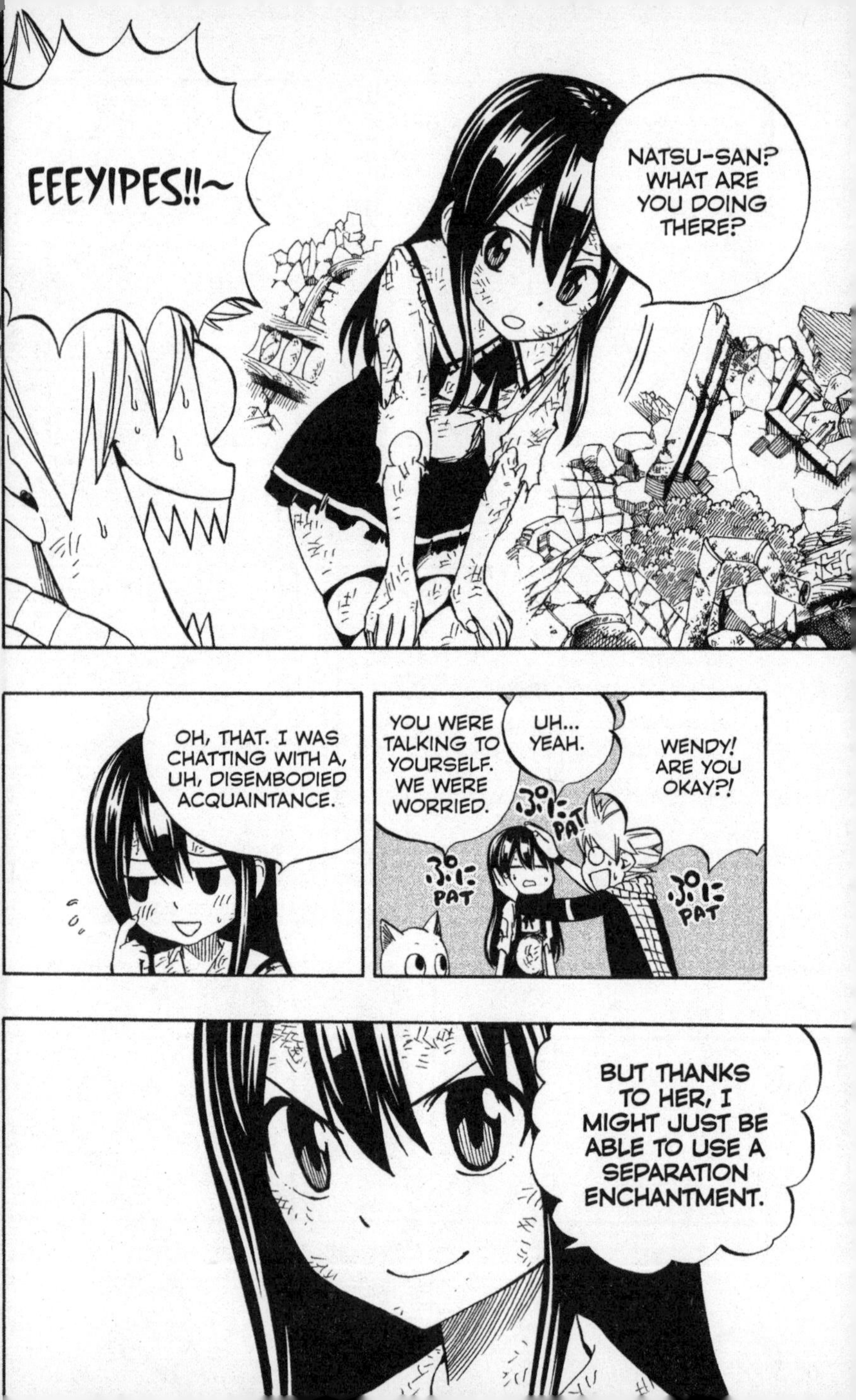
NATSU-SAN? WHAT ARE YOU DOING THERE?
EEEYIPES!!~
WENDY! ARE YOU OKAY?!
UH... YEAH.
ぷに PAT
ぷに PAT
ぷに PAT
YOU WERE TALKING TO YOURSELF. WE WERE WORRIED.
OH, THAT. I WAS CHATTING WITH A, UH, DISEMBODIED ACQUAINTANCE.
BUT THANKS TO HER, I MIGHT JUST BE ABLE TO USE A SEPARATION ENCHANTMENT.

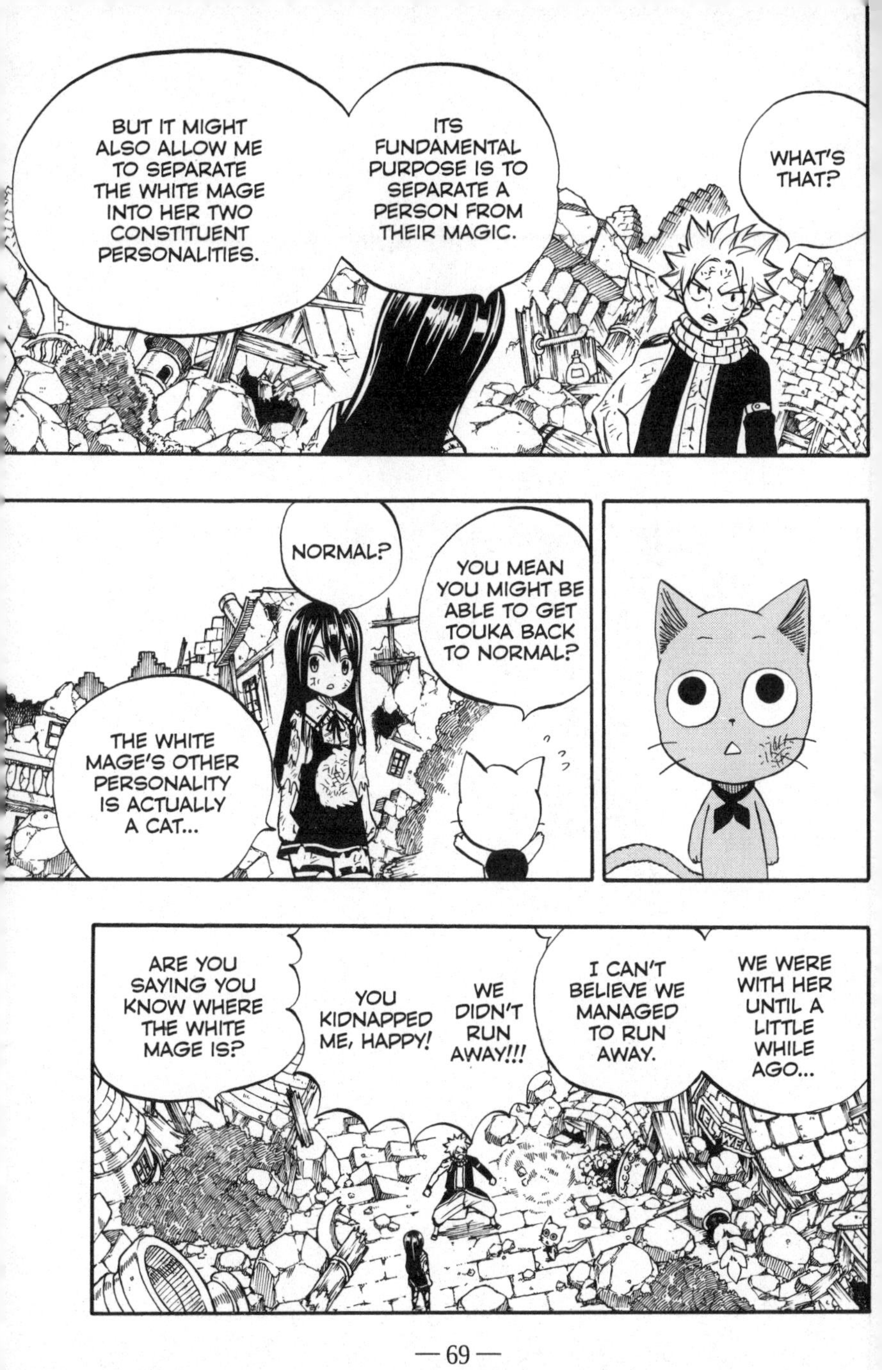
WHAT'S THAT?
ITS FUNDAMENTAL PURPOSE IS TO SEPARATE A PERSON FROM THEIR MAGIC.
BUT IT MIGHT ALSO ALLOW ME TO SEPARATE THE WHITE MAGE INTO HER TWO CONSTITUENT PERSONALITIES.
YOU MEAN YOU MIGHT BE ABLE TO GET TOUKA BACK TO NORMAL?
NORMAL?
THE WHITE MAGE'S OTHER PERSONALITY IS ACTUALLY A CAT...
WE WERE WITH HER UNTIL A LITTLE WHILE AGO...
I CAN'T BELIEVE WE MANAGED TO RUN AWAY.
WE DIDN'T RUN AWAY!!!
YOU KIDNAPPED ME, HAPPY!
ARE YOU SAYING YOU KNOW WHERE THE WHITE MAGE IS?

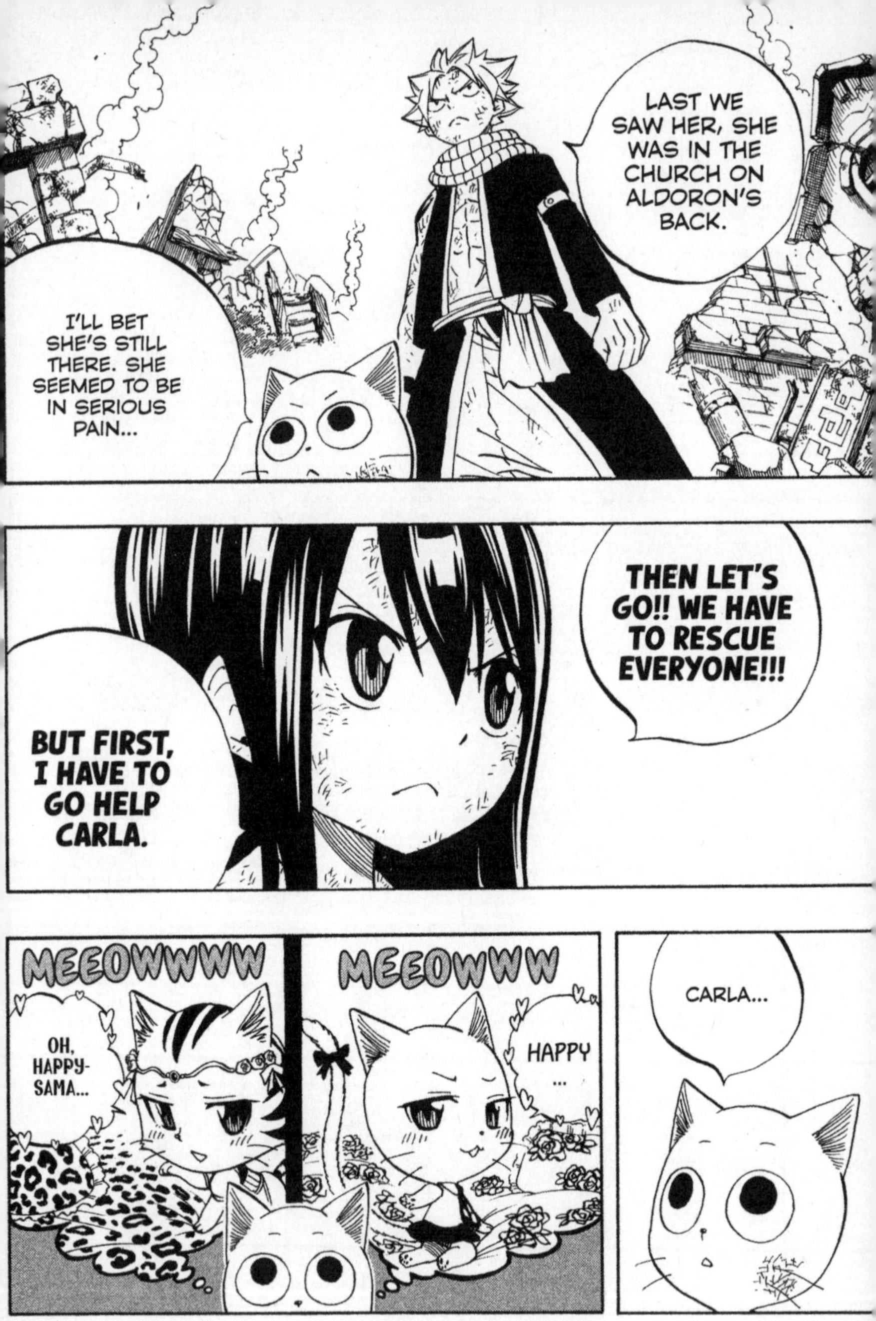
LAST WE SAW HER, SHE WAS IN THE CHURCH ON ALDORON'S BACK.
I'LL BET SHE'S STILL THERE. SHE SEEMED TO BE IN SERIOUS PAIN...
THEN LET'S GO!! WE HAVE TO RESCUE EVERYONE!!!
BUT FIRST, I HAVE TO GO HELP CARLA.
CARLA...
MEEOWWW
HAPPY ...
MEEOWWWW
OH, HAPPY-SAMA...

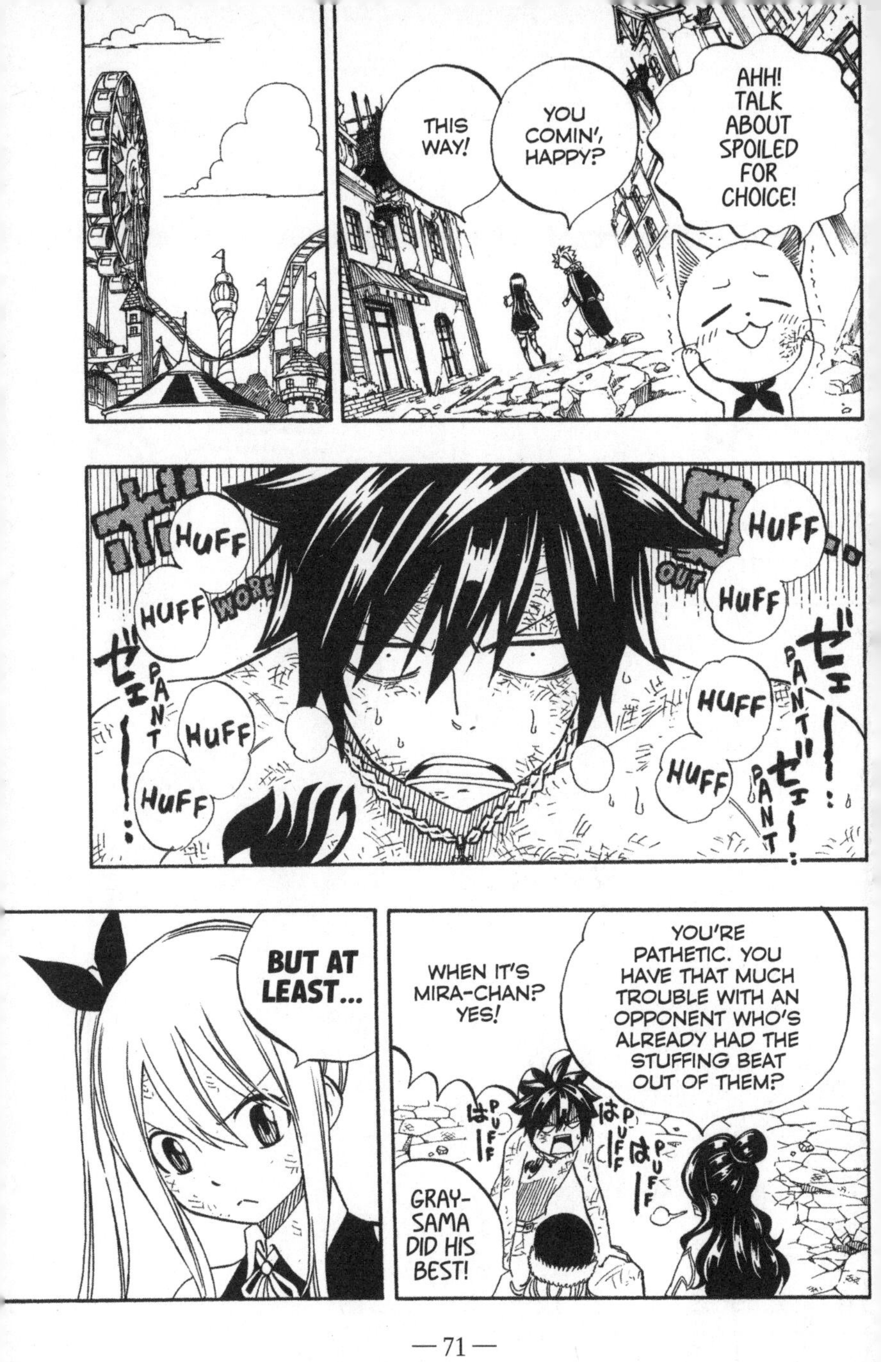

AHH! TALK ABOUT SPOILED FOR CHOICE!
YOU COMIN', HAPPY?
THIS WAY!
HUFF... HUFF
OUT
ゼェー PANT
ゼェー PANT
HUFF
HUFF
HUFF
WORE
HUFF
ゼェー PANT
HUFF
HUFF
YOU'RE PATHETIC. YOU HAVE THAT MUCH TROUBLE WITH AN OPPONENT WHO'S ALREADY HAD THE STUFFING BEAT OUT OF THEM?
WHEN IT'S MIRA-CHAN? YES!
はー PUFF
はー PUFF
はー PUFF
GRAY-SAMA DID HIS BEST!
BUT AT LEAST...

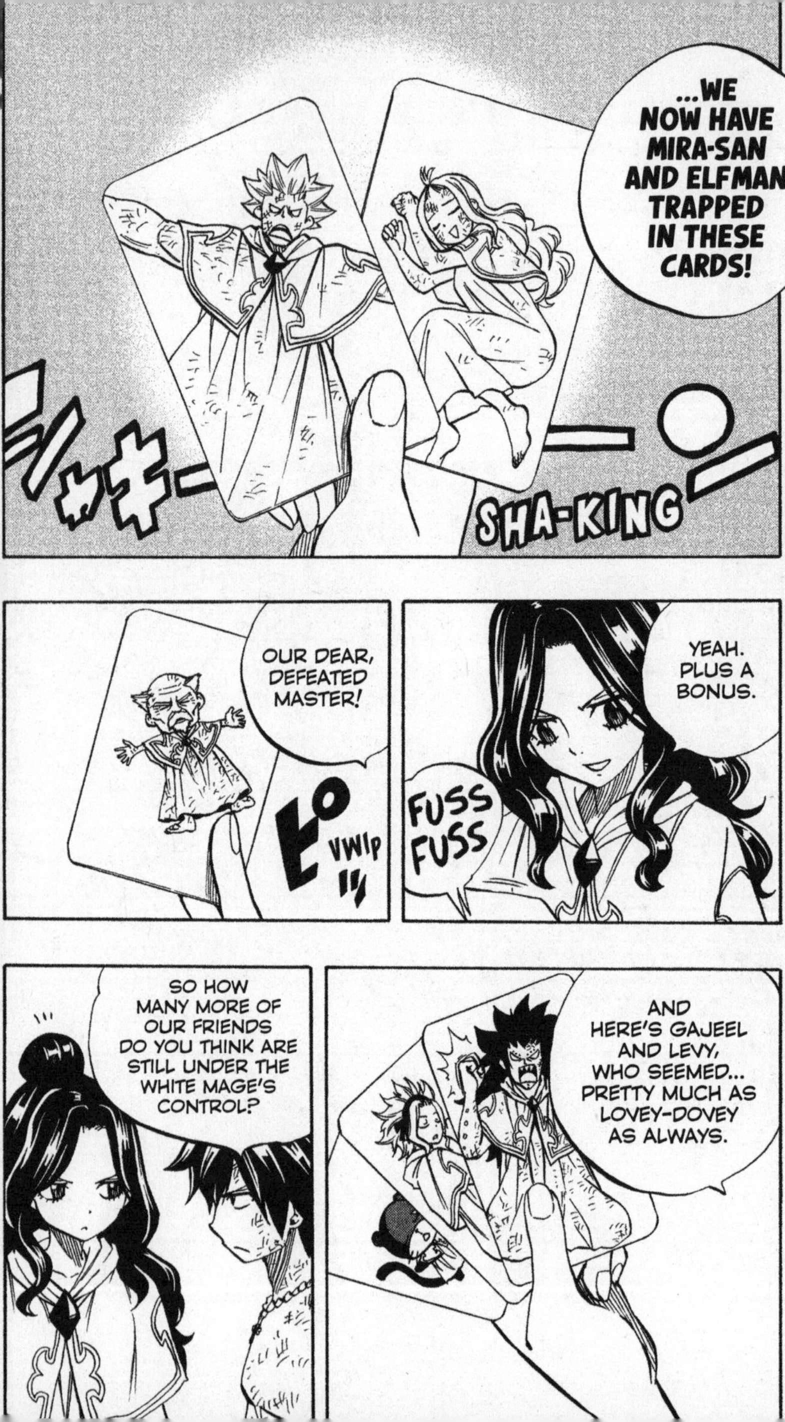
...WE NOW HAVE MIRA-SAN AND ELFMAN TRAPPED IN THESE CARDS!
SHA-KING
YEAH. PLUS A BONUS.
FUSS FUSS
OUR DEAR, DEFEATED MASTER!
VWIP
AND HERE'S GAJEEL AND LEVY, WHO SEEMED... PRETTY MUCH AS LOVEY-DOVEY AS ALWAYS.
SO HOW MANY MORE OF OUR FRIENDS DO YOU THINK ARE STILL UNDER THE WHITE MAGE'S CONTROL?

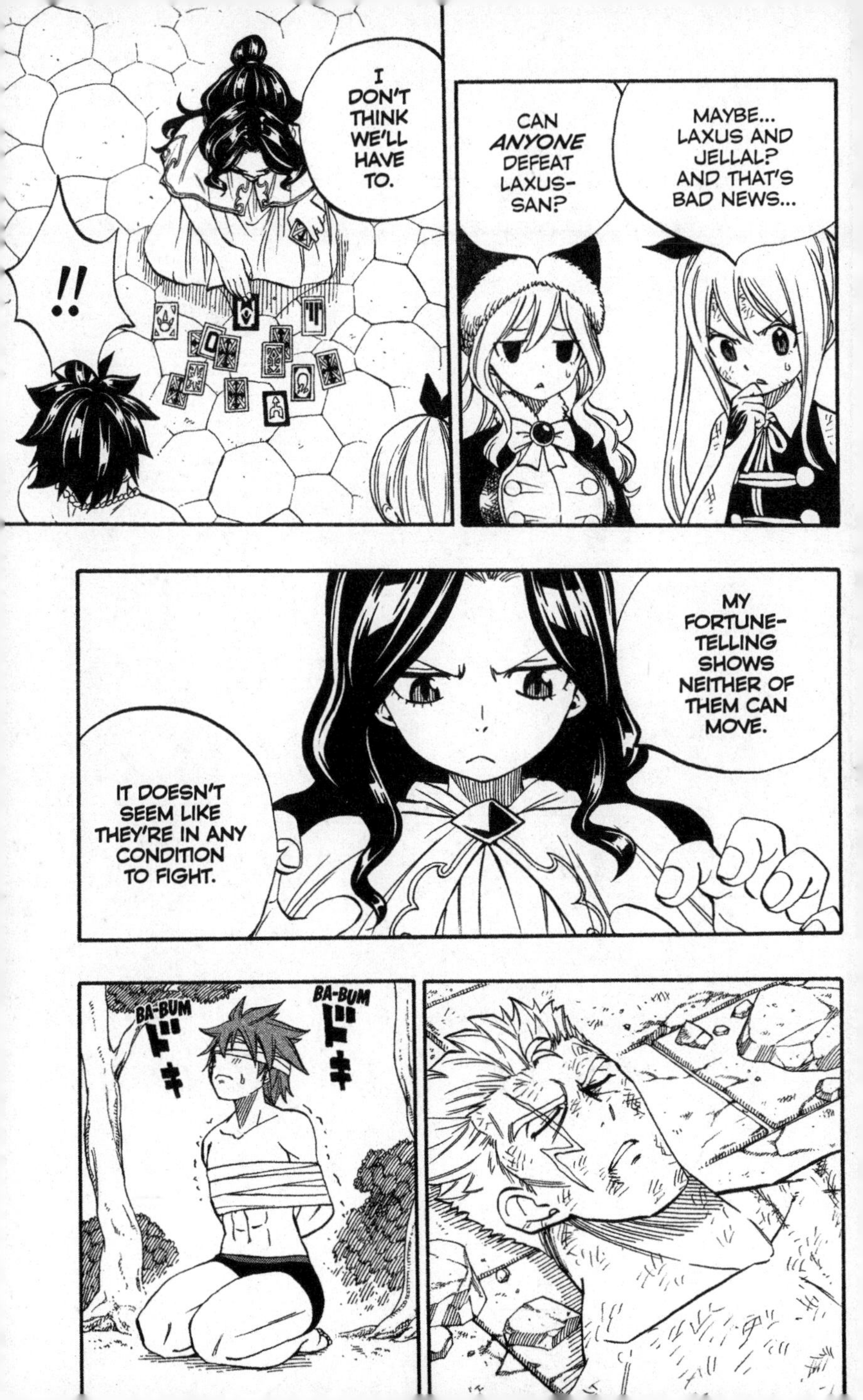
MAYBE... LAXUS AND JELLAL? AND THAT'S BAD NEWS...
CAN *ANYONE* DEFEAT LAXUS-SAN?
I DON'T THINK WE'LL HAVE TO.
!!
MY FORTUNE-TELLING SHOWS NEITHER OF THEM CAN MOVE.
IT DOESN'T SEEM LIKE THEY'RE IN ANY CONDITION TO FIGHT.
BA-BUM
ドキ
BA-BUM
ドキ

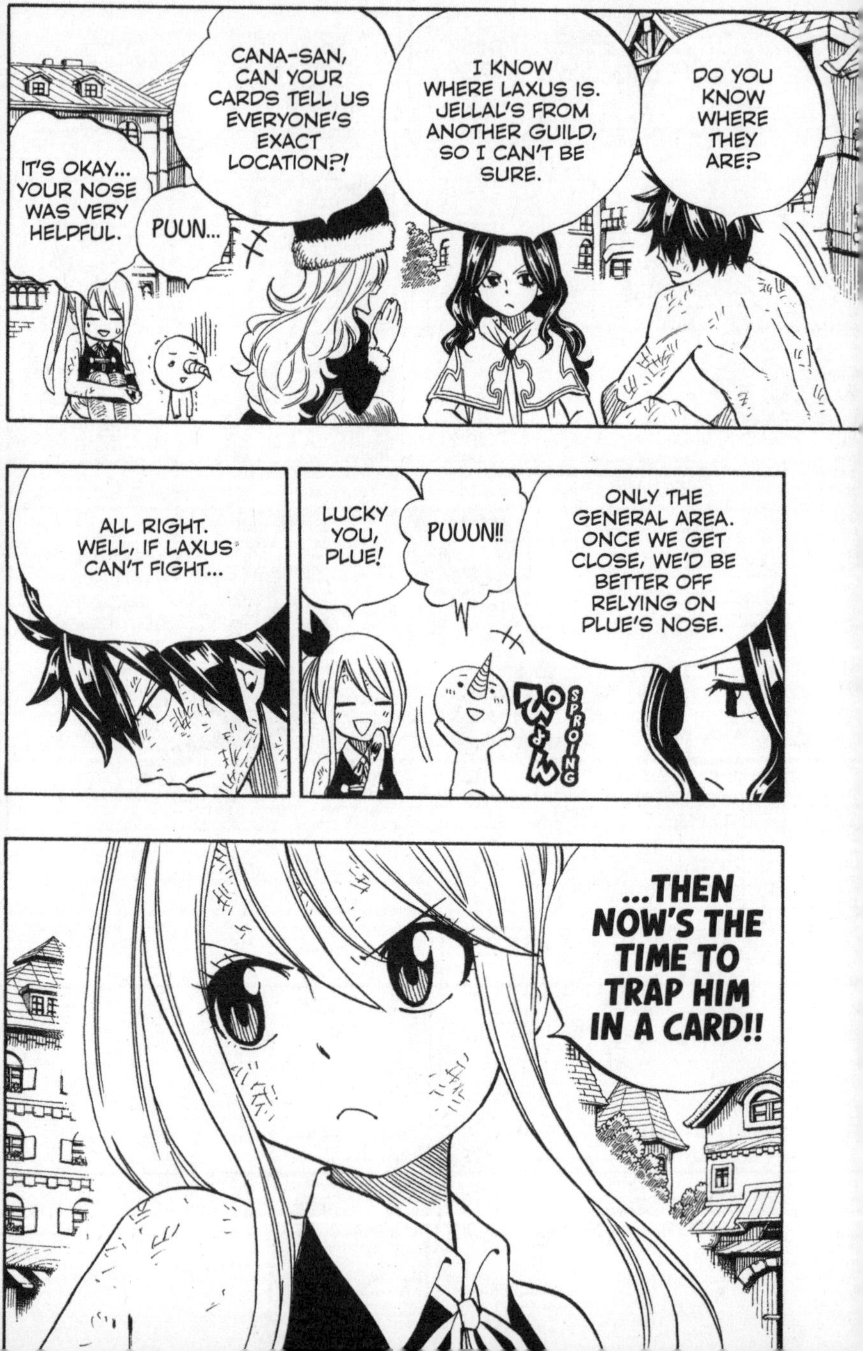
DO YOU KNOW WHERE THEY ARE?
I KNOW WHERE LAXUS IS. JELLAL'S FROM ANOTHER GUILD, SO I CAN'T BE SURE.
CANA-SAN, CAN YOUR CARDS TELL US EVERYONE'S EXACT LOCATION?!
PUUN...
IT'S OKAY... YOUR NOSE WAS VERY HELPFUL.
ONLY THE GENERAL AREA. ONCE WE GET CLOSE, WE'D BE BETTER OFF RELYING ON PLUE'S NOSE.
PUUUN!!
LUCKY YOU, PLUE!
ぴょん
SPROING
ALL RIGHT. WELL, IF LAXUS CAN'T FIGHT...
...THEN NOW'S THE TIME TO TRAP HIM IN A CARD!!

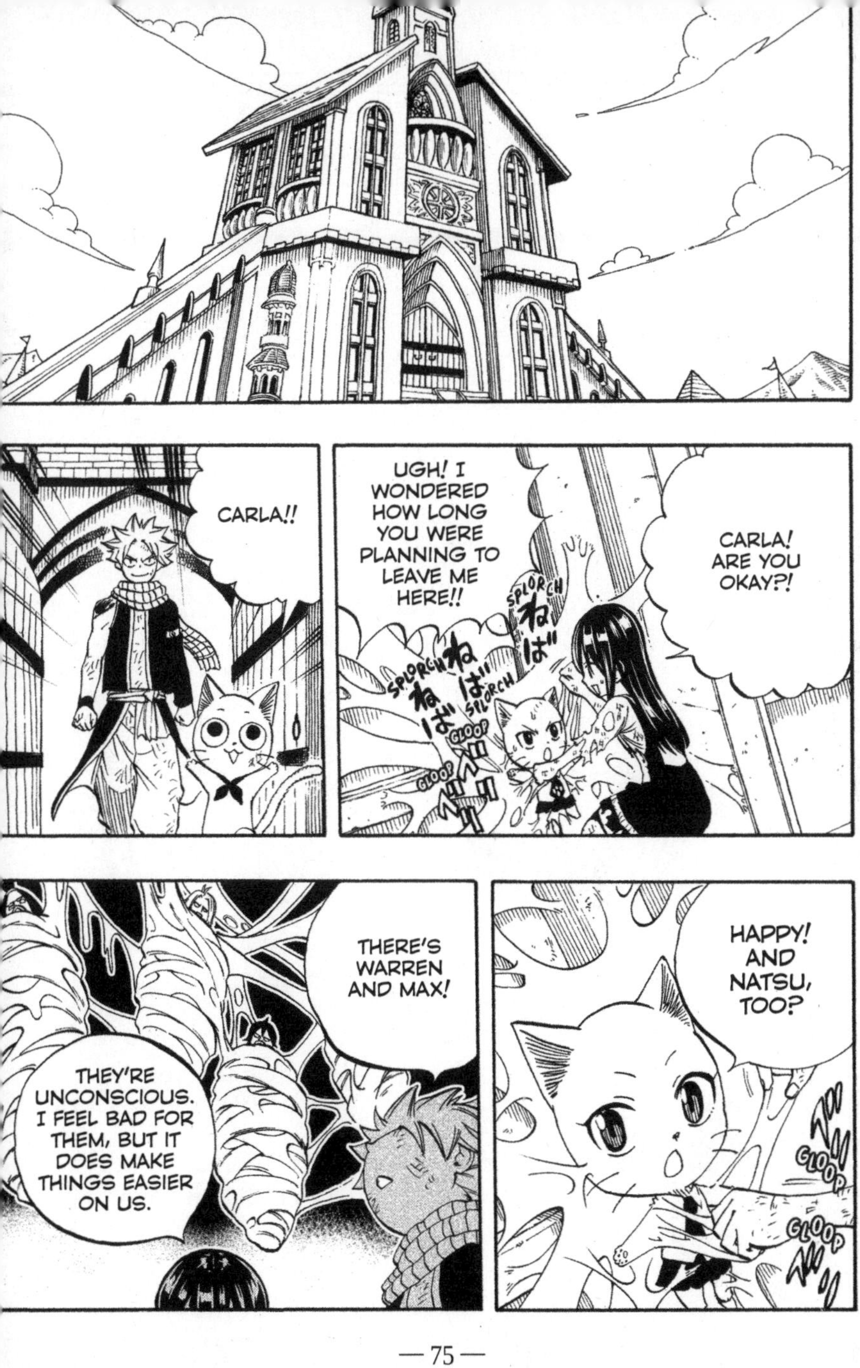
CARLA! ARE YOU OKAY?!
UGH! I WONDERED HOW LONG YOU WERE PLANNING TO LEAVE ME HERE!!
SPLORCH ねば
SPLORCH ねば
SPLORCH
GLOOP
GLOOP
CARLA!!
HAPPY! AND NATSU, TOO?
GLOOP
GLOOP
THERE'S WARREN AND MAX!
THEY'RE UNCONSCIOUS. I FEEL BAD FOR THEM, BUT IT DOES MAKE THINGS EASIER ON US.

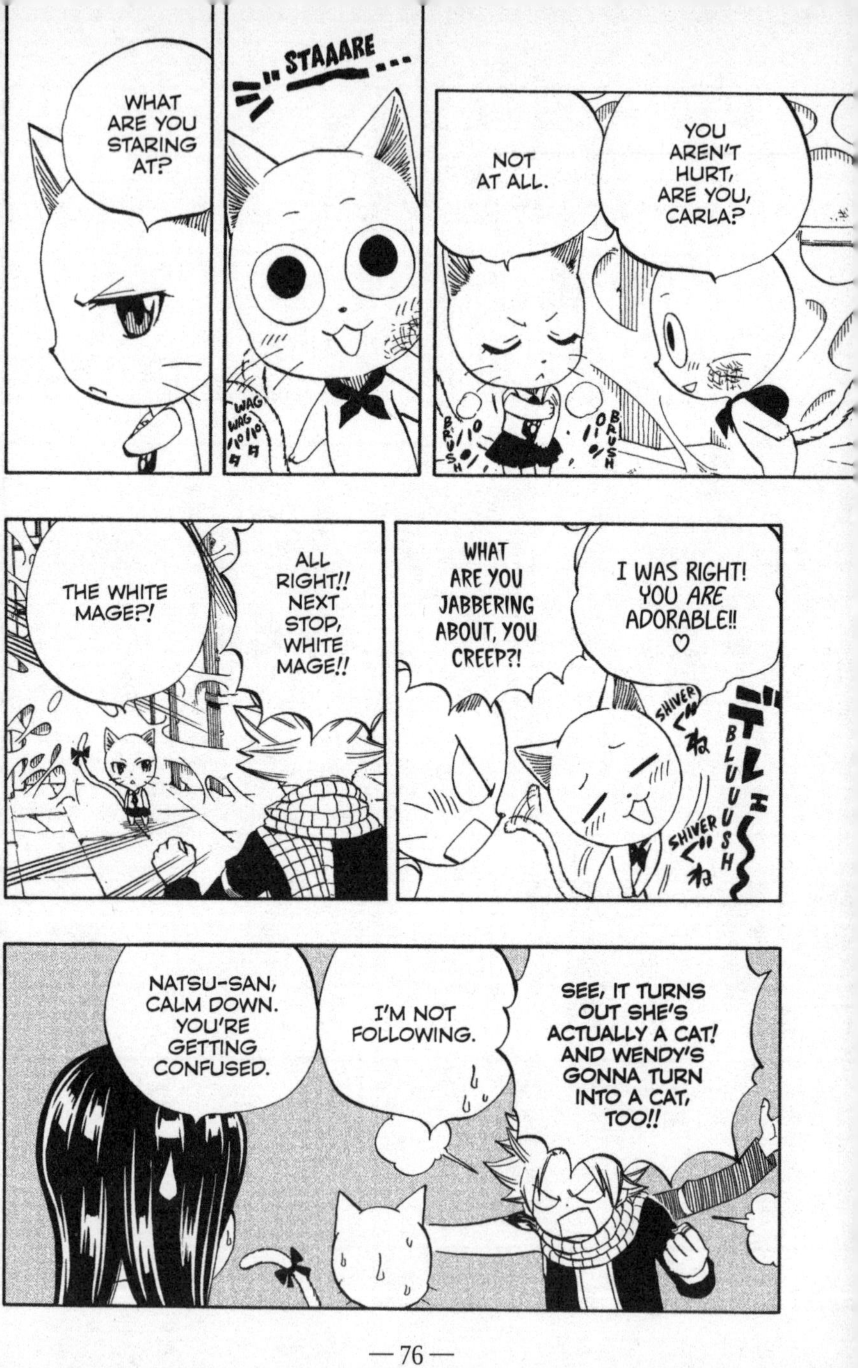
YOU AREN'T HURT, ARE YOU, CARLA?
NOT AT ALL.
BRUSH
BRUSH
STAAARE...
WAG WAG
WHAT ARE YOU STARING AT?
I WAS RIGHT! YOU *ARE* ADORABLE!! ♡
WHAT ARE YOU JABBERING ABOUT, YOU CREEP?!
SHIVER
BLUUUSH
SHIVER
ALL RIGHT!! NEXT STOP, WHITE MAGE!!
THE WHITE MAGE?!
SEE, IT TURNS OUT SHE'S ACTUALLY A CAT! AND WENDY'S GONNA TURN INTO A CAT, TOO!!
I'M NOT FOLLOWING.
NATSU-SAN, CALM DOWN. YOU'RE GETTING CONFUSED.

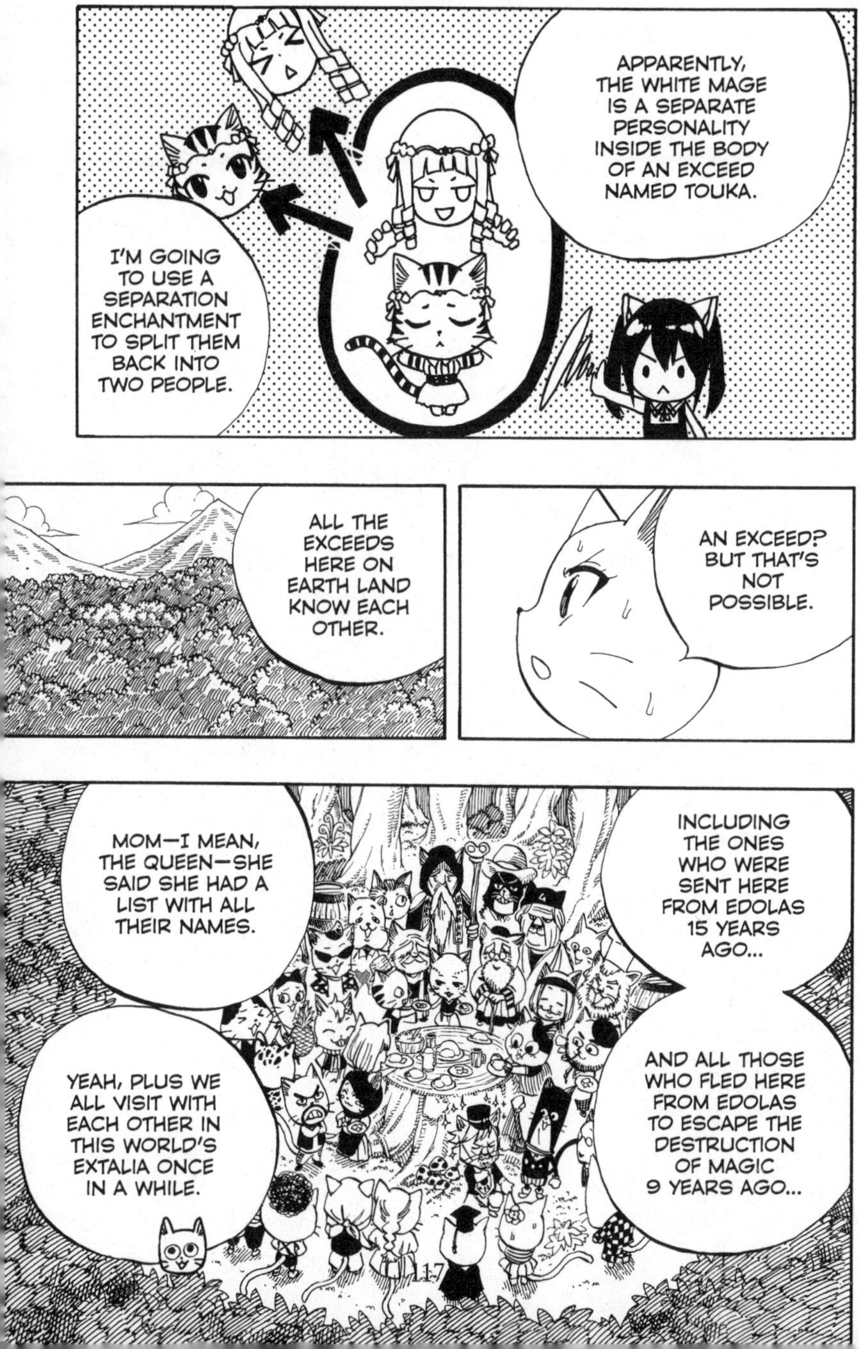
APPARENTLY, THE WHITE MAGE IS A SEPARATE PERSONALITY INSIDE THE BODY OF AN EXCEED NAMED TOUKA.
I'M GOING TO USE A SEPARATION ENCHANTMENT TO SPLIT THEM BACK INTO TWO PEOPLE.
AN EXCEED? BUT THAT'S NOT POSSIBLE.
ALL THE EXCEEDS HERE ON EARTH LAND KNOW EACH OTHER.
INCLUDING THE ONES WHO WERE SENT HERE FROM EDOLAS 15 YEARS AGO...
AND ALL THOSE WHO FLED HERE FROM EDOLAS TO ESCAPE THE DESTRUCTION OF MAGIC 9 YEARS AGO...
MOM—I MEAN, THE QUEEN—SHE SAID SHE HAD A LIST WITH ALL THEIR NAMES.
YEAH, PLUS WE ALL VISIT WITH EACH OTHER IN THIS WORLD'S EXTALIA ONCE IN A WHILE.

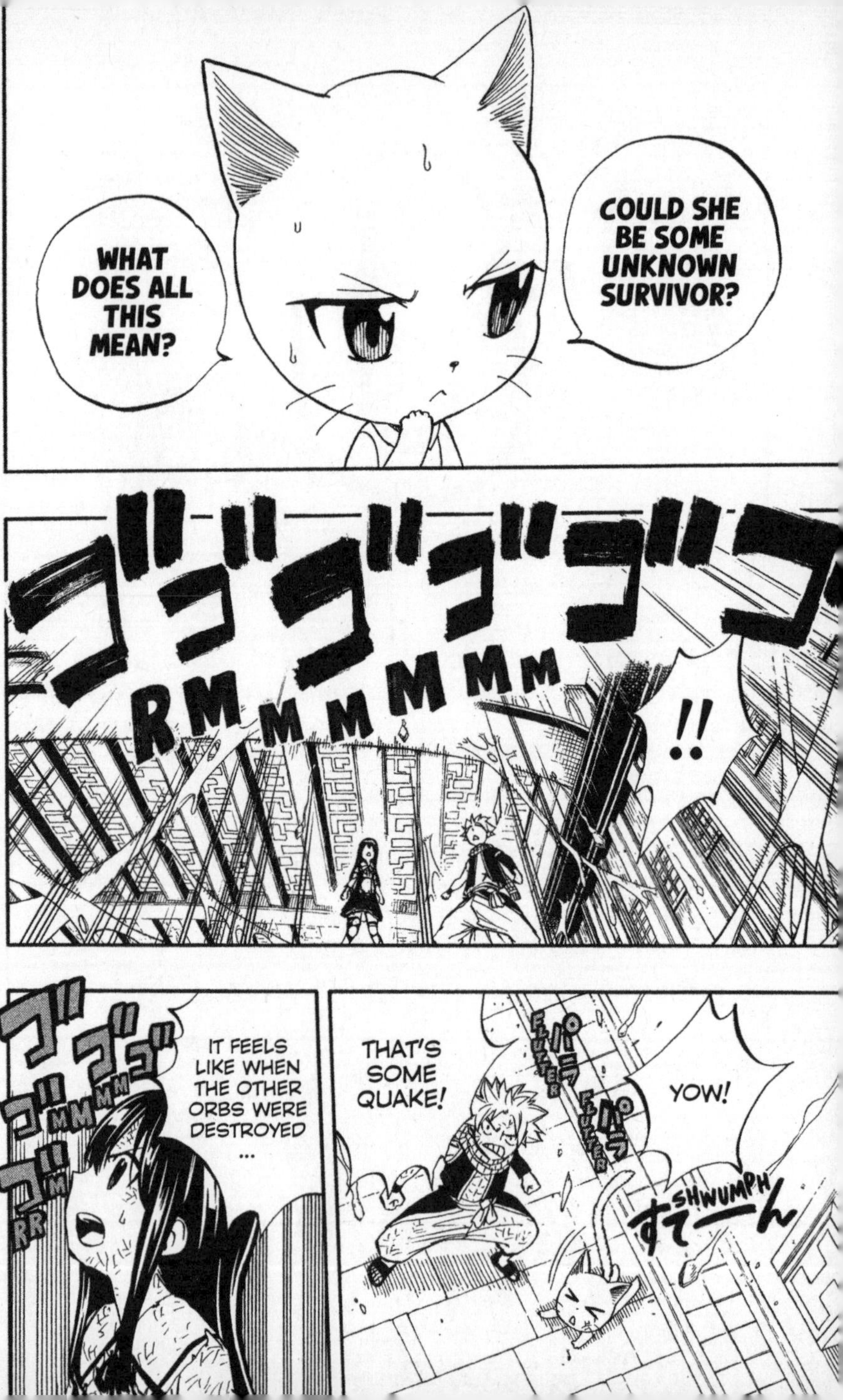
COULD SHE BE SOME UNKNOWN SURVIVOR?
WHAT DOES ALL THIS MEAN?
RMMMMMMM
!!
YOW!
FLUTTER FLUTTER
THAT'S SOME QUAKE!
SHWUMPH
RRMMMMM
IT FEELS LIKE WHEN THE OTHER ORBS WERE DESTROYED ...

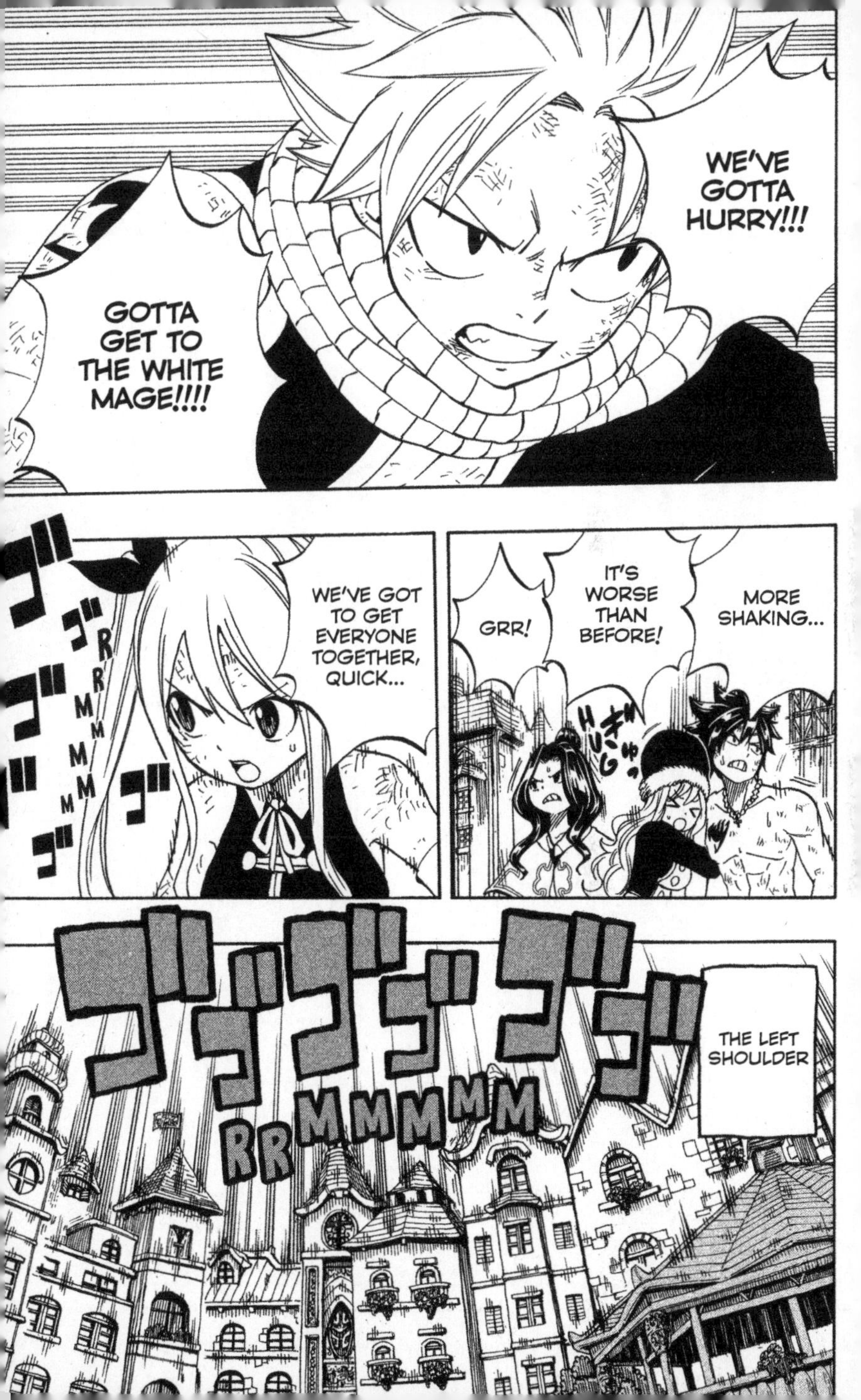
WE'VE GOTTA HURRY!!!
GOTTA GET TO THE WHITE MAGE!!!!
MORE SHAKING...
IT'S WORSE THAN BEFORE!
GRR!
ぎゅっ
HUG
WE'VE GOT TO GET EVERYONE TOGETHER, QUICK...
ゴゴゴゴゴ
RRMMMMMM
ゴゴゴゴゴゴ
THE LEFT SHOULDER
RRMMMMMM

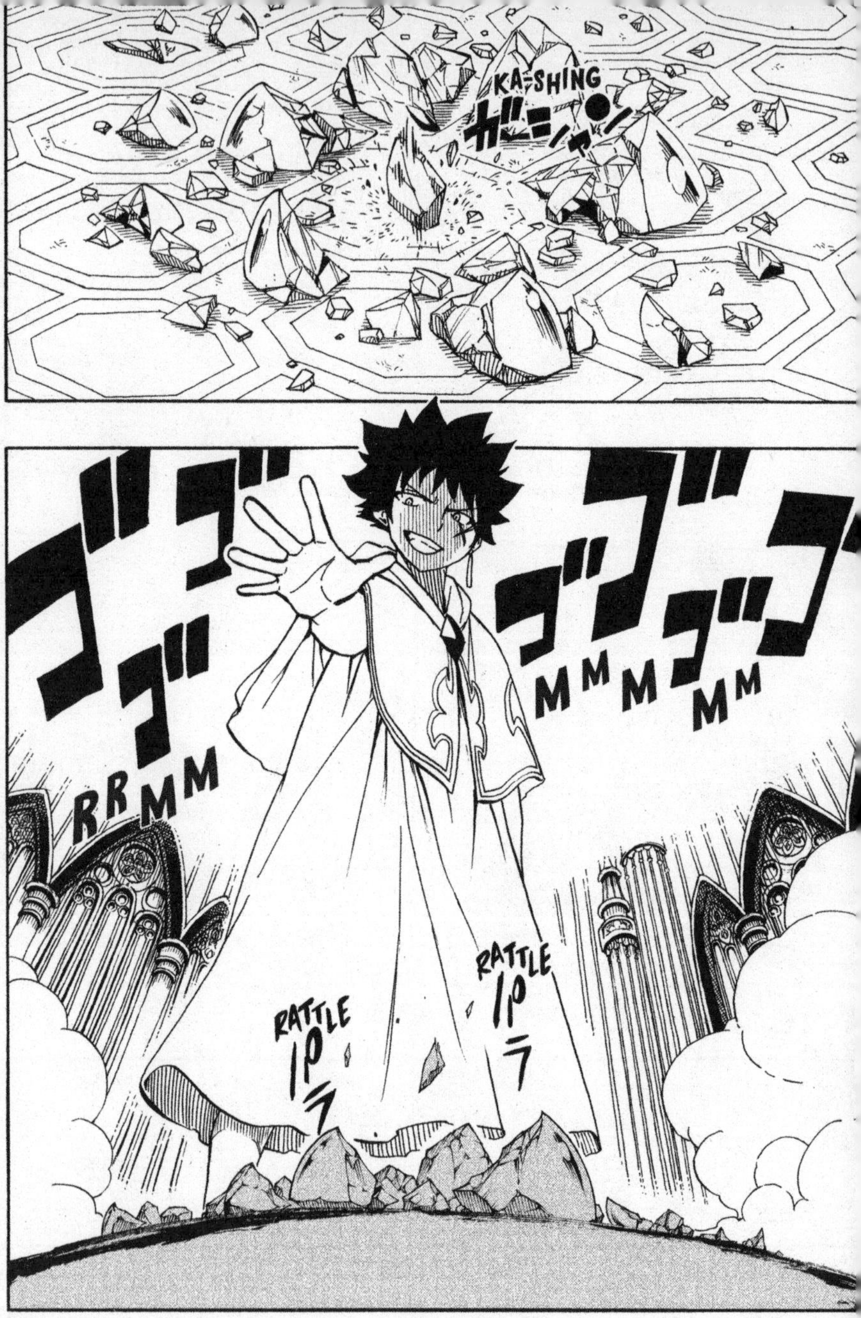
KA-SHING
RRMM
MMMMM
RATTLE
RATTLE

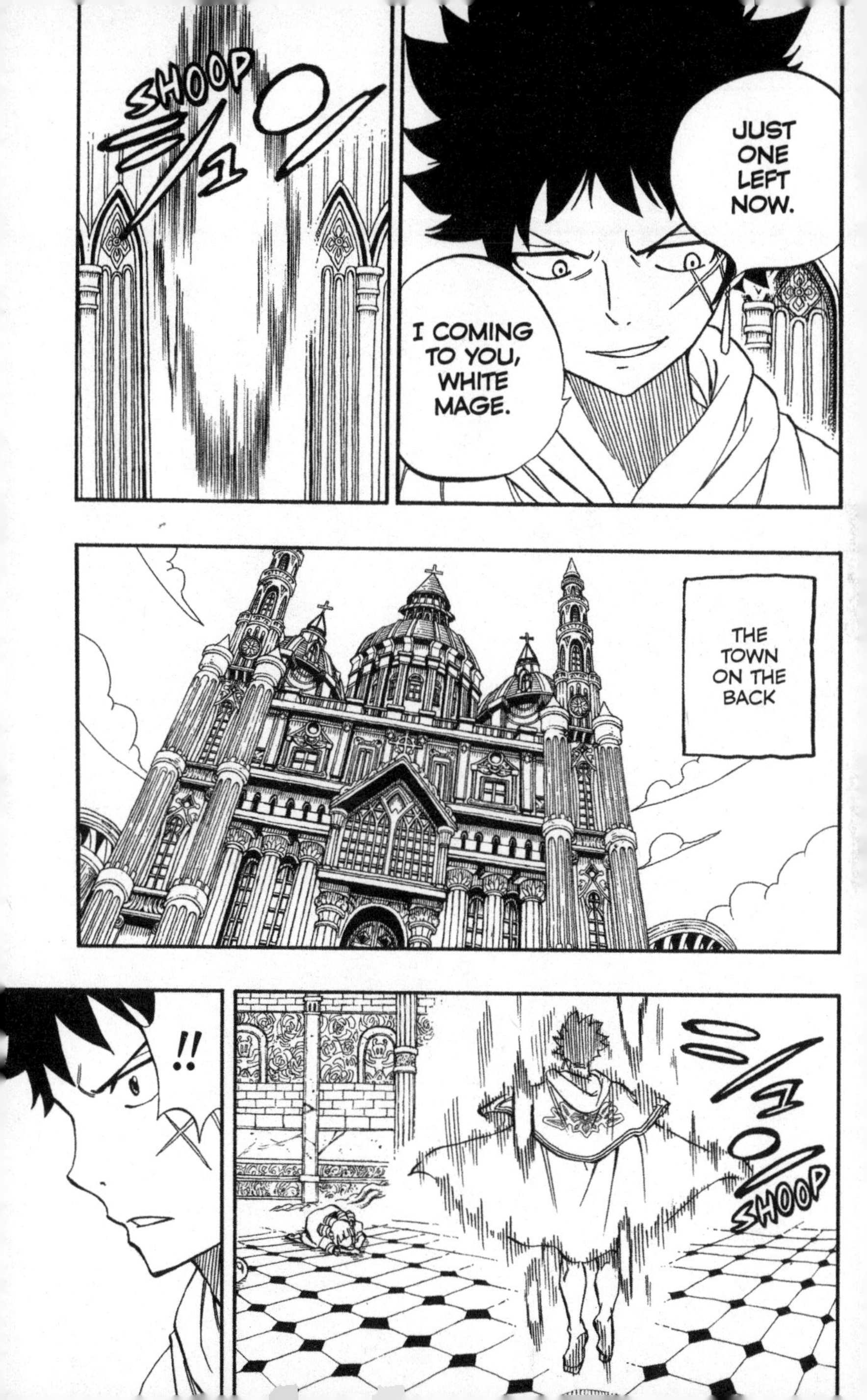
JUST ONE LEFT NOW.
I COMING TO YOU, WHITE MAGE.
SHOOP
THE TOWN ON THE BACK
SHOOP
!!

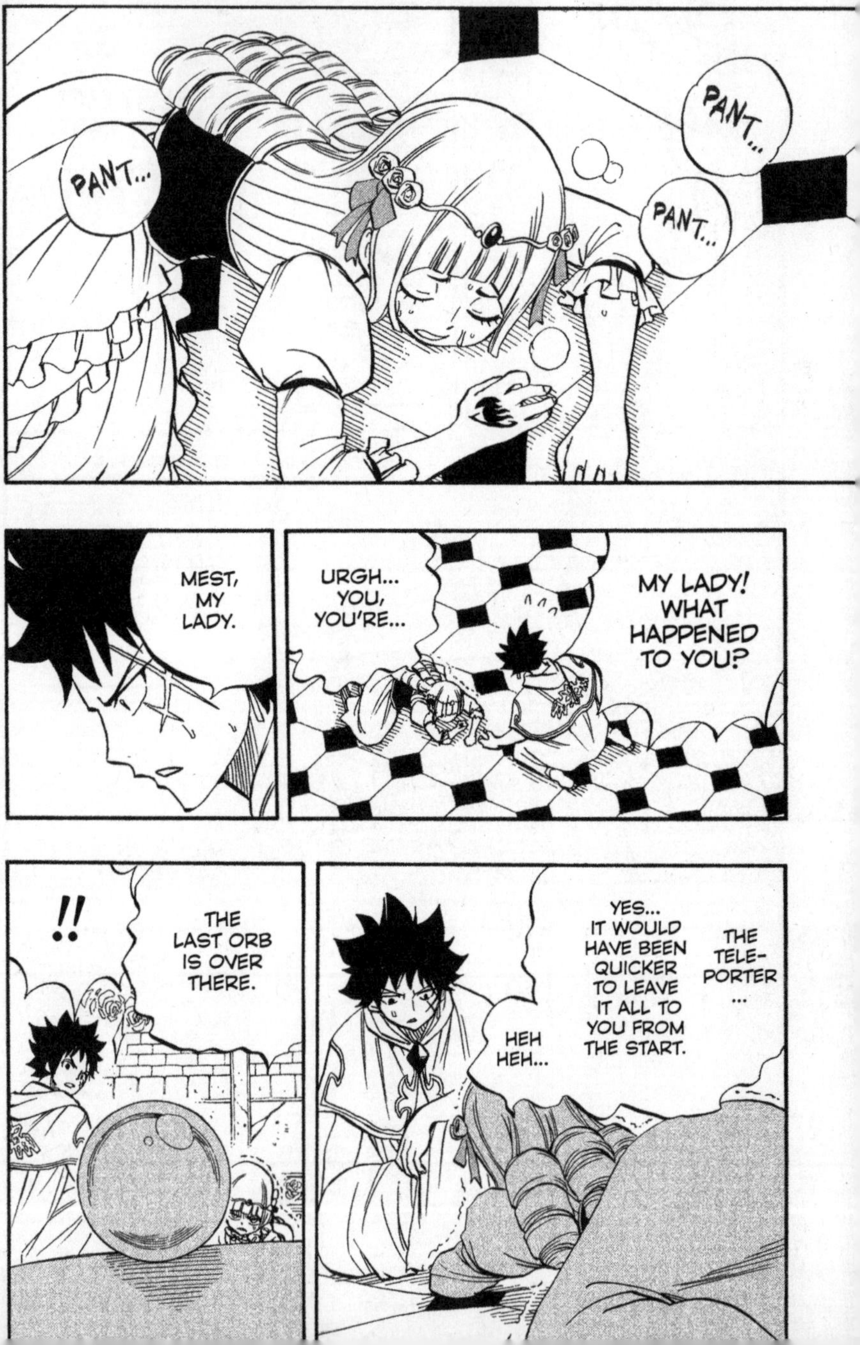
PANT...
PANT...
PANT...
MY LADY! WHAT HAPPENED TO YOU?
URGH... YOU, YOU'RE...
MEST, MY LADY.
THE TELE-PORTER ...
YES... IT WOULD HAVE BEEN QUICKER TO LEAVE IT ALL TO YOU FROM THE START.
HEH HEH...
!!
THE LAST ORB IS OVER THERE.

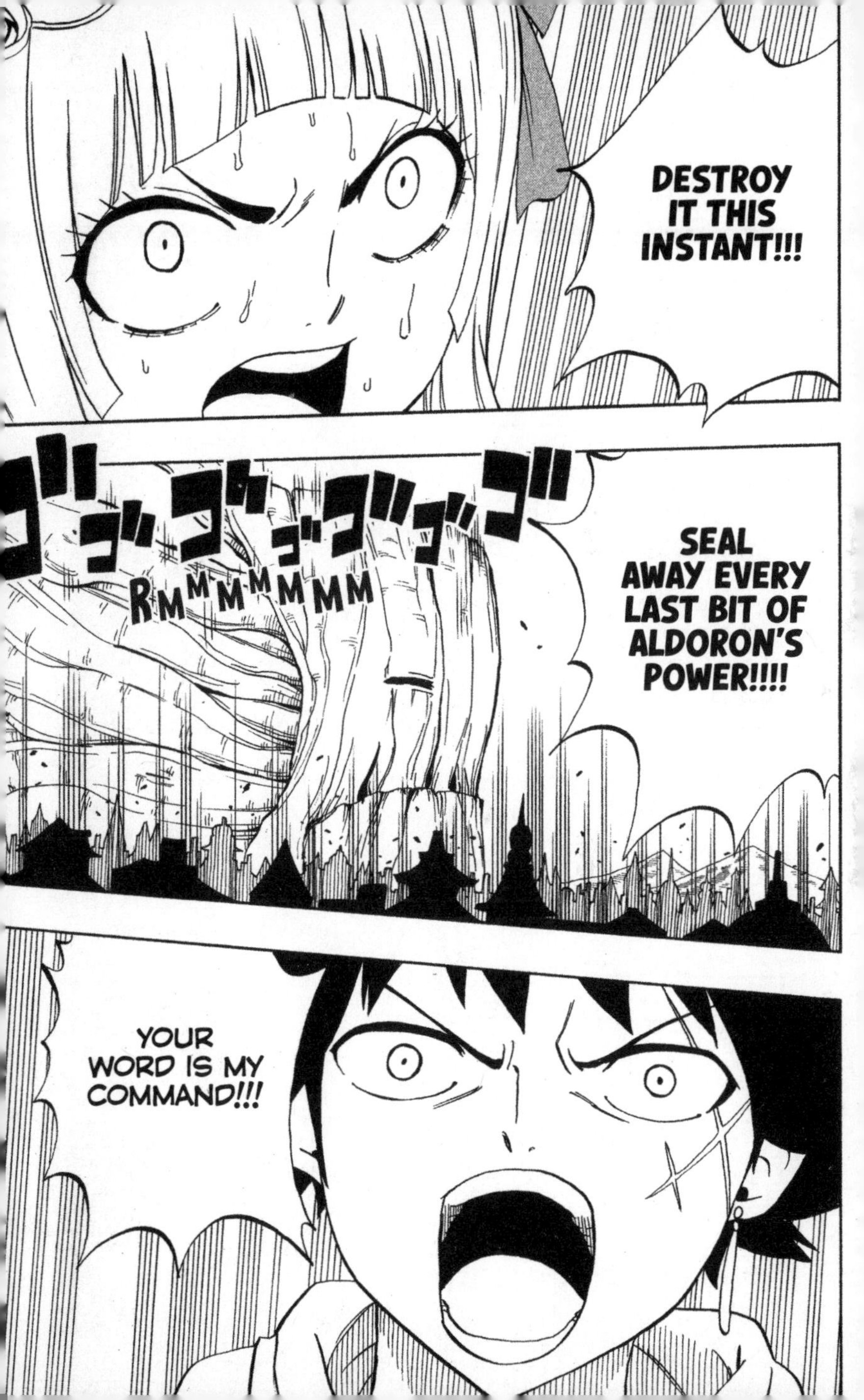
DESTROY IT THIS INSTANT!!!
RMMMMMMM
SEAL AWAY EVERY LAST BIT OF ALDORON'S POWER!!!!
YOUR WORD IS MY COMMAND!!!

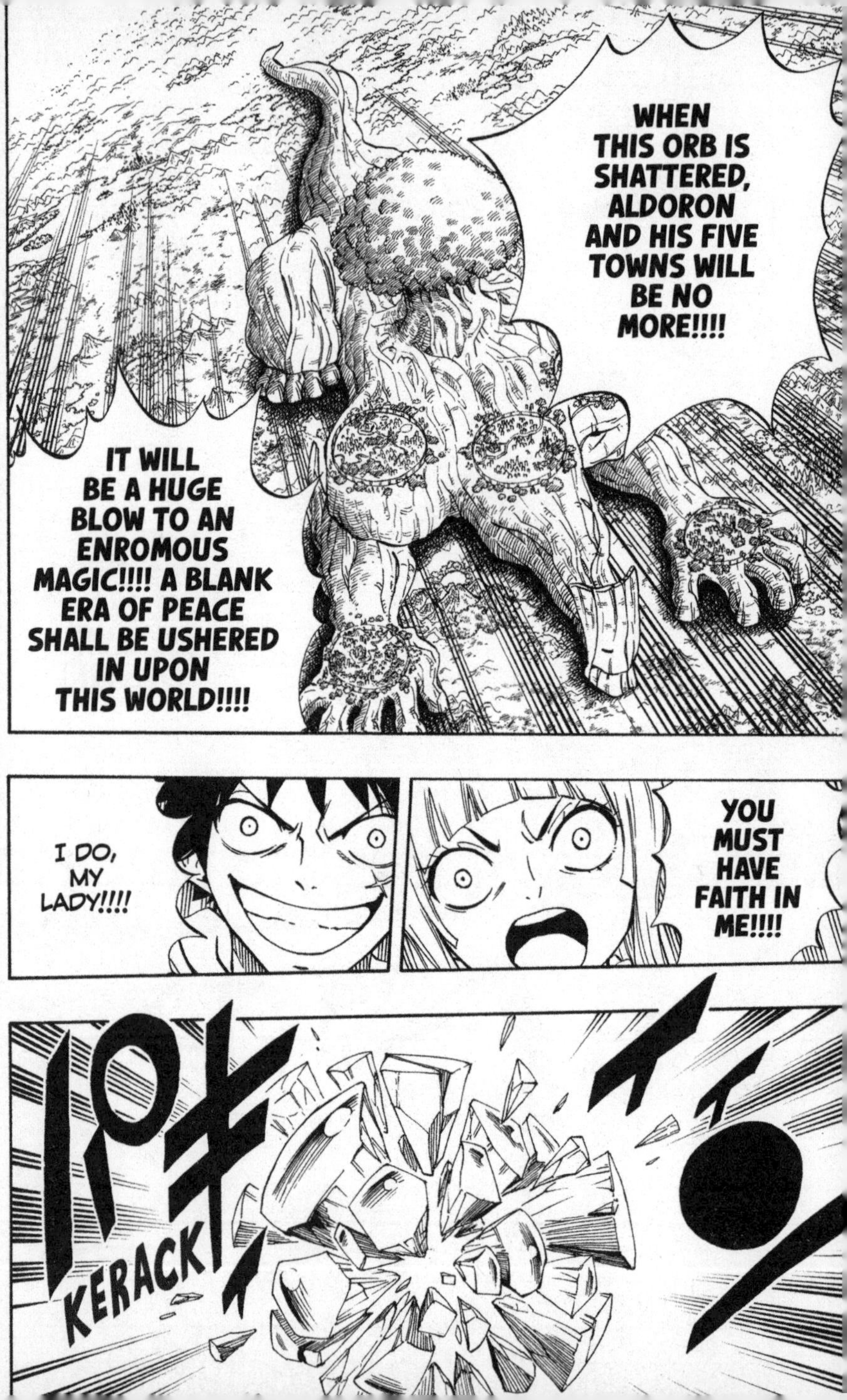
WHEN THIS ORB IS SHATTERED, ALDORON AND HIS FIVE TOWNS WILL BE NO MORE!!!!
IT WILL BE A HUGE BLOW TO AN ENROMOUS MAGIC!!!! A BLANK ERA OF PEACE SHALL BE USHERED IN UPON THIS WORLD!!!!
YOU MUST HAVE FAITH IN ME!!!!
I DO, MY LADY!!!!
KERACK

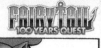

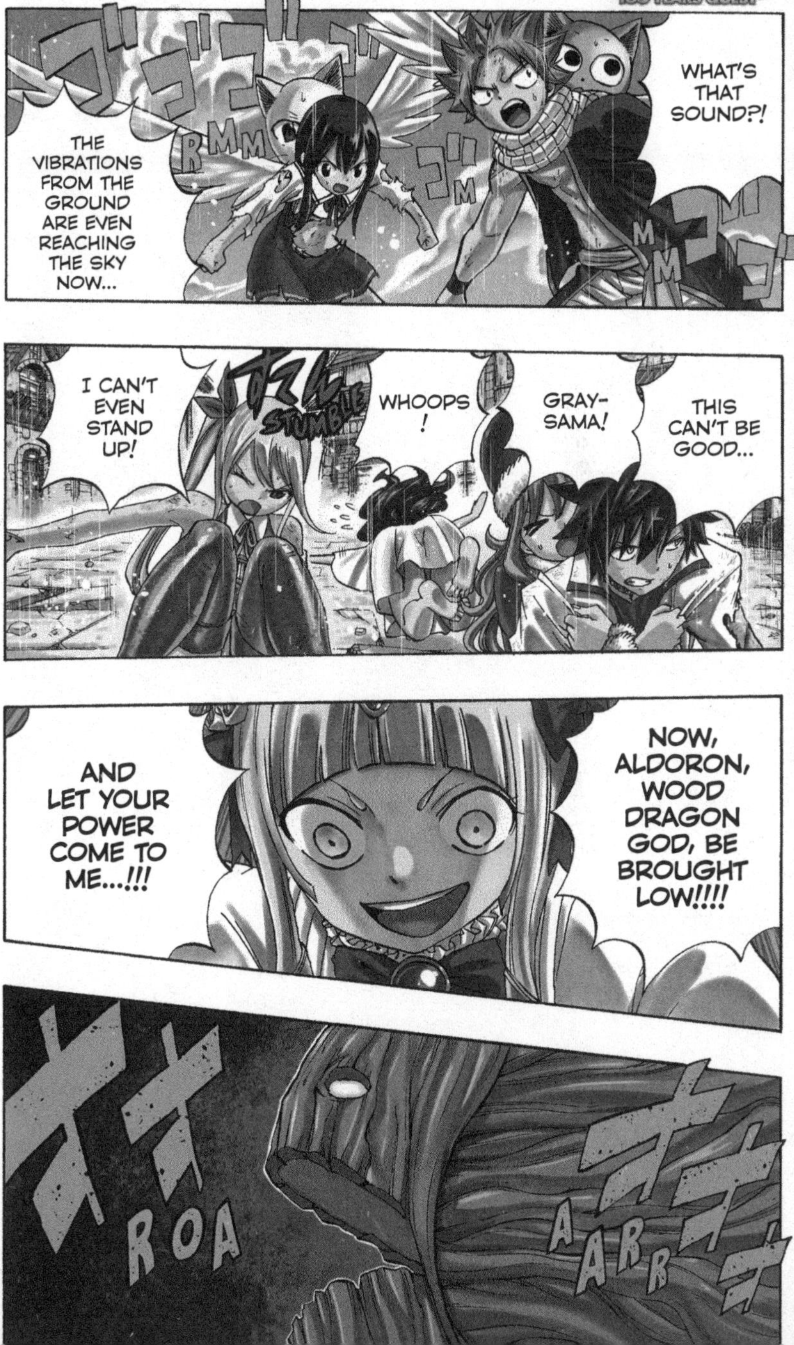
WHAT'S THAT SOUND?!
MMM
RMMM
THE VIBRATIONS FROM THE GROUND ARE EVEN REACHING THE SKY NOW...
THIS CAN'T BE GOOD...
GRAY-SAMA!
WHOOPS!
STUMBLE
I CAN'T EVEN STAND UP!
NOW, ALDORON, WOOD DRAGON GOD, BE BROUGHT LOW!!!!
AND LET YOUR POWER COME TO ME...!!!
ROA
AARR

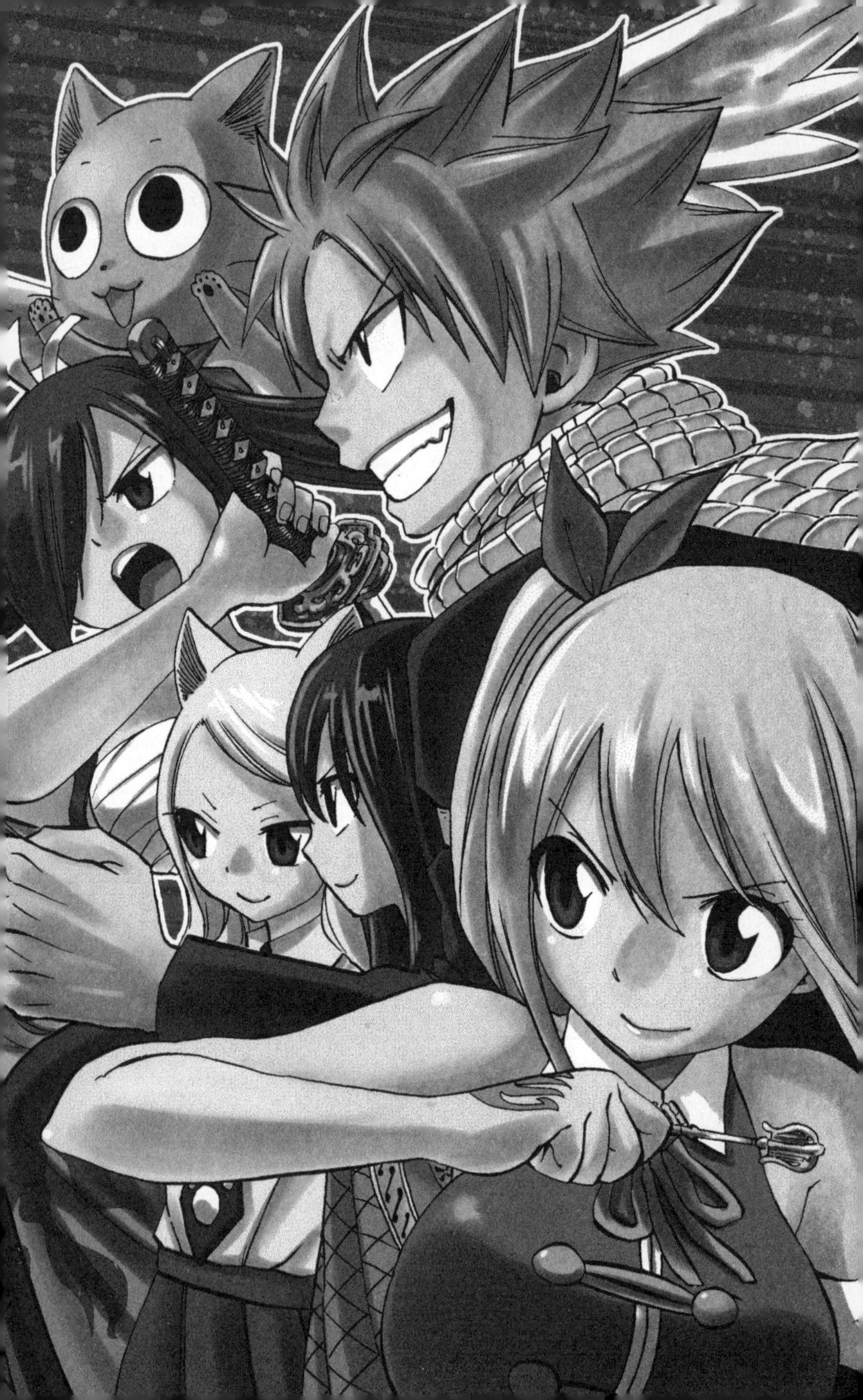

Chapter 58: The Secret of the Wood Dragon God

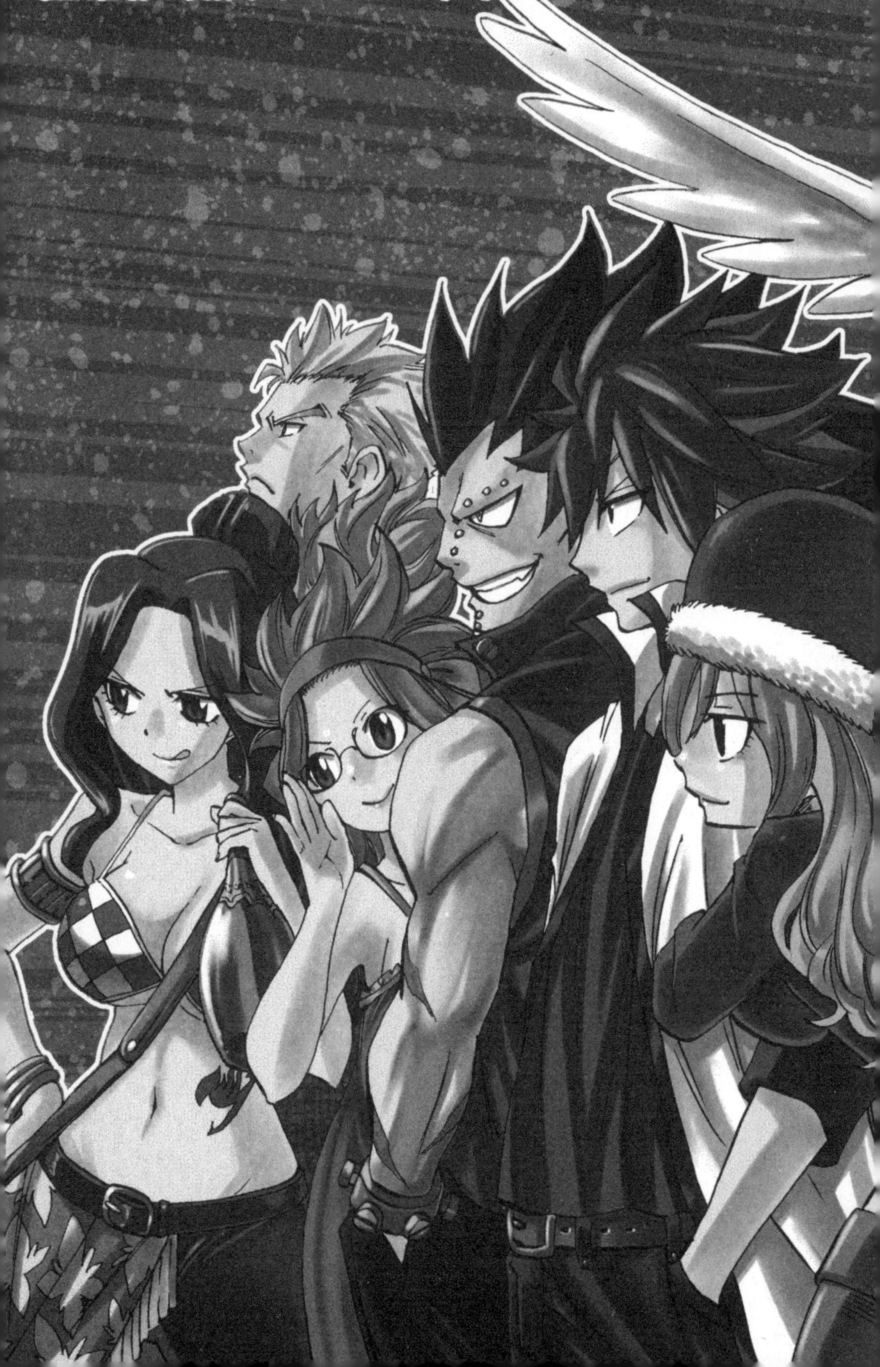

FAIRY TAIL
100 YEARS QUEST

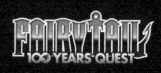

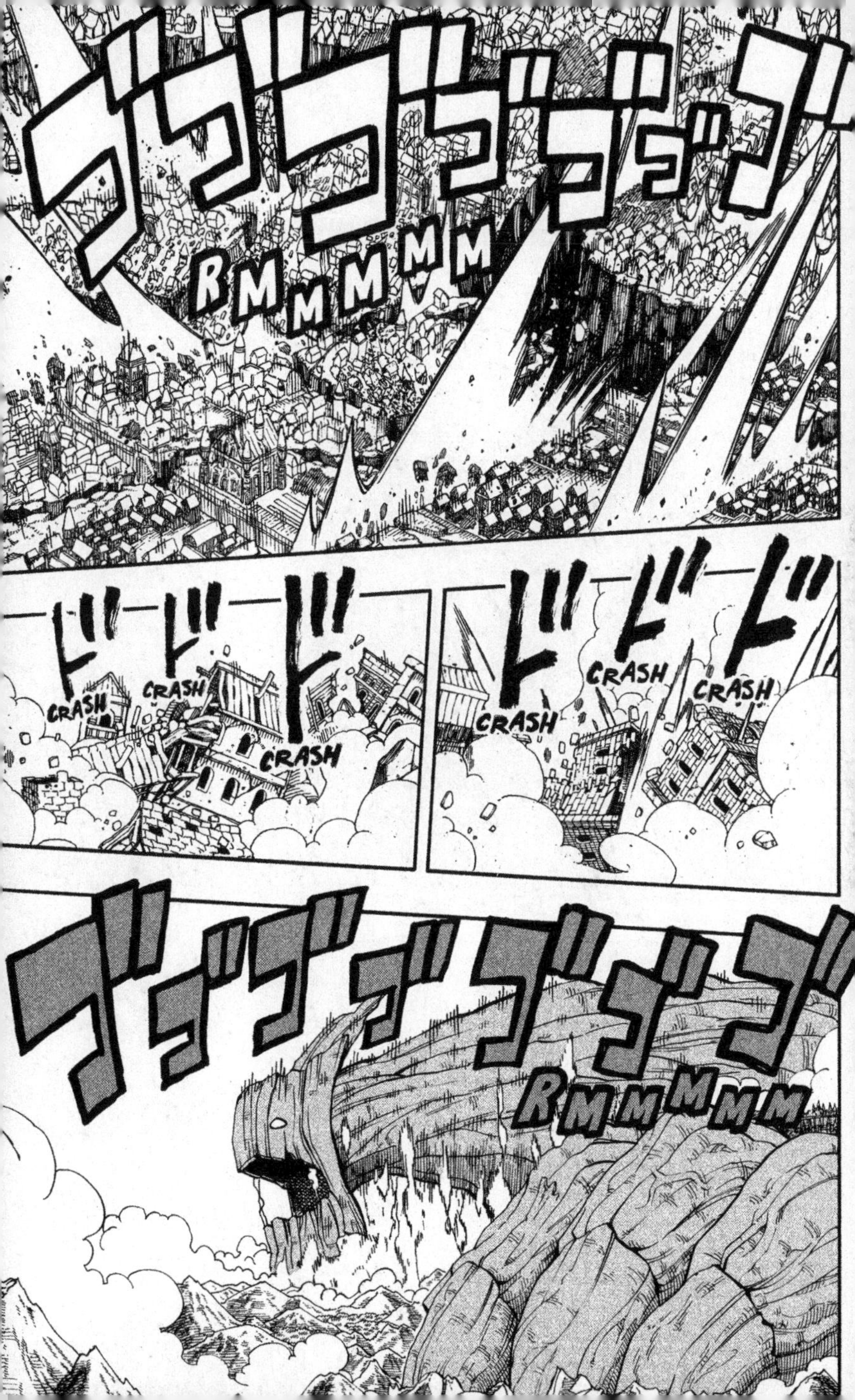
ゴゴゴゴゴゴ
RMMMMM
ドドド
CRASH
CRASH
CRASH
ドドド
CRASH
CRASH
CRASH
ゴゴゴゴゴゴ
RMMMMMM

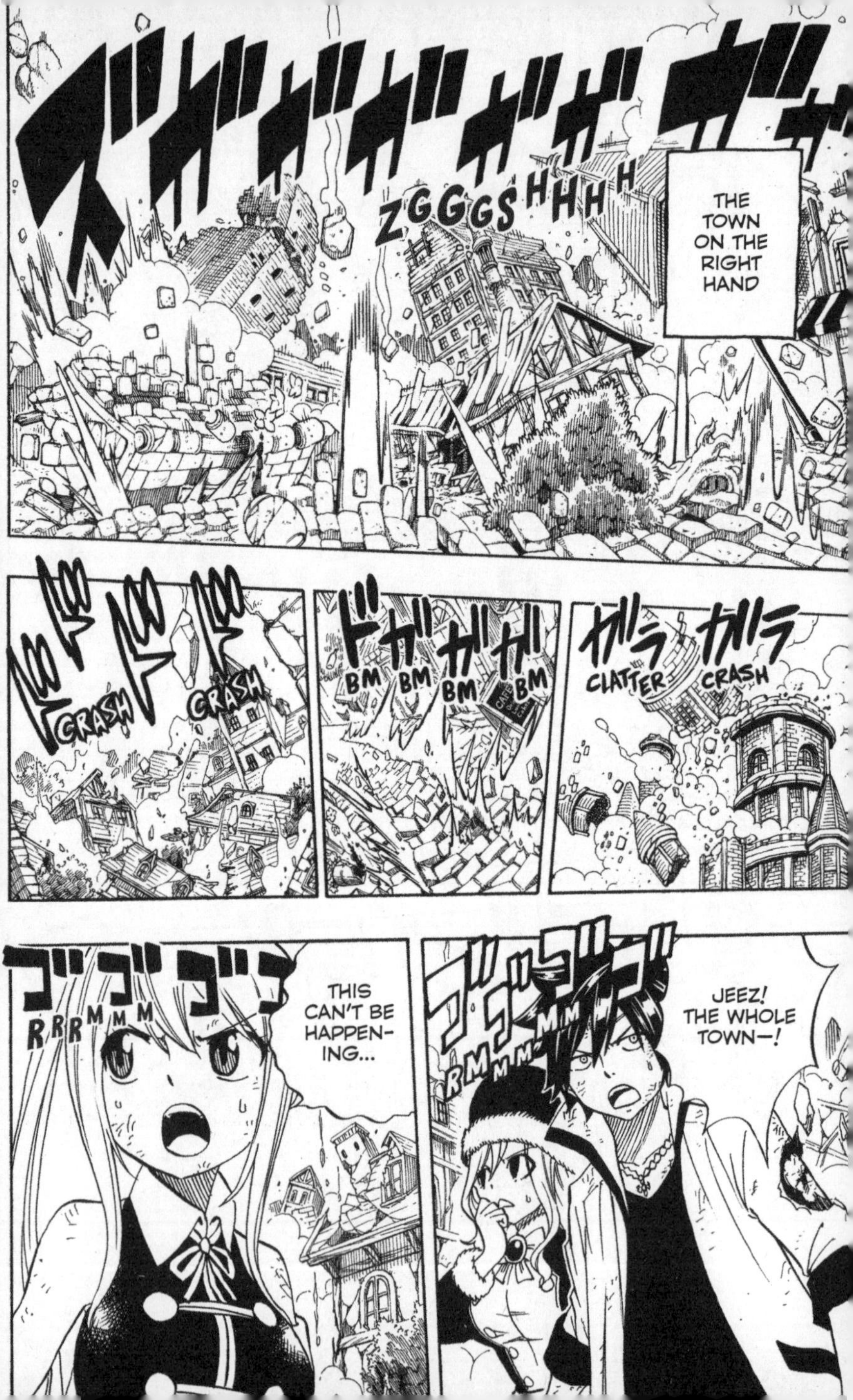
ズガガガガガガガガ
ZGGGSHHHH
THE TOWN ON THE RIGHT HAND
ガラ ガラ
CLATTER CRASH
ドガガガ
BM BM BM BM
ドド ドド
CRASH CRASH
JEEZ! THE WHOLE TOWN—!
ゴゴゴゴ
RMMMMM
THIS CAN'T BE HAPPEN-ING...
ゴゴゴゴ
RRRMMM

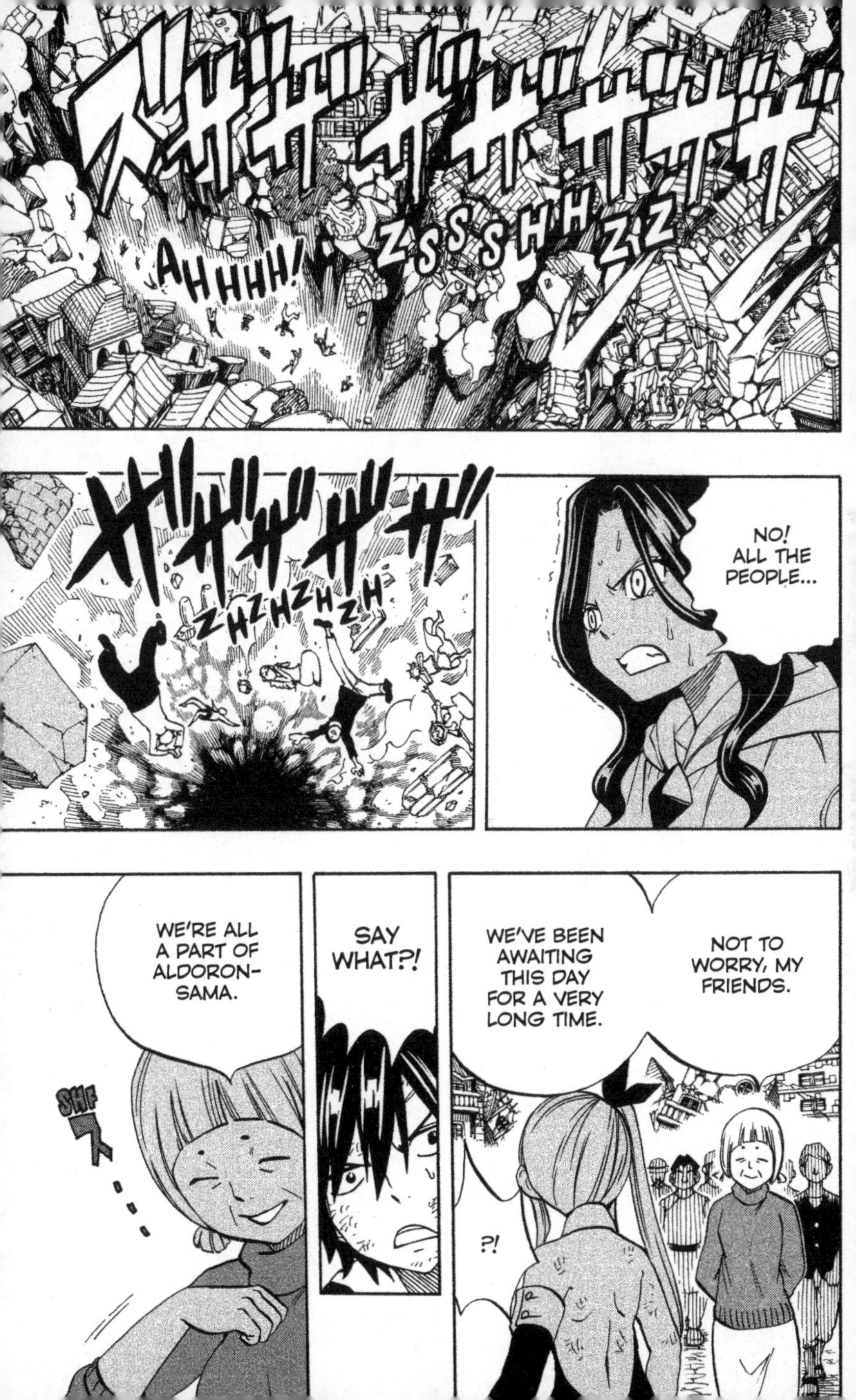
ZSSSHHZZ
AHHHH!
NO! ALL THE PEOPLE...
ZHZHZHZH
NOT TO WORRY, MY FRIENDS.
WE'VE BEEN AWAITING THIS DAY FOR A VERY LONG TIME.
?!
SAY WHAT?!
WE'RE ALL A PART OF ALDORON-SAMA.
SHF

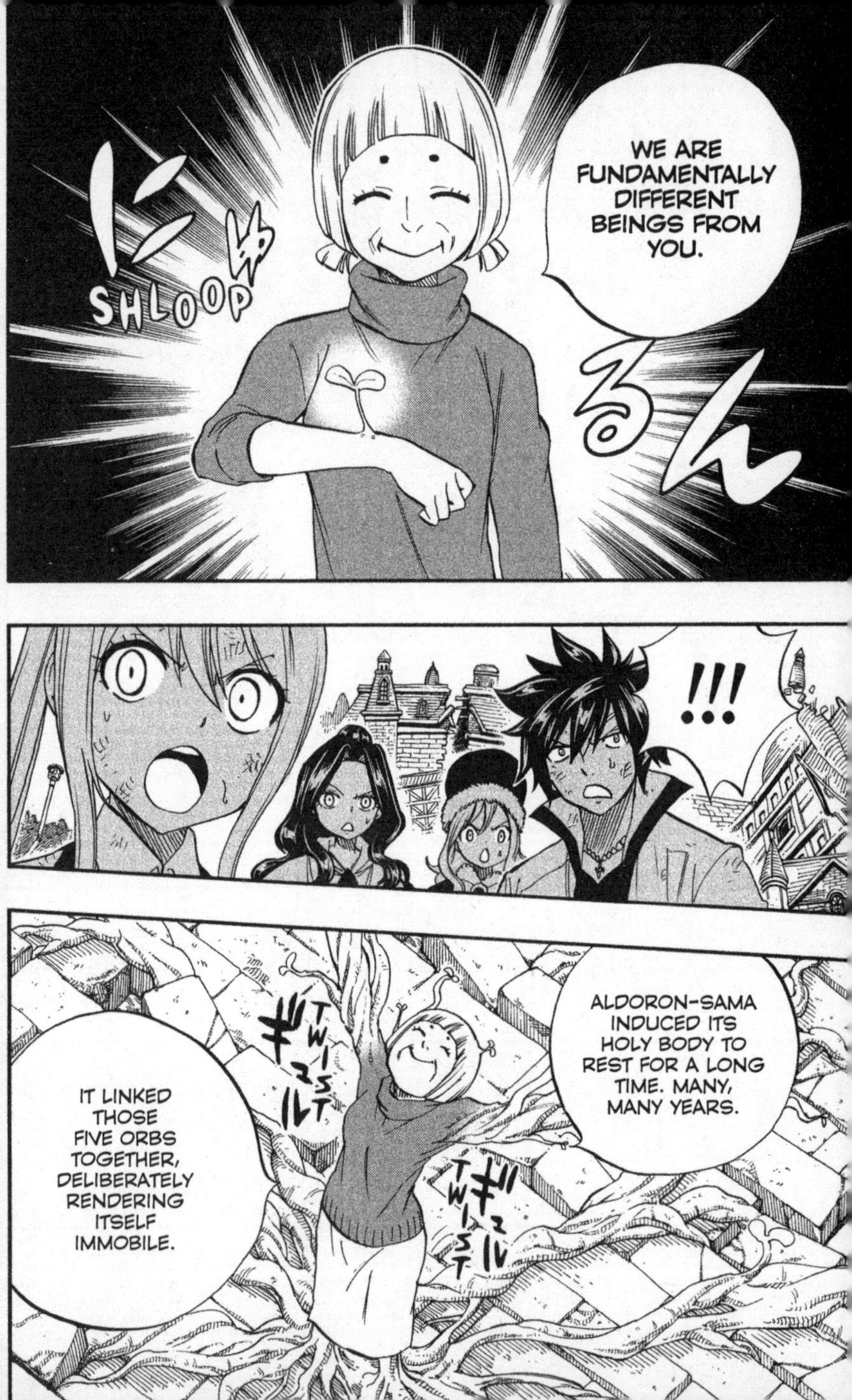
WE ARE FUNDAMENTALLY DIFFERENT BEINGS FROM YOU.
るん
にゅ
SHLOOP
!!!
ALDORON-SAMA INDUCED ITS HOLY BODY TO REST FOR A LONG TIME. MANY, MANY YEARS.
ギュル
TWIST
ギュル
TWIST
IT LINKED THOSE FIVE ORBS TOGETHER, DELIBERATELY RENDERING ITSELF IMMOBILE.

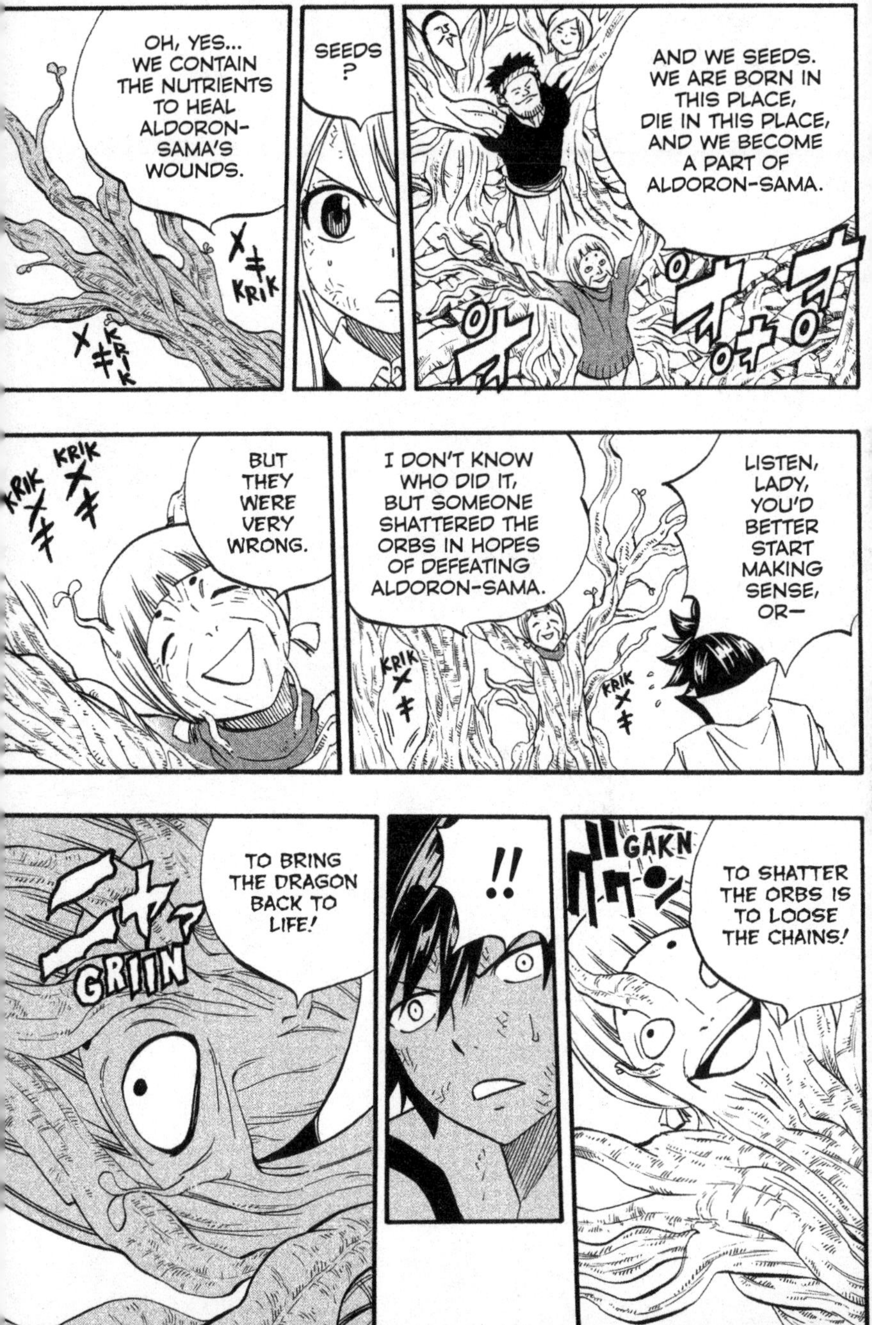
AND WE SEEDS. WE ARE BORN IN THIS PLACE, DIE IN THIS PLACE, AND WE BECOME A PART OF ALDORON-SAMA.
SEEDS ?
OH, YES... WE CONTAIN THE NUTRIENTS TO HEAL ALDORON-SAMA'S WOUNDS.
KRIK
KRIK
LISTEN, LADY, YOU'D BETTER START MAKING SENSE, OR—
I DON'T KNOW WHO DID IT, BUT SOMEONE SHATTERED THE ORBS IN HOPES OF DEFEATING ALDORON-SAMA.
KRIK
KRIK
KRIK
KRIK
BUT THEY WERE VERY WRONG.
GAKN
TO SHATTER THE ORBS IS TO LOOSE THE CHAINS!
!!
GRIIN
TO BRING THE DRAGON BACK TO LIFE!

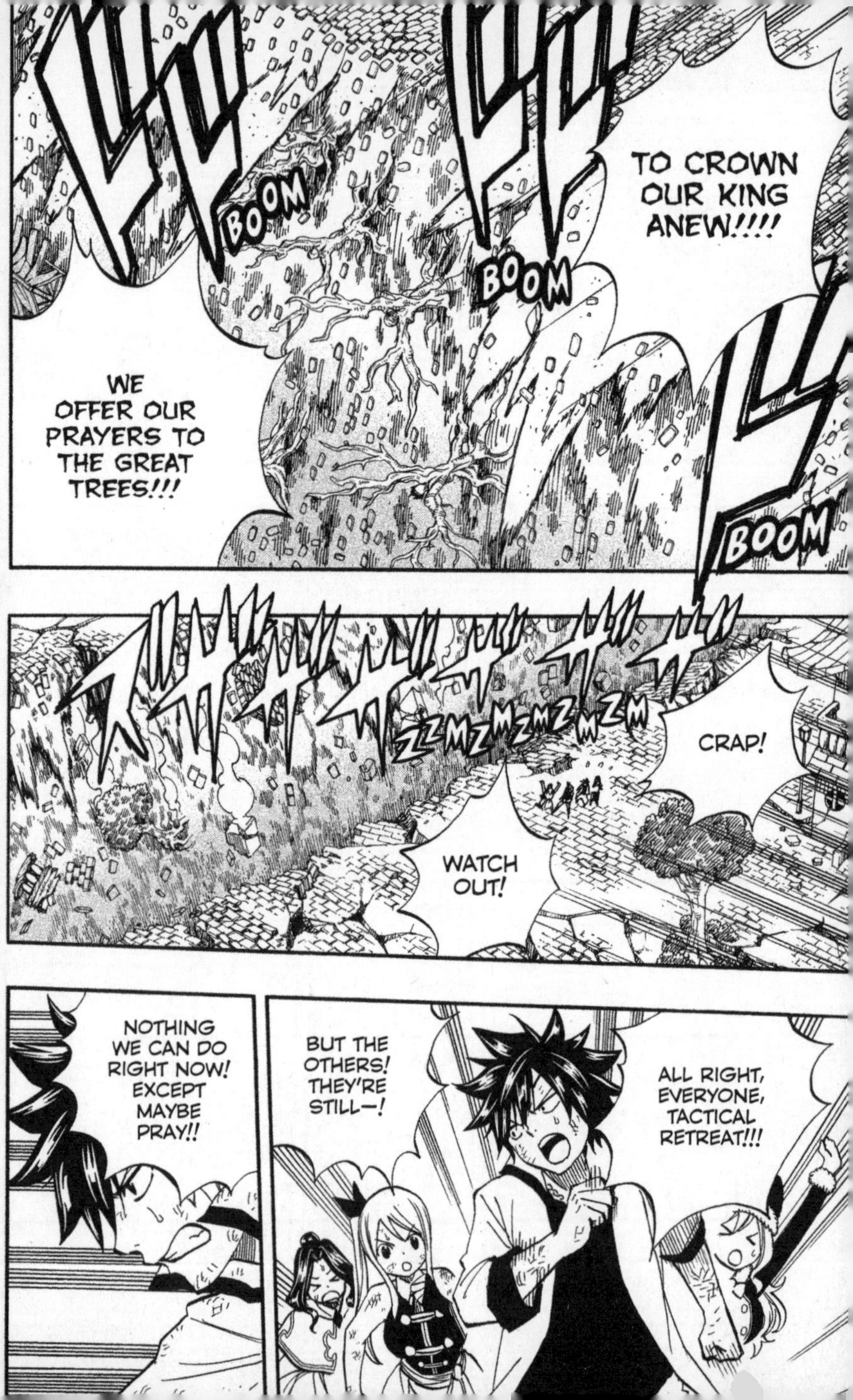
TO CROWN OUR KING ANEW!!!!
BOOM
BOOM
WE OFFER OUR PRAYERS TO THE GREAT TREES!!!
BOOM
ZZMZMZMZMZM
CRAP!
WATCH OUT!
ALL RIGHT, EVERYONE, TACTICAL RETREAT!!!
BUT THE OTHERS! THEY'RE STILL—!
NOTHING WE CAN DO RIGHT NOW! EXCEPT MAYBE PRAY!!

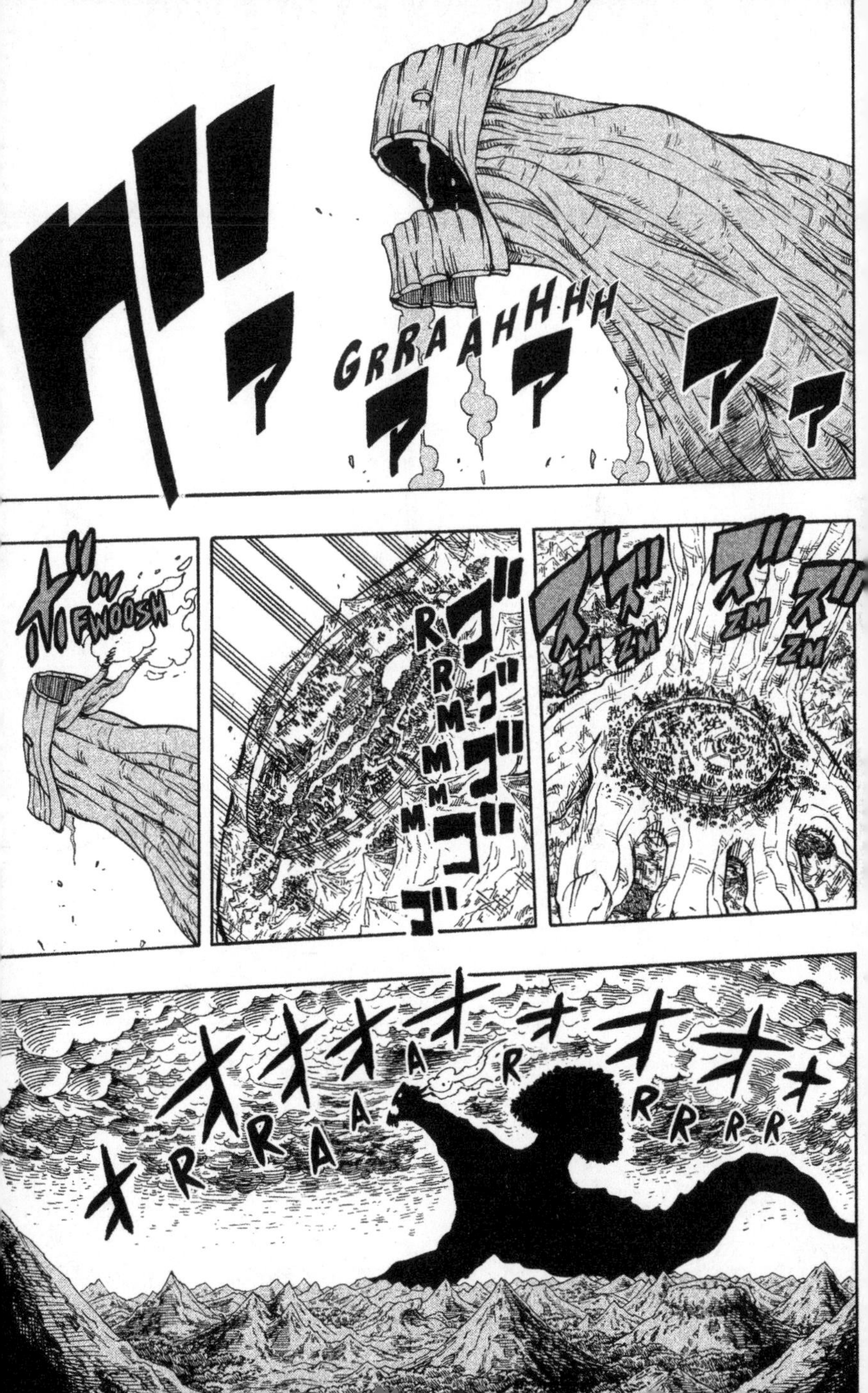
GRRAAHHHH
ZM ZM ZM ZM
RRMMMM
FWOOSH
RRAAARRRRR

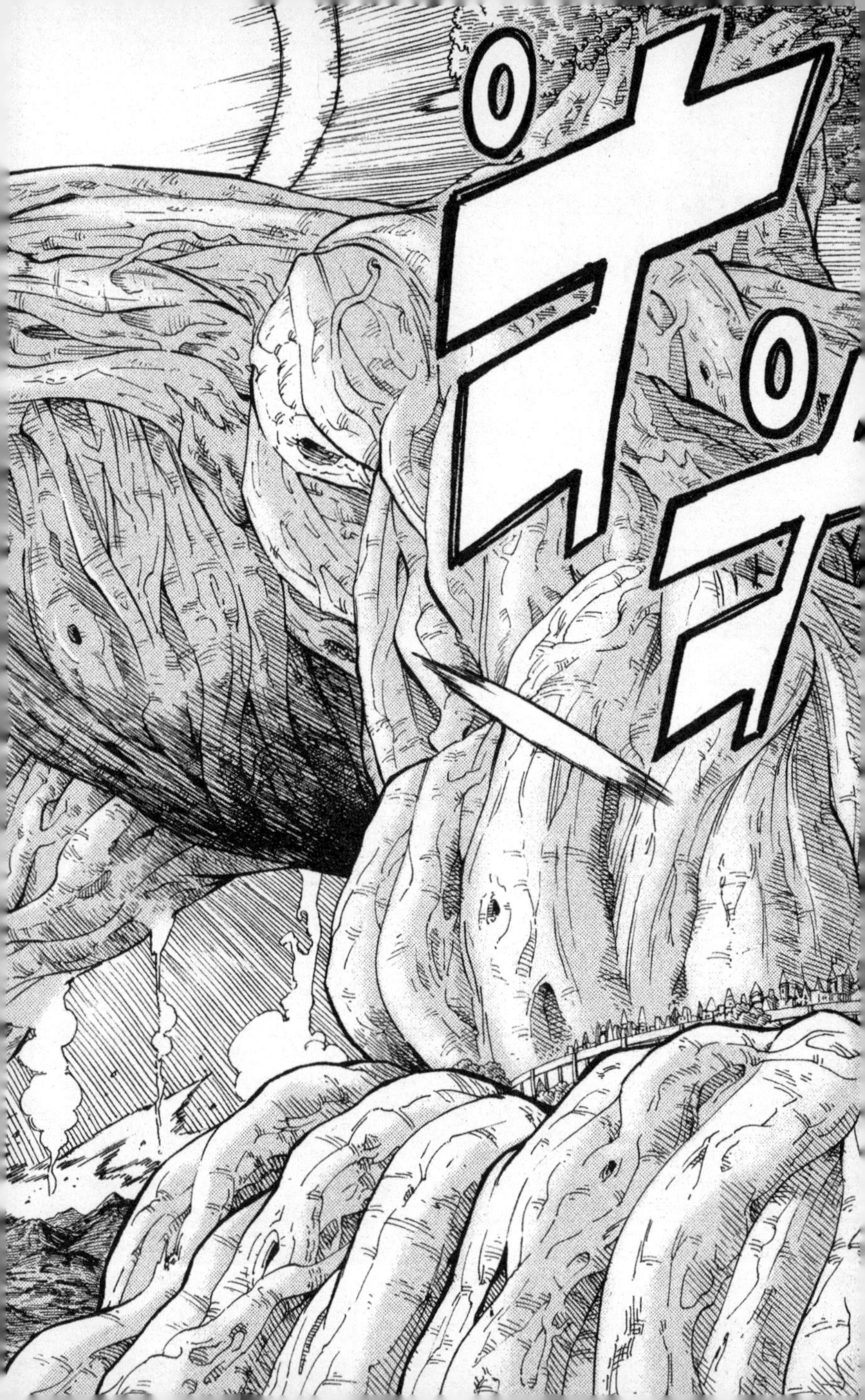

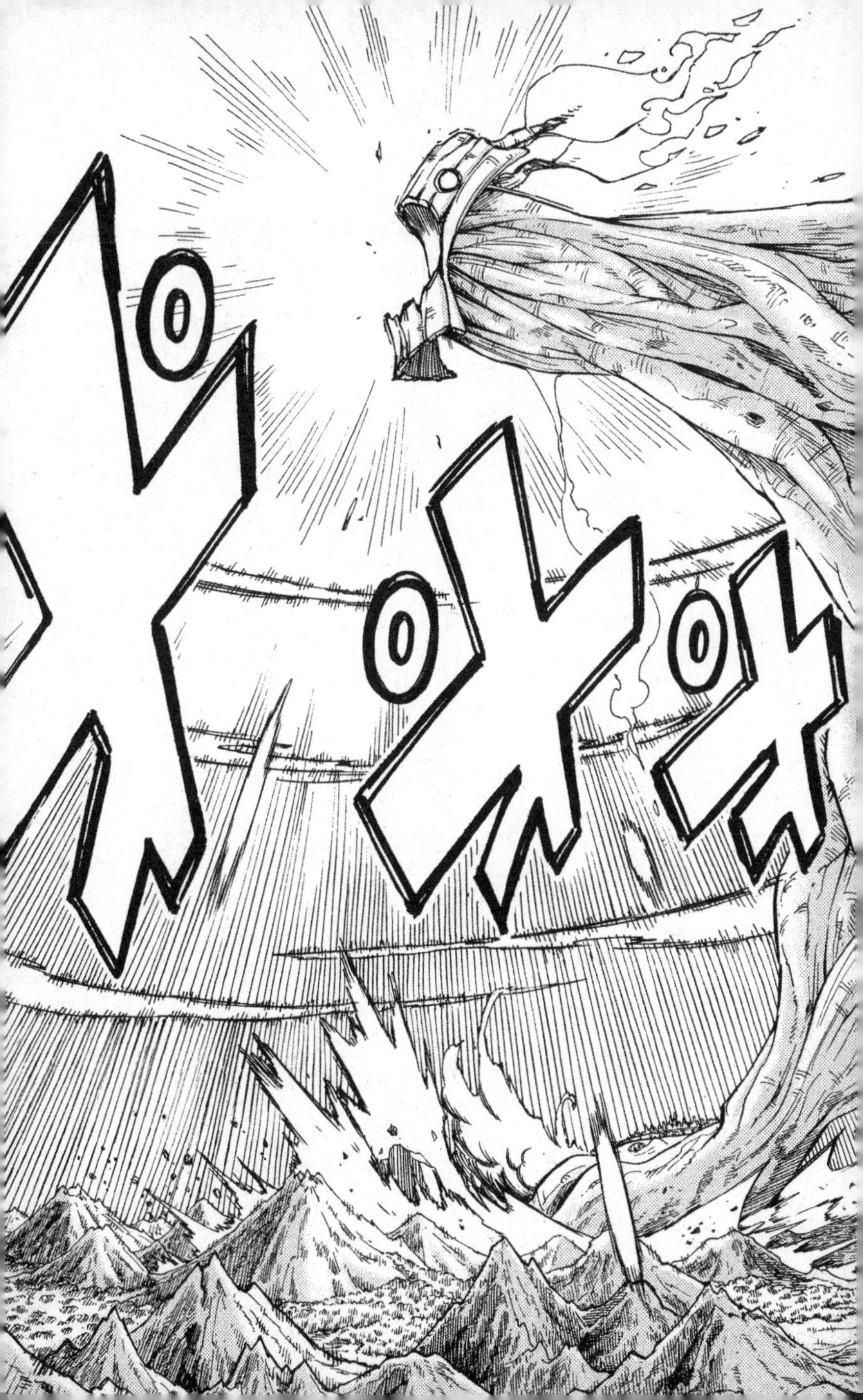

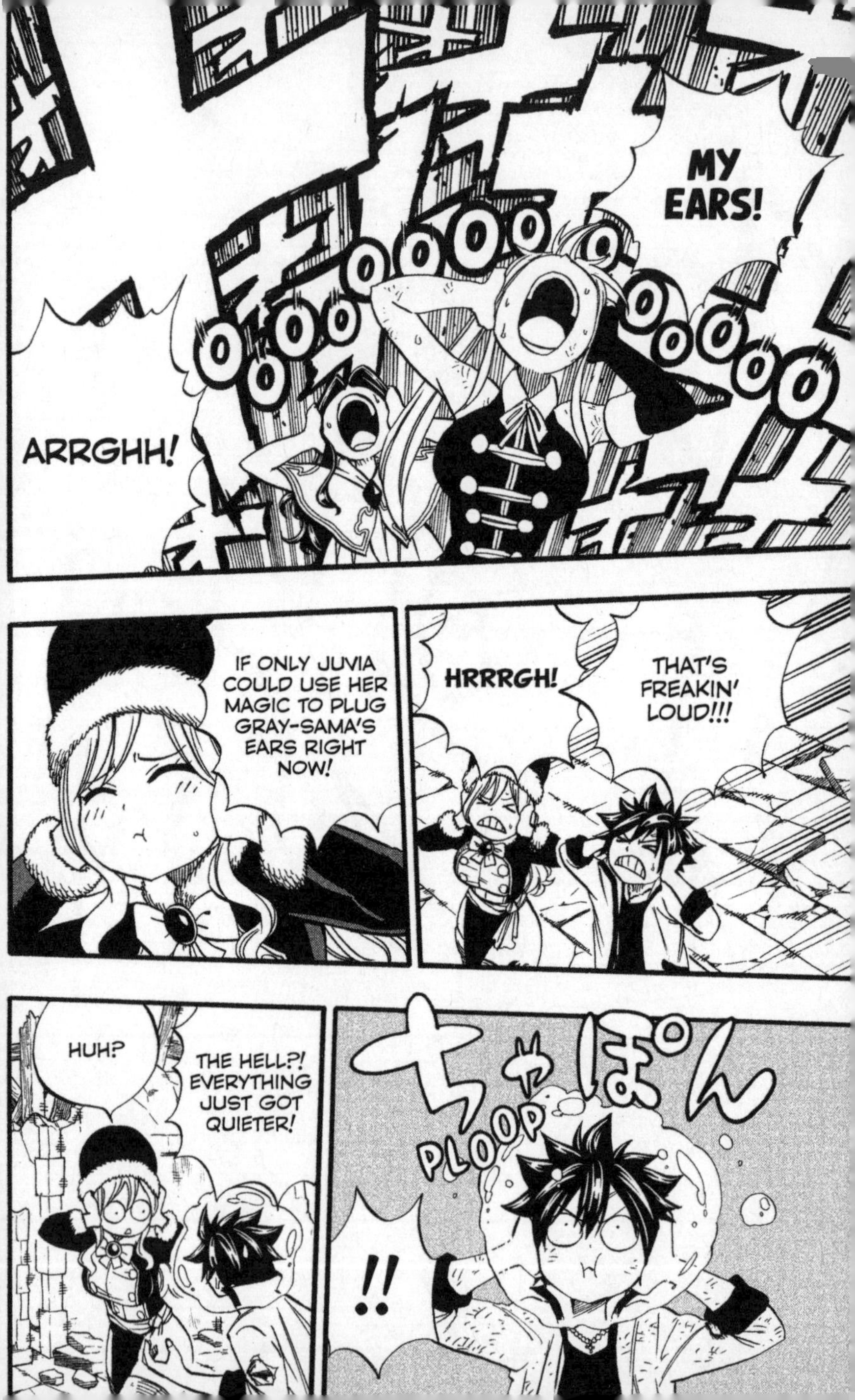
MY EARS!
ARRGHH!
THAT'S FREAKIN' LOUD!!!
HRRRGH!
IF ONLY JUVIA COULD USE HER MAGIC TO PLUG GRAY-SAMA'S EARS RIGHT NOW!
ちゃぽん
PLOOP
!!
THE HELL?! EVERYTHING JUST GOT QUIETER!
HUH?

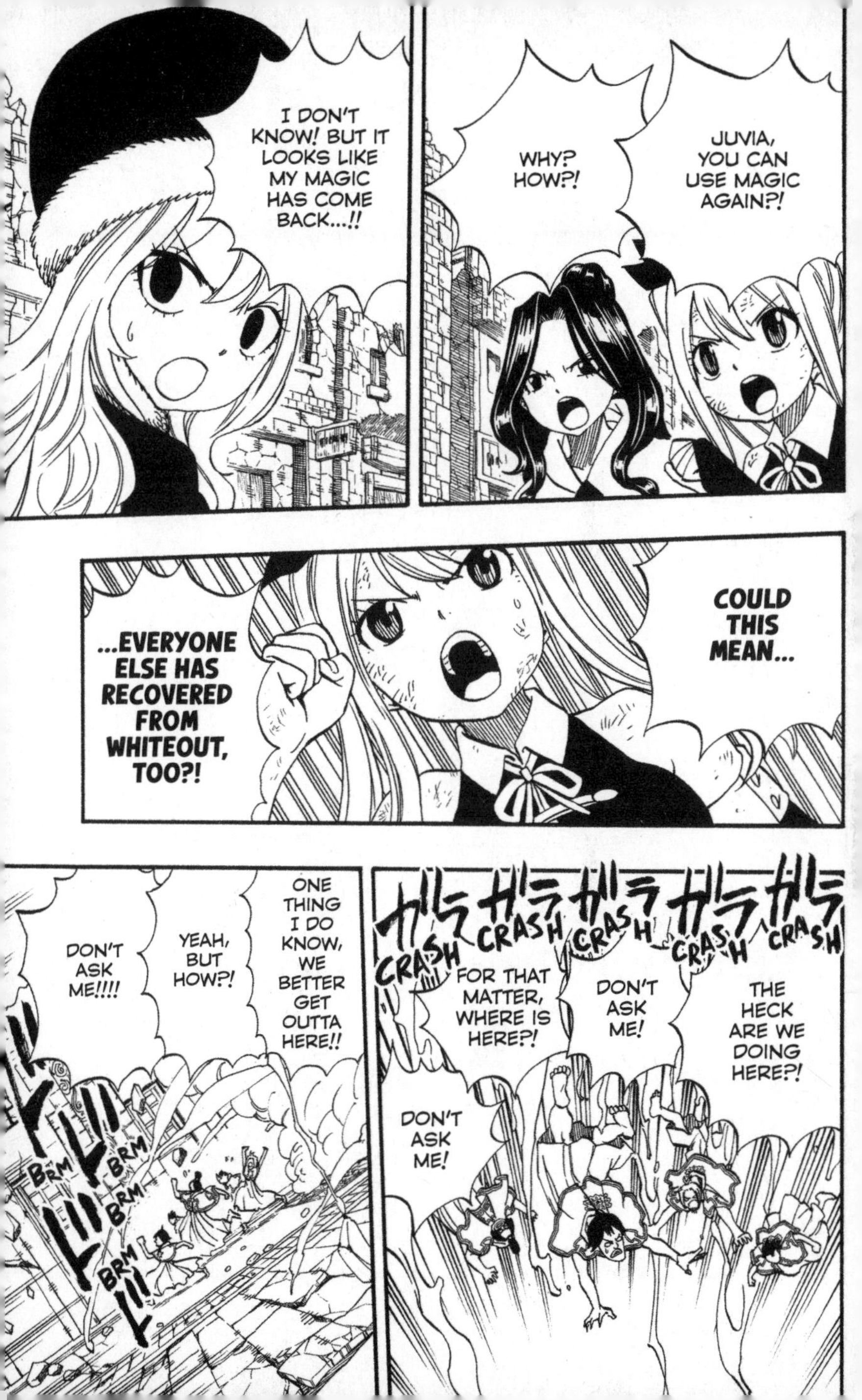
JUVIA, YOU CAN USE MAGIC AGAIN?!
WHY? HOW?!
I DON'T KNOW! BUT IT LOOKS LIKE MY MAGIC HAS COME BACK...!!
COULD THIS MEAN...
...EVERYONE ELSE HAS RECOVERED FROM WHITEOUT, TOO?!
ガラガラガラガラガラ
CRASH CRASH CRASH CRASH CRASH
THE HECK ARE WE DOING HERE?!
DON'T ASK ME!
FOR THAT MATTER, WHERE IS HERE?!
DON'T ASK ME!
ONE THING I DO KNOW, WE BETTER GET OUTTA HERE!!
YEAH, BUT HOW?!
DON'T ASK ME!!!!
BRM BRM BRM BRM

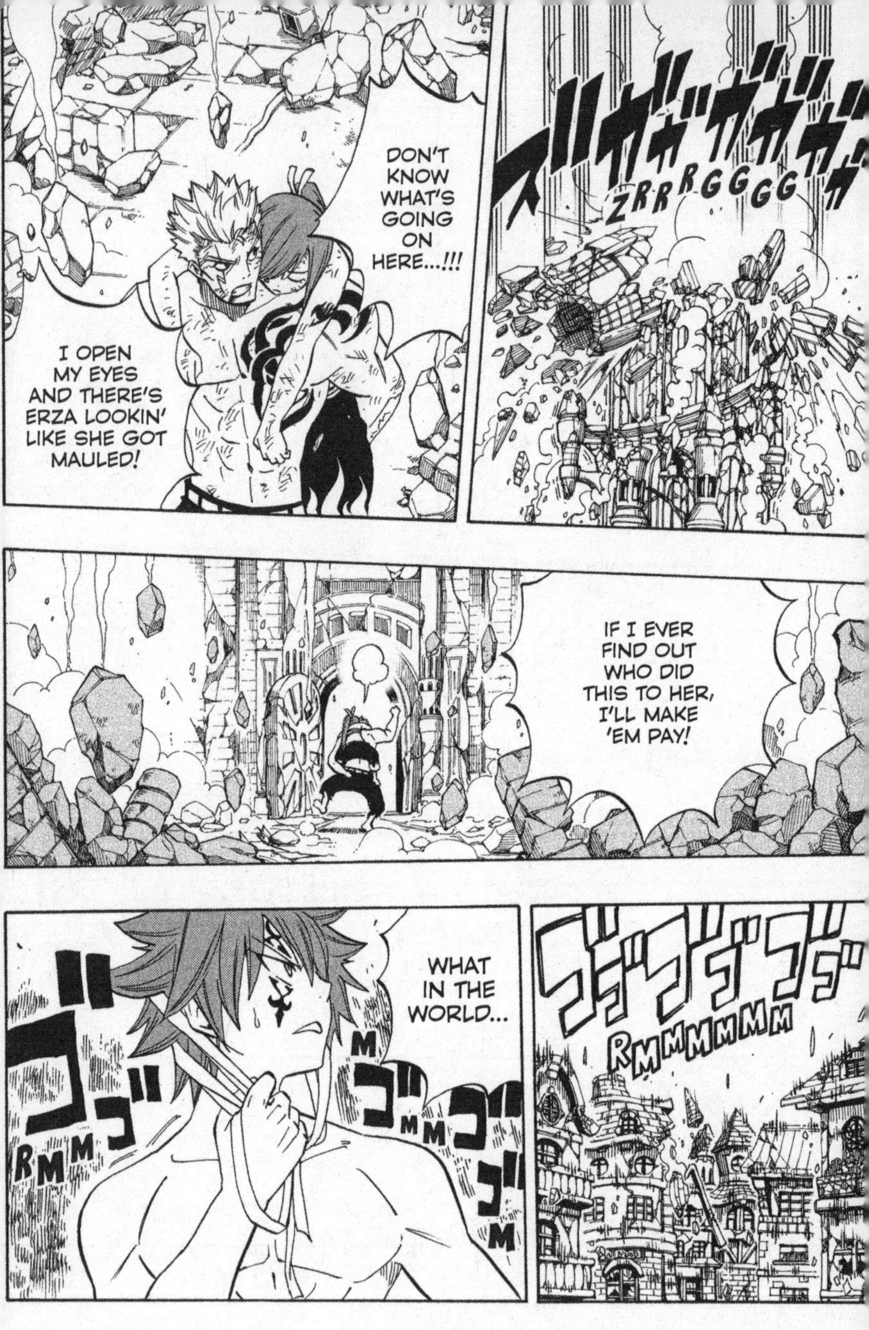
ZRRRGGGGG
DON'T KNOW WHAT'S GOING ON HERE...!!!
I OPEN MY EYES AND THERE'S ERZA LOOKIN' LIKE SHE GOT MAULED!
IF I EVER FIND OUT WHO DID THIS TO HER, I'LL MAKE 'EM PAY!
RMMMMMMM
WHAT IN THE WORLD...
RMMM

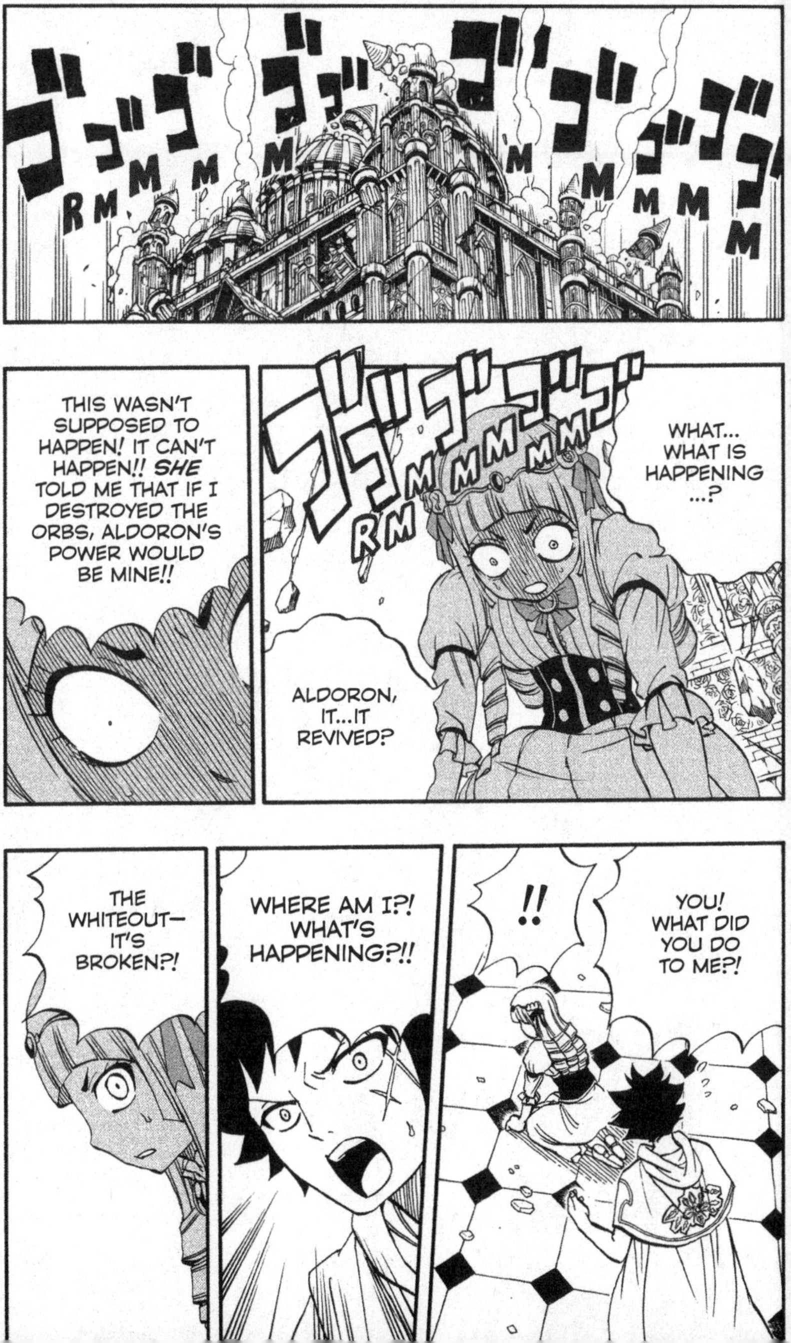
RMMMMMMMMMM
WHAT... WHAT IS HAPPENING ...?
RMMMMMMM
ALDORON, IT...IT REVIVED?
THIS WASN'T SUPPOSED TO HAPPEN! IT CAN'T HAPPEN!! *SHE* TOLD ME THAT IF I DESTROYED THE ORBS, ALDORON'S POWER WOULD BE MINE!!
!!
YOU! WHAT DID YOU DO TO ME?!
WHERE AM I?! WHAT'S HAPPENING?!!
THE WHITEOUT— IT'S BROKEN?!

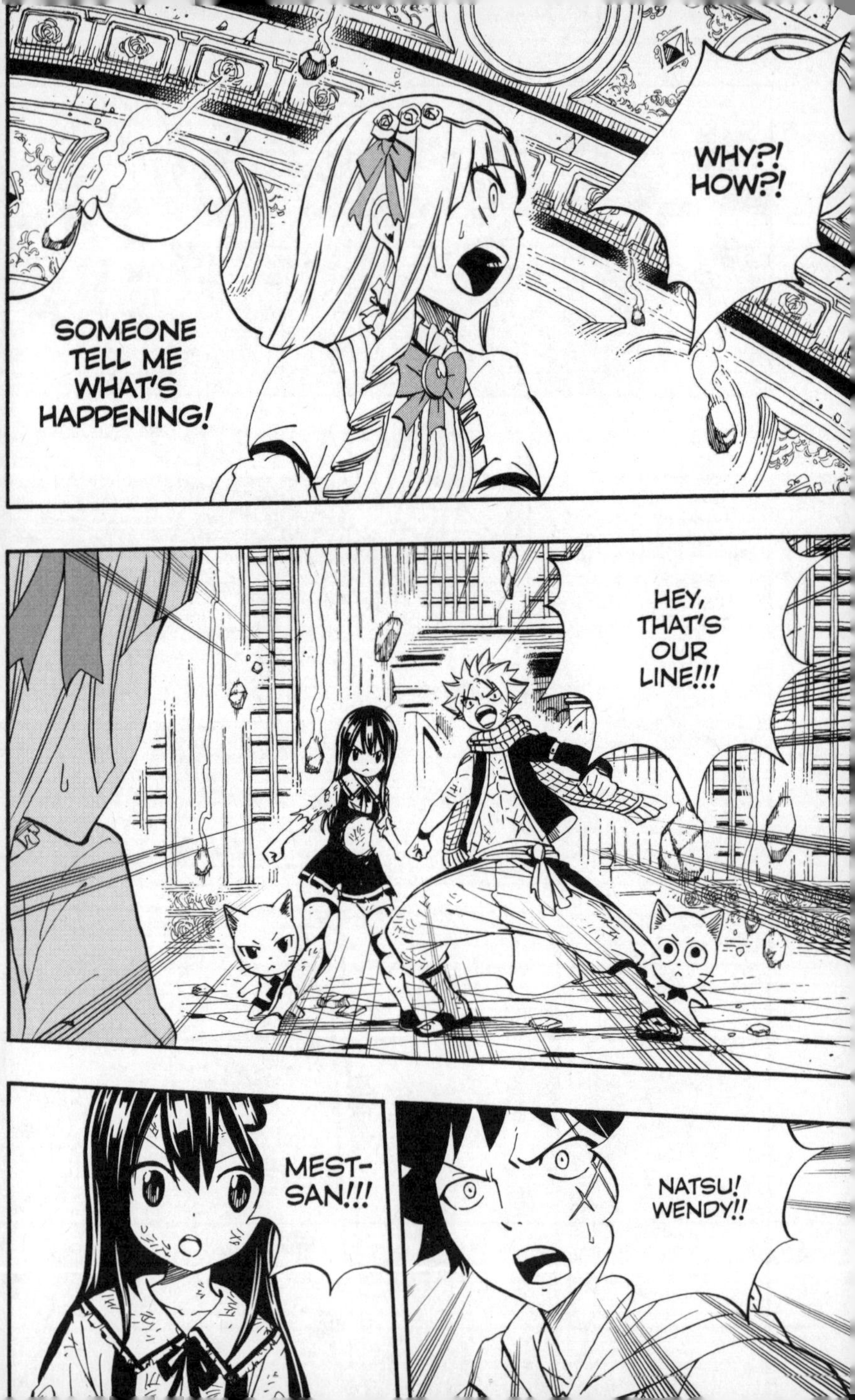
WHY?! HOW?!
SOMEONE TELL ME WHAT'S HAPPENING!
HEY, THAT'S OUR LINE!!!
NATSU! WENDY!!
MEST-SAN!!!

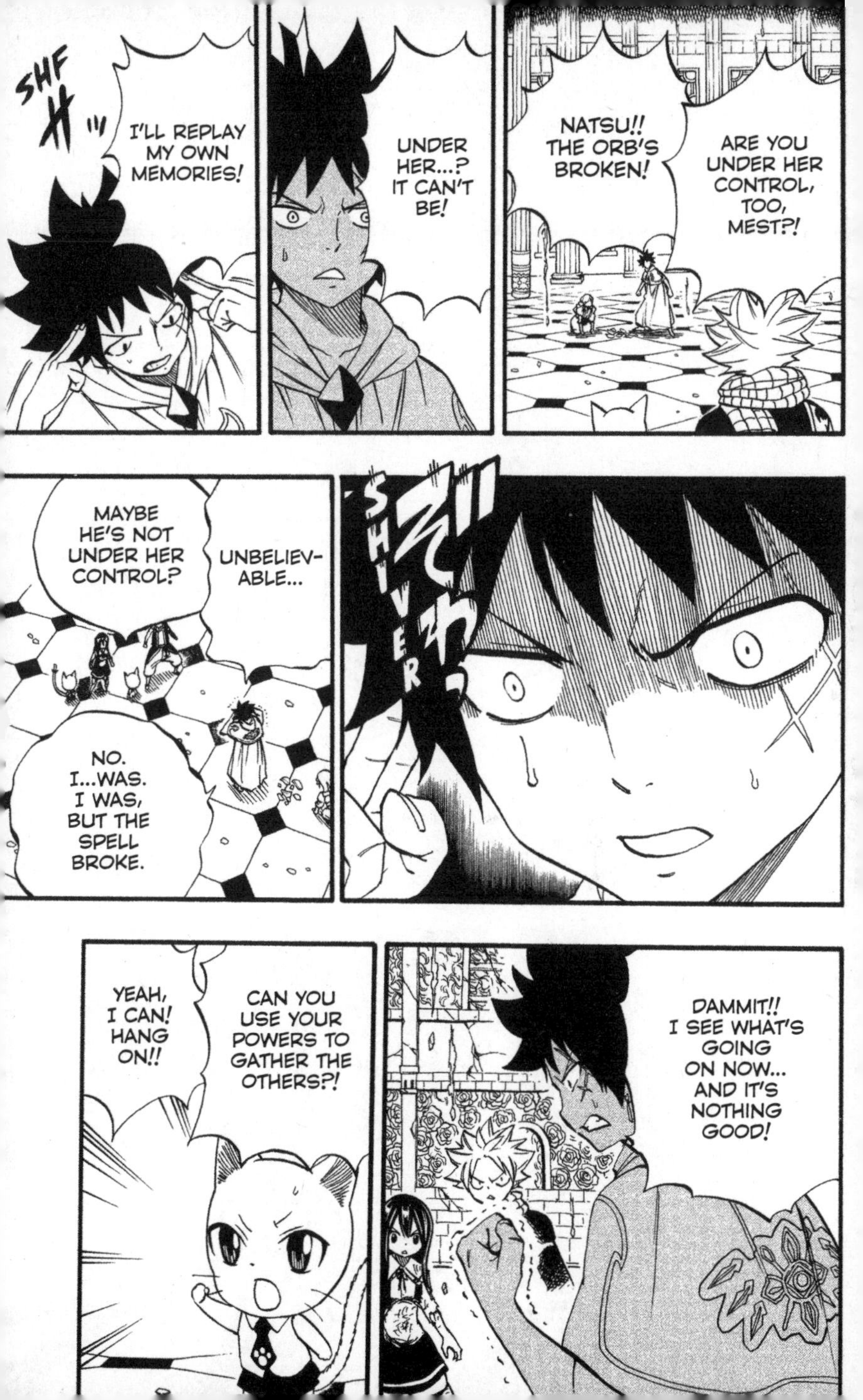
ARE YOU UNDER HER CONTROL, TOO, MEST?!
NATSU!! THE ORB'S BROKEN!
UNDER HER...? IT CAN'T BE!
SHFF
I'LL REPLAY MY OWN MEMORIES!
SHIVER
UNBELIEV-ABLE...
MAYBE HE'S NOT UNDER HER CONTROL?
NO. I...WAS. I WAS, BUT THE SPELL BROKE.
DAMMIT!! I SEE WHAT'S GOING ON NOW... AND IT'S NOTHING GOOD!
CAN YOU USE YOUR POWERS TO GATHER THE OTHERS?!
YEAH, I CAN! HANG ON!!

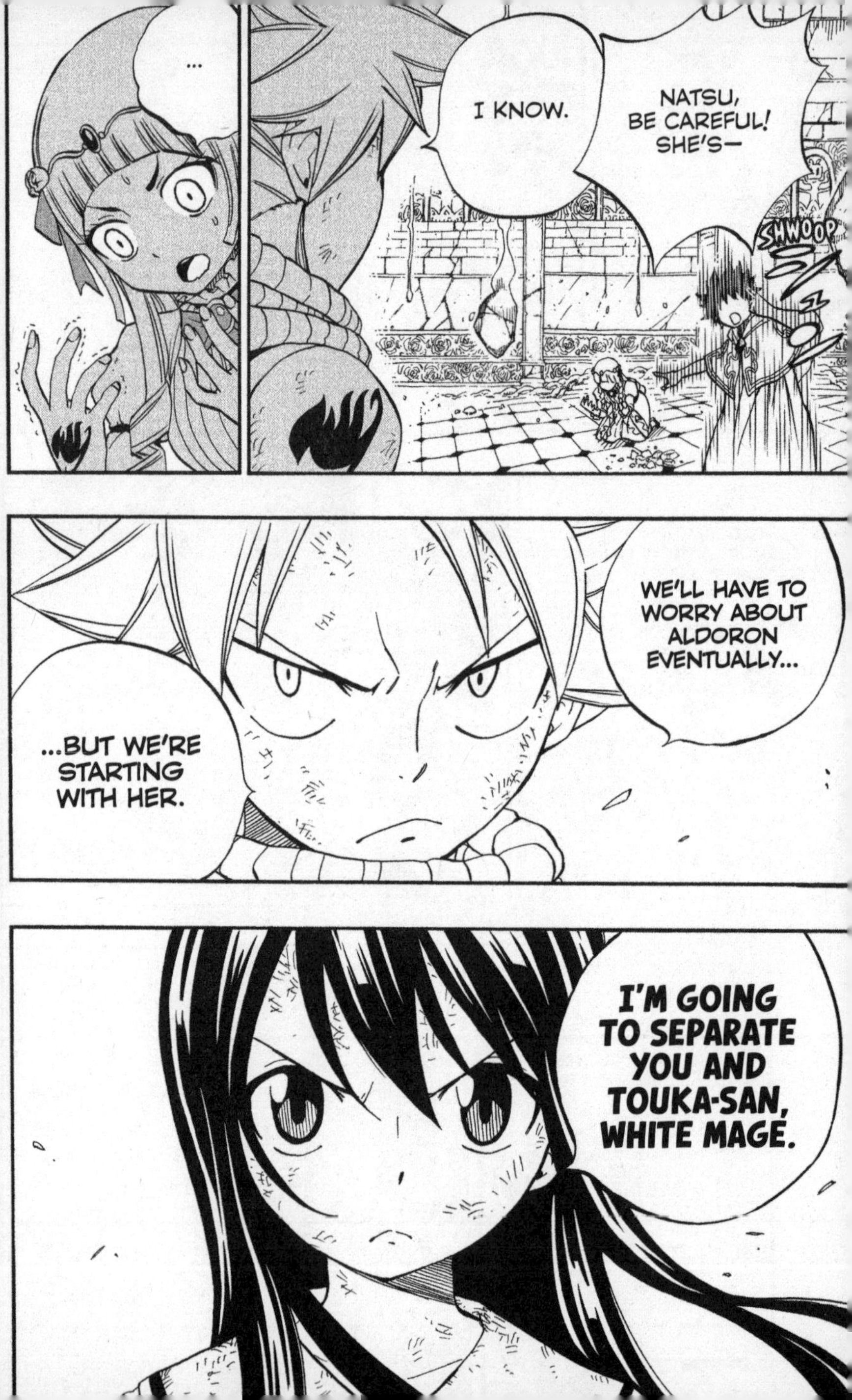
NATSU, BE CAREFUL! SHE'S—
I KNOW.
SHWOOP
...
WE'LL HAVE TO WORRY ABOUT ALDORON EVENTUALLY...
...BUT WE'RE STARTING WITH HER.
I'M GOING TO SEPARATE YOU AND TOUKA-SAN, WHITE MAGE.

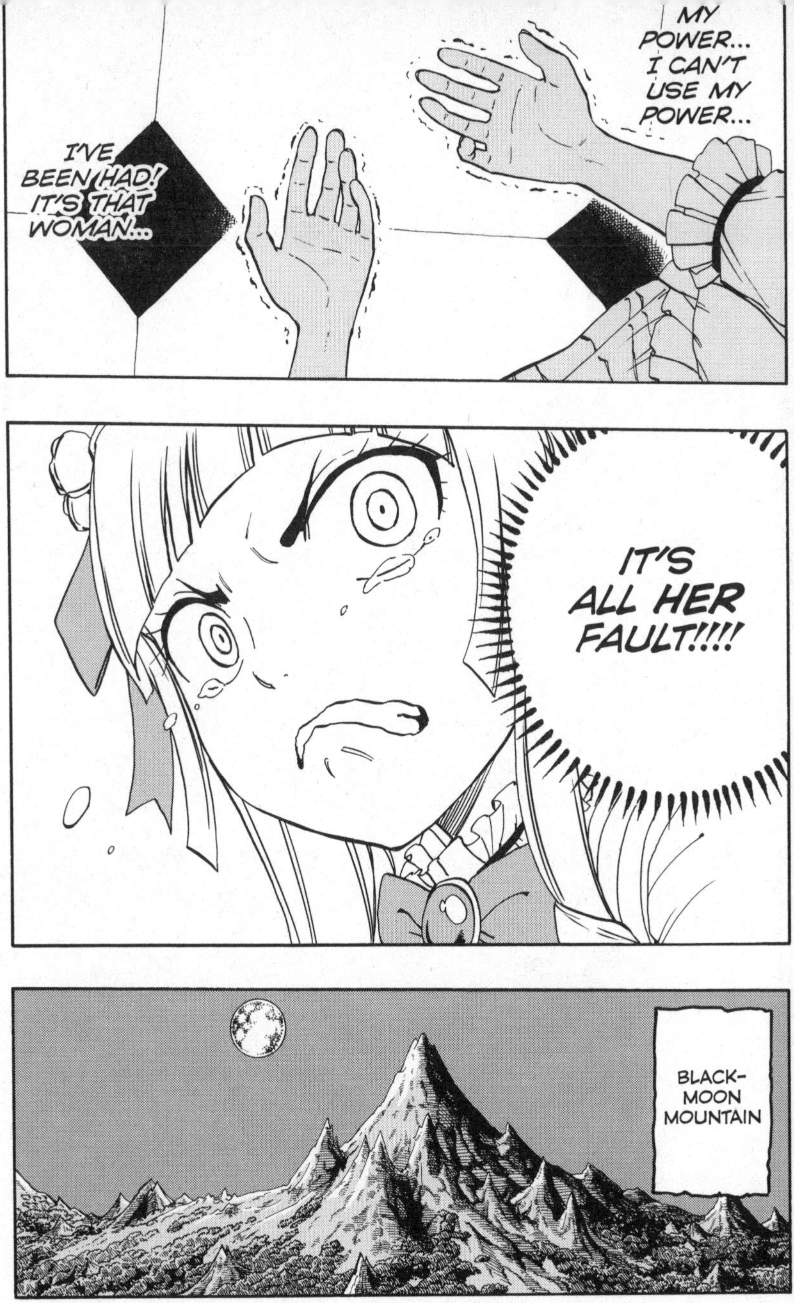
MY POWER... I CAN'T USE MY POWER...
I'VE BEEN HAD! IT'S THAT WOMAN...
IT'S ALL HER FAULT!!!!
BLACK-MOON MOUNTAIN

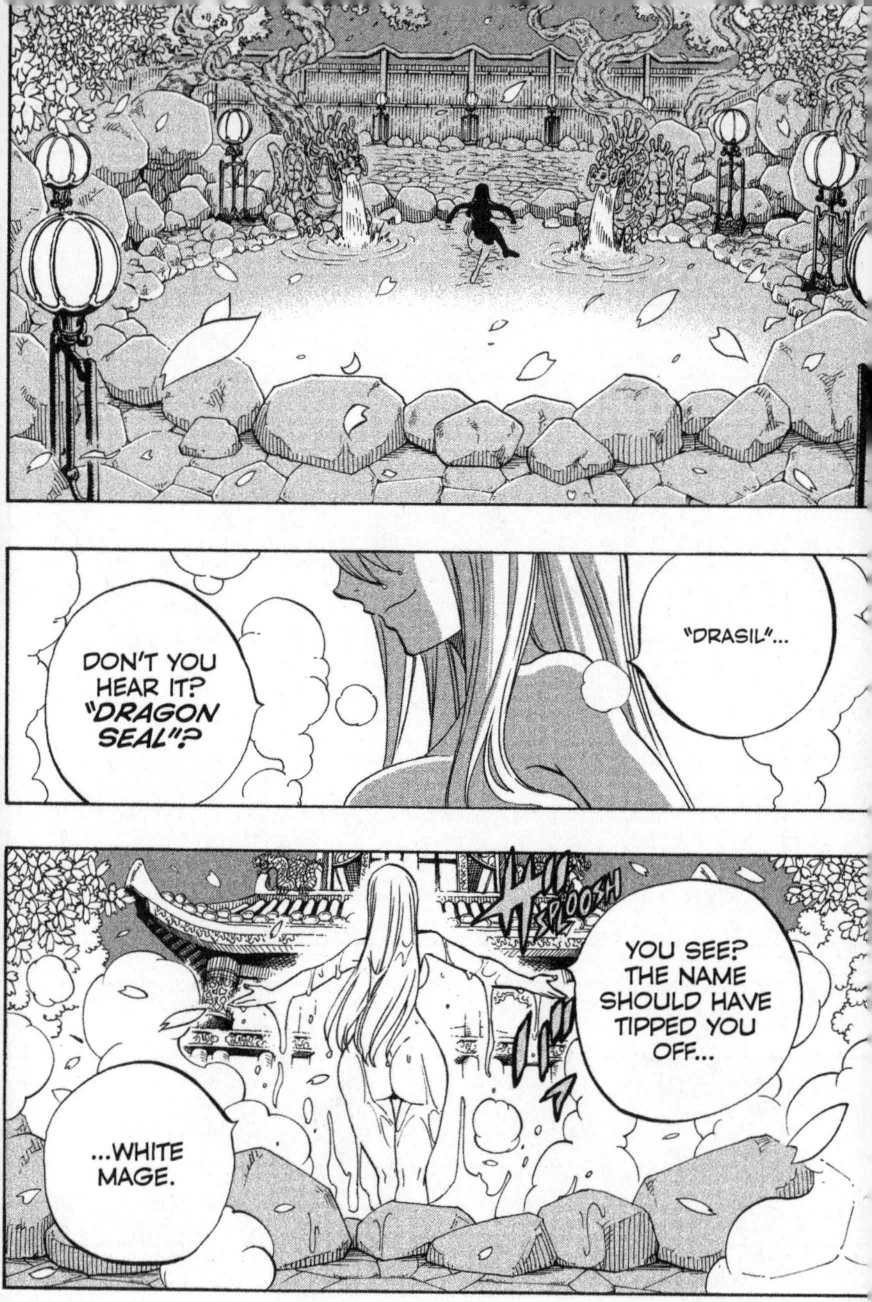
"DRASIL"...
DON'T YOU HEAR IT? "DRAGON SEAL"?
SPLOOSH
YOU SEE? THE NAME SHOULD HAVE TIPPED YOU OFF...
...WHITE MAGE.

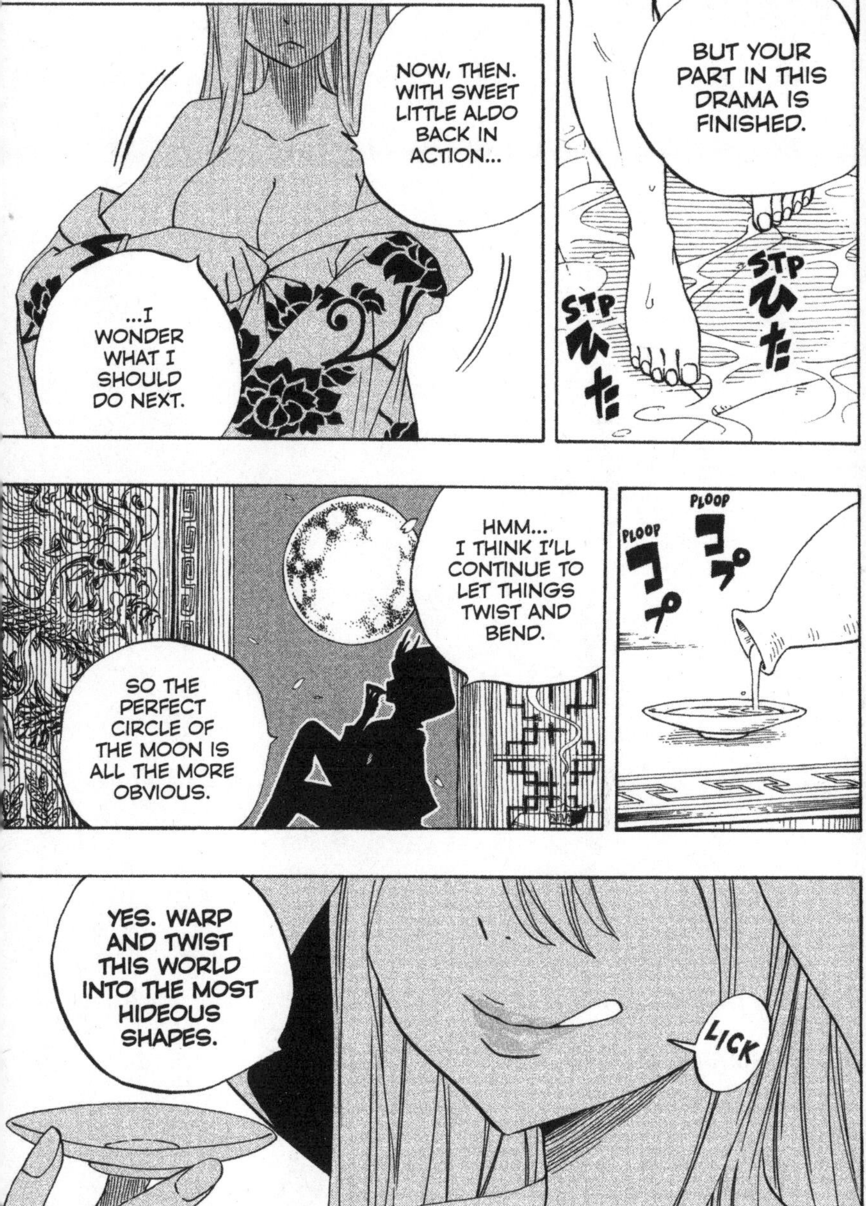
BUT YOUR PART IN THIS DRAMA IS FINISHED.
STP ひた
STP ひた
NOW, THEN. WITH SWEET LITTLE ALDO BACK IN ACTION...
...I WONDER WHAT I SHOULD DO NEXT.
PLOOP
PLOOP
HMM... I THINK I'LL CONTINUE TO LET THINGS TWIST AND BEND.
SO THE PERFECT CIRCLE OF THE MOON IS ALL THE MORE OBVIOUS.
YES. WARP AND TWIST THIS WORLD INTO THE MOST HIDEOUS SHAPES.
LICK

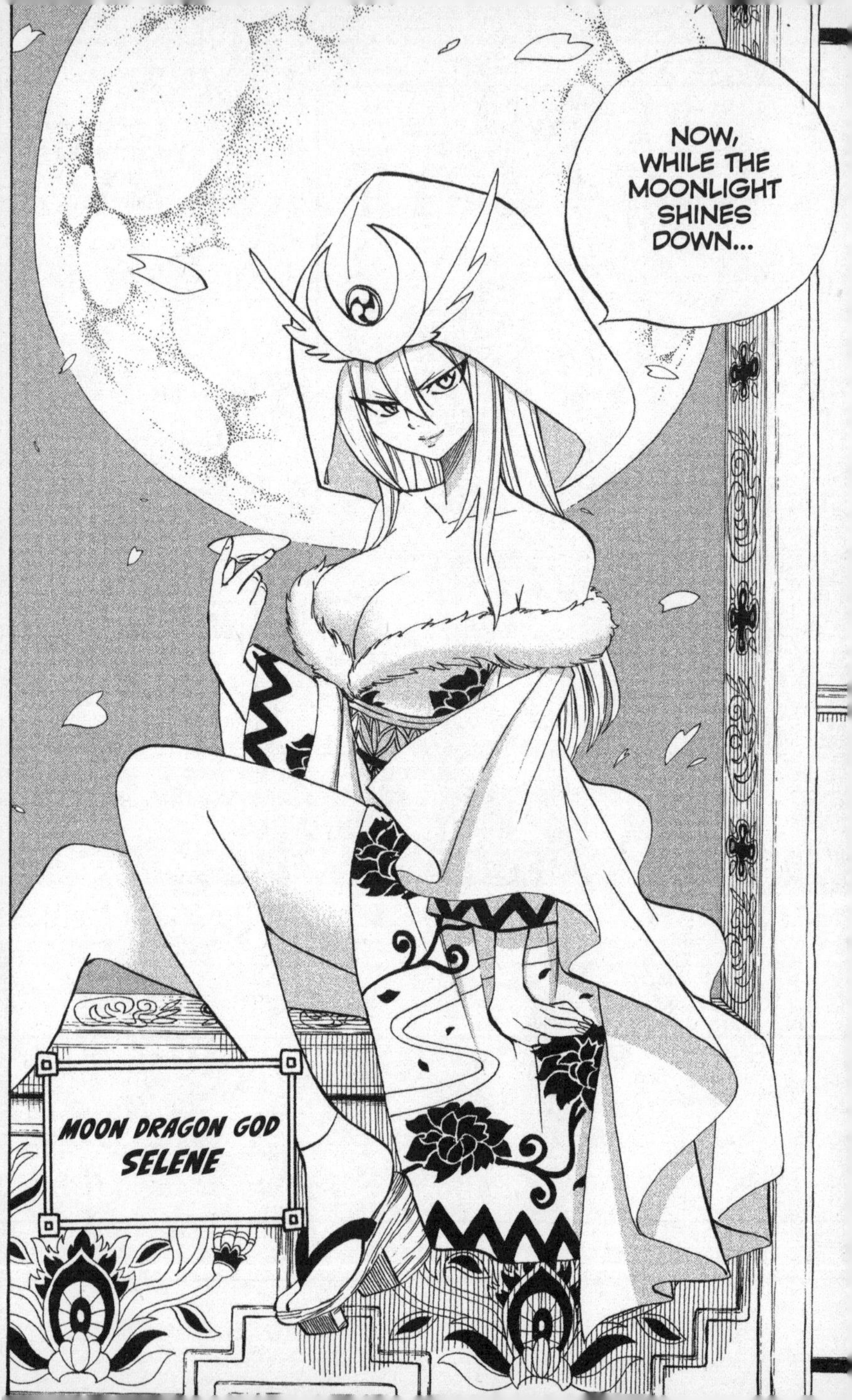
NOW, WHILE THE MOONLIGHT SHINES DOWN...
MOON DRAGON GOD SELENE

FAIRY TAIL 100 YEARS QUEST

Chapter 51: The Howling Earth

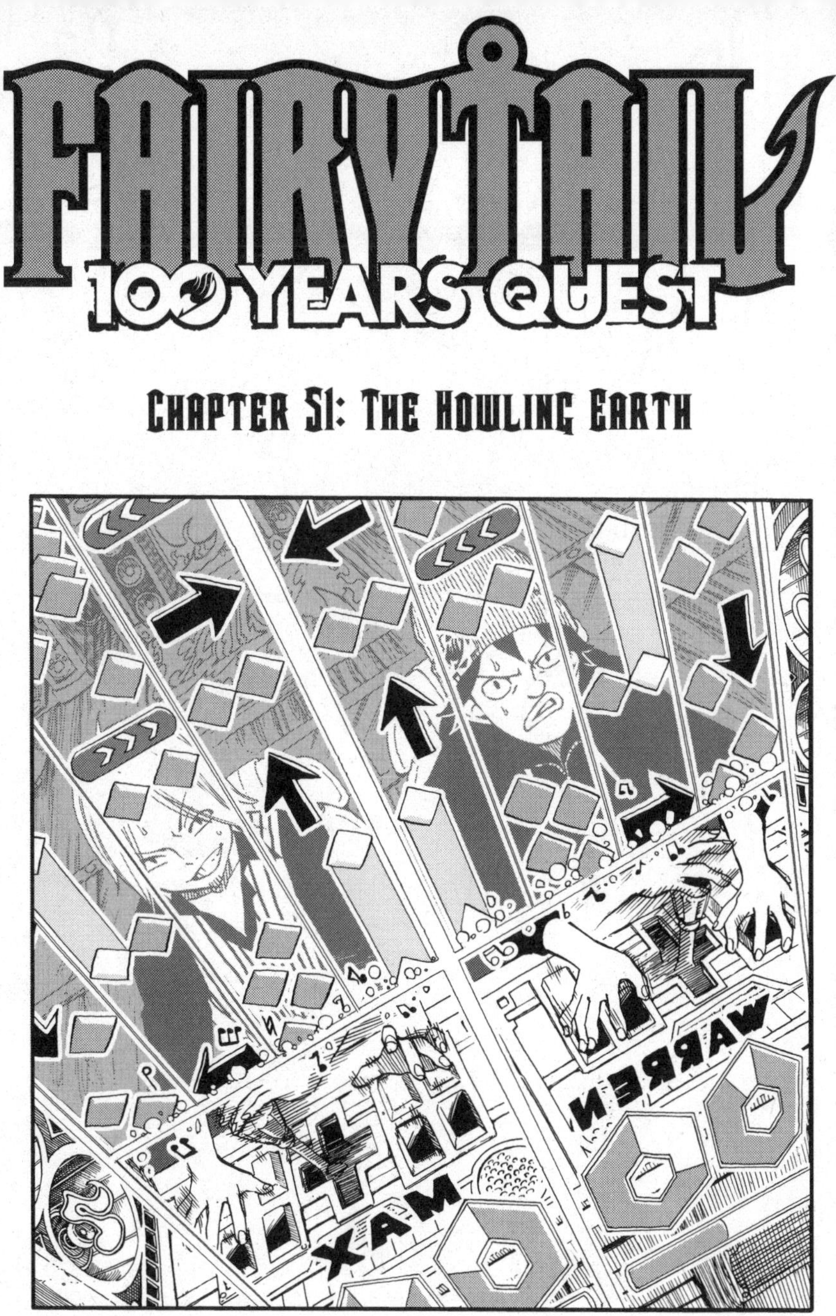
WARREN
MAX

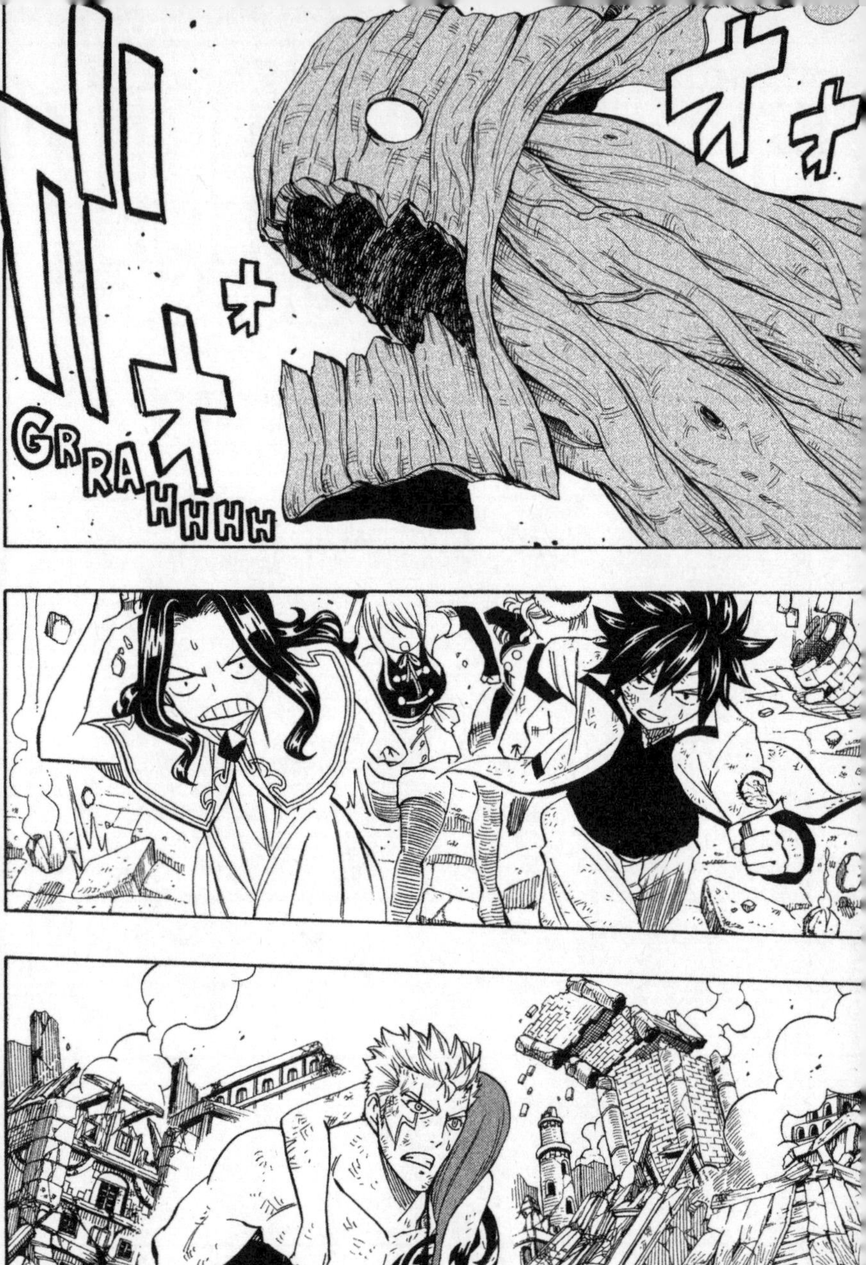
GRRAHHHH

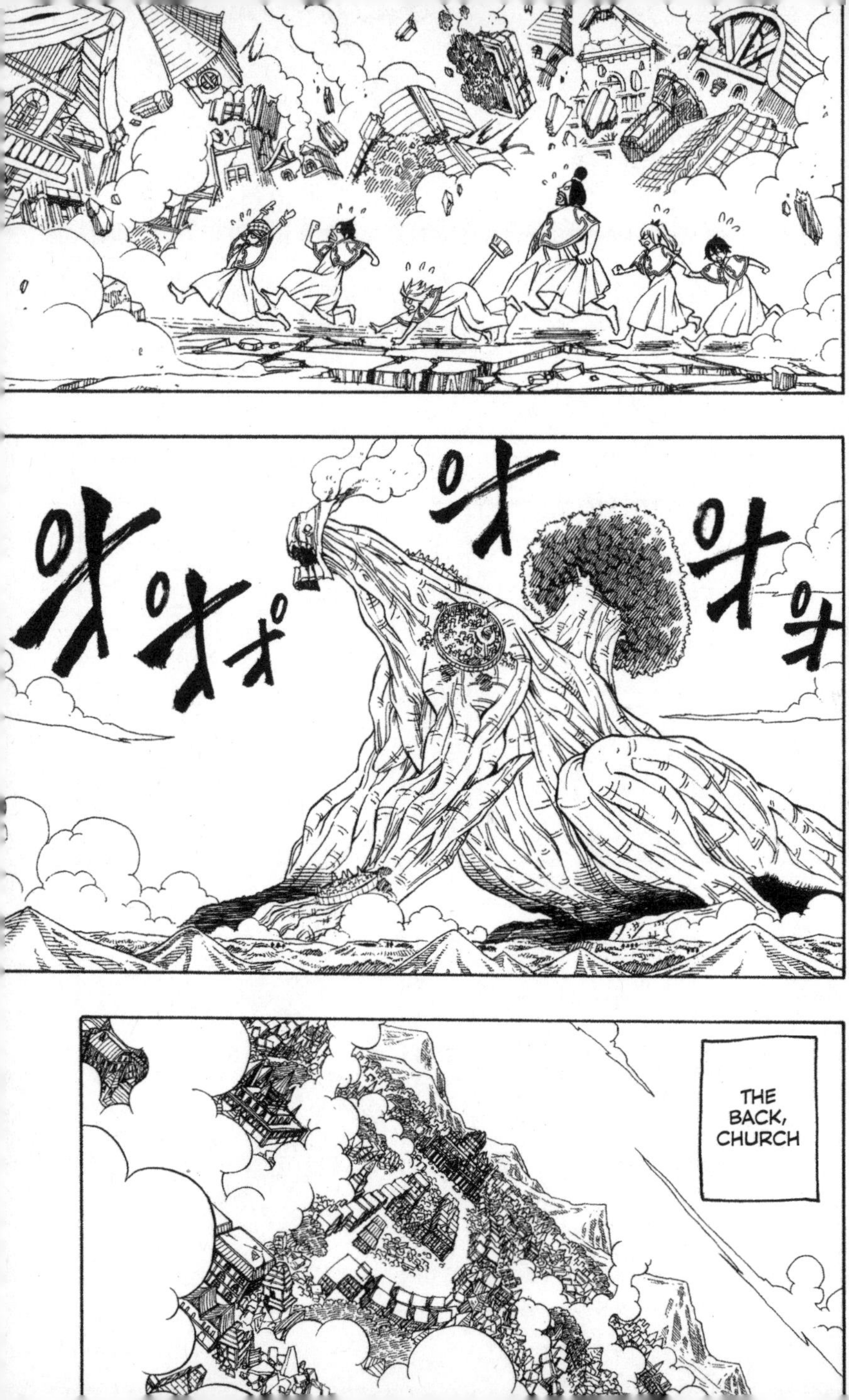
THE BACK, CHURCH

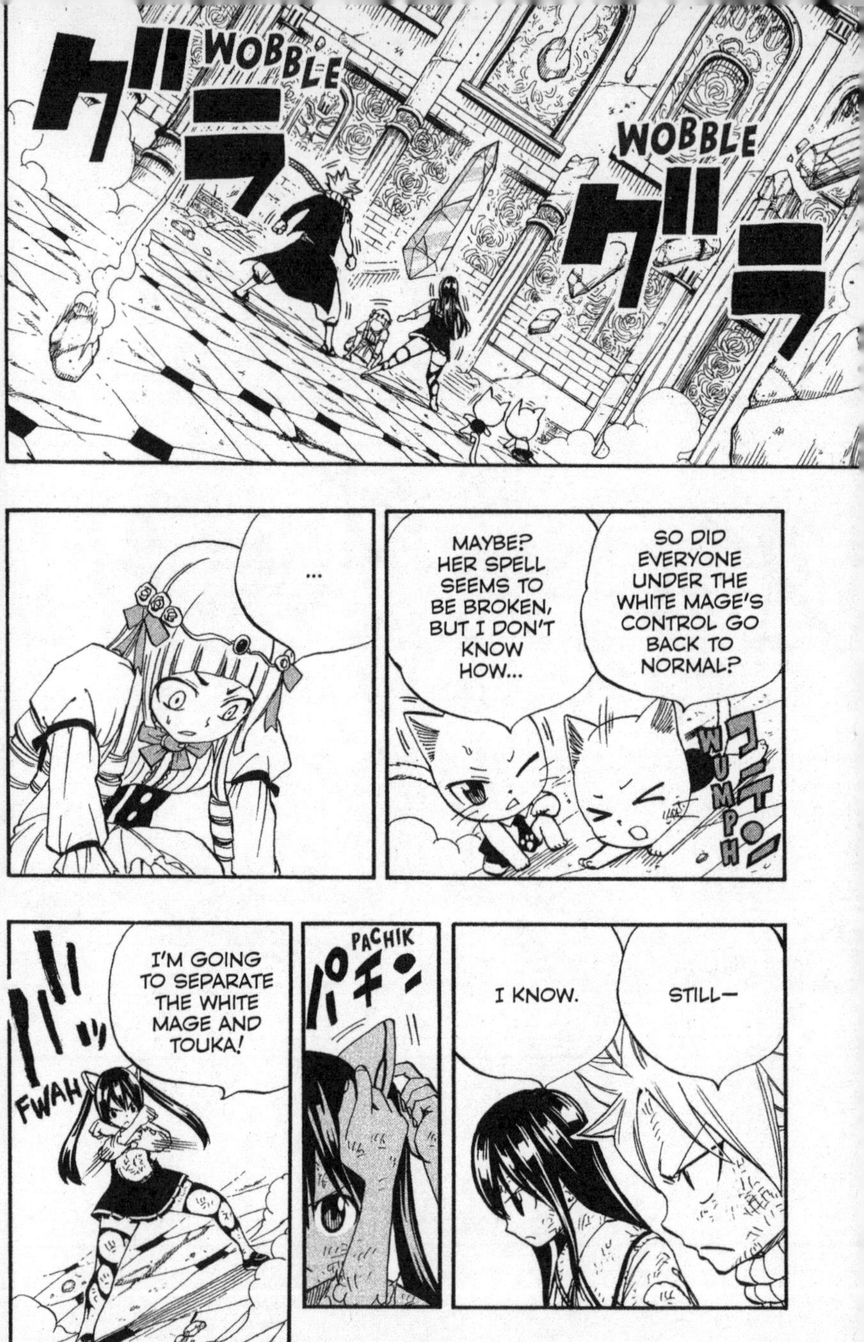
WOBBLE
グラ
WOBBLE
グラ
SO DID EVERYONE UNDER THE WHITE MAGE'S CONTROL GO BACK TO NORMAL?
WUMPH
コテッ
MAYBE? HER SPELL SEEMS TO BE BROKEN, BUT I DON'T KNOW HOW...
...
STILL—
I KNOW.
PACHIK
パチン
I'M GOING TO SEPARATE THE WHITE MAGE AND TOUKA!
FWAH
バッ

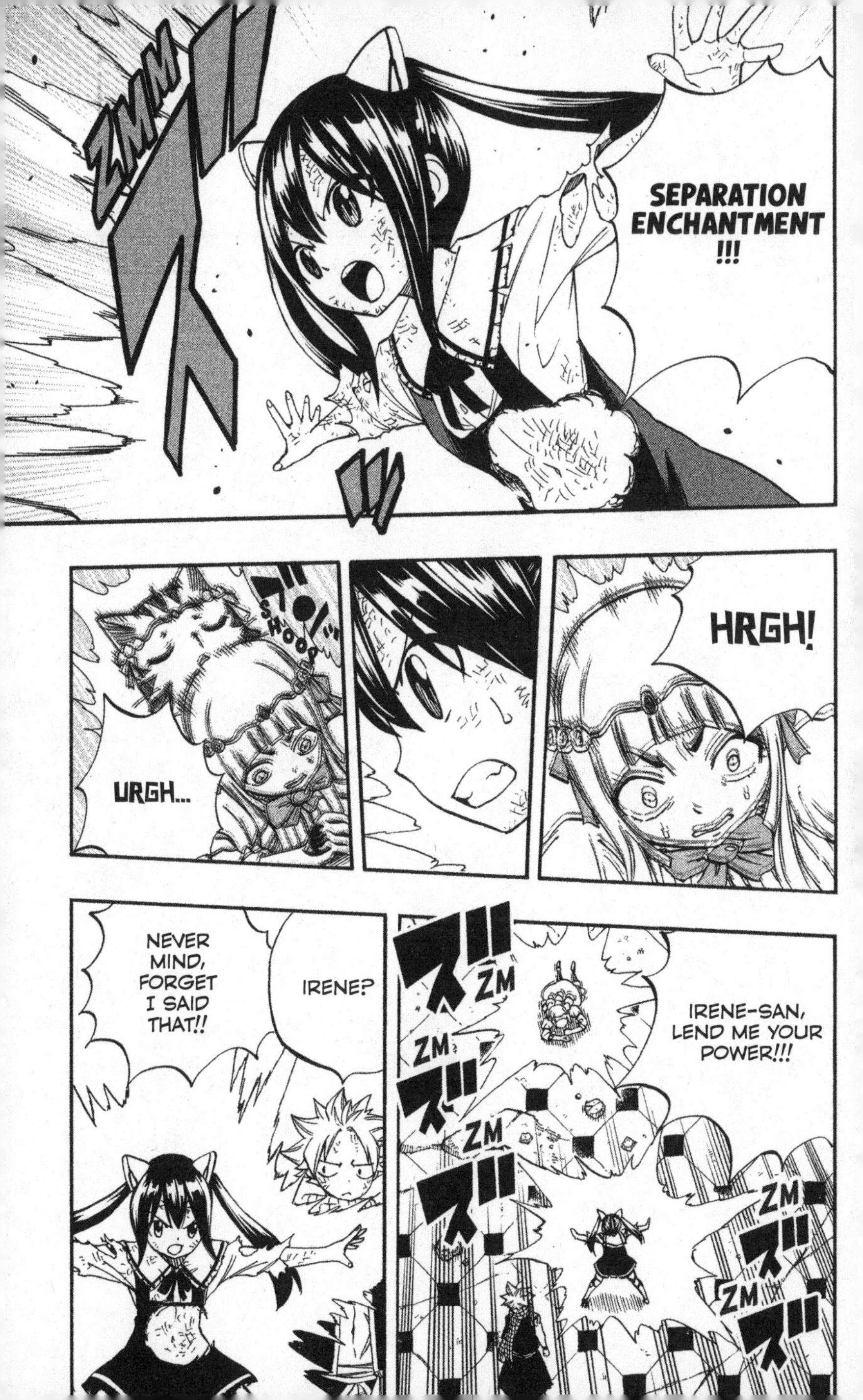
ZMM
SEPARATION ENCHANTMENT !!!
HRGH!
SHOOP
URGH...
ZM
ZM
ZM
IRENE-SAN, LEND ME YOUR POWER!!!
ZM
ZM
IRENE?
NEVER MIND, FORGET I SAID THAT!!

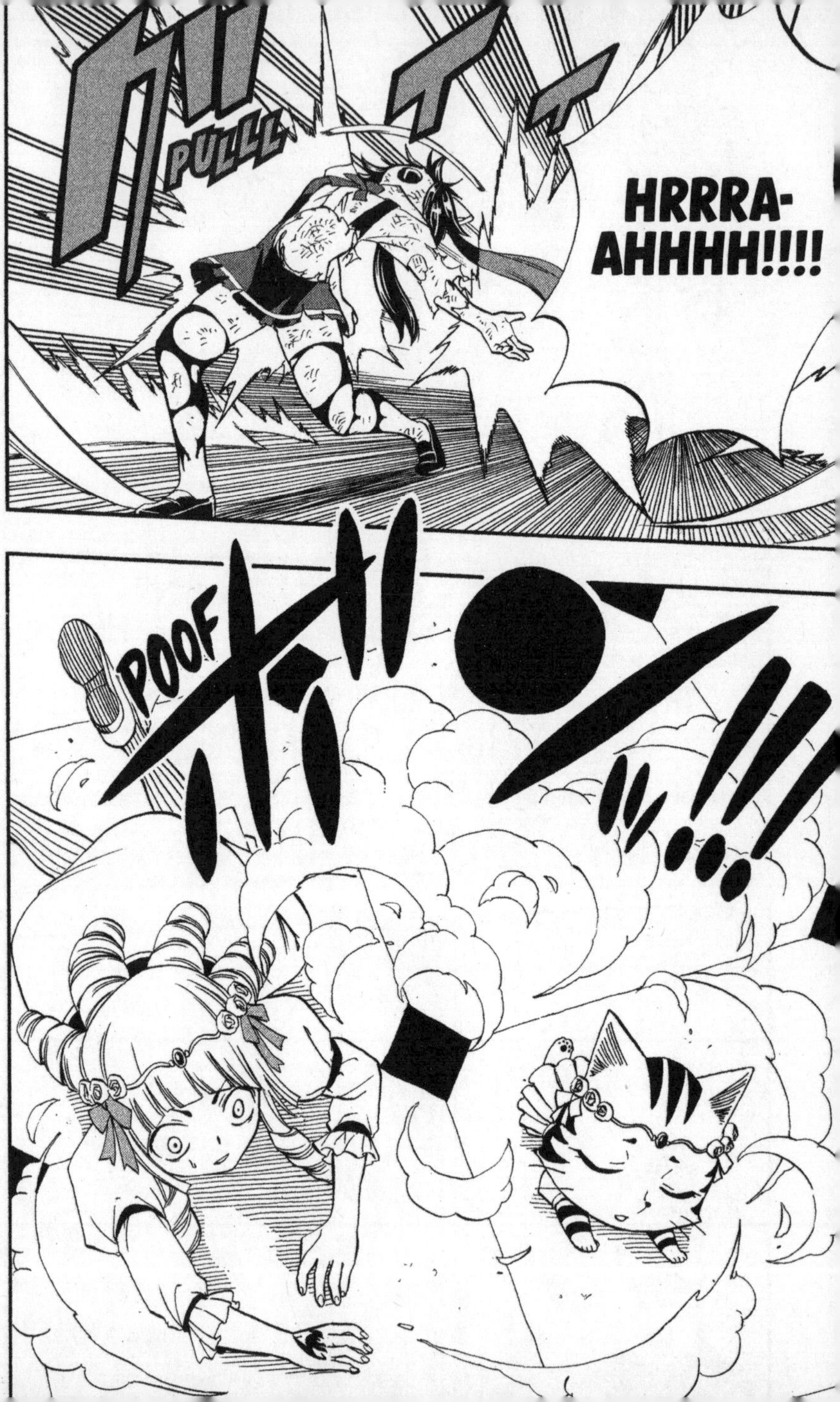
HRRRA-AHHHH!!!!
PULLL
POOF

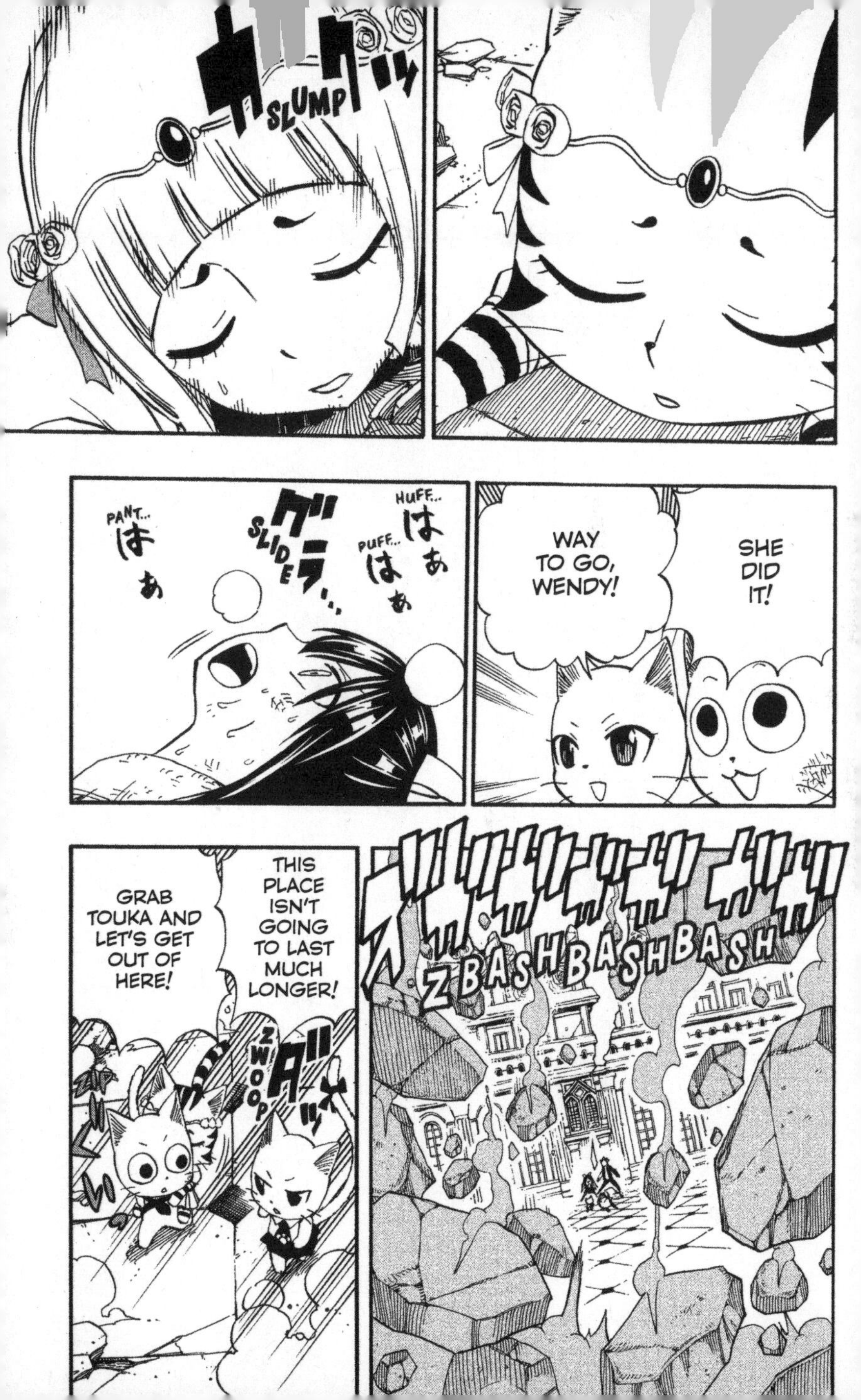
SLUMP
SHE DID IT!
WAY TO GO, WENDY!
HUFF...
PUFF...
SLIDE
PANT...
ZBASHBASHBASH
THIS PLACE ISN'T GOING TO LAST MUCH LONGER!
GRAB TOUKA AND LET'S GET OUT OF HERE!
ZWOOP

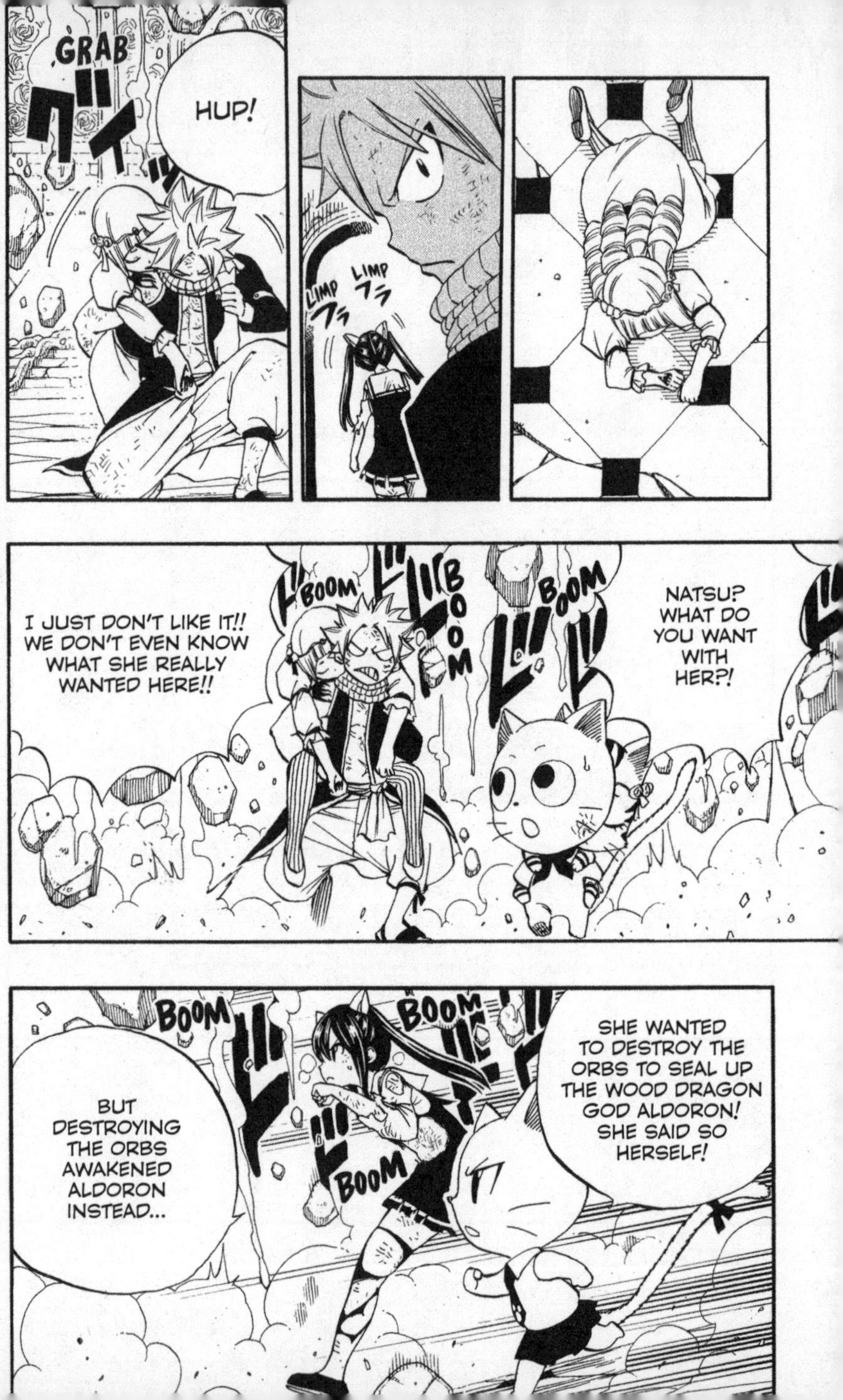
LIMP
LIMP
GRAB
HUP!
NATSU? WHAT DO YOU WANT WITH HER?!
BOOM
BOOM
BOOM
I JUST DON'T LIKE IT!! WE DON'T EVEN KNOW WHAT SHE REALLY WANTED HERE!!
SHE WANTED TO DESTROY THE ORBS TO SEAL UP THE WOOD DRAGON GOD ALDORON! SHE SAID SO HERSELF!
BOOM
BOOM
BOOM
BUT DESTROYING THE ORBS AWAKENED ALDORON INSTEAD...

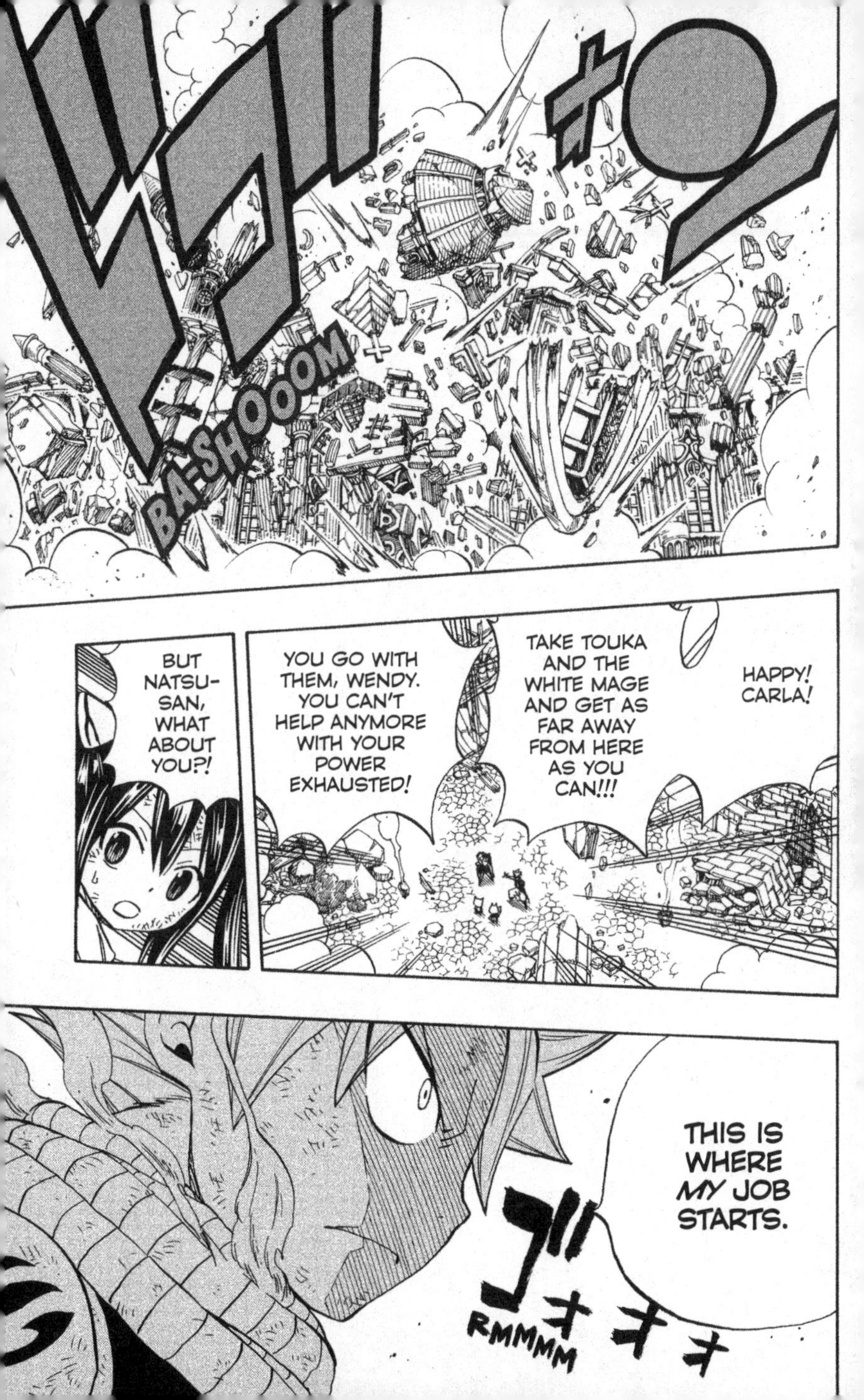
BA-SHOOOM
HAPPY! CARLA!
TAKE TOUKA AND THE WHITE MAGE AND GET AS FAR AWAY FROM HERE AS YOU CAN!!!
YOU GO WITH THEM, WENDY. YOU CAN'T HELP ANYMORE WITH YOUR POWER EXHAUSTED!
BUT NATSU-SAN, WHAT ABOUT YOU?!
THIS IS WHERE *MY* JOB STARTS.
RMMMM

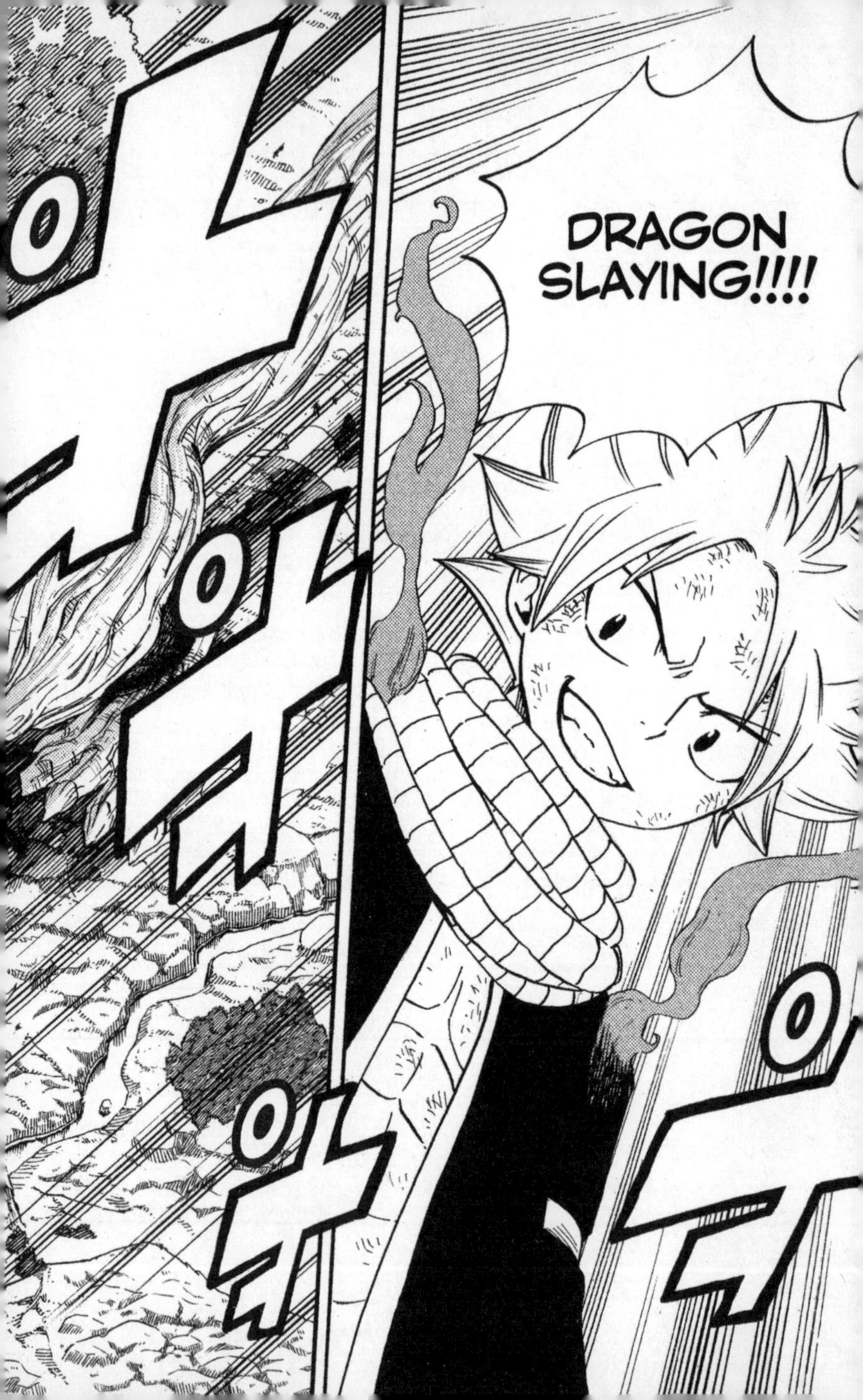
DRAGON SLAYING!!!!

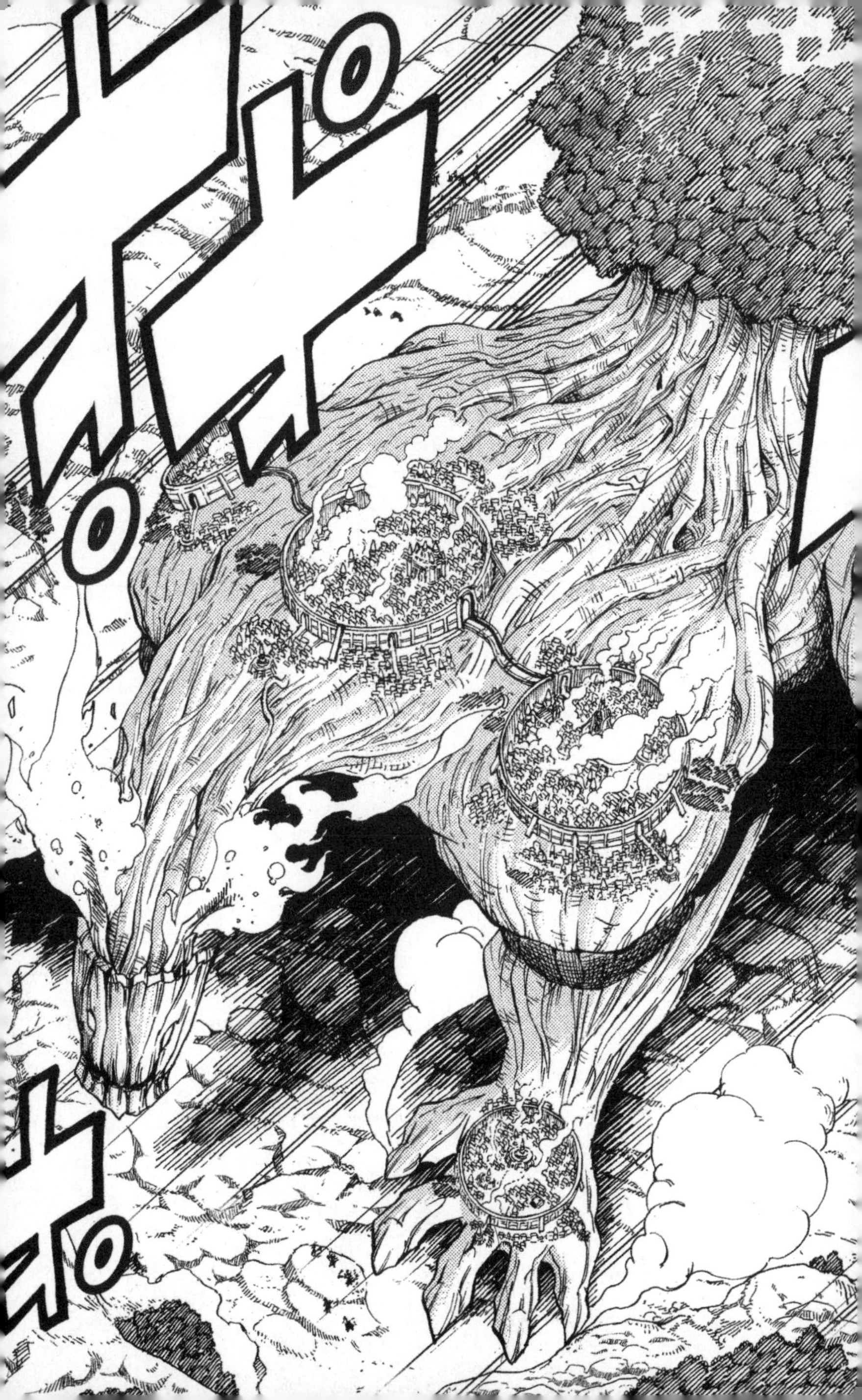

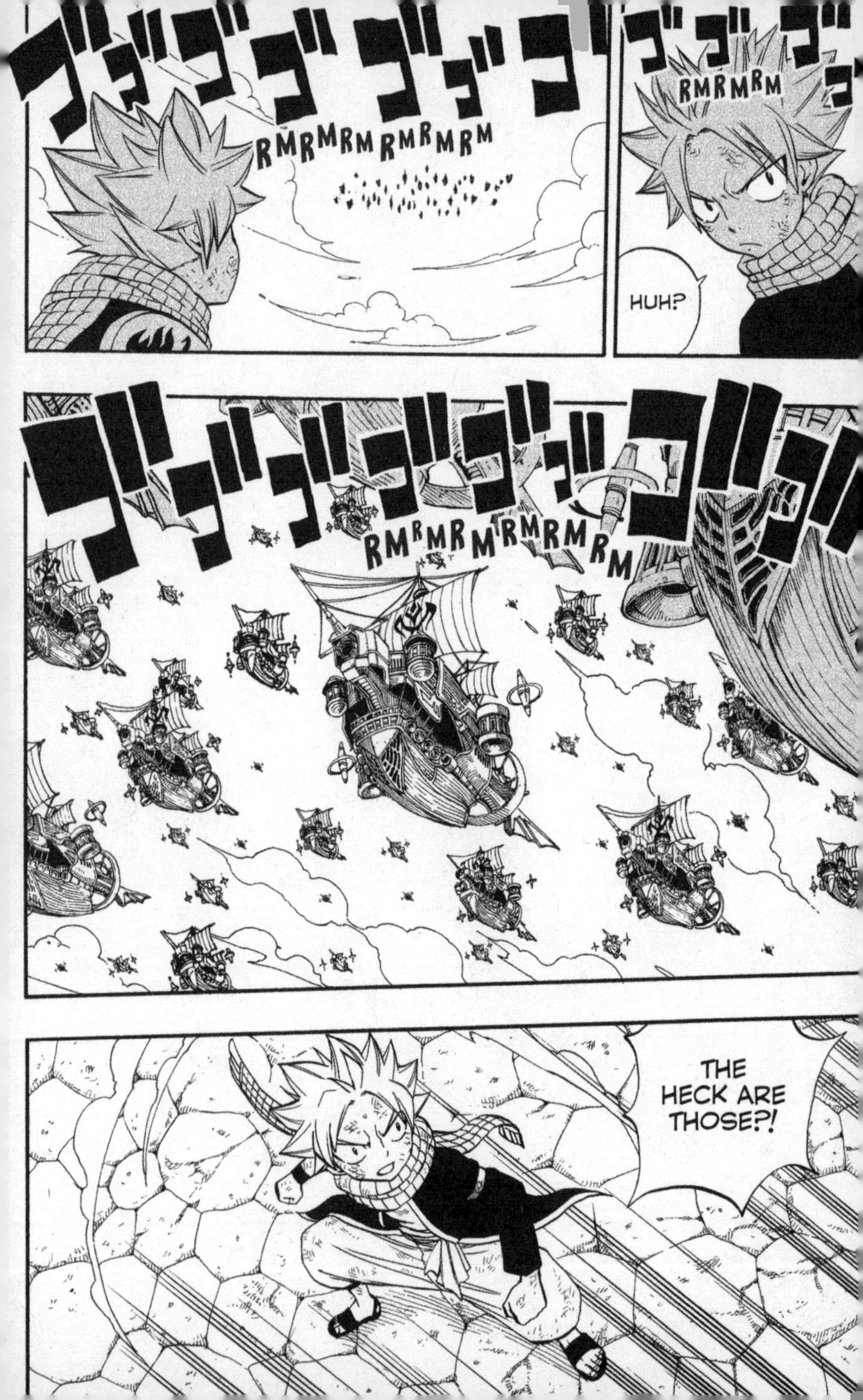
RMRMRM
HUH?
RMRMRMRMRMRMRM
RMRMRMRMRMRMRM
THE HECK ARE THOSE?!

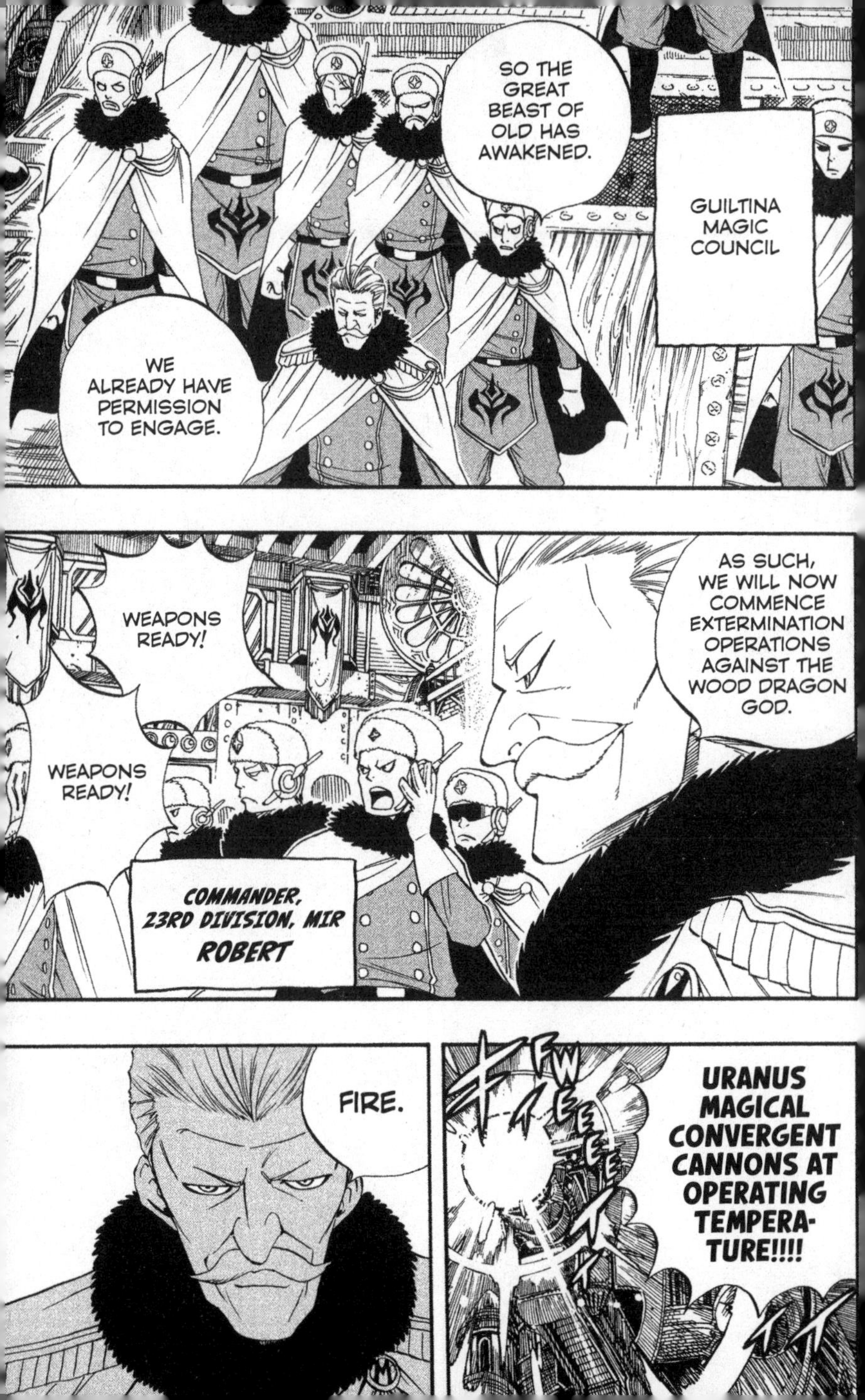

GUILTINA MAGIC COUNCIL
SO THE GREAT BEAST OF OLD HAS AWAKENED.
WE ALREADY HAVE PERMISSION TO ENGAGE.
AS SUCH, WE WILL NOW COMMENCE EXTERMINATION OPERATIONS AGAINST THE WOOD DRAGON GOD.
WEAPONS READY!
WEAPONS READY!
COMMANDER, 23RD DIVISION, MIR
ROBERT
FWEEEEE
URANUS MAGICAL CONVERGENT CANNONS AT OPERATING TEMPERA-TURE!!!!
FIRE.

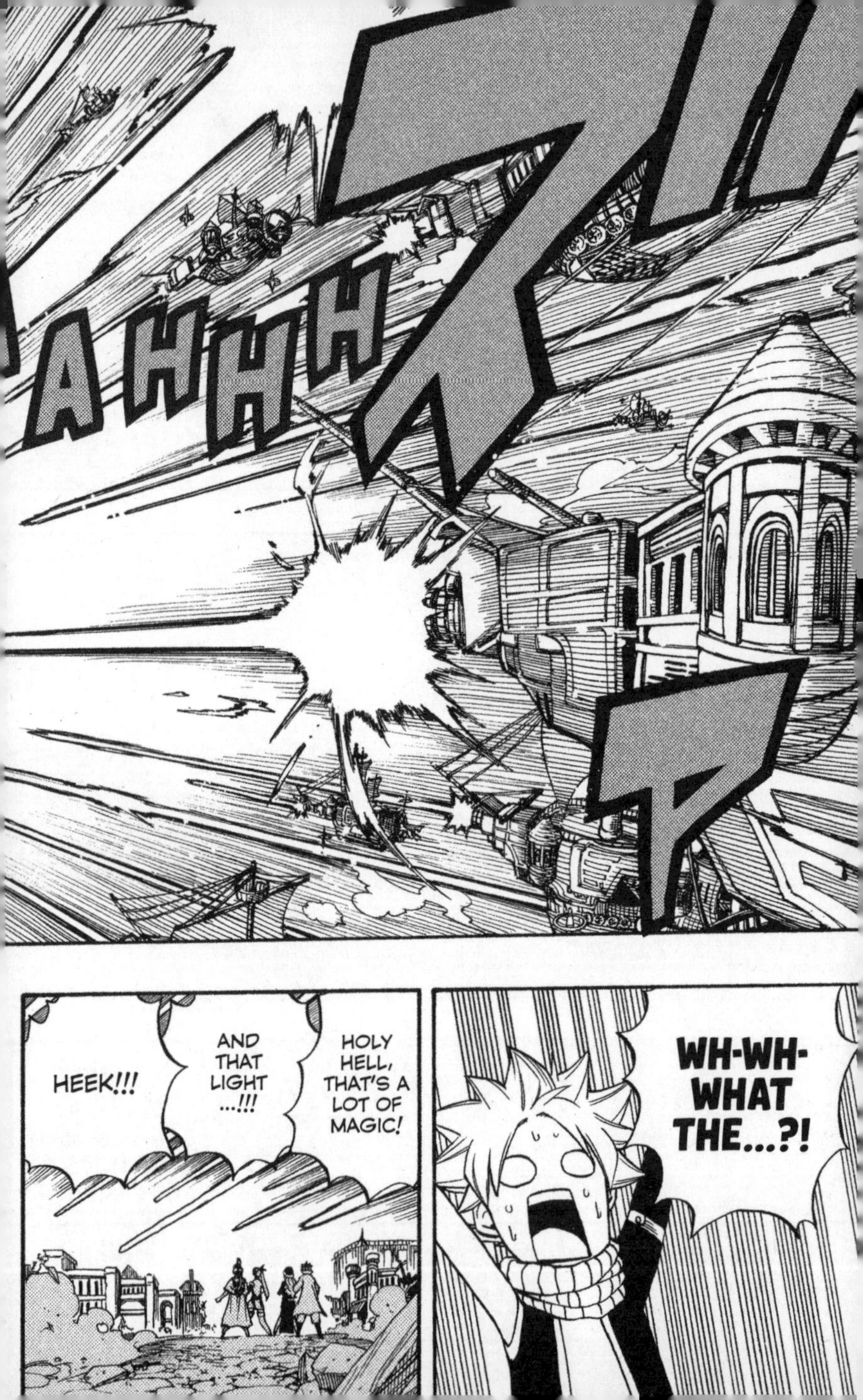
AHHHH
WH-WH-WHAT THE...?!
HOLY HELL, THAT'S A LOT OF MAGIC!
AND THAT LIGHT ...!!!
HEEK!!!

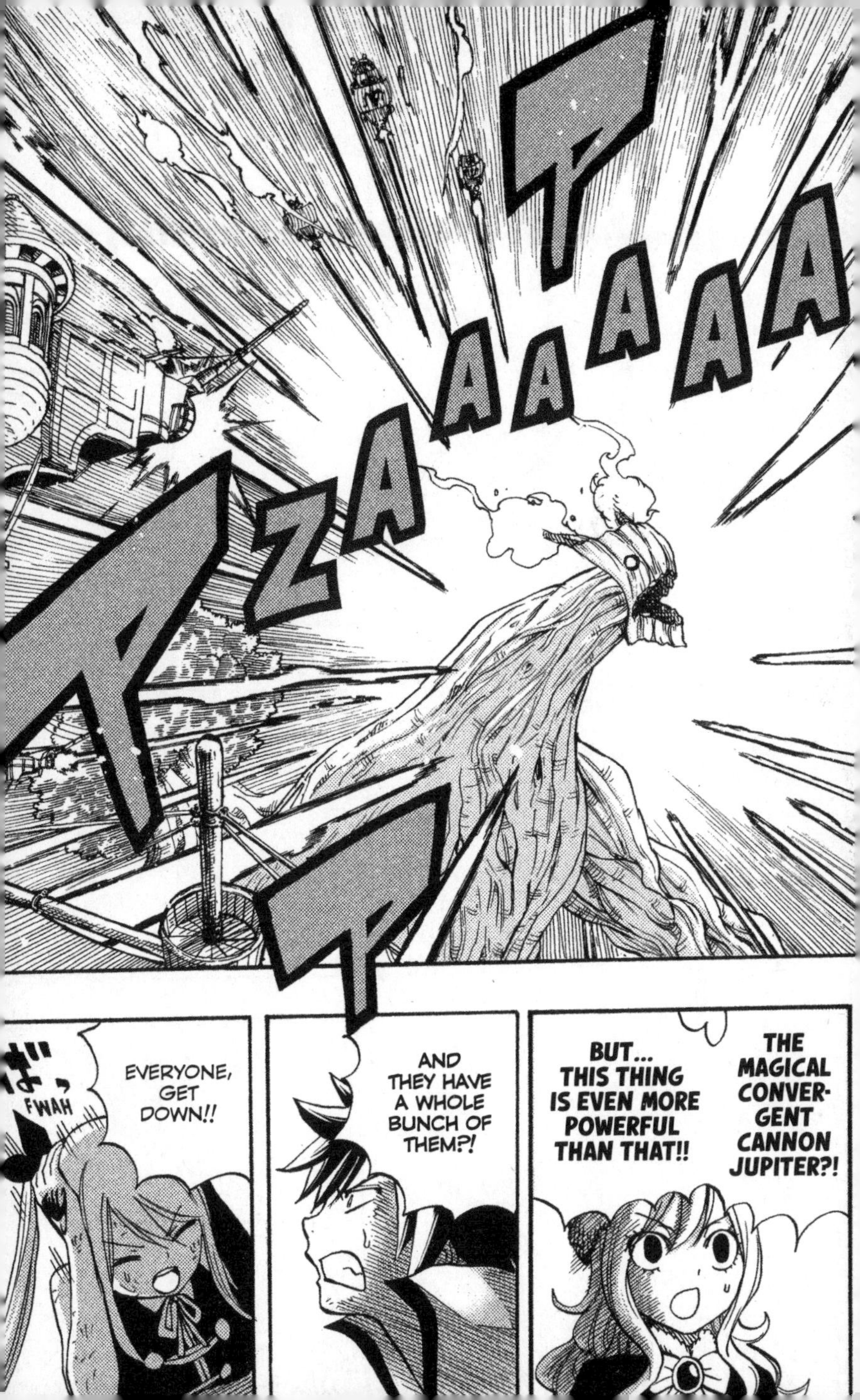
ZAAAAAA
THE MAGICAL CONVERGENT CANNON JUPITER?!
BUT... THIS THING IS EVEN MORE POWERFUL THAN THAT!!
AND THEY HAVE A WHOLE BUNCH OF THEM?!
EVERYONE, GET DOWN!!
FWAH

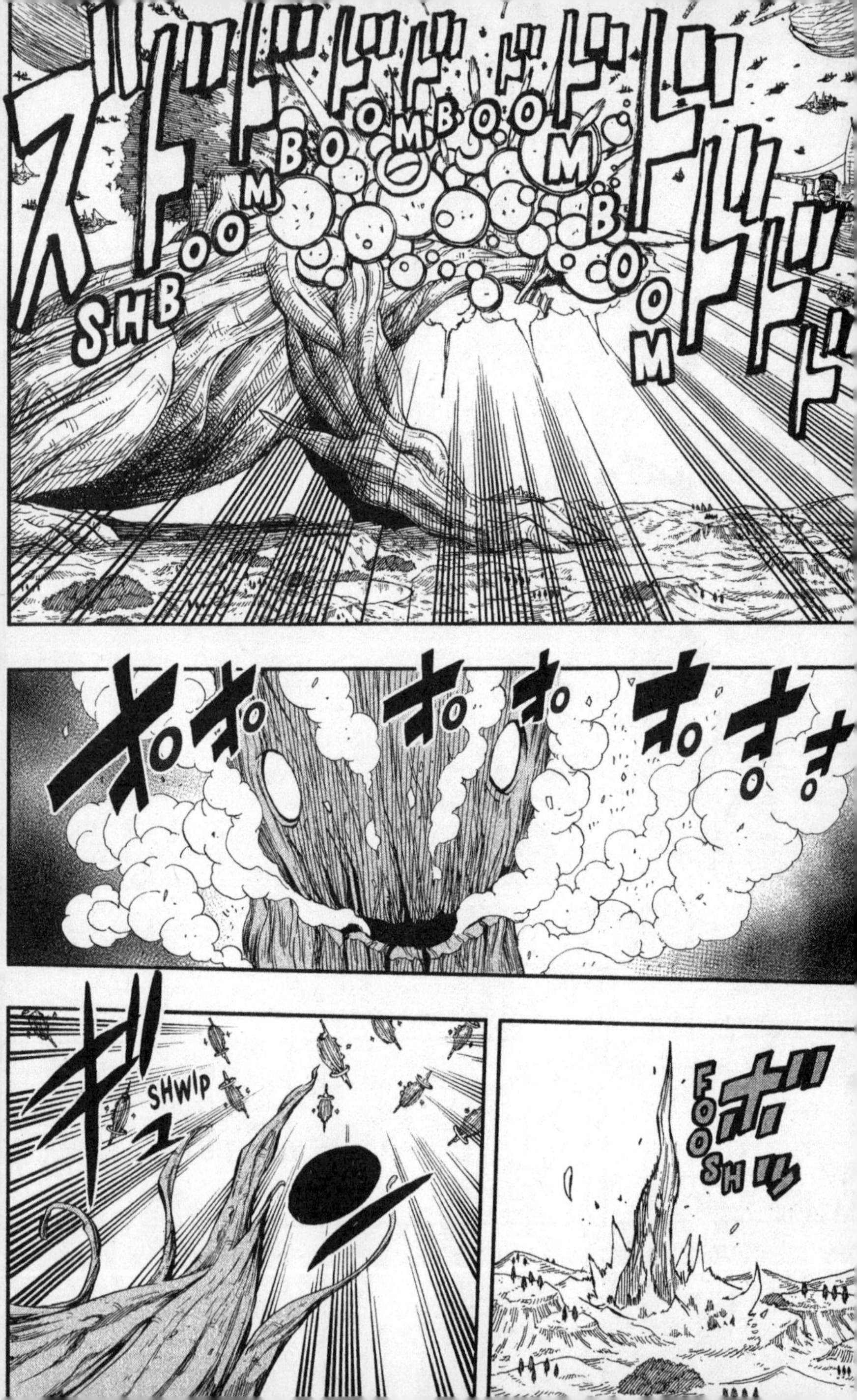
SHBOOMBOOMBOOMBOOM
FOOSH
SHWIP

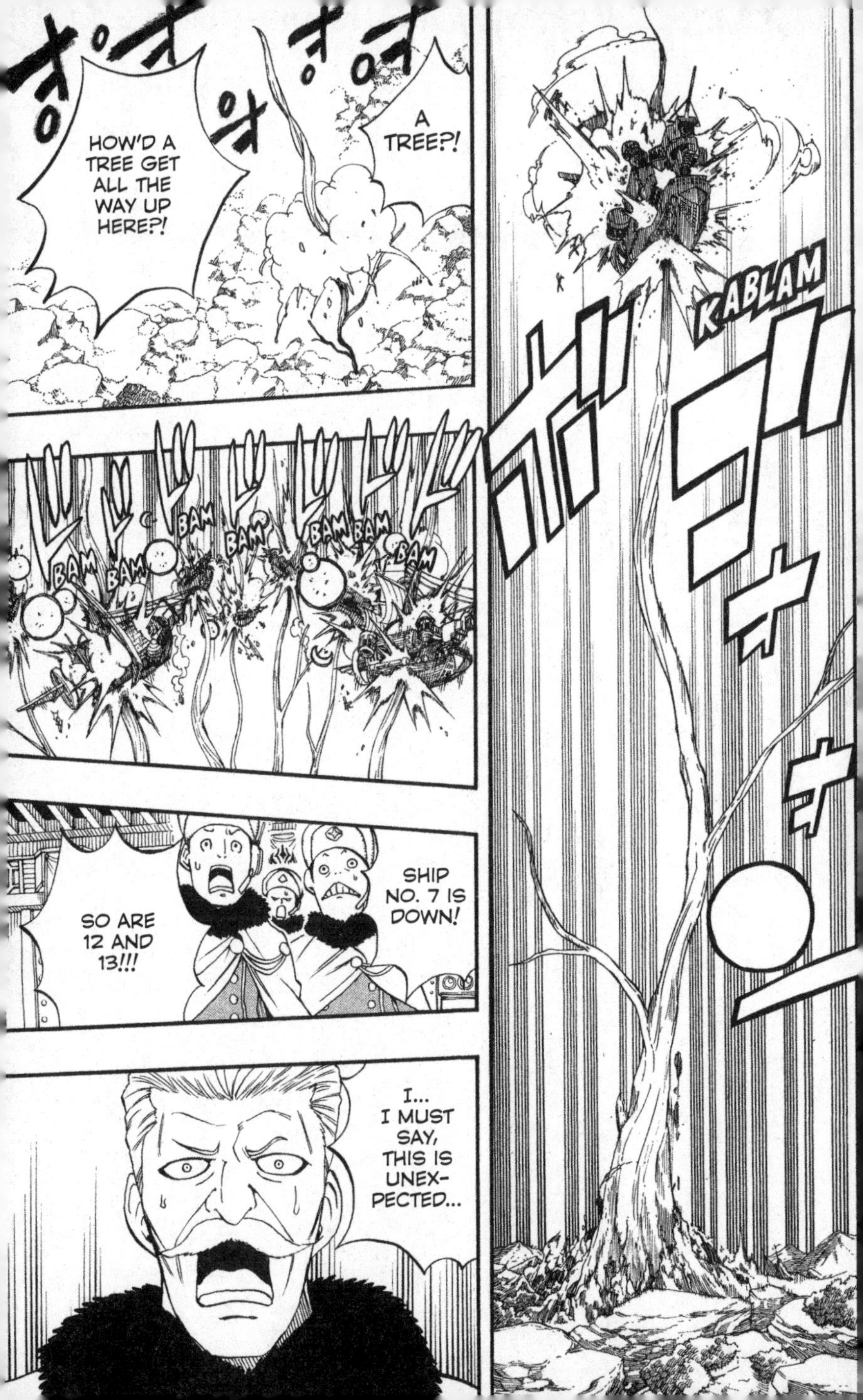
KABLAM
A TREE?!
HOW'D A TREE GET ALL THE WAY UP HERE?!
BAM BAM BAM BAM BAM BAM BAM
SHIP NO. 7 IS DOWN!
SO ARE 12 AND 13!!!
I... I MUST SAY, THIS IS UNEXPECTED...

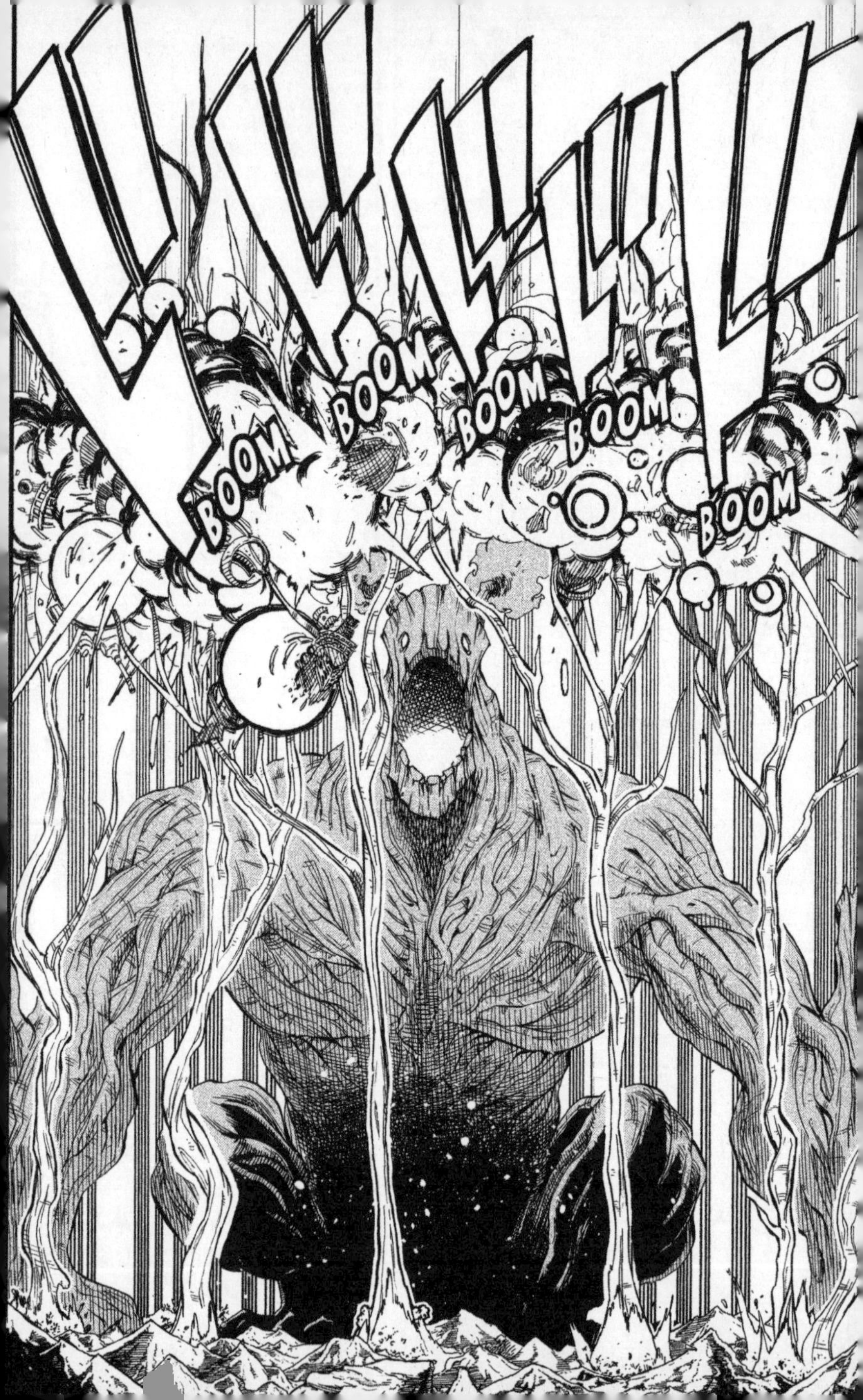
BOOM
BOOM
BOOM
BOOM
BOOM
BOOM

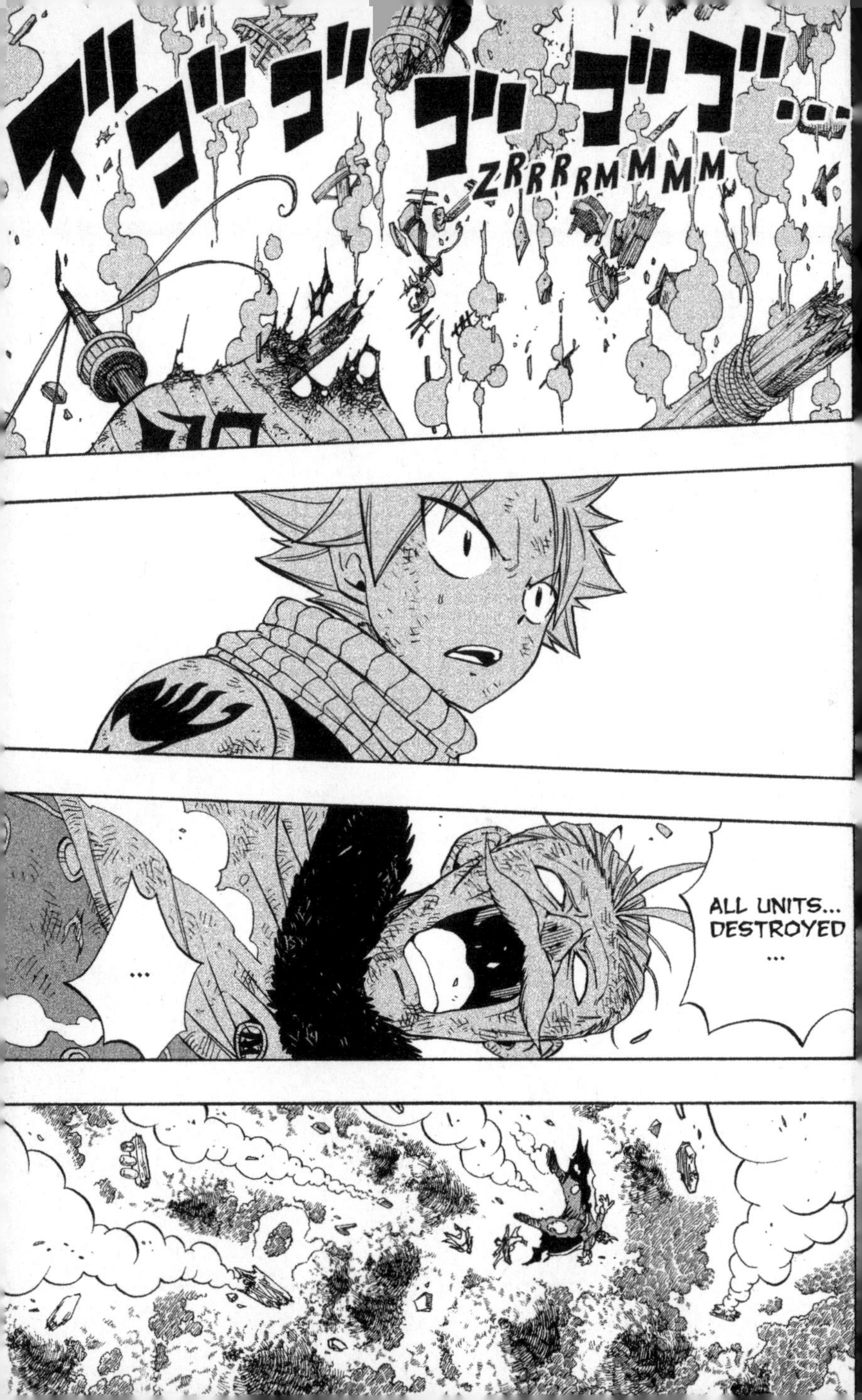
ズゴゴゴゴ…
ZRRRRMMMM
ALL UNITS... DESTROYED ...
...

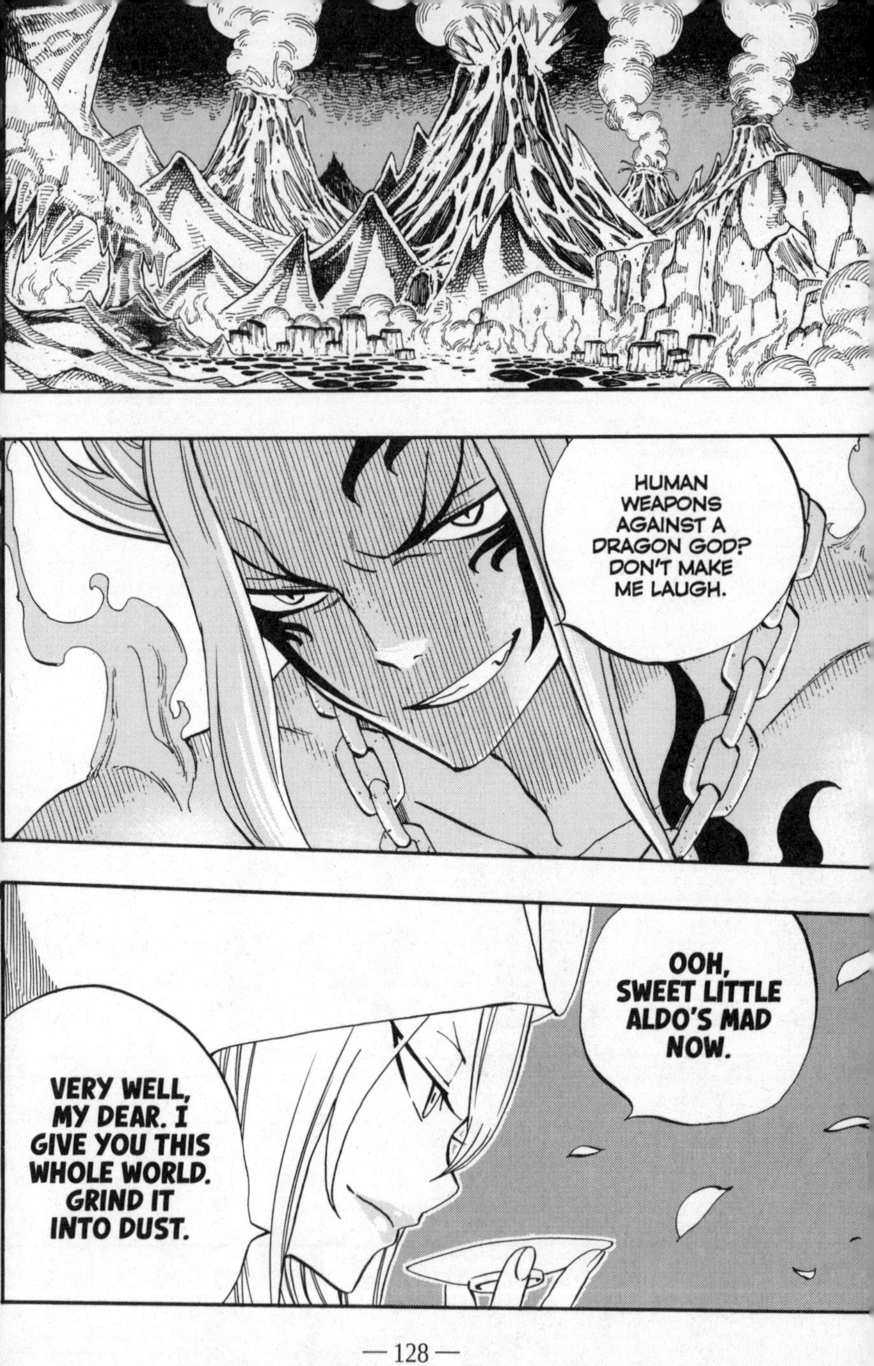
HUMAN WEAPONS AGAINST A DRAGON GOD? DON'T MAKE ME LAUGH.
OOH, SWEET LITTLE ALDO'S MAD NOW.
VERY WELL, MY DEAR. I GIVE YOU THIS WHOLE WORLD. GRIND IT INTO DUST.

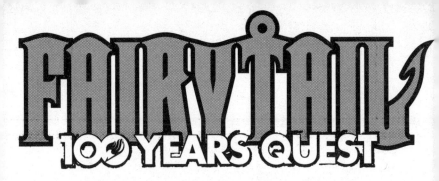

100 YEARS QUEST

Chapter 52: Telepathic Trees

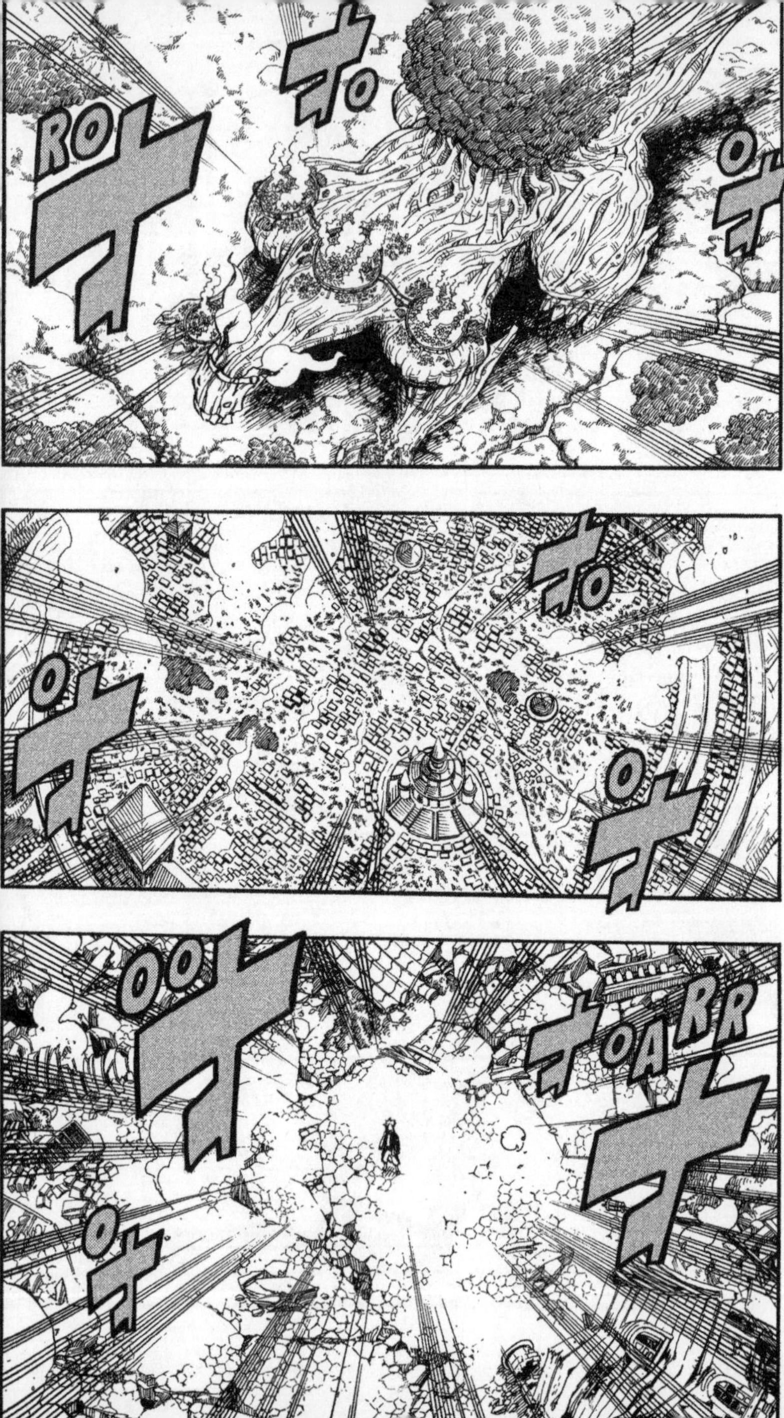
O
O
RO
O
O
O
OARR
OO
O

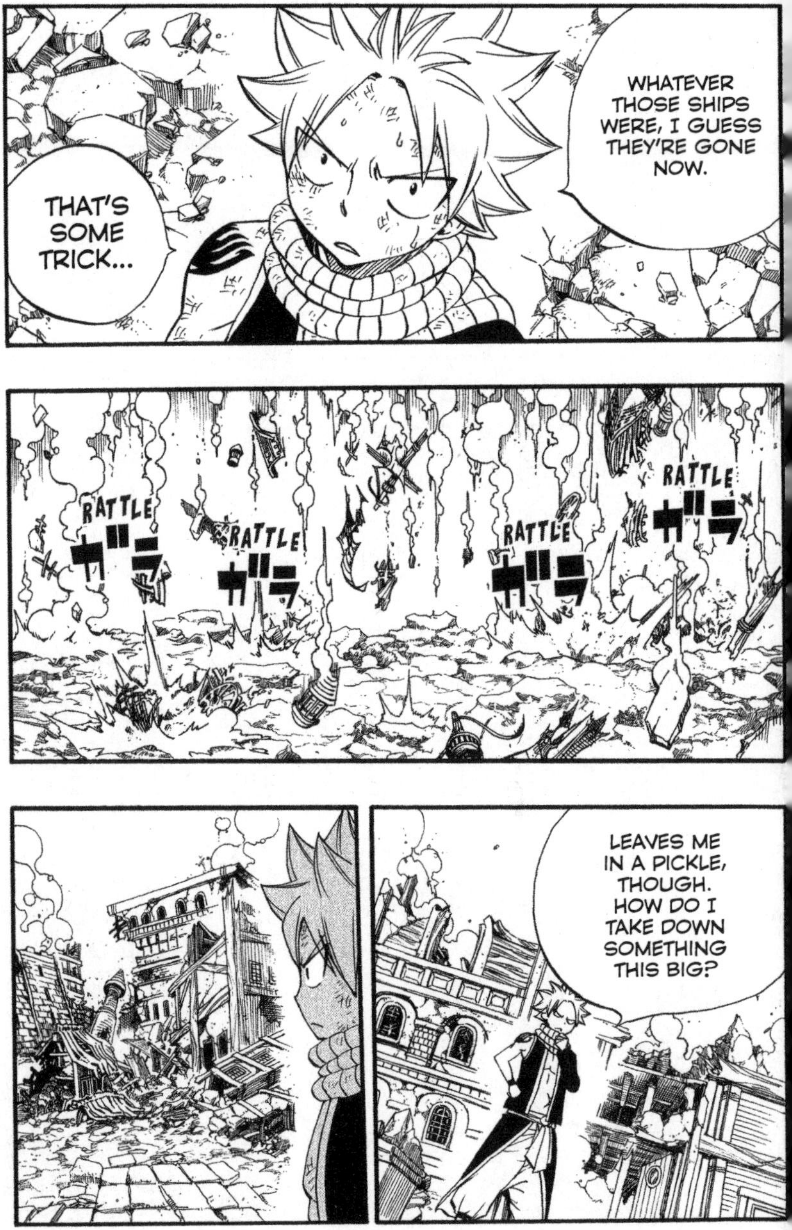
WHATEVER THOSE SHIPS WERE, I GUESS THEY'RE GONE NOW.
THAT'S SOME TRICK...
RATTLE
ガラ
RATTLE
ガラ
RATTLE
ガラ
RATTLE
ガラ
LEAVES ME IN A PICKLE, THOUGH. HOW DO I TAKE DOWN SOMETHING THIS BIG?

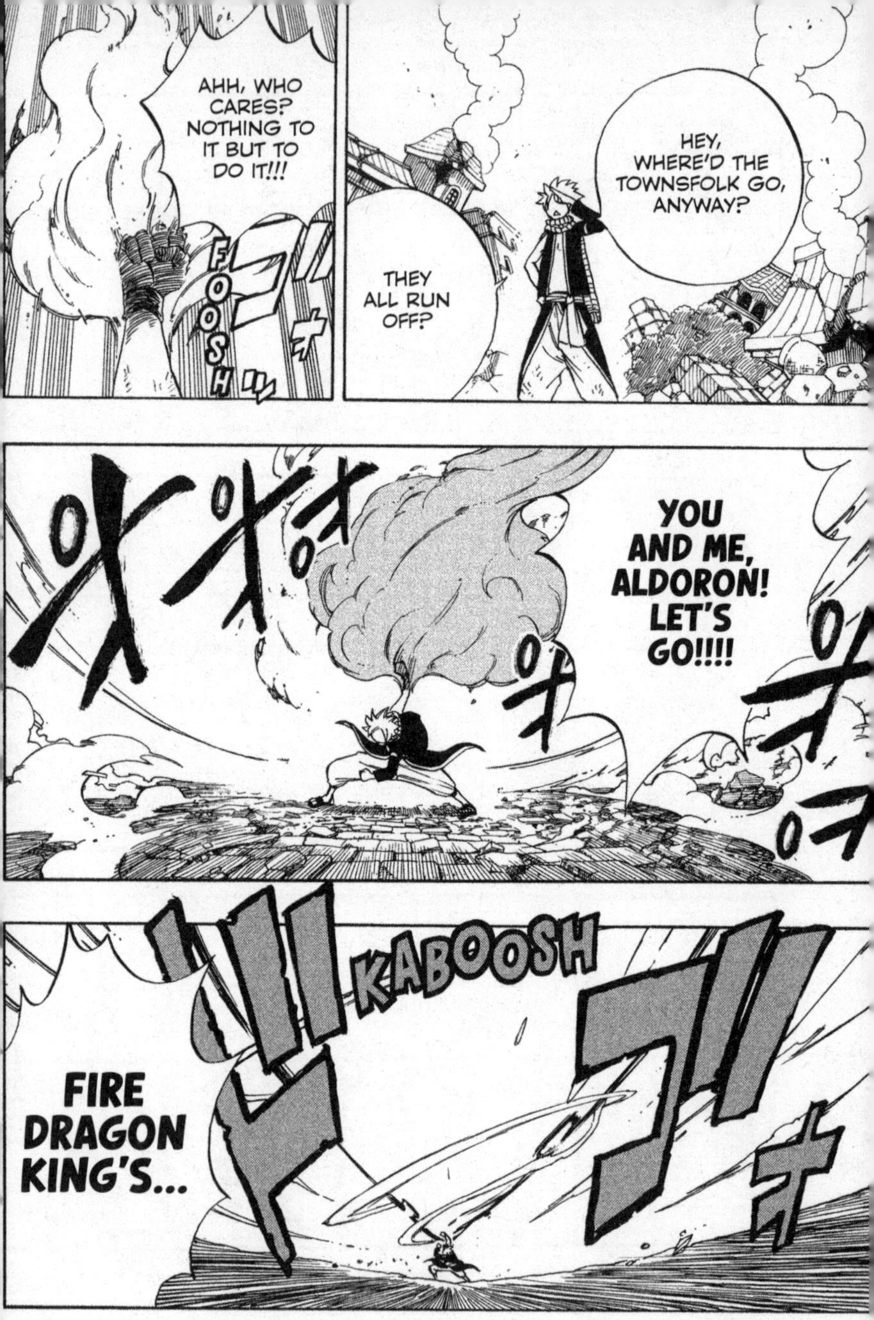
HEY, WHERE'D THE TOWNSFOLK GO, ANYWAY?
THEY ALL RUN OFF?
AHH, WHO CARES? NOTHING TO IT BUT TO DO IT!!!
FOOSH
YOU AND ME, ALDORON! LET'S GO!!!!
KABOOSH
FIRE DRAGON KING'S...

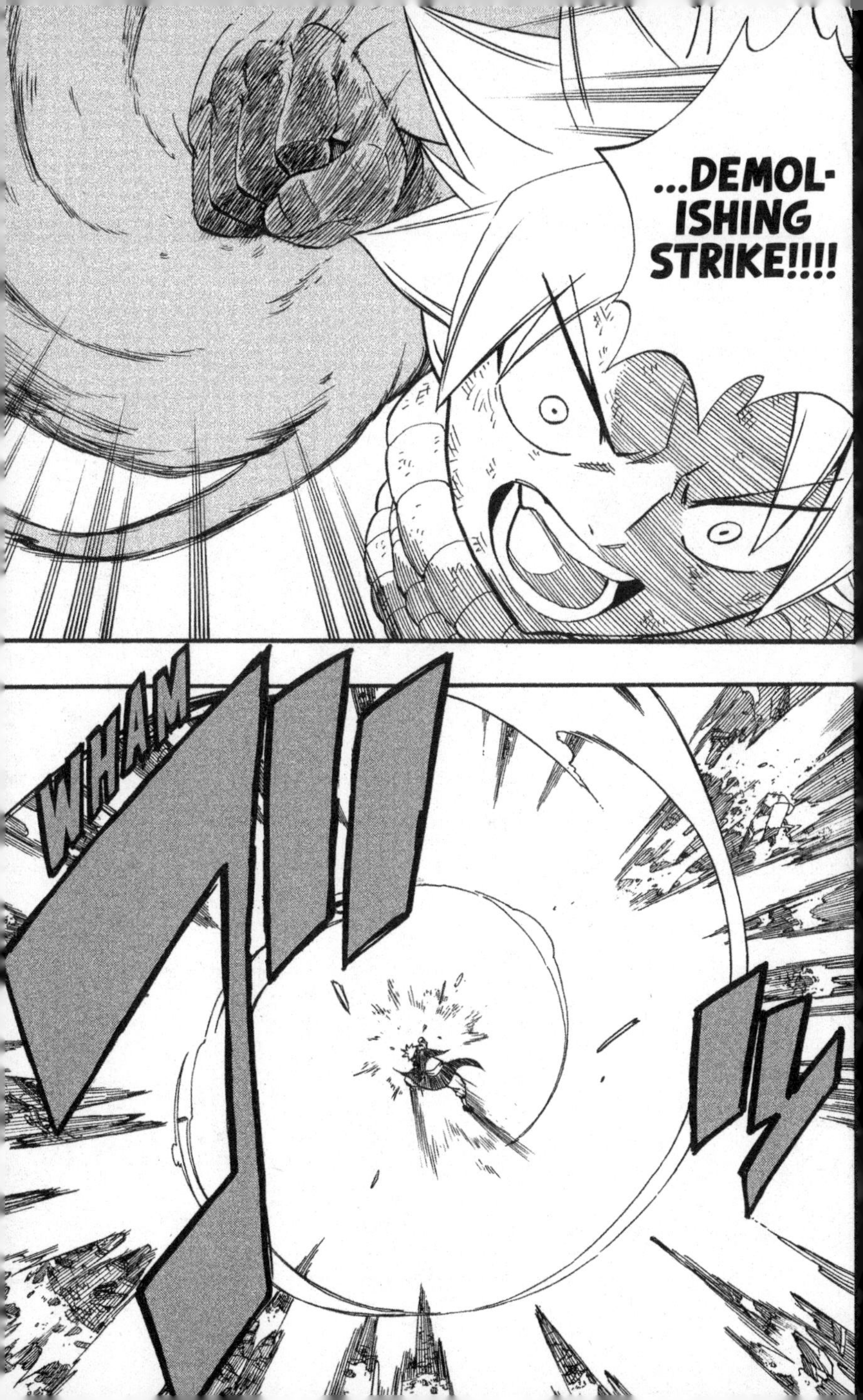
...DEMOL-
ISHING
STRIKE!!!!
WHAM

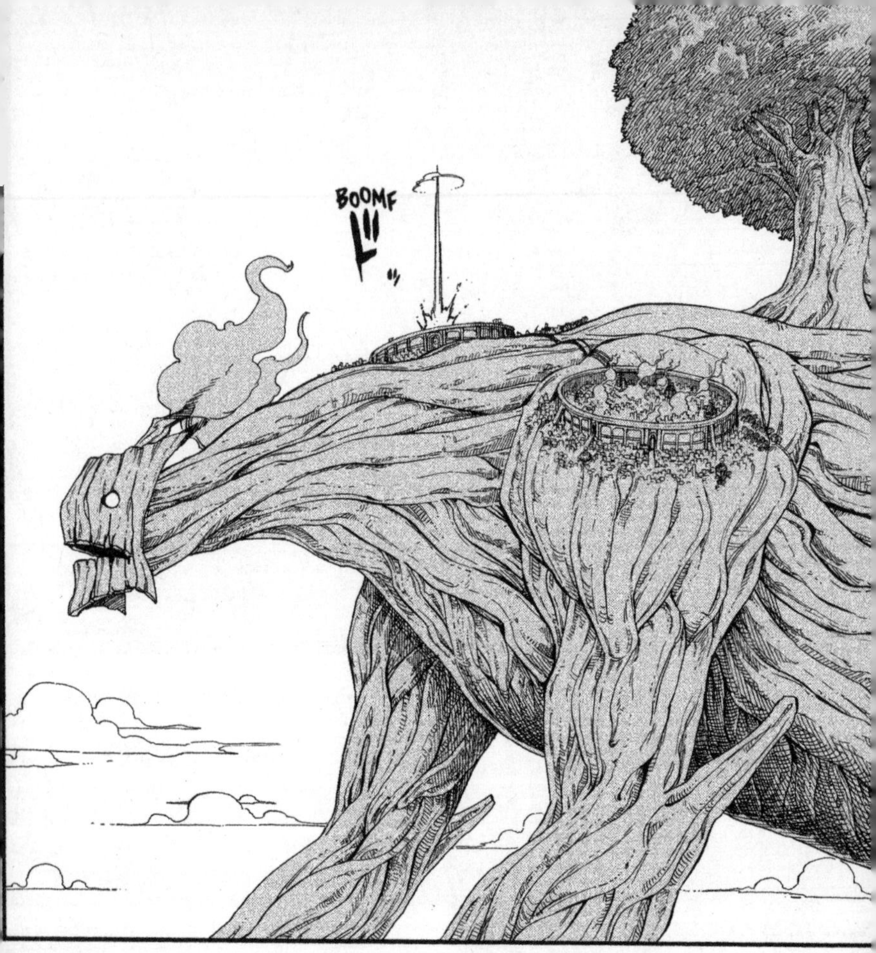
BOOMF

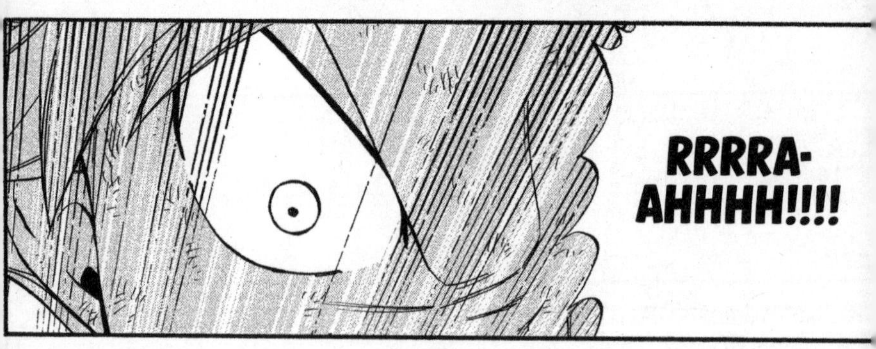
RRRRA-
AHHHH!!!!

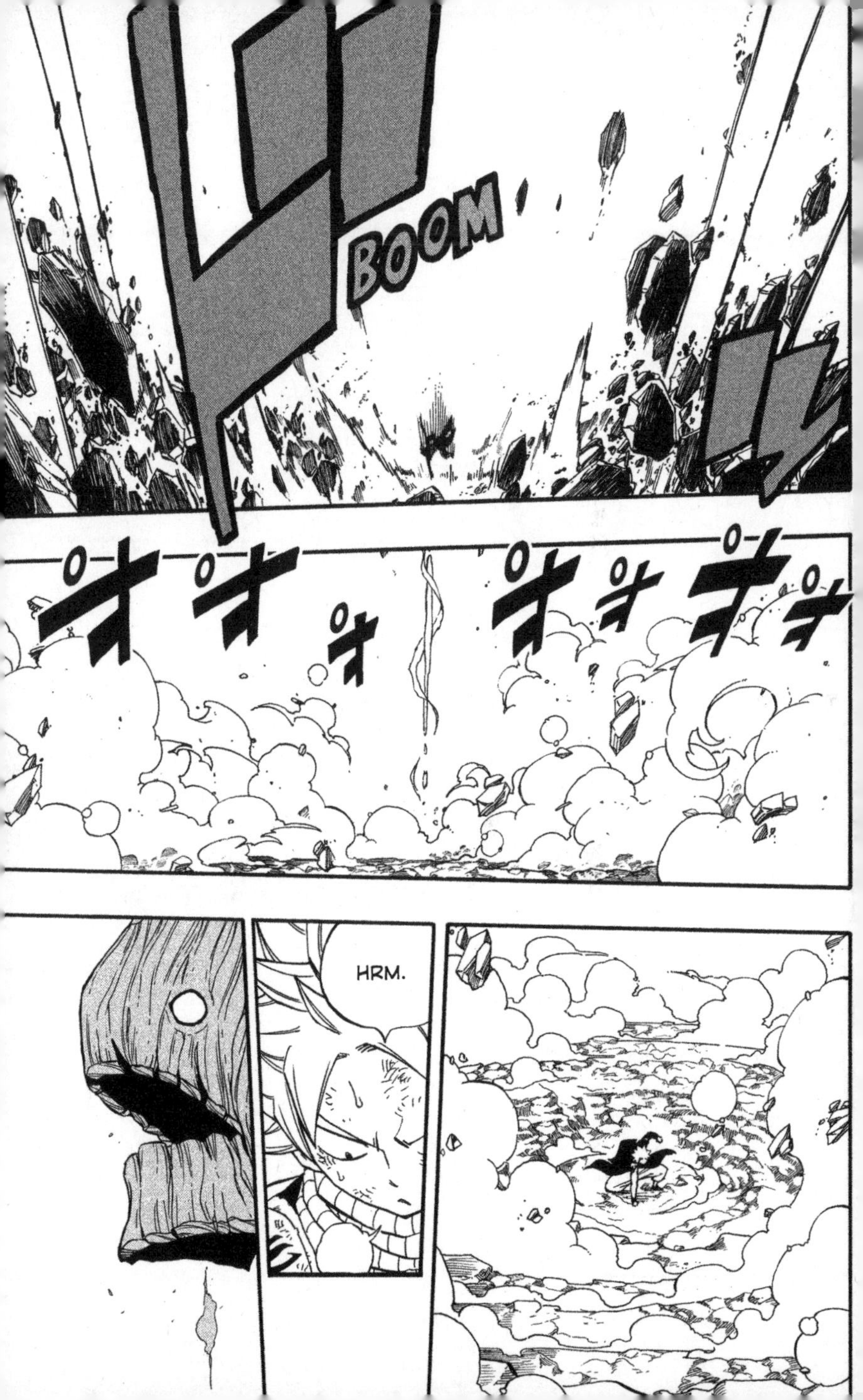
BOOM
HRM.

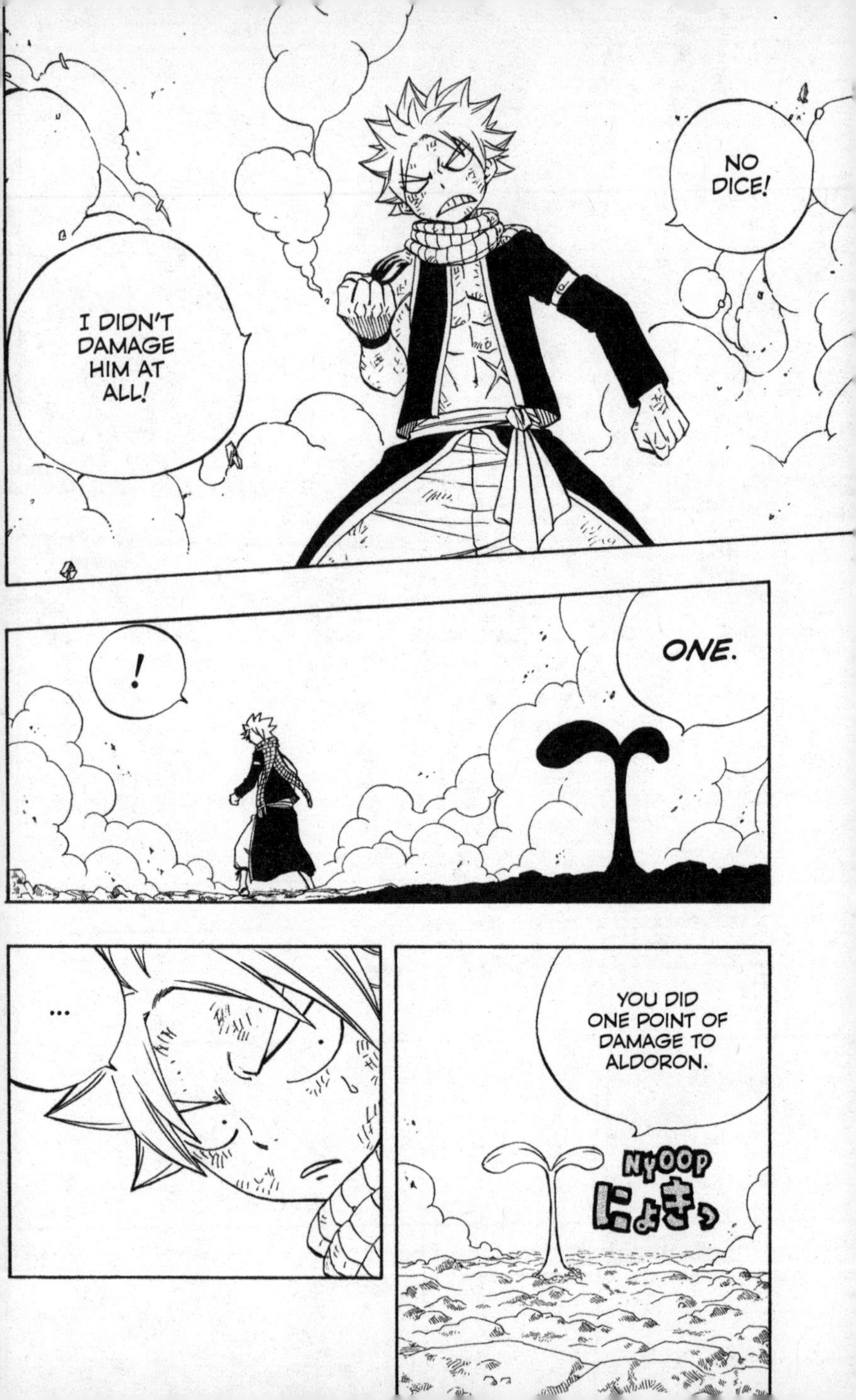
NO DICE!
I DIDN'T DAMAGE HIM AT ALL!
ONE.
!
YOU DID ONE POINT OF DAMAGE TO ALDORON.
NYOOP
にょきっ
...

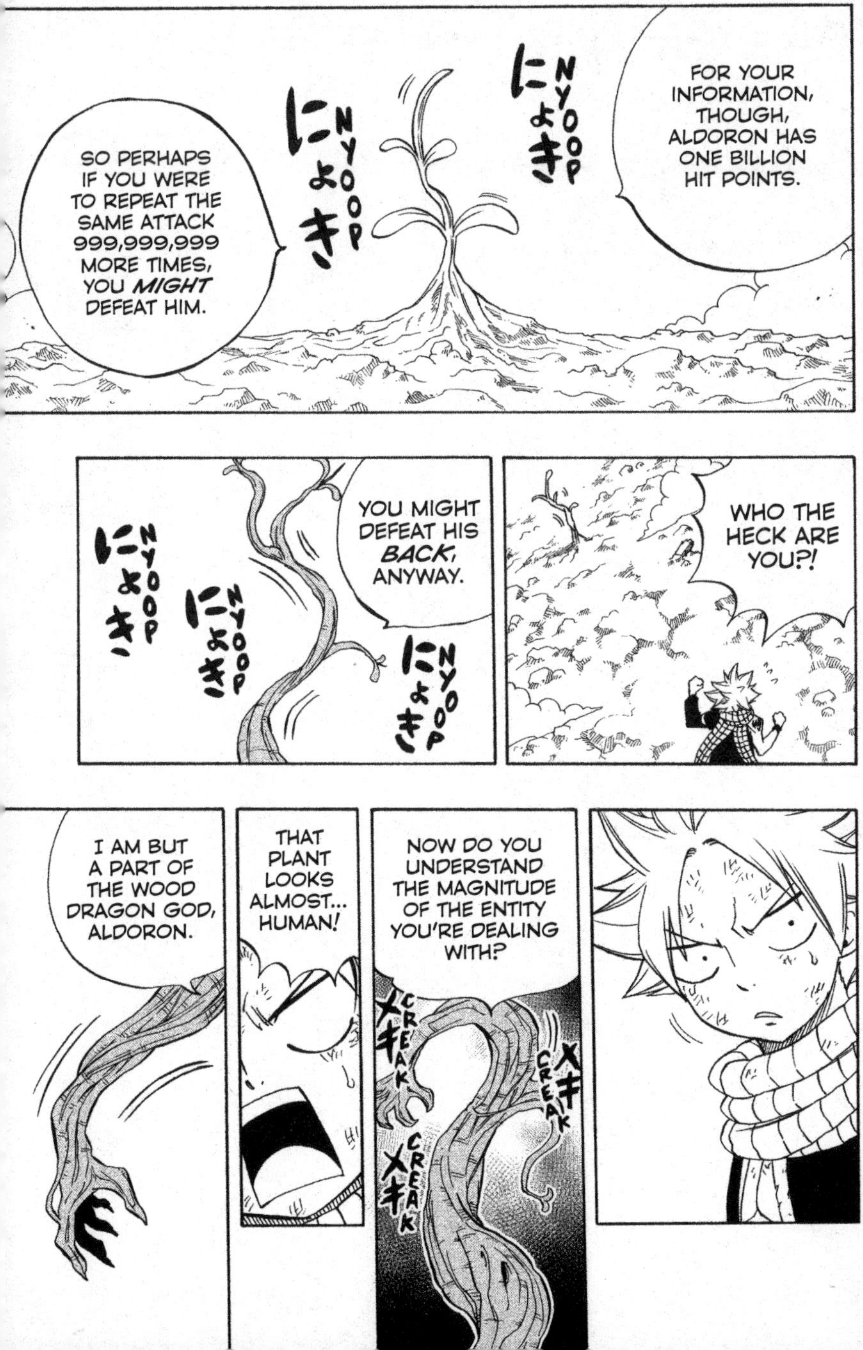
FOR YOUR INFORMATION, THOUGH, ALDORON HAS ONE BILLION HIT POINTS.
にょき NYOOP
にょき NYOOP
SO PERHAPS IF YOU WERE TO REPEAT THE SAME ATTACK 999,999,999 MORE TIMES, YOU *MIGHT* DEFEAT HIM.
WHO THE HECK ARE YOU?!
YOU MIGHT DEFEAT HIS *BACK*, ANYWAY.
にょき NYOOP
にょき NYOOP
にょき NYOOP
NOW DO YOU UNDERSTAND THE MAGNITUDE OF THE ENTITY YOU'RE DEALING WITH?
メキ CREAK
メキ CREAK
メキ CREAK
THAT PLANT LOOKS ALMOST... HUMAN!
I AM BUT A PART OF THE WOOD DRAGON GOD, ALDORON.

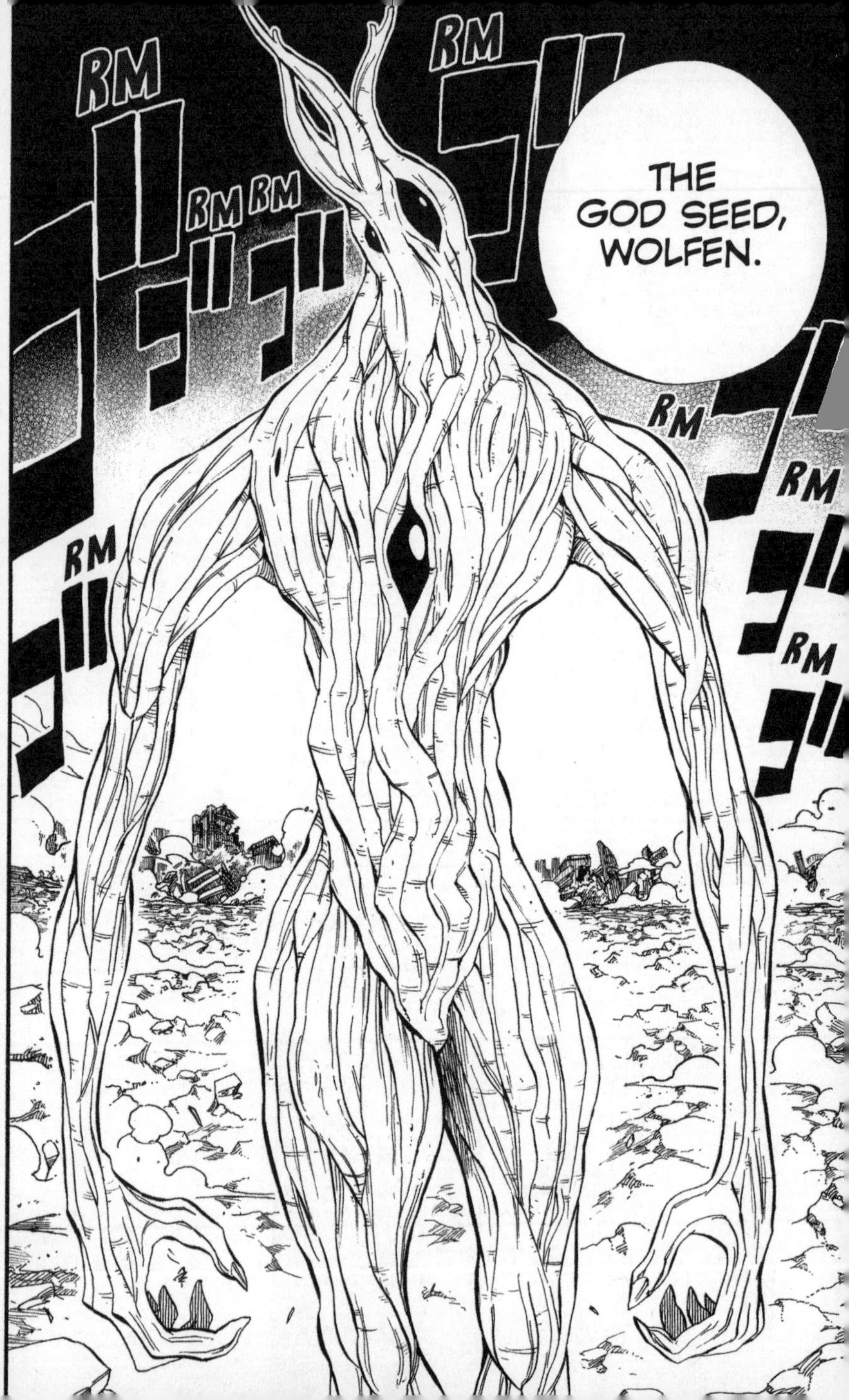
RM
THE GOD SEED, WOLFEN.
RM
RM
RM
RM
RM RM
RM

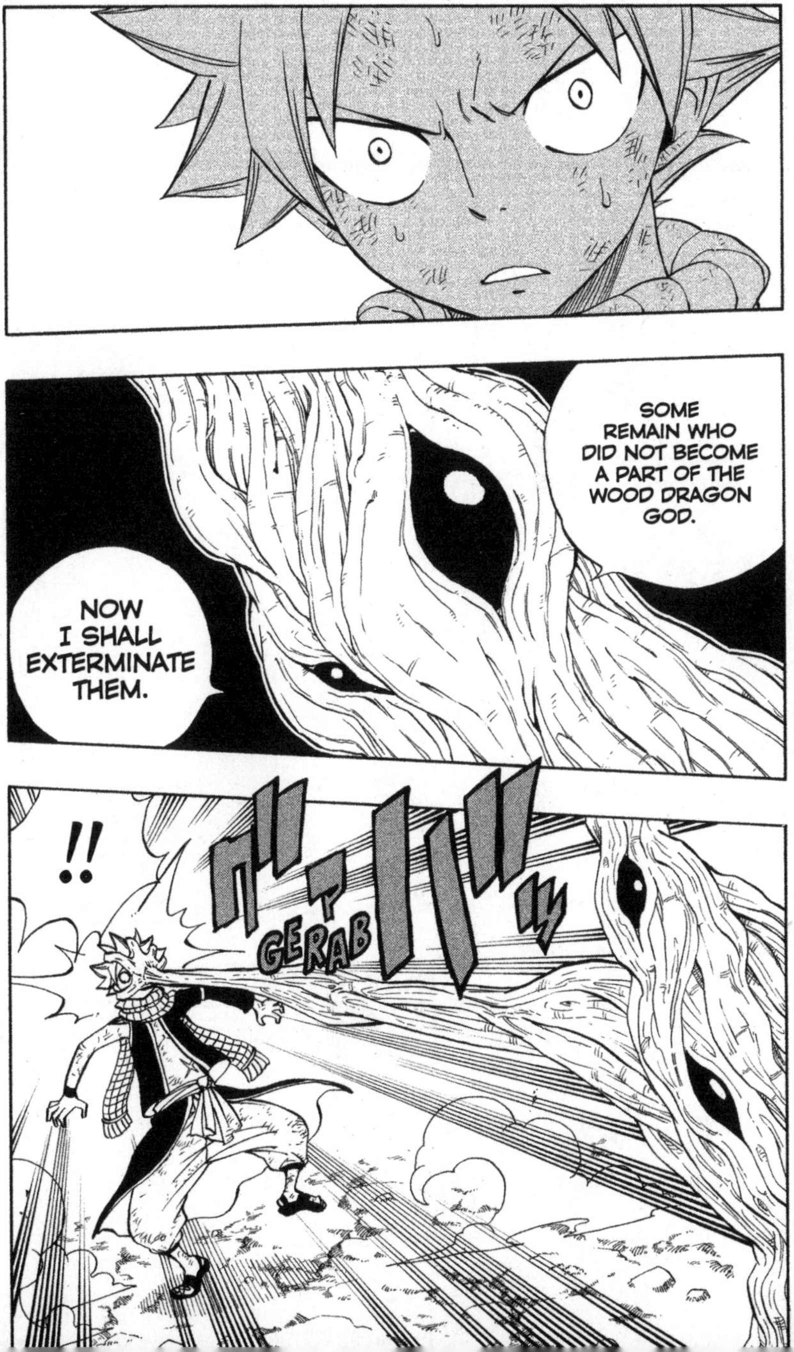
SOME REMAIN WHO DID NOT BECOME A PART OF THE WOOD DRAGON GOD.
NOW I SHALL EXTERMINATE THEM.
GERAB
!!

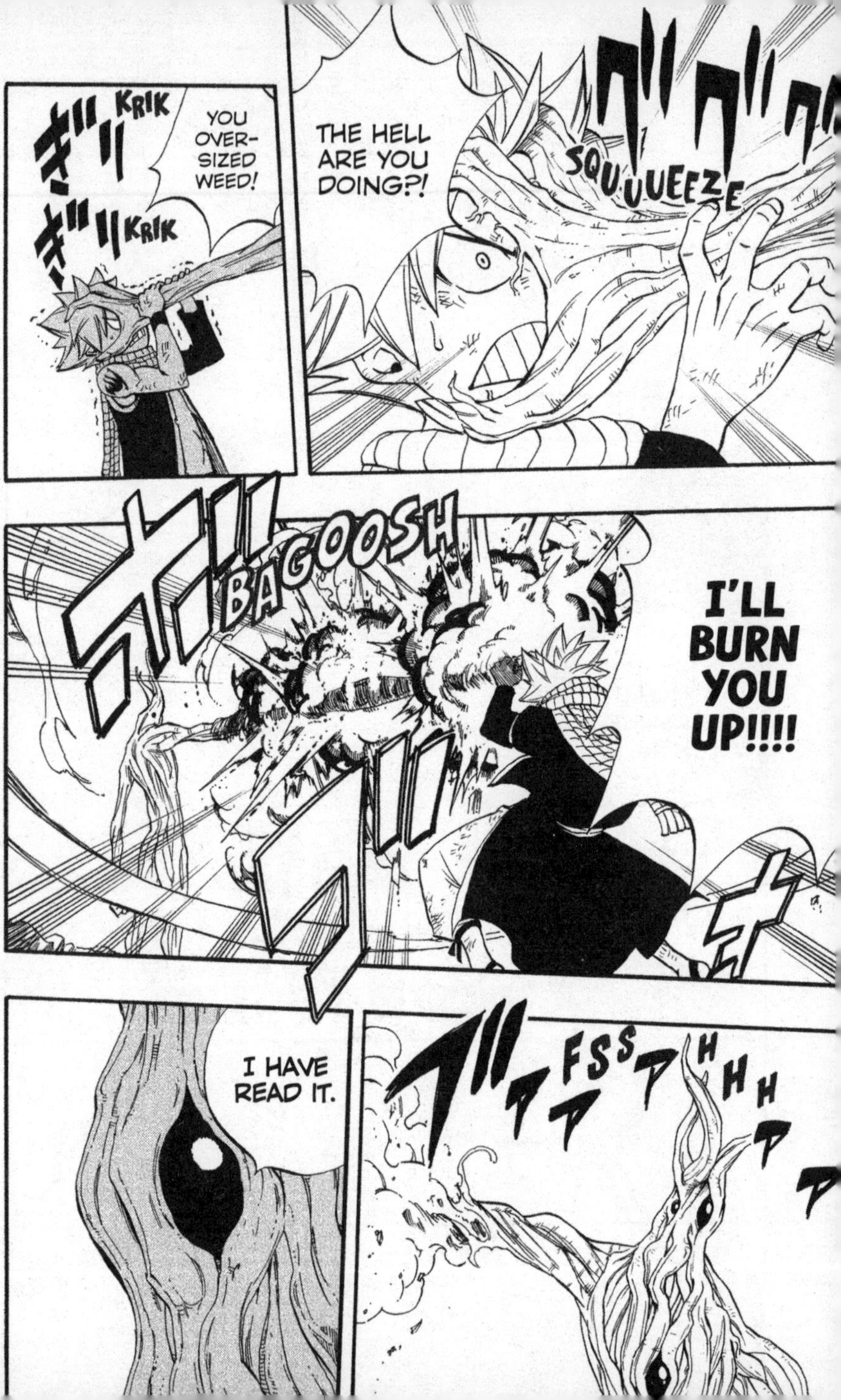
SQUUUEEZE
THE HELL ARE YOU DOING?!
YOU OVER-SIZED WEED!
KRIK
KRIK
BAGOOSH
I'LL BURN YOU UP!!!!
FSSHHH
I HAVE READ IT.

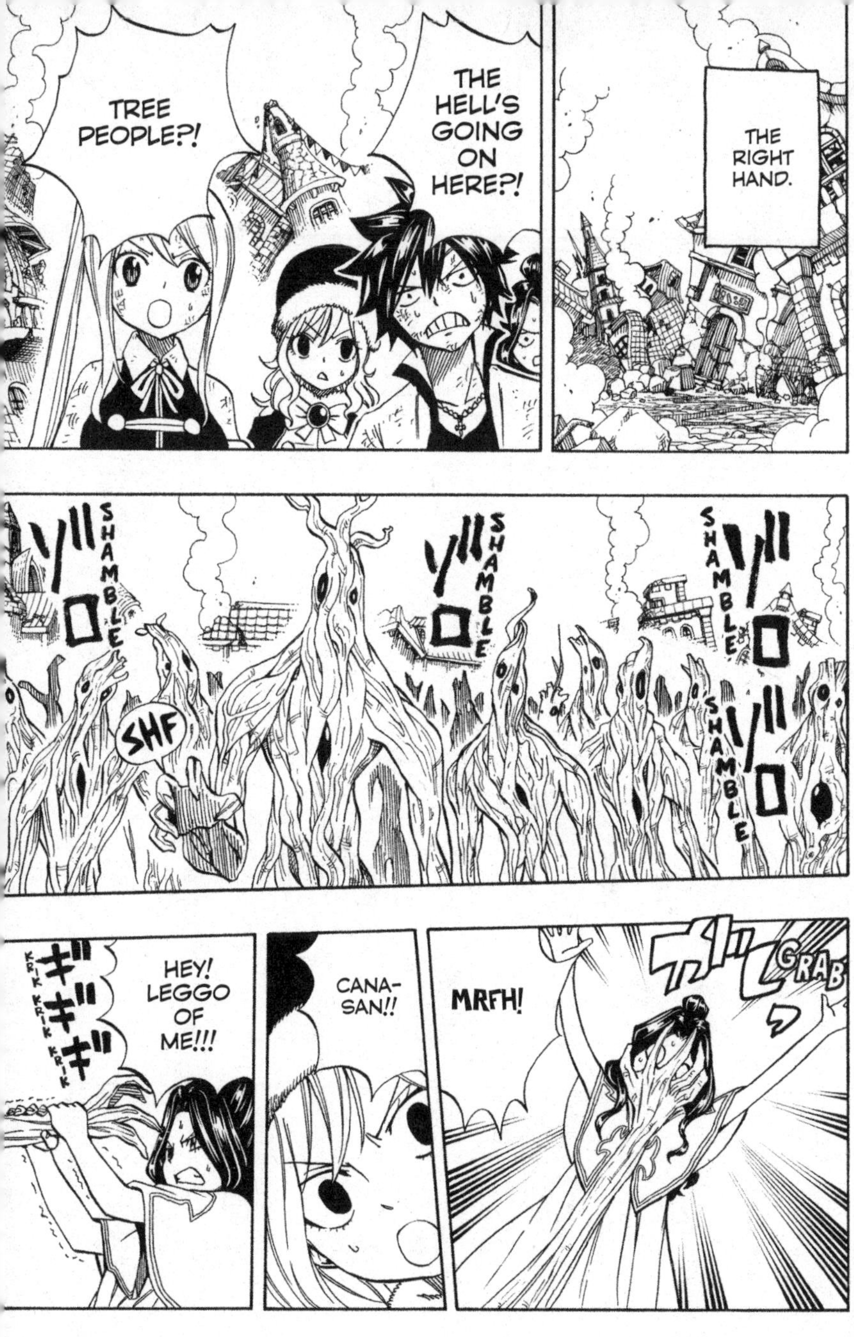
THE RIGHT HAND.
THE HELL'S GOING ON HERE?!
TREE PEOPLE?!
SHAMBLE
SHAMBLE
SHAMBLE
SHAMBLE
SHF
GRAB
MRFH!
CANA-SAN!!
HEY! LEGGO OF ME!!!
KRIK KRIK KRIK

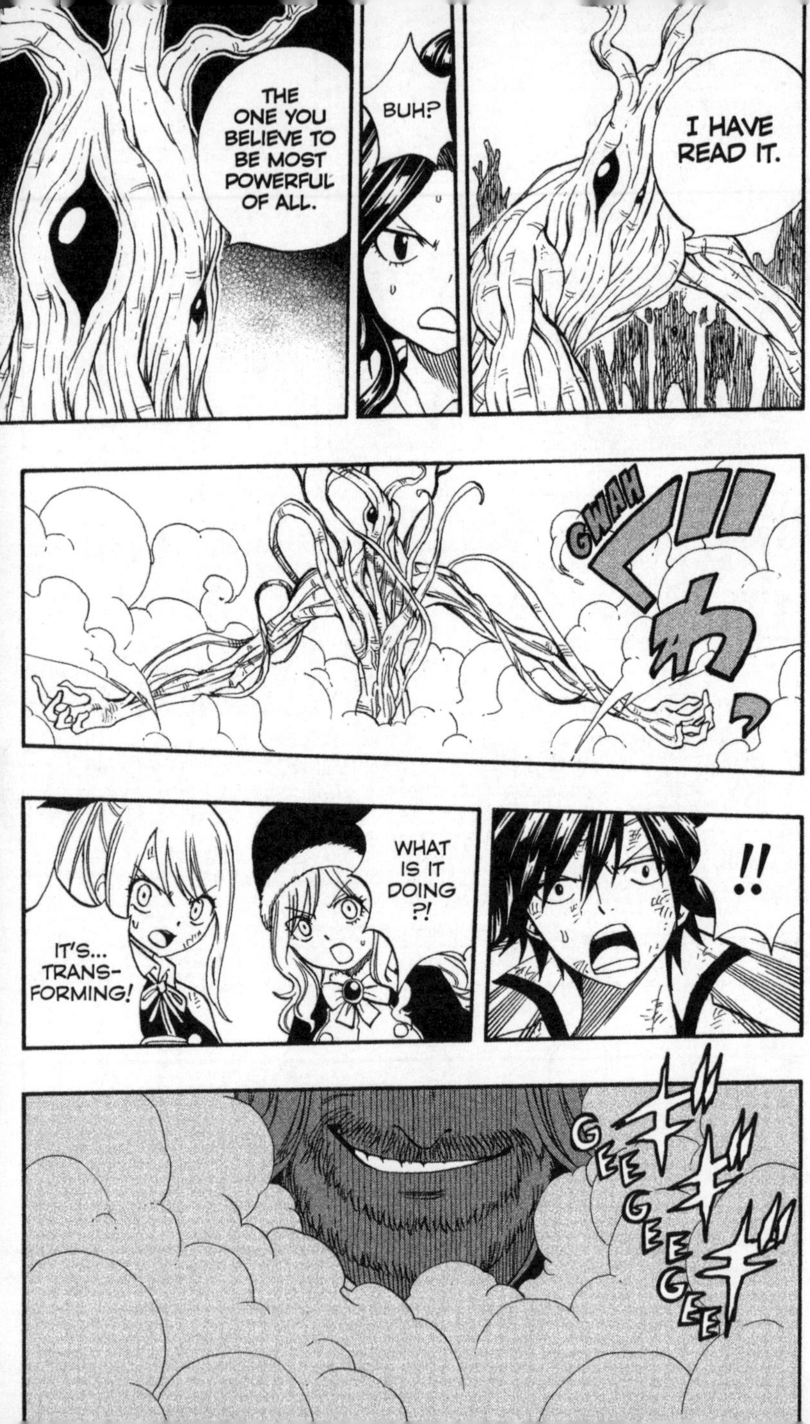
I HAVE READ IT.
BUH?
THE ONE YOU BELIEVE TO BE MOST POWERFUL OF ALL.
GWAH
!!
WHAT IS IT DOING?!
IT'S... TRANS-FORMING!
GEEGEEGEE

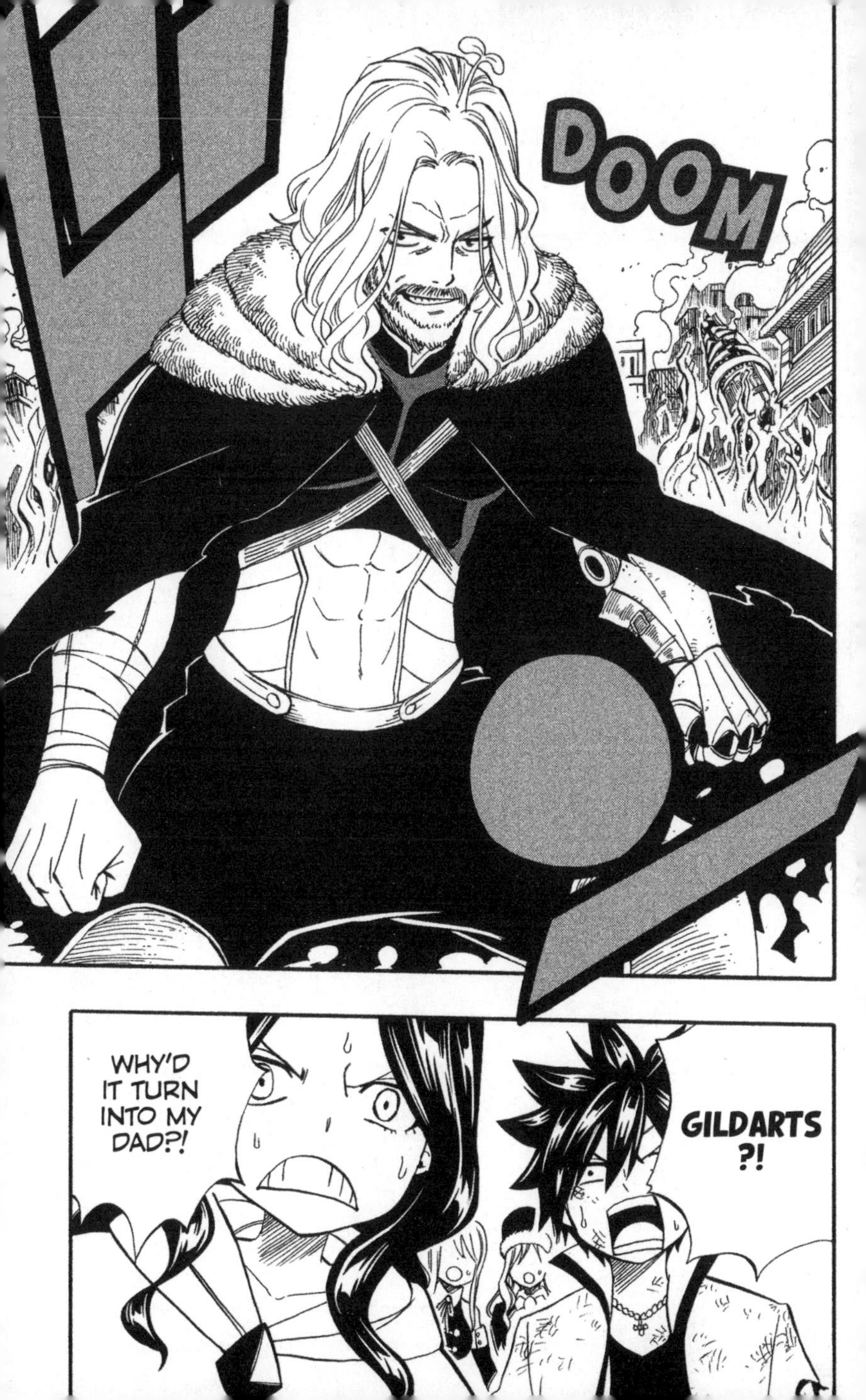
DOOM
GILDARTS ?!
WHY'D IT TURN INTO MY DAD?!

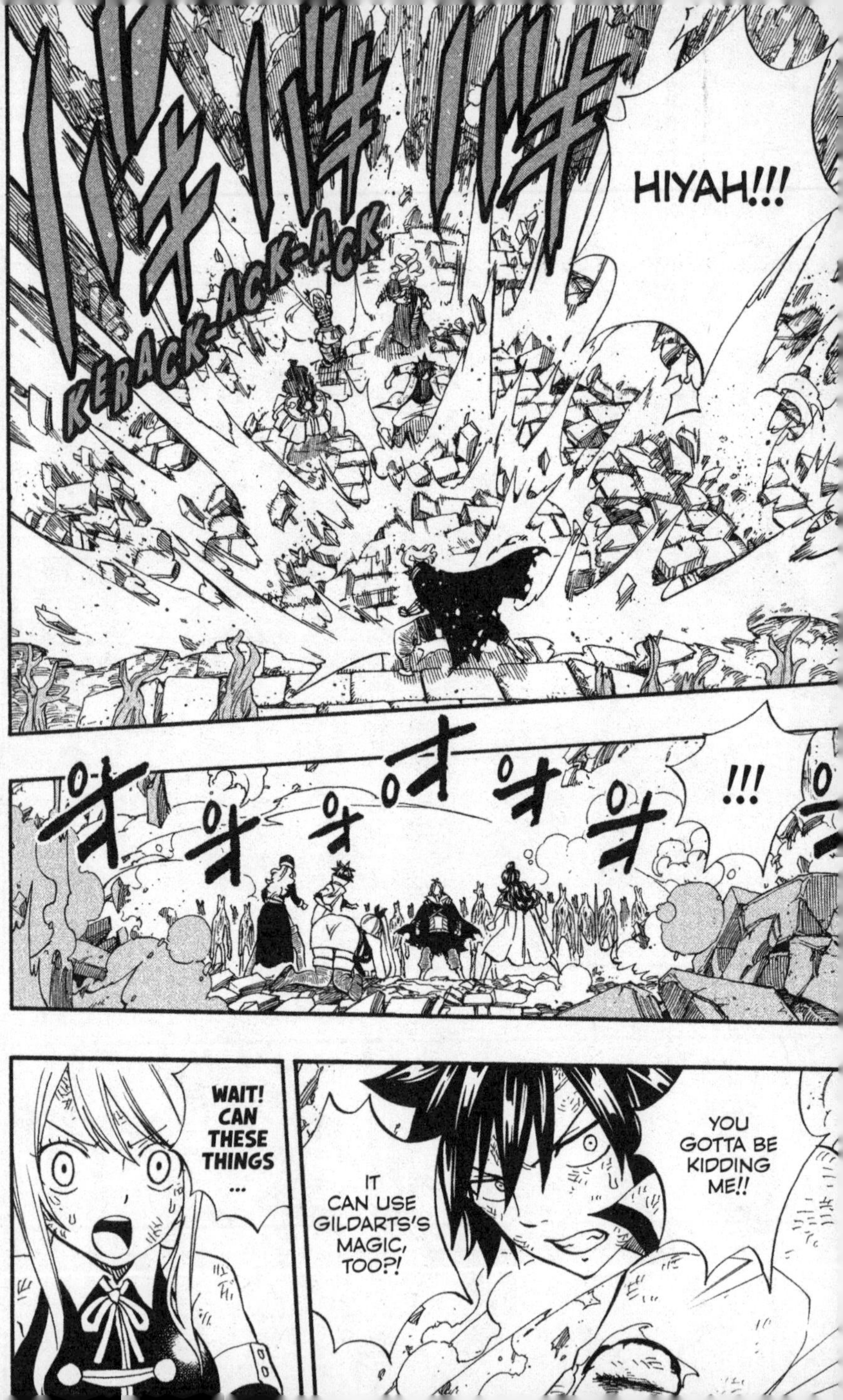
HIYAH!!!
KERACK-ACK-ACK
!!!
YOU GOTTA BE KIDDING ME!!
IT CAN USE GILDARTS'S MAGIC, TOO?!
WAIT! CAN THESE THINGS ...

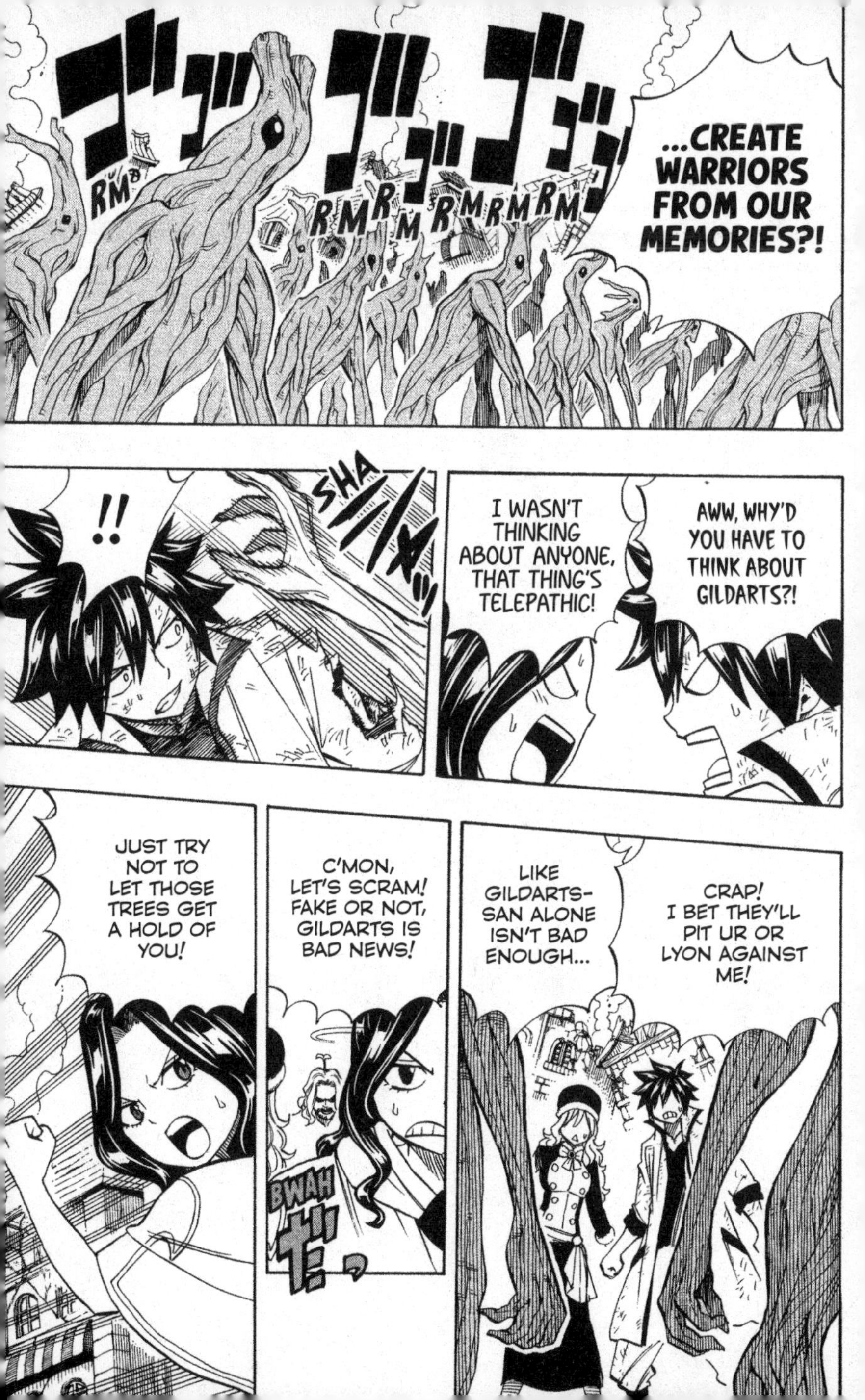
...CREATE WARRIORS FROM OUR MEMORIES?!
RM
RMRMRMRMRM
AWW, WHY'D YOU HAVE TO THINK ABOUT GILDARTS?!
I WASN'T THINKING ABOUT ANYONE, THAT THING'S TELEPATHIC!
SHA
!!
CRAP! I BET THEY'LL PIT UR OR LYON AGAINST ME!
LIKE GILDARTS-SAN ALONE ISN'T BAD ENOUGH...
C'MON, LET'S SCRAM! FAKE OR NOT, GILDARTS IS BAD NEWS!
BWAH
JUST TRY NOT TO LET THOSE TREES GET A HOLD OF YOU!

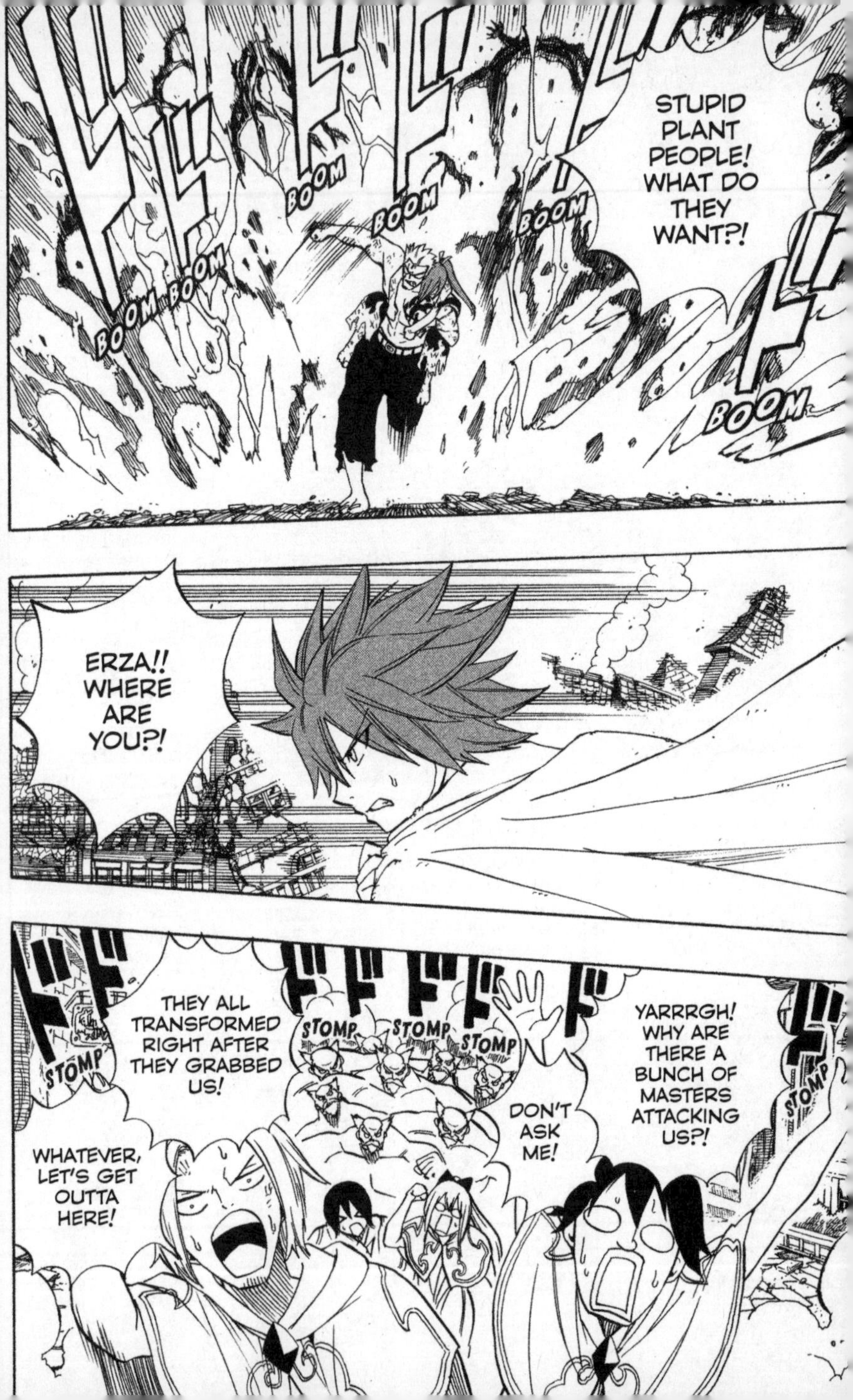
STUPID PLANT PEOPLE! WHAT DO THEY WANT?!
BOOM
BOOM
BOOM
BOOM
BOOM BOOM
ERZA!! WHERE ARE YOU?!
STOMP
YARRRGH! WHY ARE THERE A BUNCH OF MASTERS ATTACKING US?!
DON'T ASK ME!
STOMP
STOMP
STOMP
THEY ALL TRANSFORMED RIGHT AFTER THEY GRABBED US!
STOMP
WHATEVER, LET'S GET OUTTA HERE!

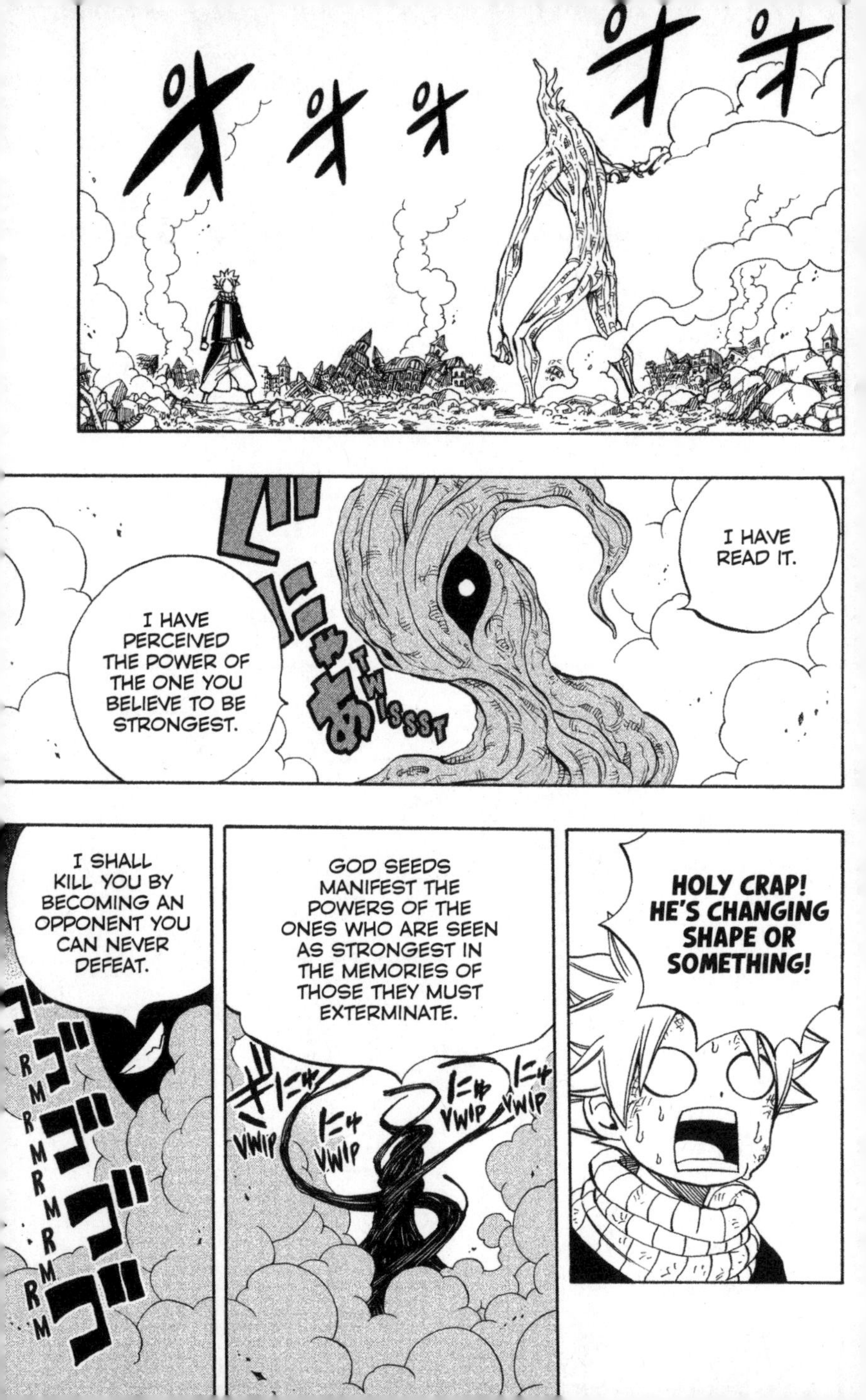
I HAVE READ IT.
I HAVE PERCEIVED THE POWER OF THE ONE YOU BELIEVE TO BE STRONGEST.
TWISSST
HOLY CRAP! HE'S CHANGING SHAPE OR SOMETHING!
GOD SEEDS MANIFEST THE POWERS OF THE ONES WHO ARE SEEN AS STRONGEST IN THE MEMORIES OF THOSE THEY MUST EXTERMINATE.
VWIP
VWIP
VWIP
VWIP
I SHALL KILL YOU BY BECOMING AN OPPONENT YOU CAN NEVER DEFEAT.
RMRMRMRMRM

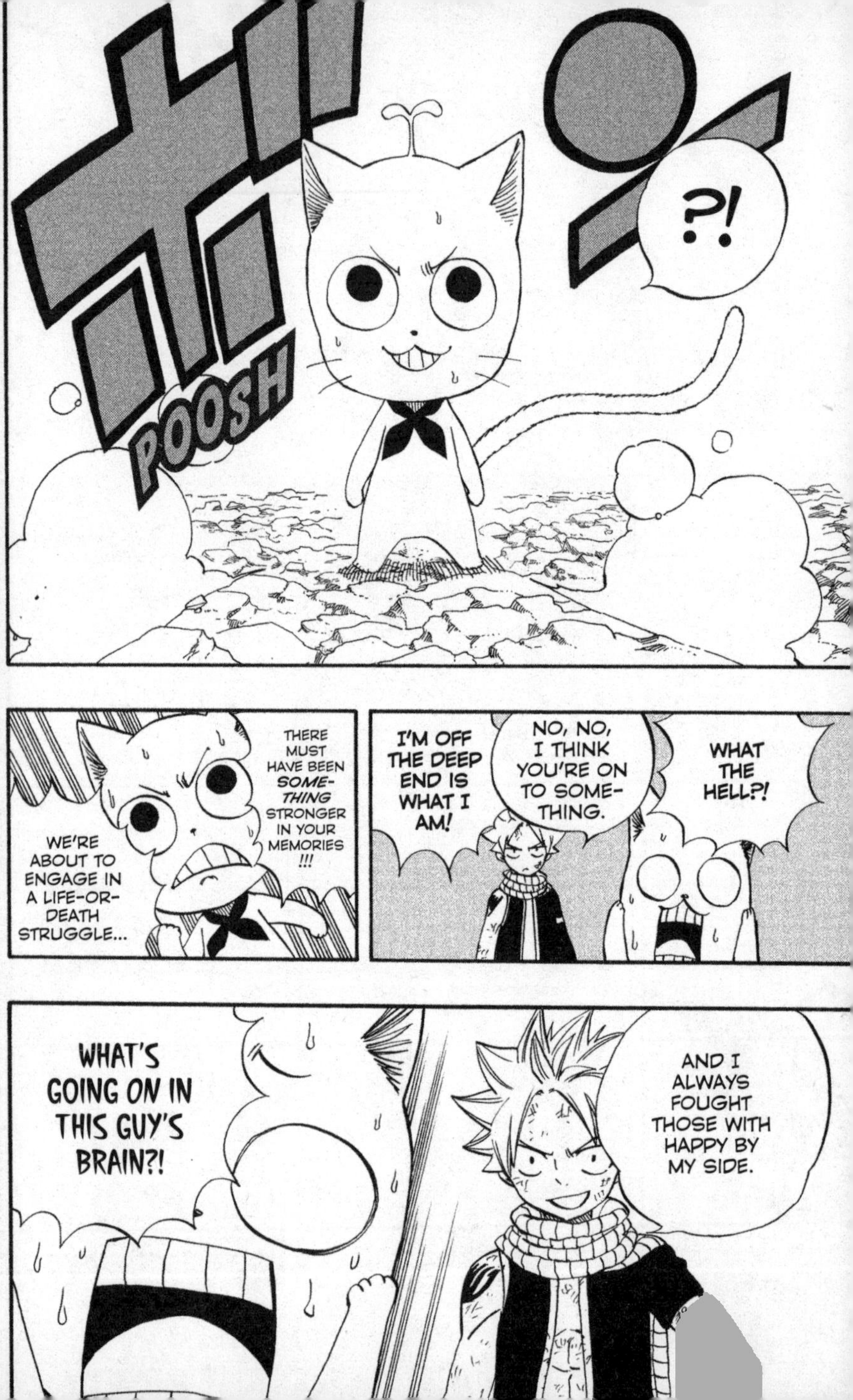
?!
POOSH
WHAT THE HELL?!
NO, NO, I THINK YOU'RE ON TO SOME-THING.
I'M OFF THE DEEP END IS WHAT I AM!
THERE MUST HAVE BEEN *SOME-THING* STRONGER IN YOUR MEMORIES!!!
WE'RE ABOUT TO ENGAGE IN A LIFE-OR-DEATH STRUGGLE...
AND I ALWAYS FOUGHT THOSE WITH HAPPY BY MY SIDE.
WHAT'S GOING ON IN THIS GUY'S BRAIN?!

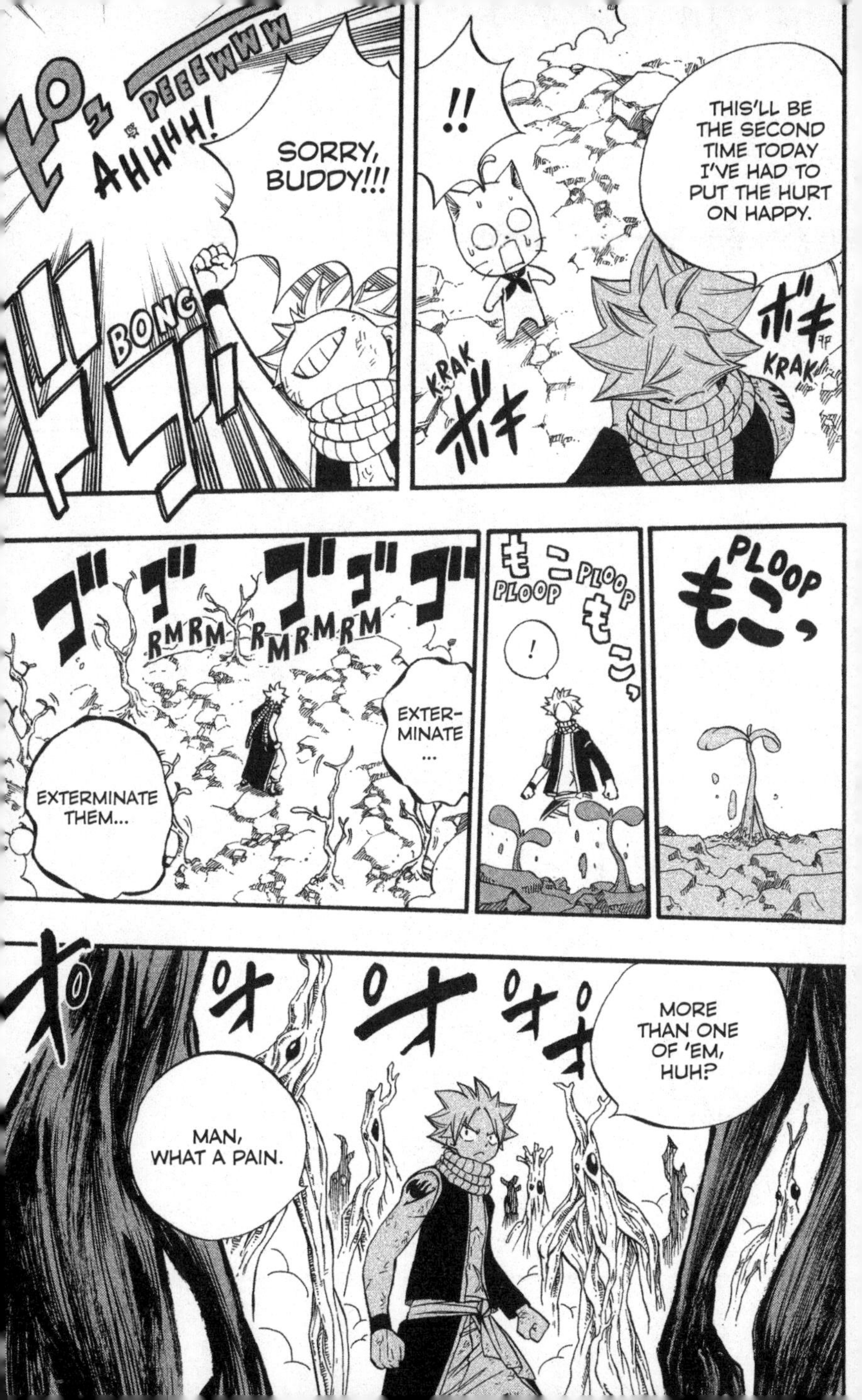
!!
THIS'LL BE THE SECOND TIME TODAY I'VE HAD TO PUT THE HURT ON HAPPY.
KRAK
KRAK
PEEEWWW
AHHHH!
SORRY, BUDDY!!!
BONG
PLOOP
PLOOP
PLOOP
!
RMRM
RMRMRM
EXTERMINATE...
EXTERMINATE THEM...
MORE THAN ONE OF 'EM, HUH?
MAN, WHAT A PAIN.

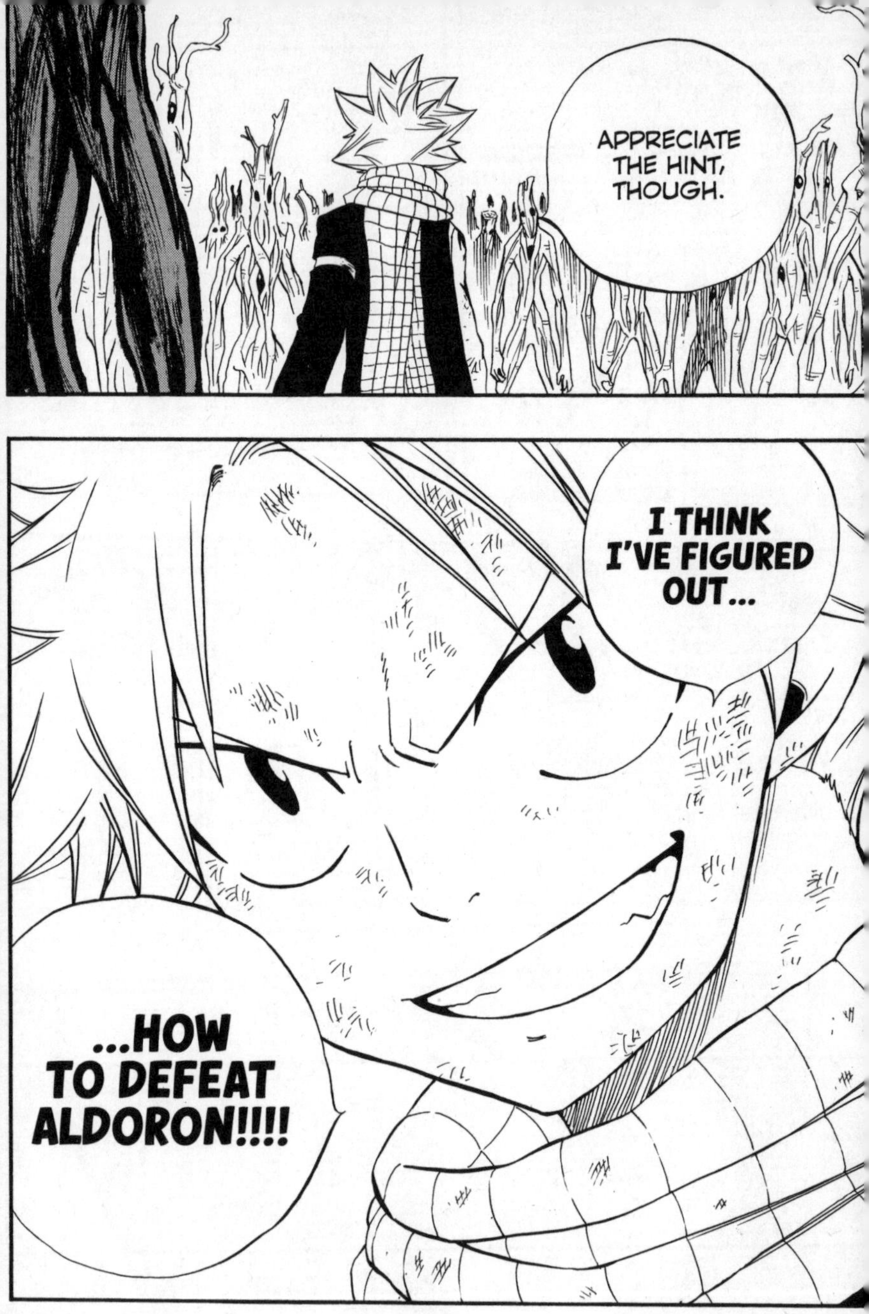
APPRECIATE THE HINT, THOUGH.
I THINK I'VE FIGURED OUT...
...HOW TO DEFEAT ALDORON!!!!

FAIRY TAIL 100 YEARS QUEST

CHAPTER 53: THE MOST PRECIOUS CURSE

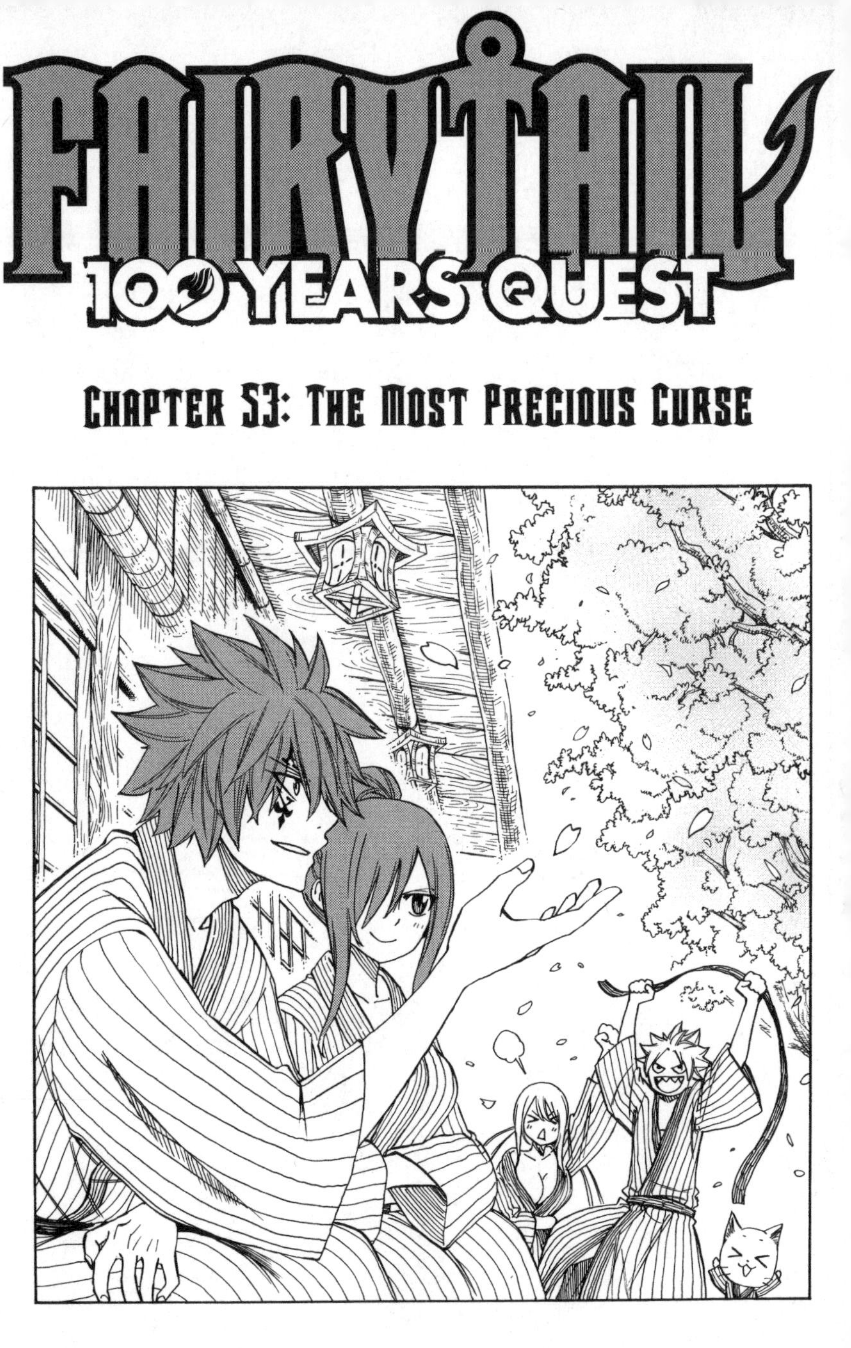

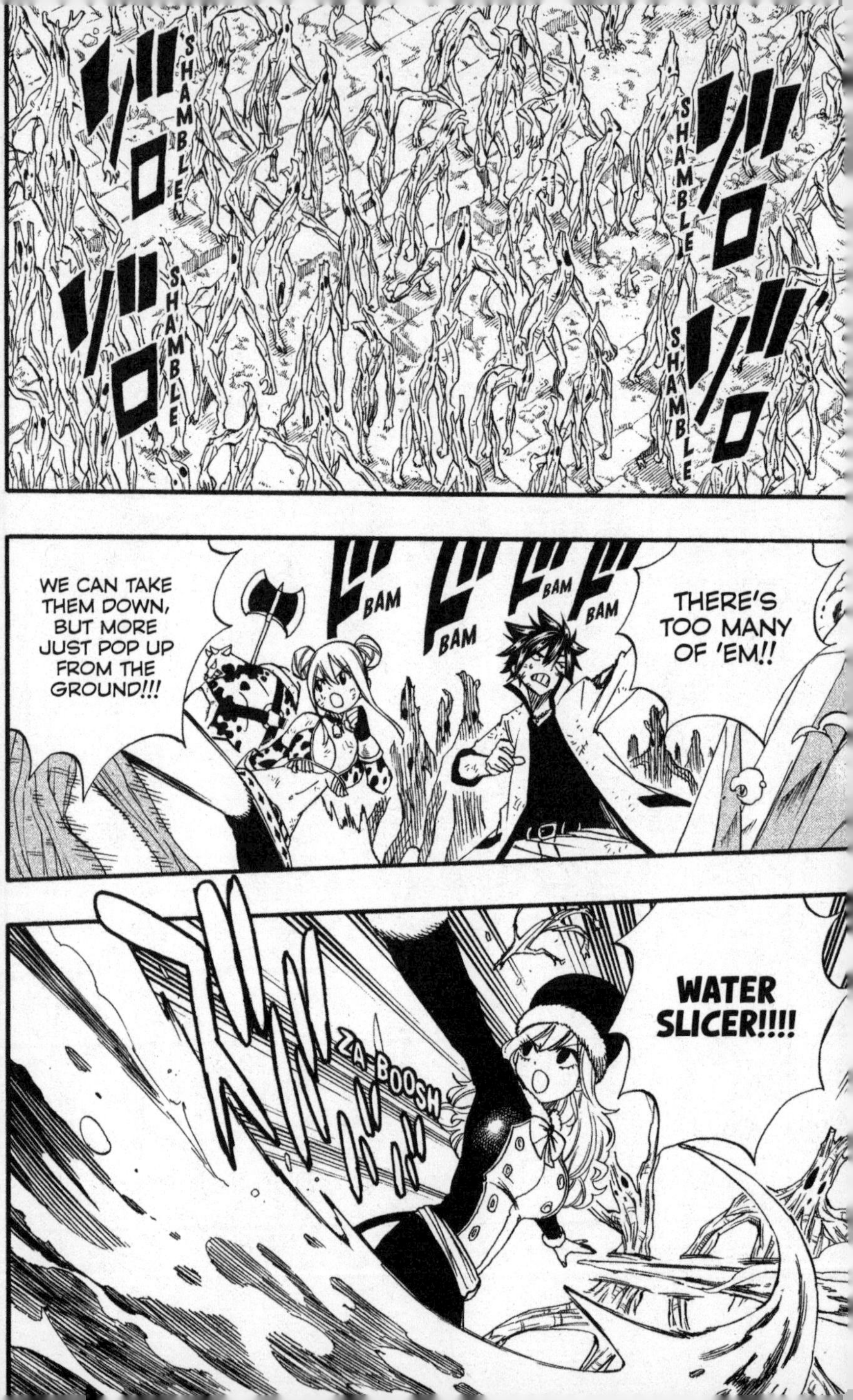
SHAMBLE
SHAMBLE
SHAMBLE
SHAMBLE
BAM
BAM
BAM
BAM
THERE'S TOO MANY OF 'EM!!
WE CAN TAKE THEM DOWN, BUT MORE JUST POP UP FROM THE GROUND!!!
WATER SLICER!!!!
ZA-BOOSH

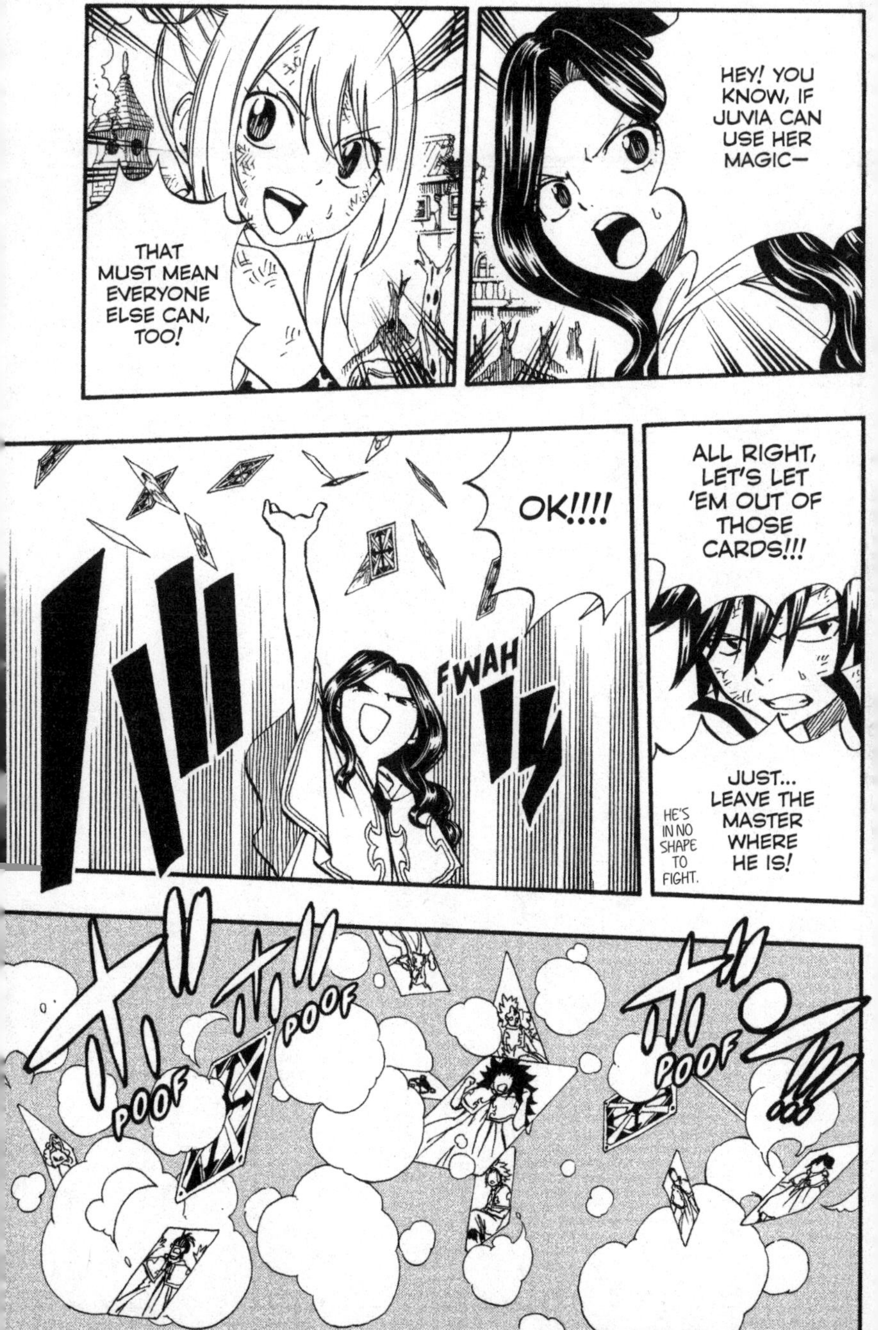
HEY! YOU KNOW, IF JUVIA CAN USE HER MAGIC—
THAT MUST MEAN EVERYONE ELSE CAN, TOO!
ALL RIGHT, LET'S LET 'EM OUT OF THOSE CARDS!!!
JUST... LEAVE THE MASTER WHERE HE IS!
HE'S IN NO SHAPE TO FIGHT.
OK!!!!
FWAH
POOF
POOF
POOF
POOF

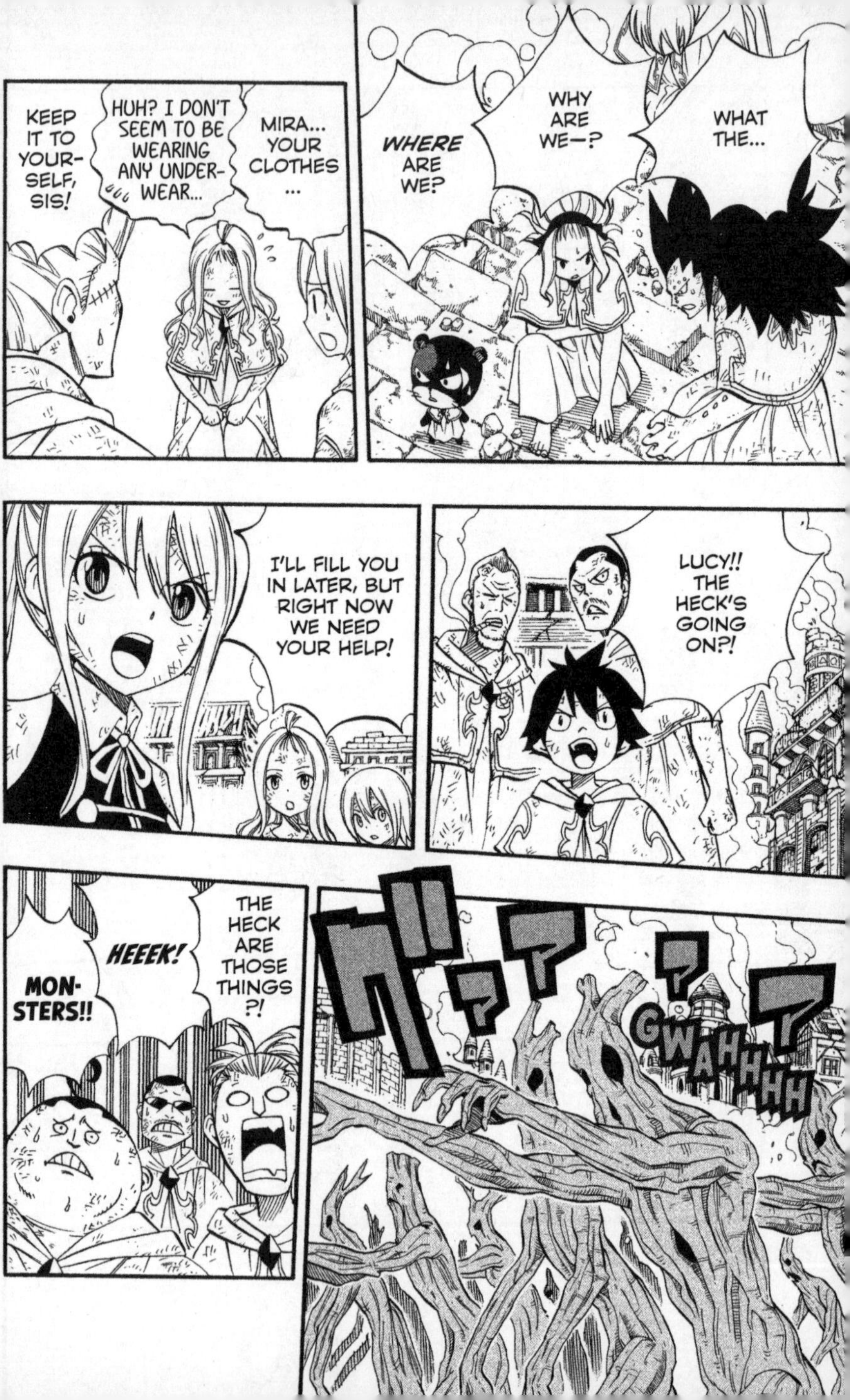
WHAT THE...
WHY ARE WE—?
WHERE ARE WE?
MIRA... YOUR CLOTHES ...
HUH? I DON'T SEEM TO BE WEARING ANY UNDER-WEAR...
KEEP IT TO YOUR-SELF, SIS!
LUCY!! THE HECK'S GOING ON?!
I'LL FILL YOU IN LATER, BUT RIGHT NOW WE NEED YOUR HELP!
GWAHHHH
THE HECK ARE THOSE THINGS ?!
HEEEK!
MON-STERS!!

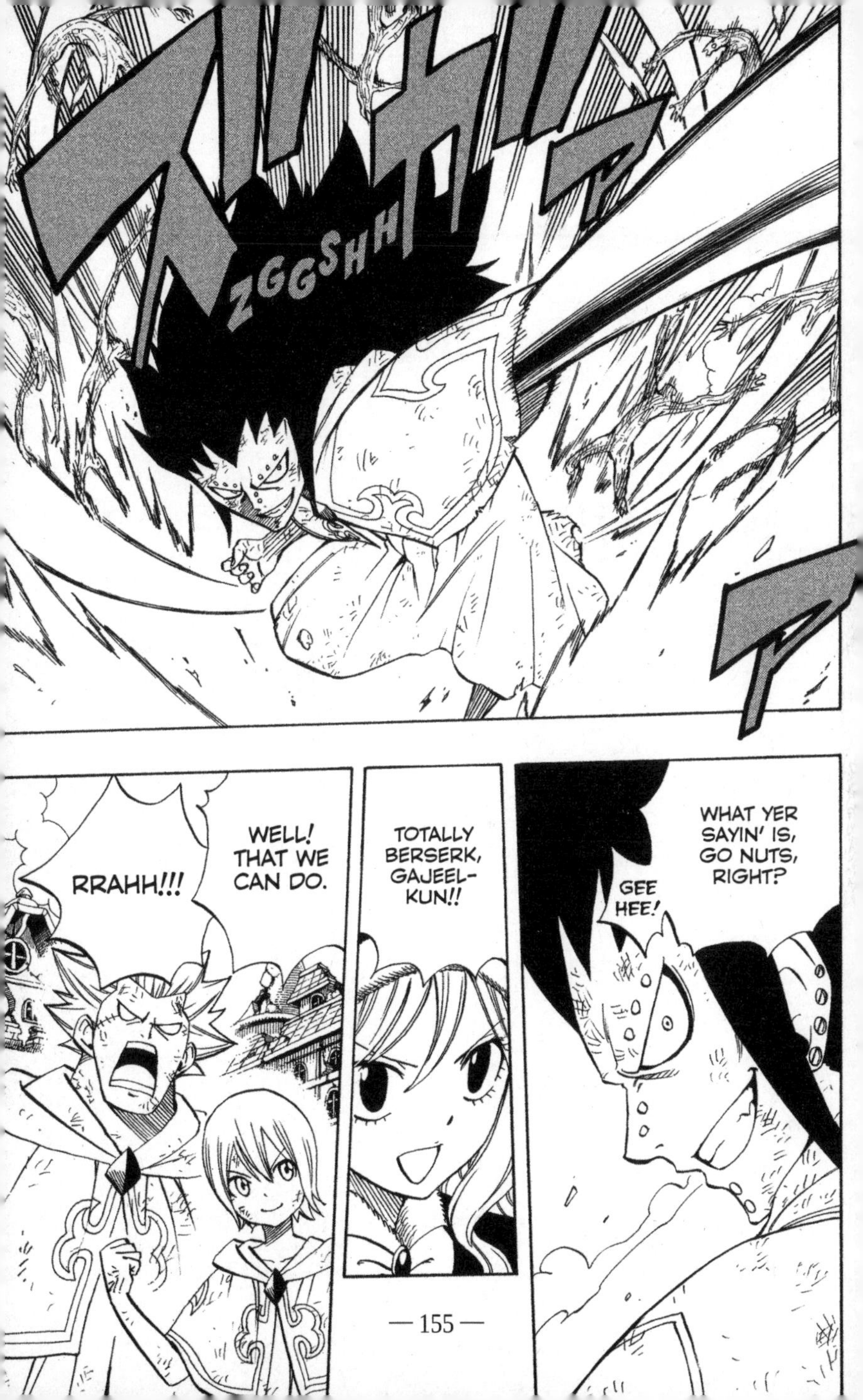
ZGGSHH
WHAT YER SAYIN' IS, GO NUTS, RIGHT?
GEE HEE!
TOTALLY BERSERK, GAJEEL-KUN!!
WELL! THAT WE CAN DO.
RRAHH!!!

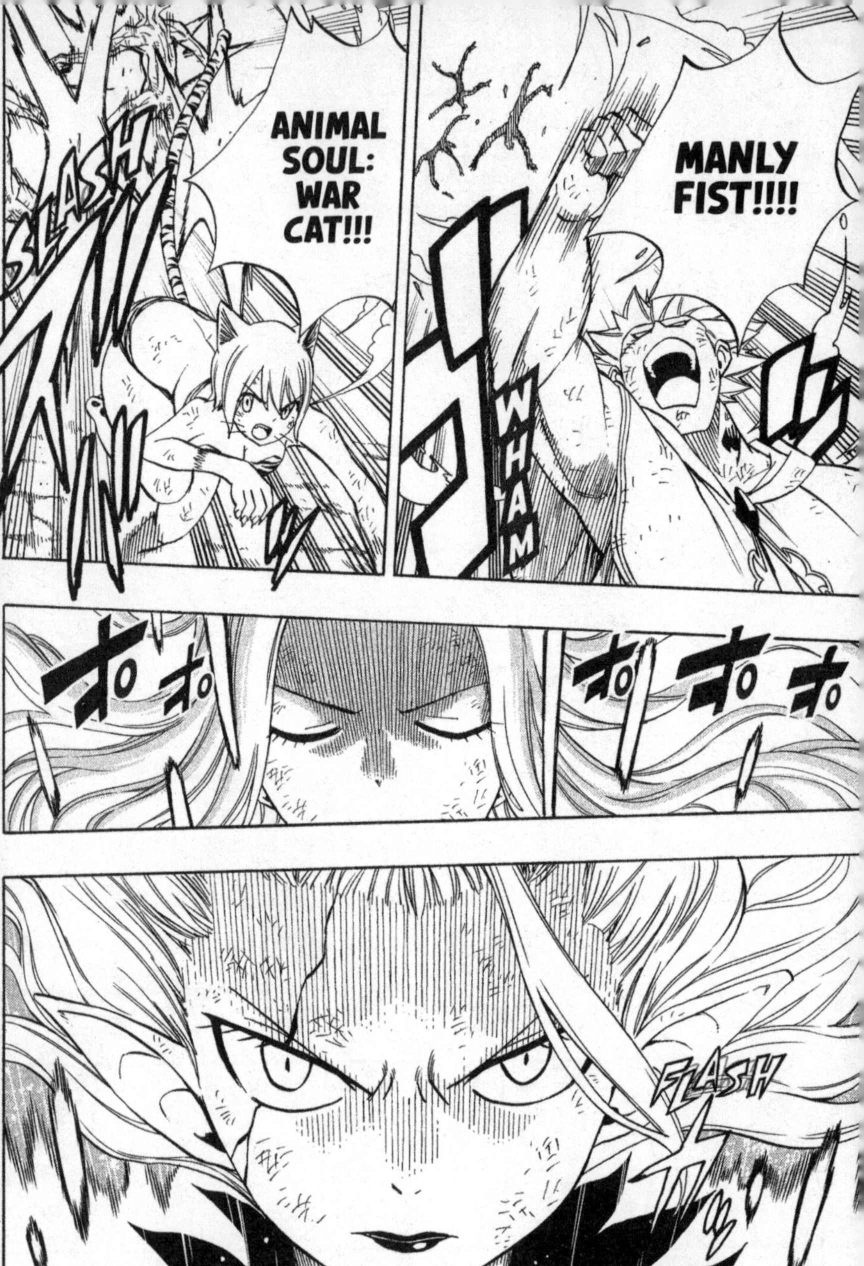
MANLY FIST!!!!
WHAM
ANIMAL SOUL: WAR CAT!!!
SLASH
FLASH

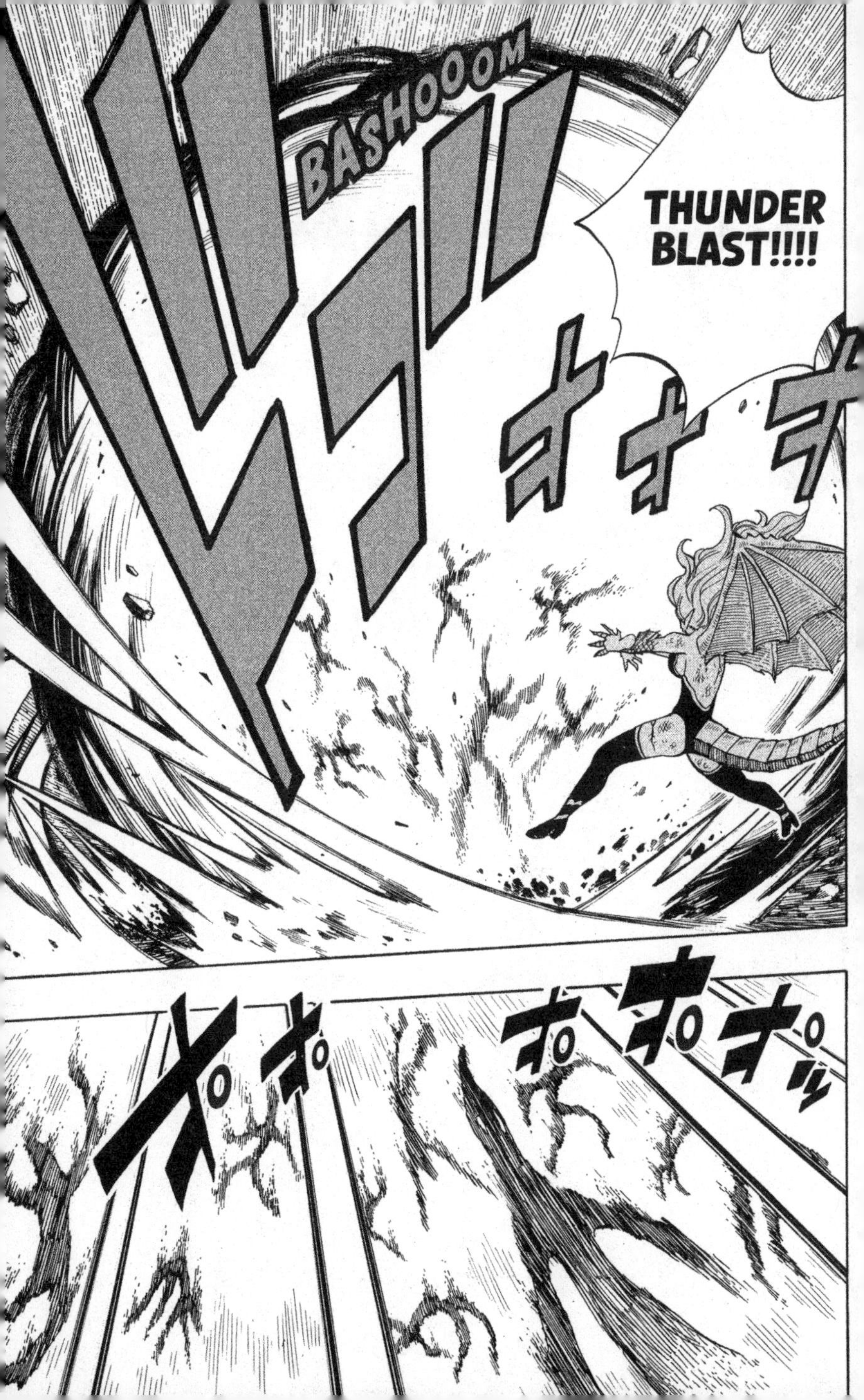
THUNDER BLAST!!!!
BASHOOOM

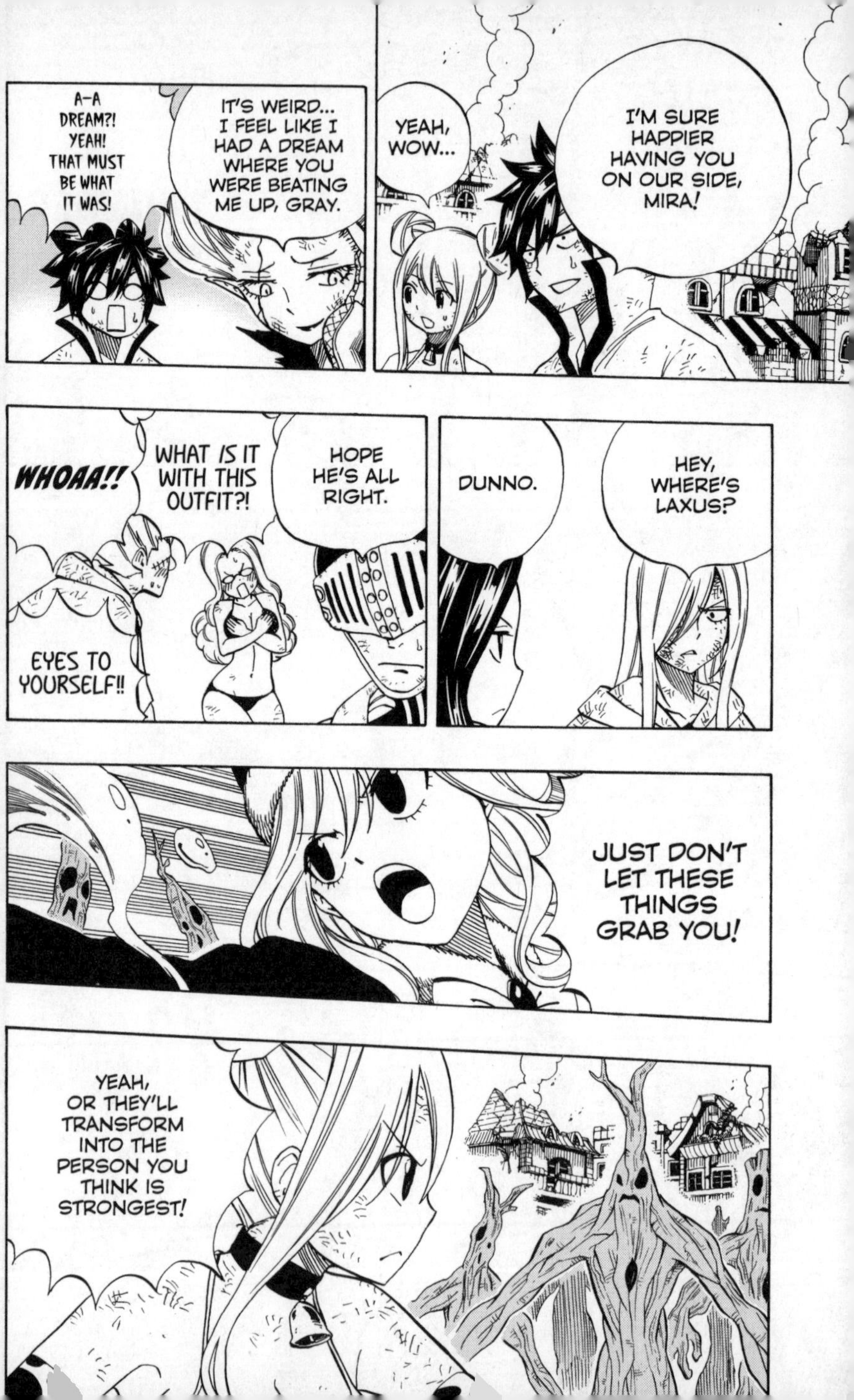
I'M SURE HAPPIER HAVING YOU ON OUR SIDE, MIRA!
YEAH, WOW...
IT'S WEIRD... I FEEL LIKE I HAD A DREAM WHERE YOU WERE BEATING ME UP, GRAY.
A-A DREAM?! YEAH! THAT MUST BE WHAT IT WAS!
HEY, WHERE'S LAXUS?
DUNNO.
HOPE HE'S ALL RIGHT.
WHAT *IS* IT WITH THIS OUTFIT?!
WHOAA!!
EYES TO YOURSELF!!
JUST DON'T LET THESE THINGS GRAB YOU!
YEAH, OR THEY'LL TRANSFORM INTO THE PERSON YOU THINK IS STRONGEST!

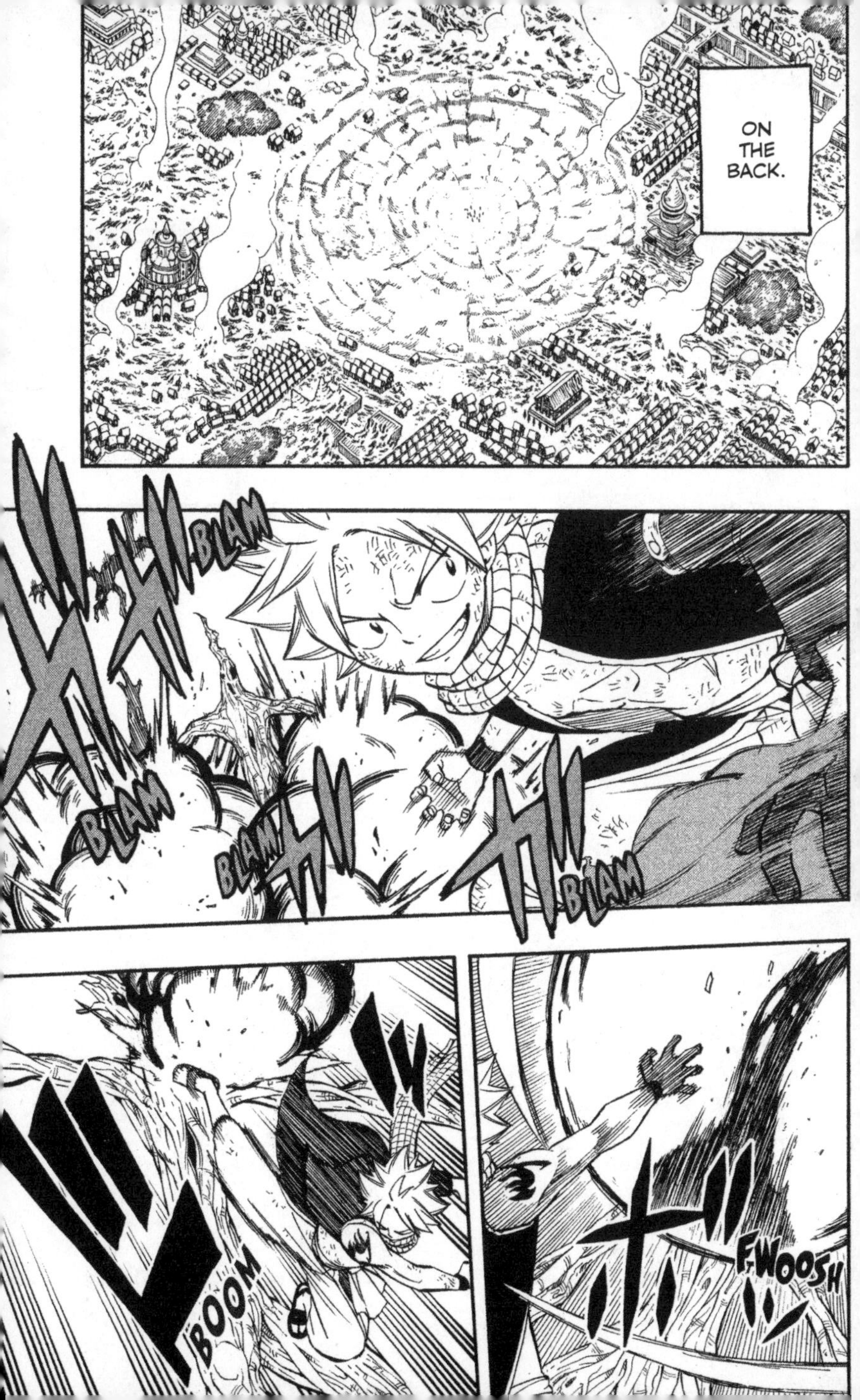

ON THE BACK.
BLAM
BLAM
BLAM
BLAM
FWOOSH
BOOM

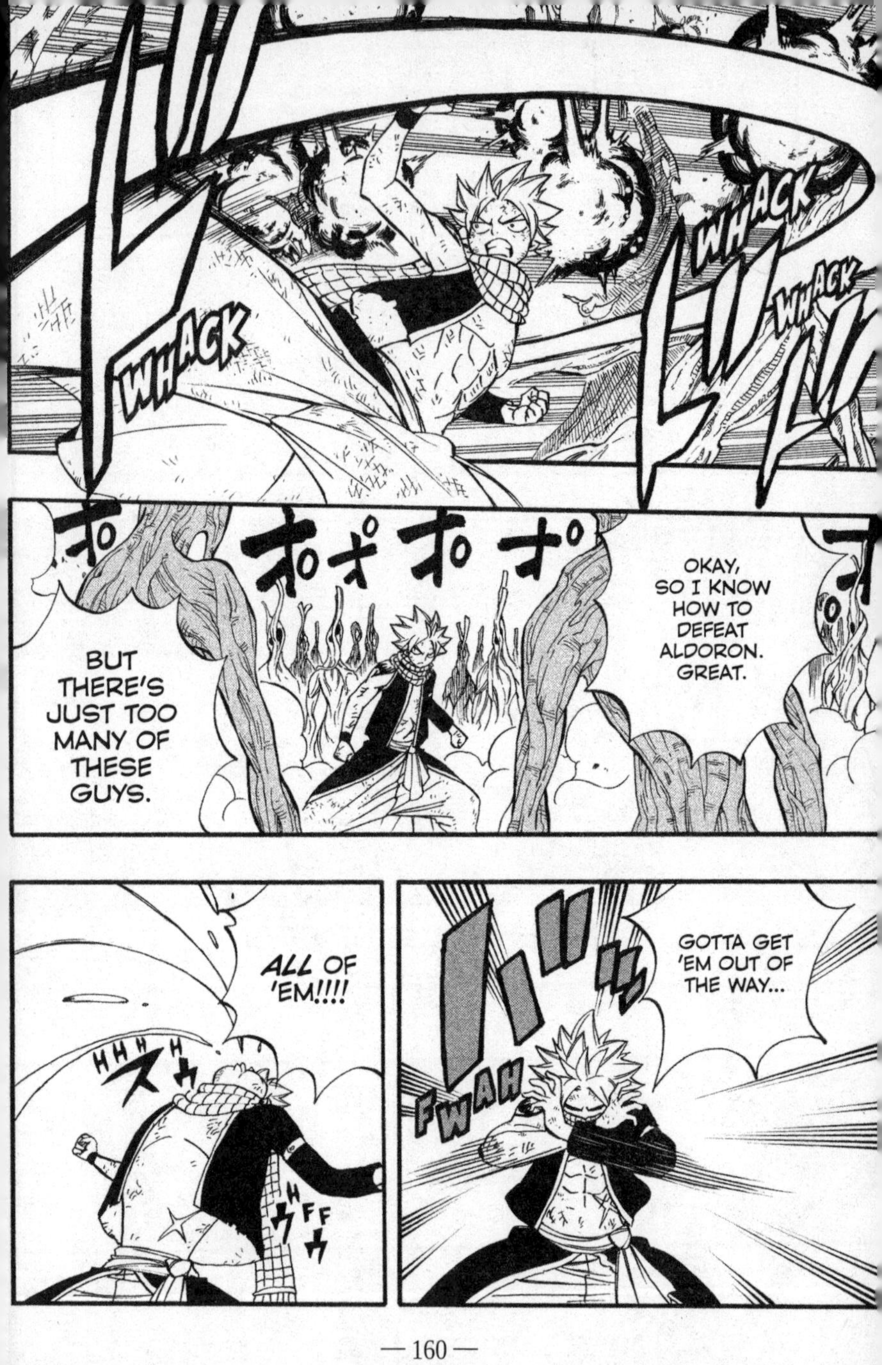

WHACK
WHACK
WHACK
OKAY, SO I KNOW HOW TO DEFEAT ALDORON. GREAT.
BUT THERE'S JUST TOO MANY OF THESE GUYS.
GOTTA GET 'EM OUT OF THE WAY...
FWAH
ALL OF 'EM!!!!

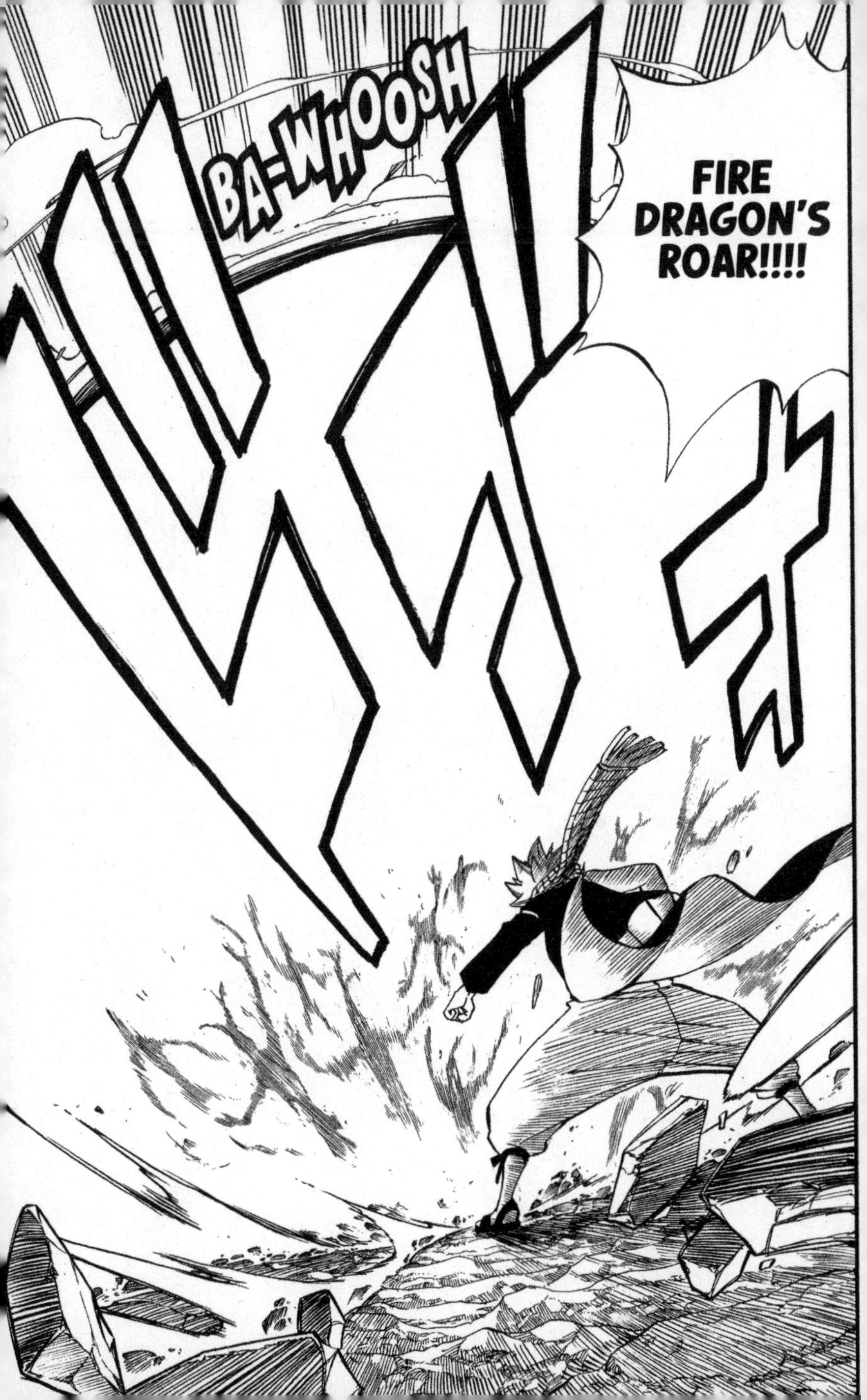
FIRE DRAGON'S ROAR!!!!
BA-WHOOSH

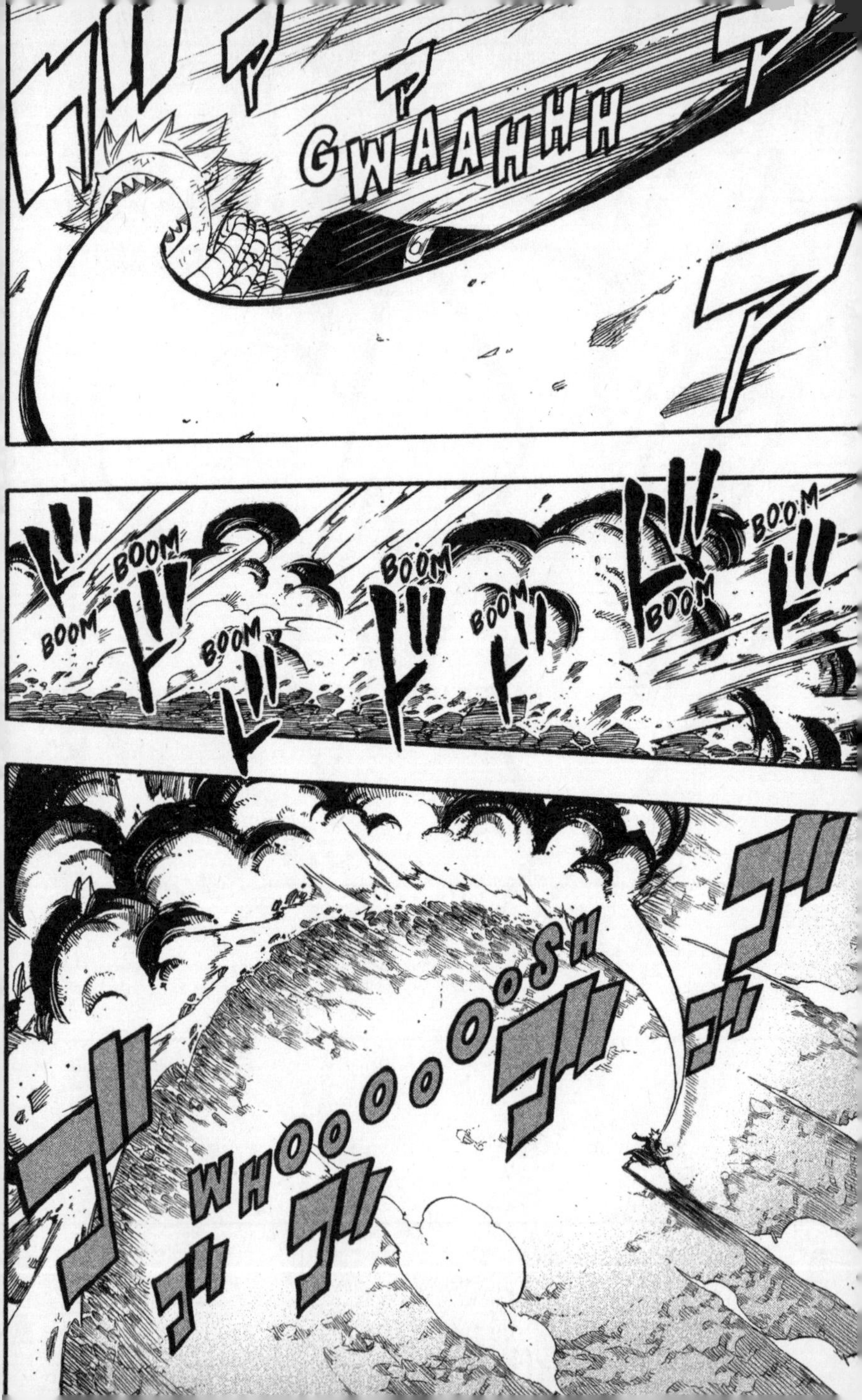
GWAAHHH
BOOM
BOOM
BOOM
BOOM
BOOM
BOOM
BOOM
WHOOOOOOSH

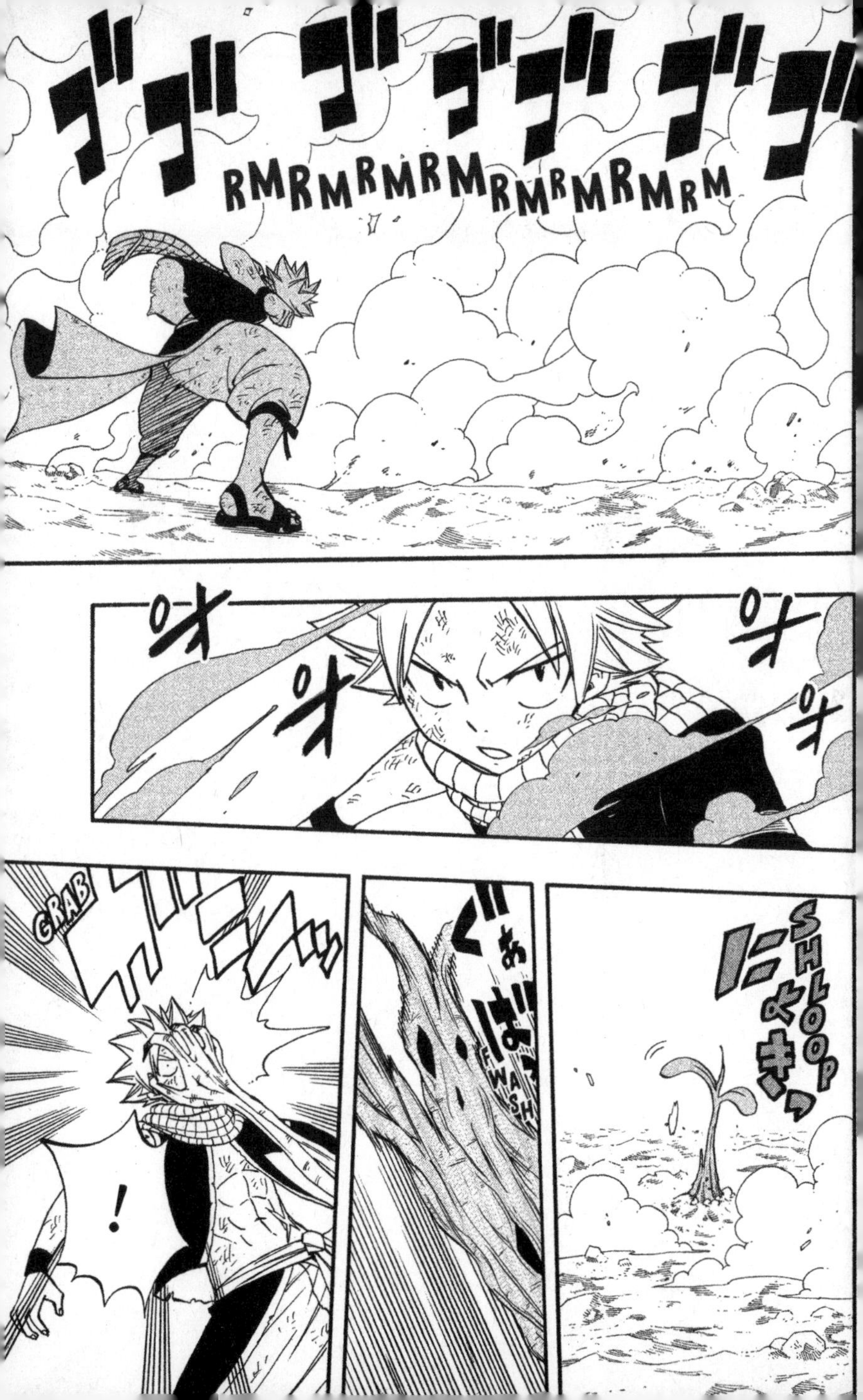
RMRMRMRMRMRMRMRMRM
SHLOOP
FWASH
GRAB
!

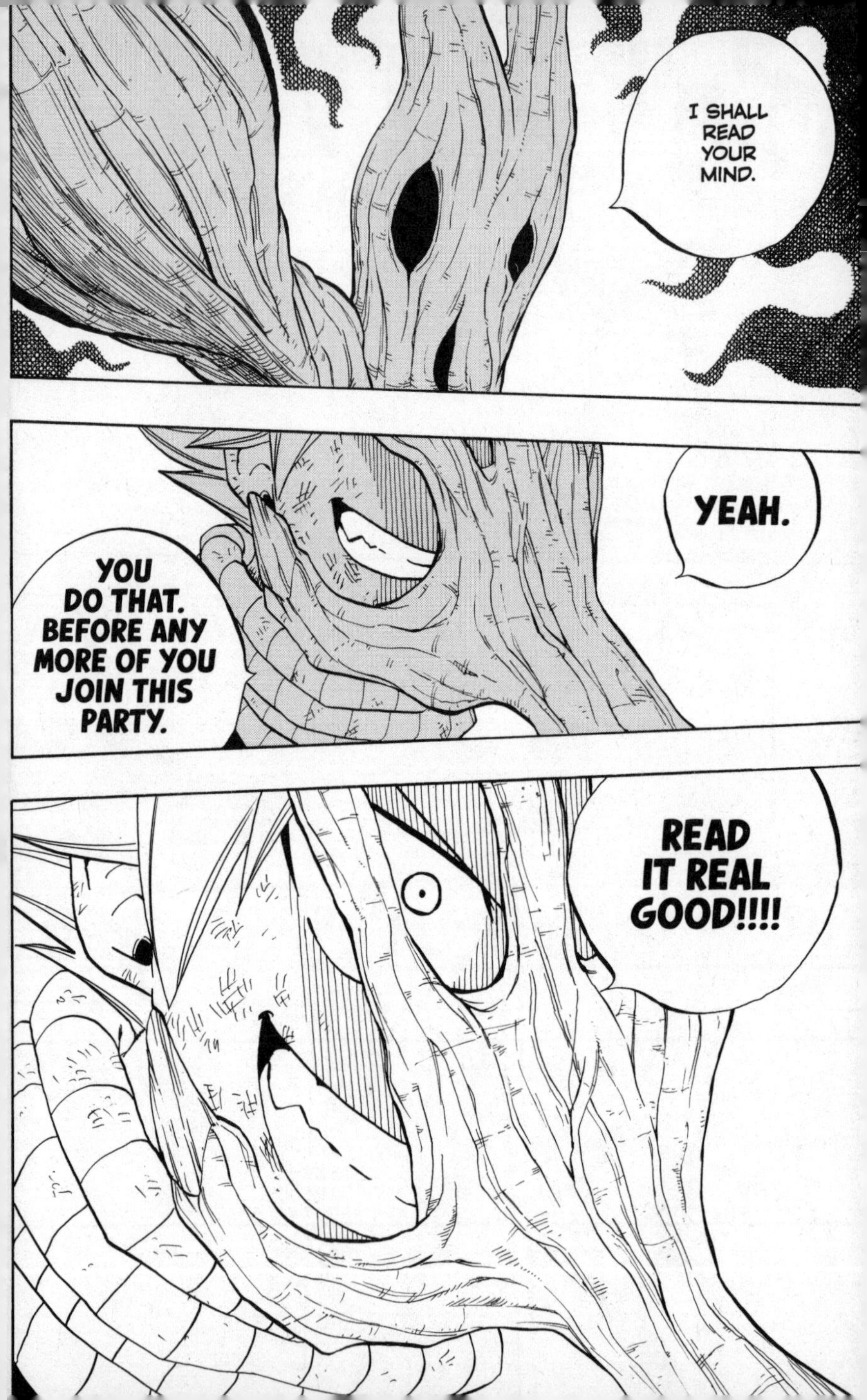
I SHALL READ YOUR MIND.
YEAH.
YOU DO THAT. BEFORE ANY MORE OF YOU JOIN THIS PARTY.
READ IT REAL GOOD!!!!

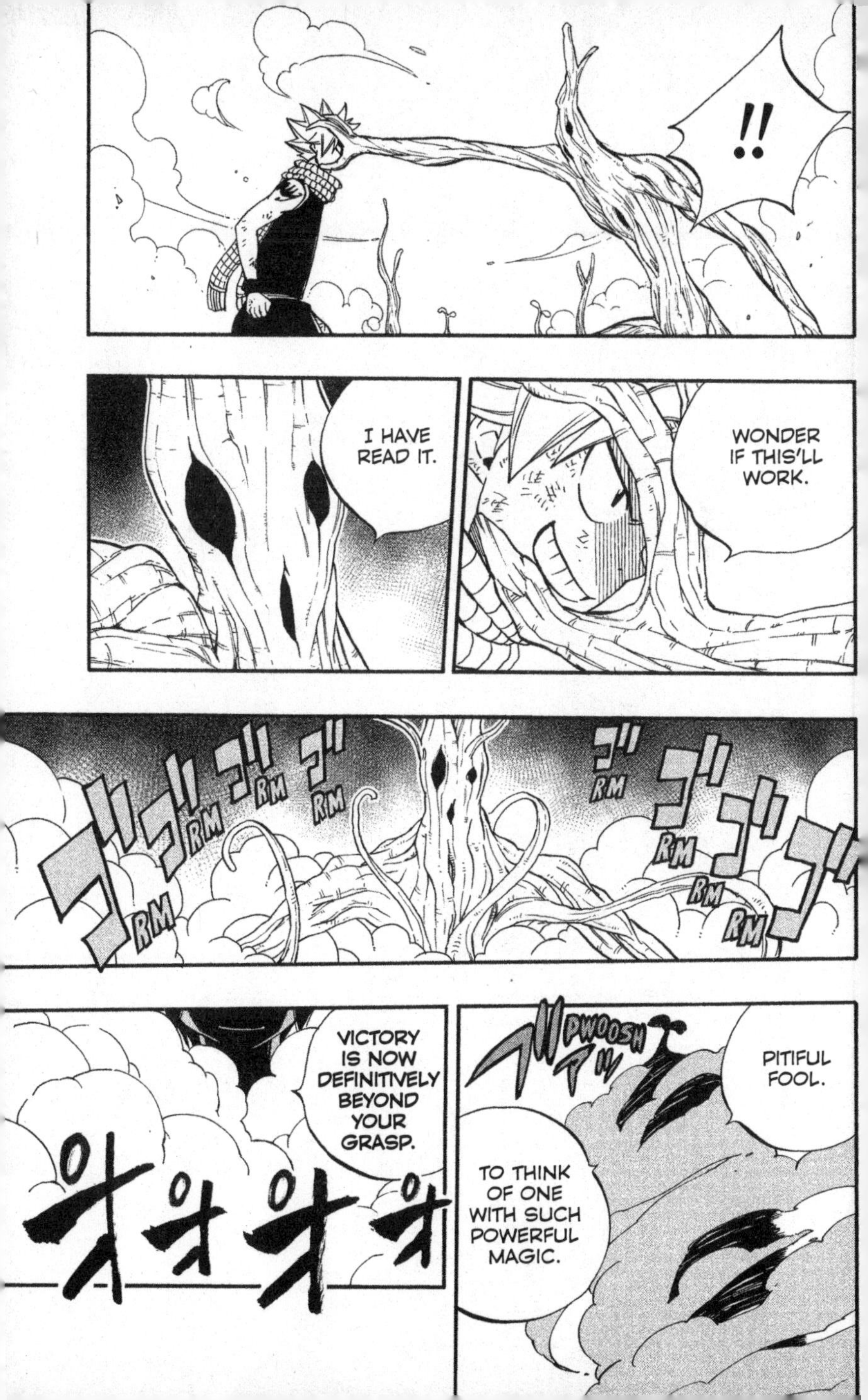
!!
WONDER IF THIS'LL WORK.
I HAVE READ IT.
RM RM RM RM RM RM RM RM RM
PITIFUL FOOL.
PWOOSH
TO THINK OF ONE WITH SUCH POWERFUL MAGIC.
VICTORY IS NOW DEFINITIVELY BEYOND YOUR GRASP.

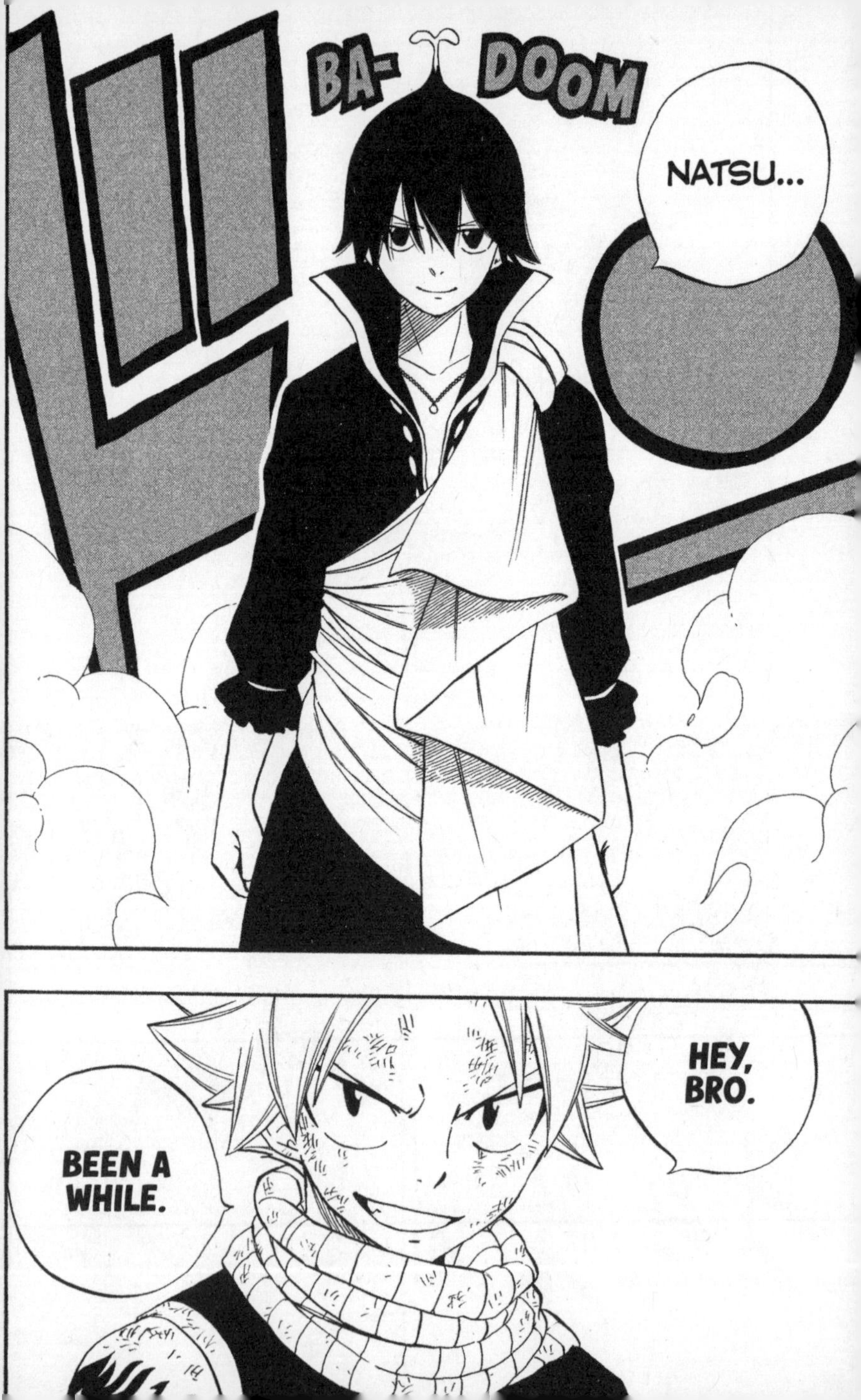
BA-DOOM
NATSU...
HEY, BRO.
BEEN A WHILE.

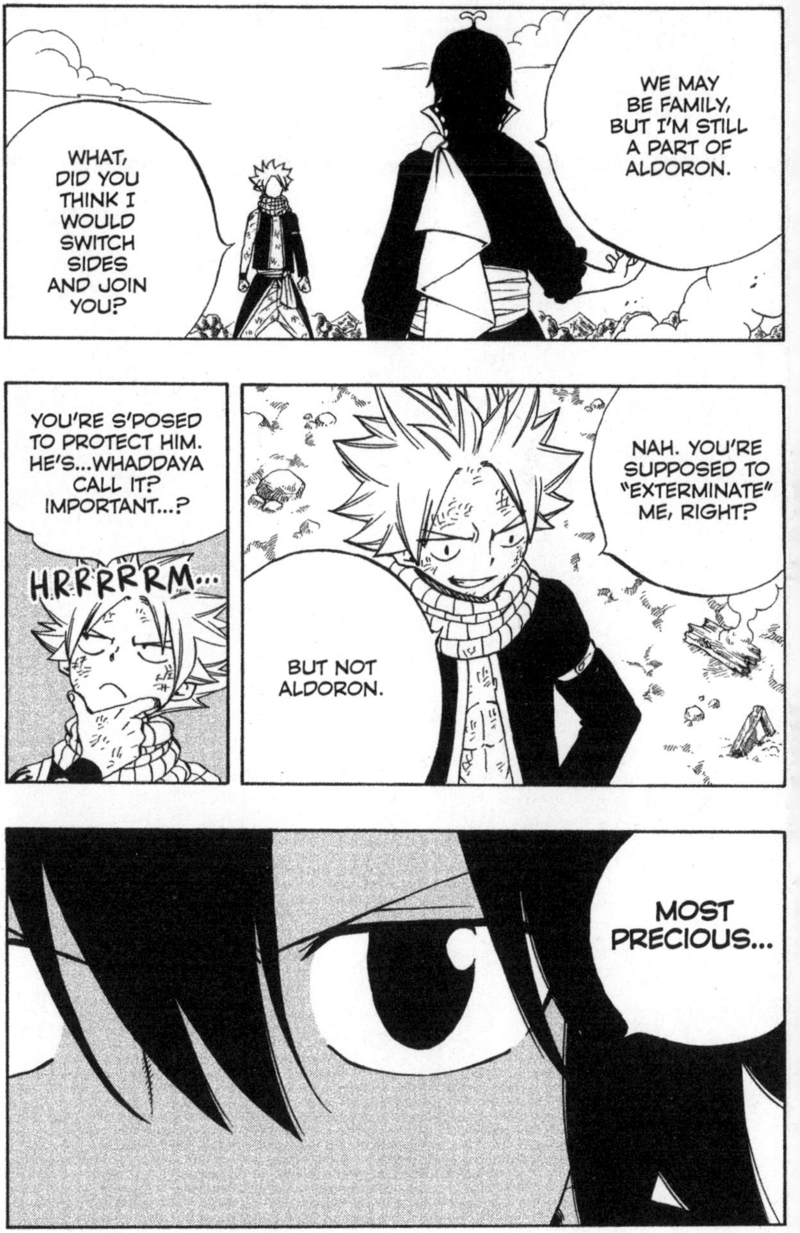
WE MAY BE FAMILY, BUT I'M STILL A PART OF ALDORON.
WHAT, DID YOU THINK I WOULD SWITCH SIDES AND JOIN YOU?
NAH. YOU'RE SUPPOSED TO "EXTERMINATE" ME, RIGHT?
BUT NOT ALDORON.
YOU'RE S'POSED TO PROTECT HIM. HE'S...WHADDAYA CALL IT? IMPORTANT...?
HRRRRRM...
MOST PRECIOUS...

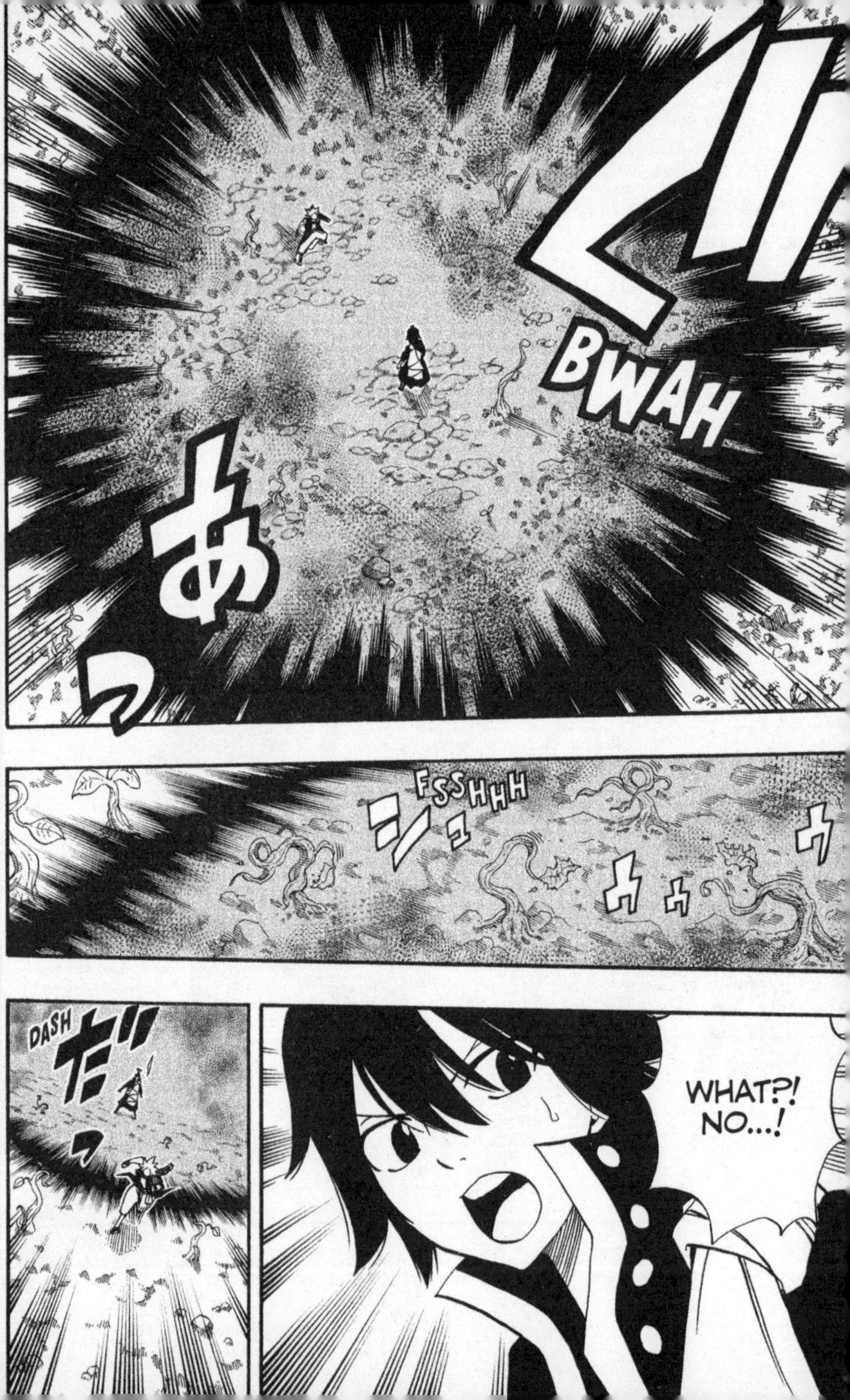
BWAH
FSSHHH
WHAT?! NO...!
DASH

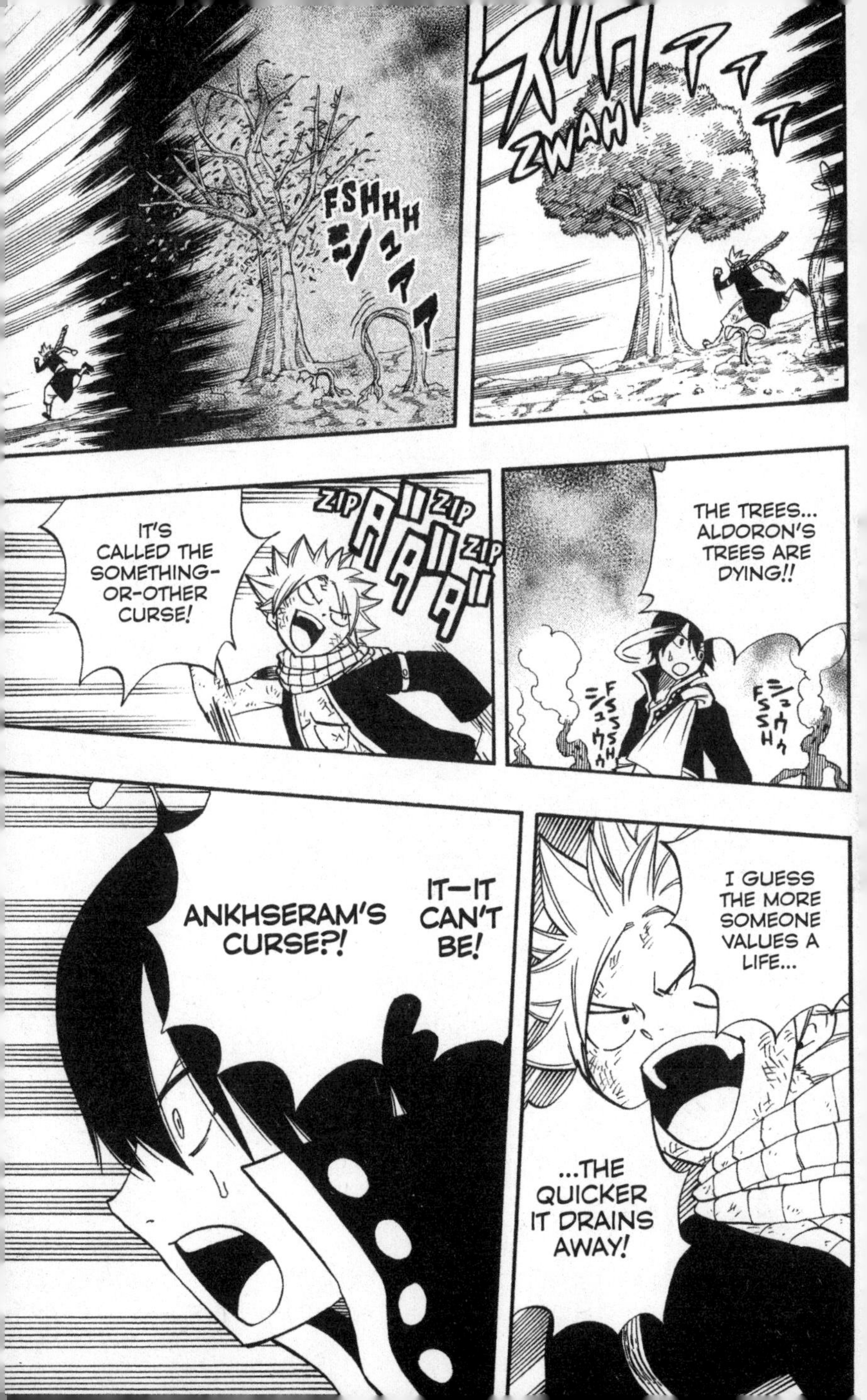
ZWAH
FSHHH
THE TREES... ALDORON'S TREES ARE DYING!!
FSSSH
FSSSH
ZIP
ZIP
ZIP
IT'S CALLED THE SOMETHING-OR-OTHER CURSE!
I GUESS THE MORE SOMEONE VALUES A LIFE...
...THE QUICKER IT DRAINS AWAY!
IT—IT CAN'T BE!
ANKHSERAM'S CURSE?!

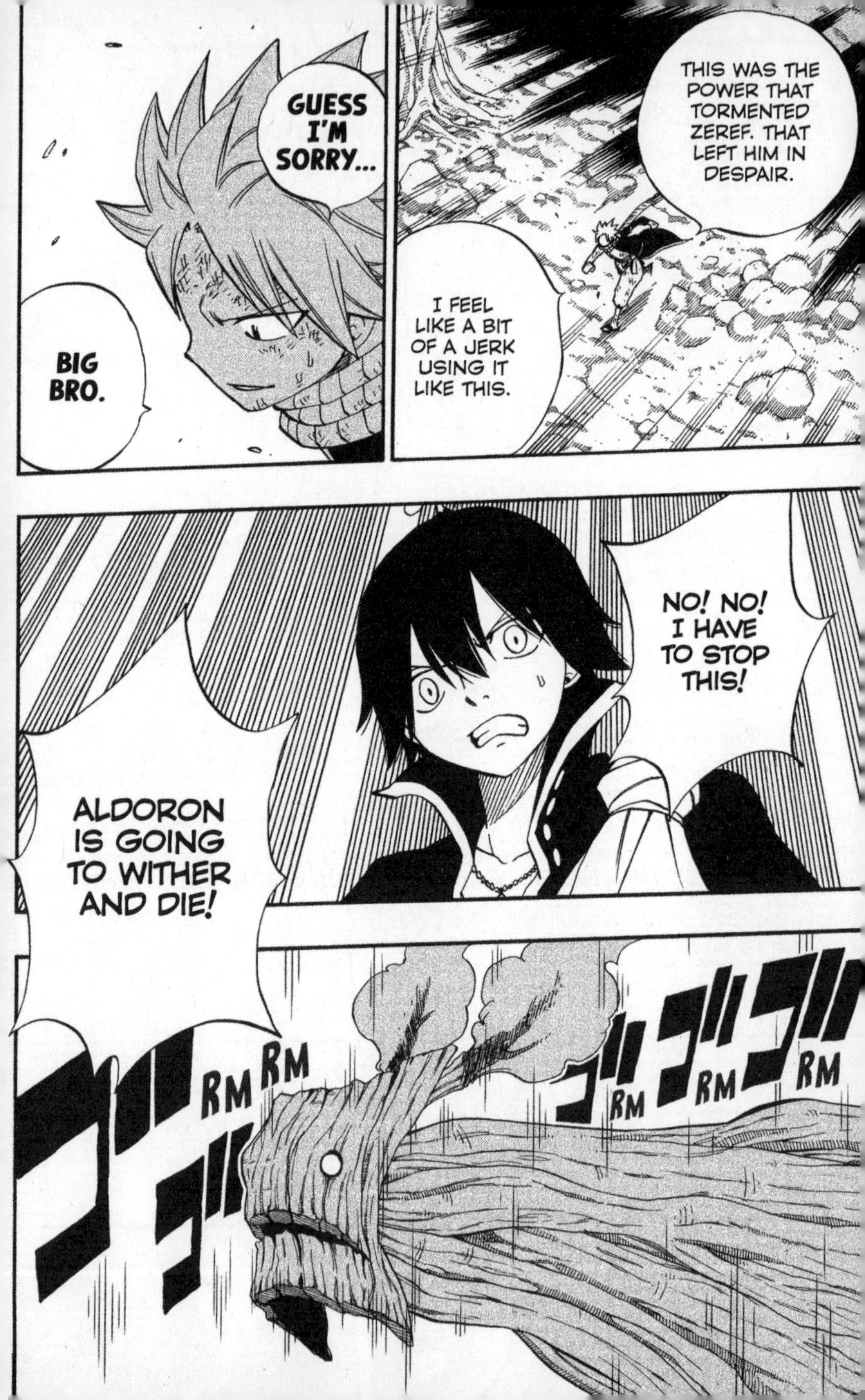
THIS WAS THE POWER THAT TORMENTED ZEREF. THAT LEFT HIM IN DESPAIR.
I FEEL LIKE A BIT OF A JERK USING IT LIKE THIS.
GUESS I'M SORRY...
BIG BRO.
NO! NO! I HAVE TO STOP THIS!
ALDORON IS GOING TO WITHER AND DIE!
RM RM RM RM
RM RM

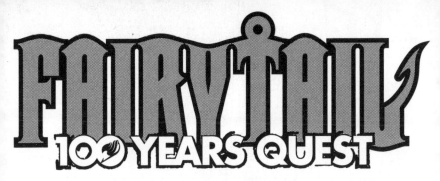

FAIRY TAIL
100 YEARS QUEST

Chapter 54: God Seeds

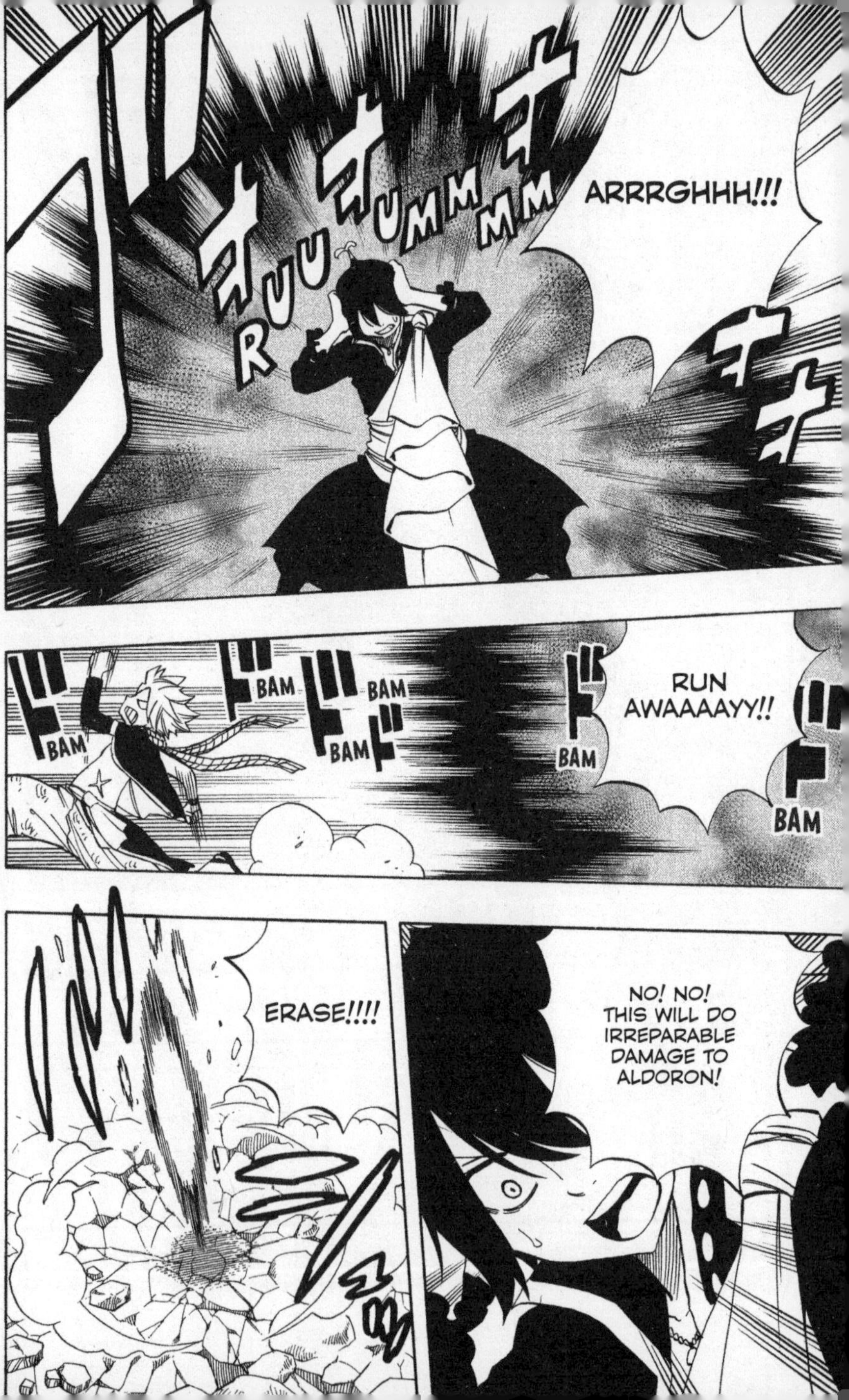
RUUUMMMMM
ARRRGHHH!!!
BAM
BAM
RUN AWAAAAYY!!
BAM
BAM
BAM
BAM
NO! NO! THIS WILL DO IRREPARABLE DAMAGE TO ALDORON!
ERASE!!!!

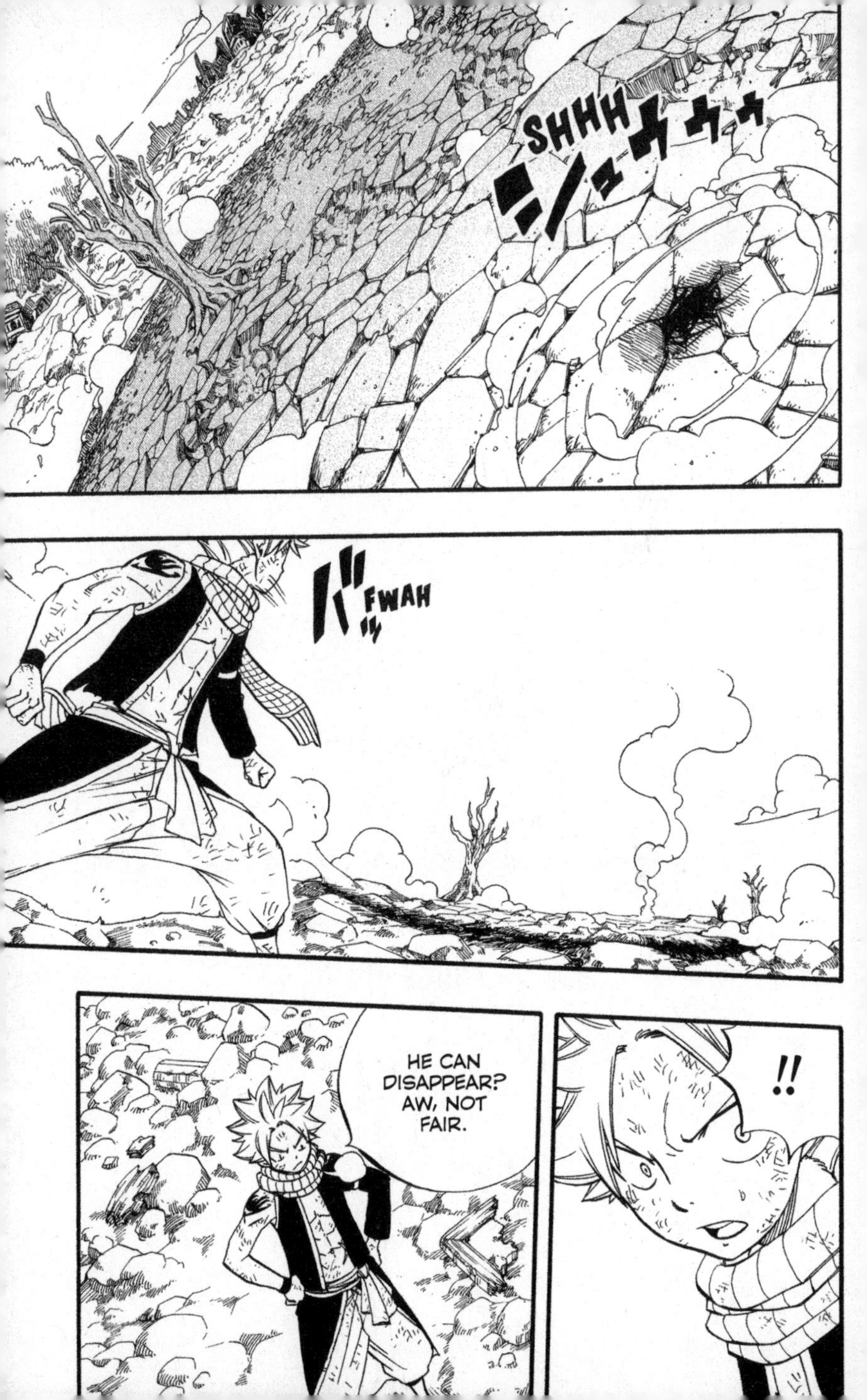
SHHH
FWAH
!!
HE CAN DISAPPEAR? AW, NOT FAIR.

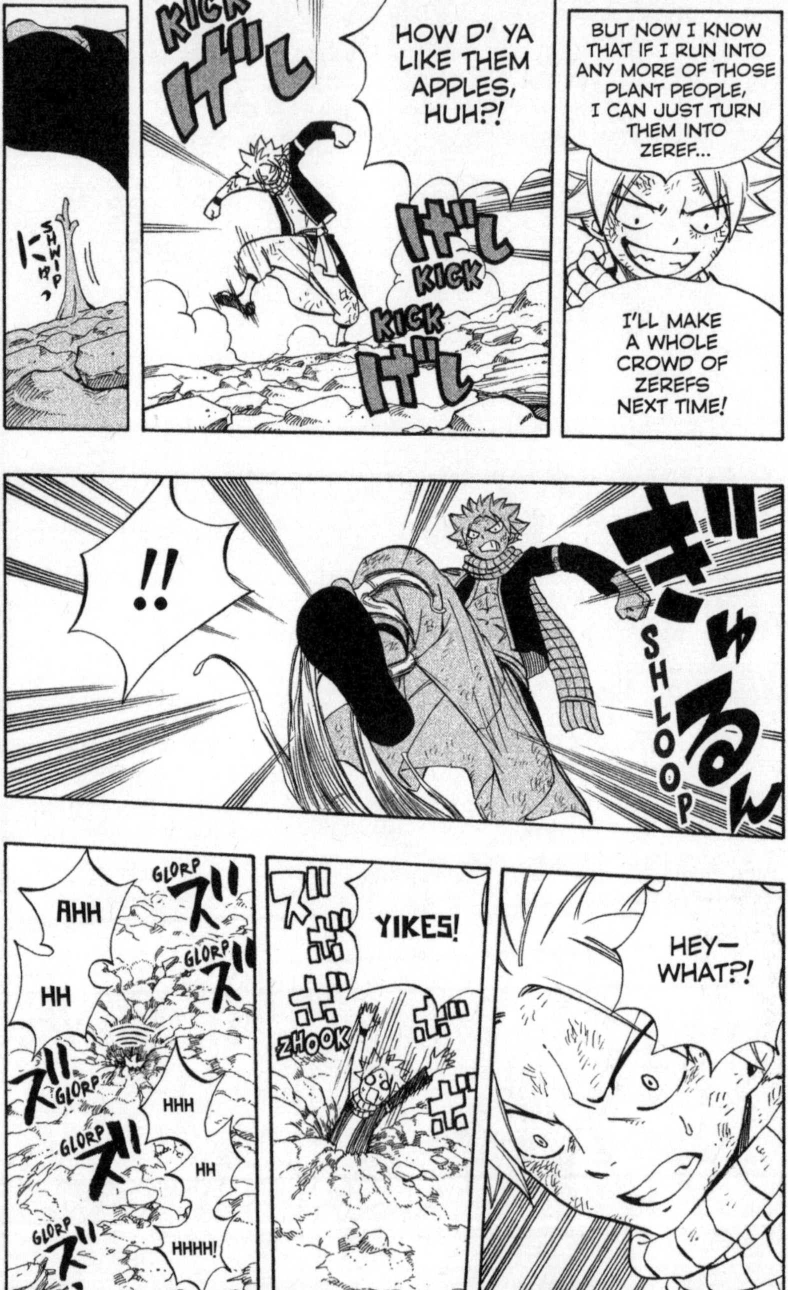
BUT NOW I KNOW THAT IF I RUN INTO ANY MORE OF THOSE PLANT PEOPLE, I CAN JUST TURN THEM INTO ZEREF...
I'LL MAKE A WHOLE CROWD OF ZEREFS NEXT TIME!
KICK
HOW D' YA LIKE THEM APPLES, HUH?!
KICK
KICK
SHWIP
SHLOOP
!!
HEY—WHAT?!
YIKES!
ZHOOK
GLORP
AHH
GLORP
HH
GLORP
HHH
GLORP
HH
GLORP
HHHH!

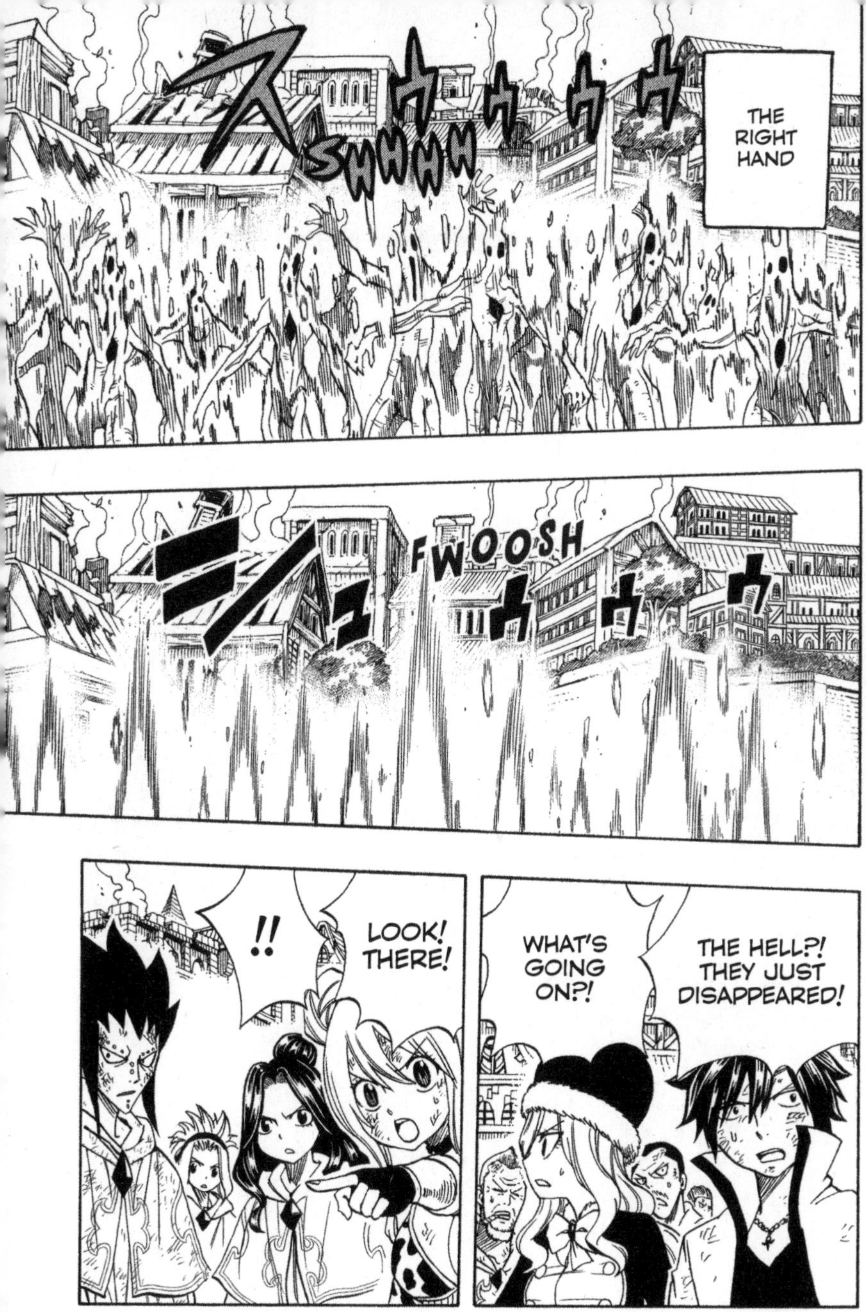
THE RIGHT HAND
SHHHH
FWOOSH
THE HELL?! THEY JUST DISAPPEARED!
WHAT'S GOING ON?!
LOOK! THERE!
!!

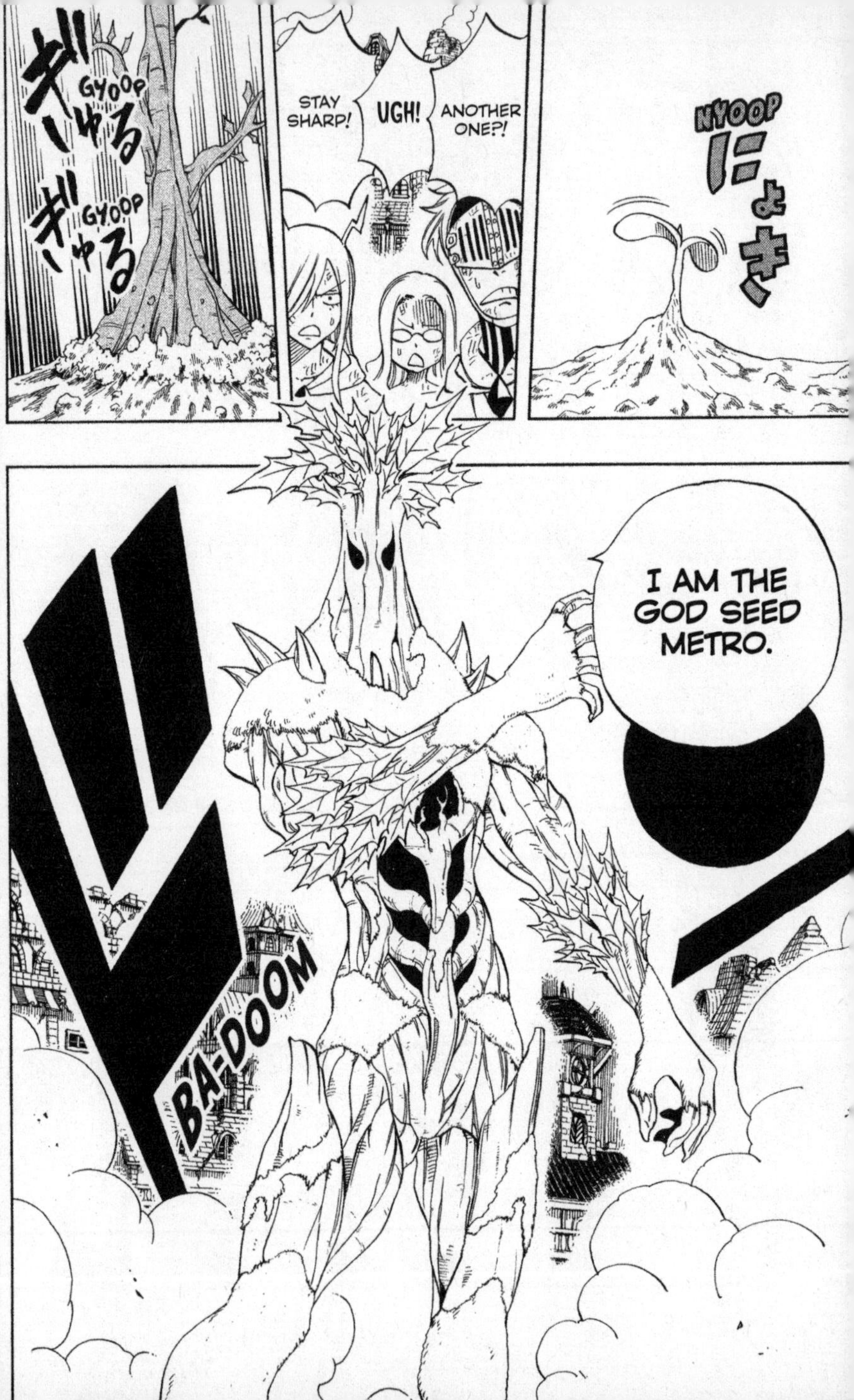
NYOOP
にょき
ANOTHER ONE?!
UGH!
STAY SHARP!
GYOOP
ぎゅる
GYOOP
ぎゅる
I AM THE GOD SEED METRO.
BA-DOOM

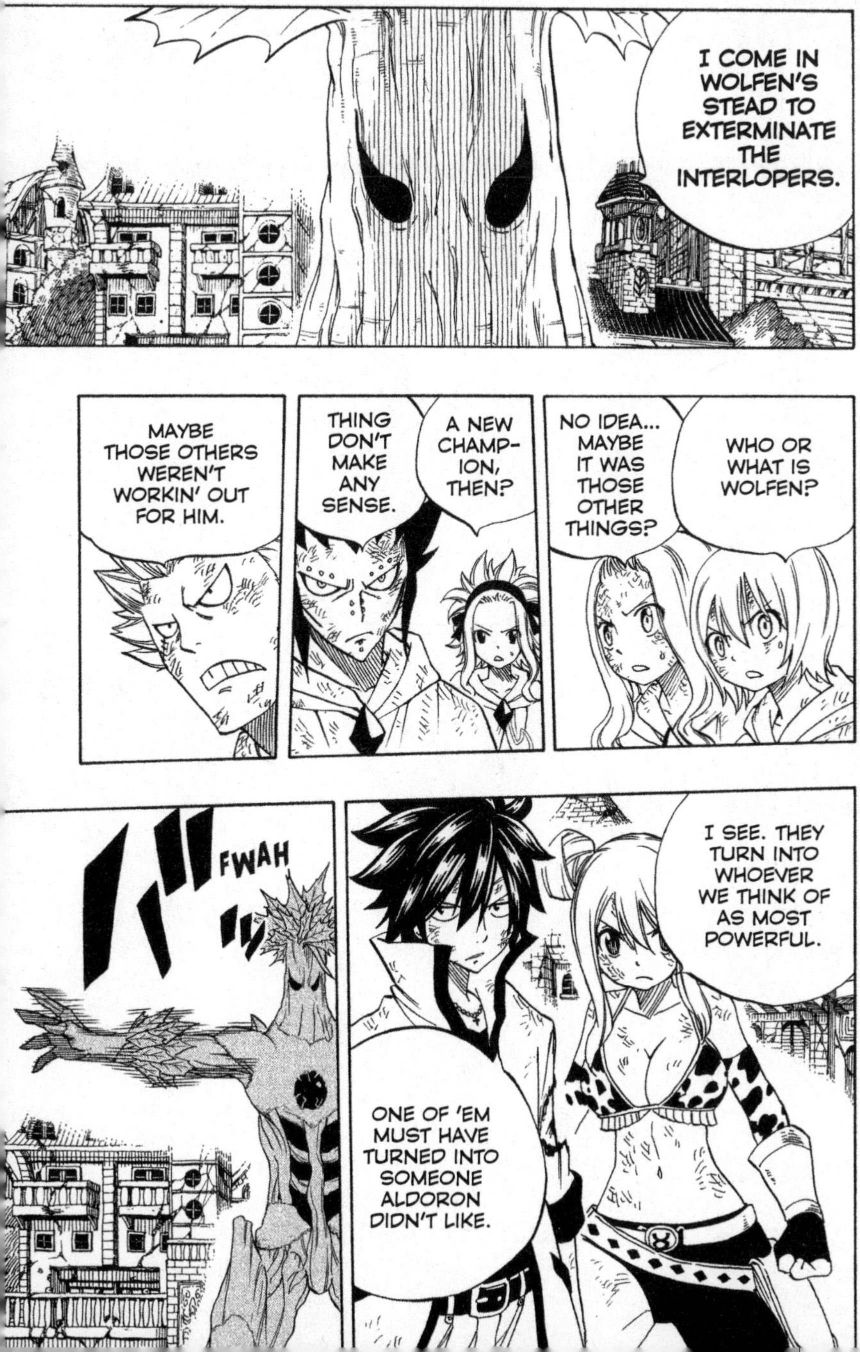
I COME IN WOLFEN'S STEAD TO EXTERMINATE THE INTERLOPERS.
WHO OR WHAT IS WOLFEN?
NO IDEA... MAYBE IT WAS THOSE OTHER THINGS?
A NEW CHAMPION, THEN?
THING DON'T MAKE ANY SENSE.
MAYBE THOSE OTHERS WEREN'T WORKIN' OUT FOR HIM.
I SEE. THEY TURN INTO WHOEVER WE THINK OF AS MOST POWERFUL.
ONE OF 'EM MUST HAVE TURNED INTO SOMEONE ALDORON DIDN'T LIKE.
FWAH

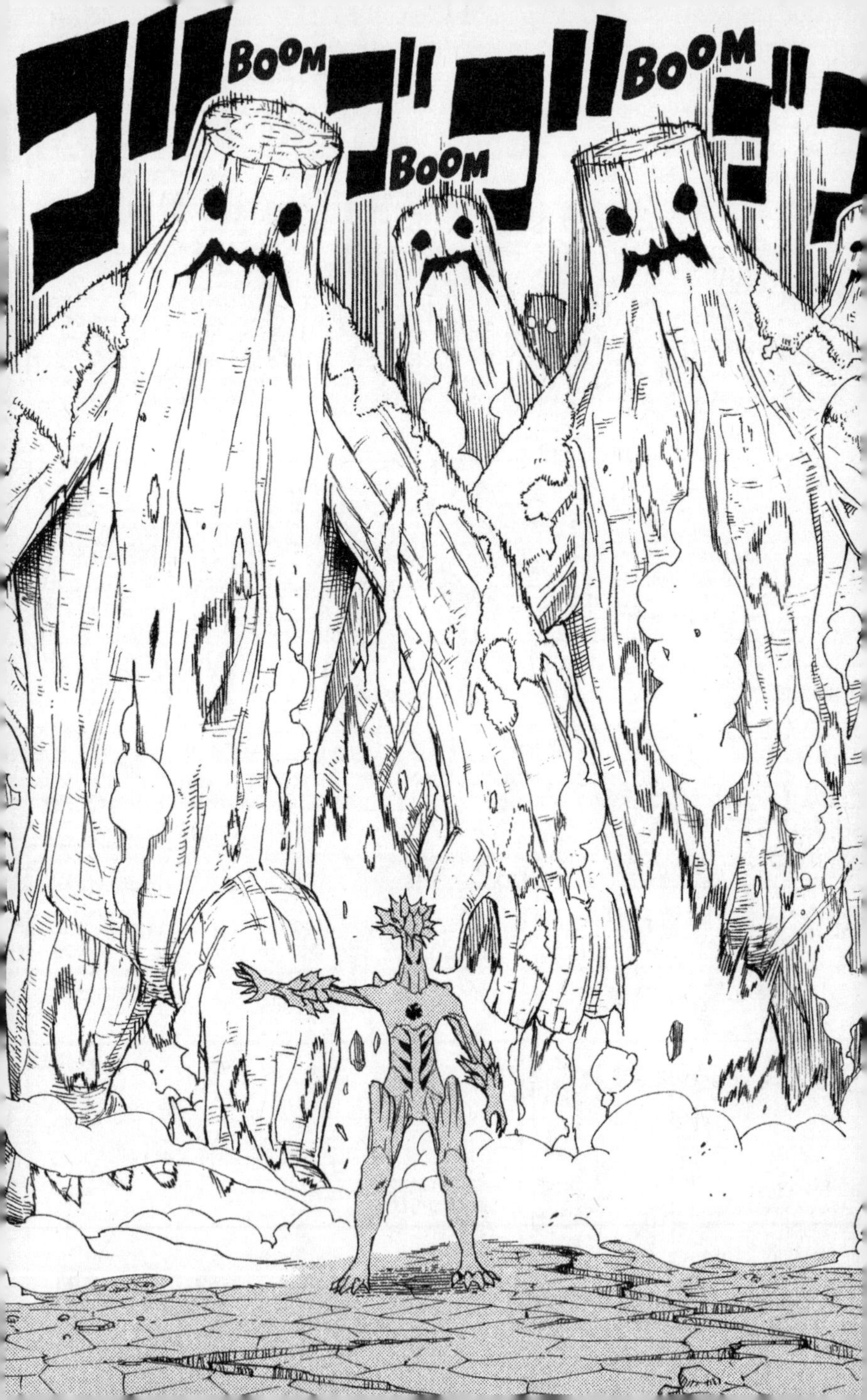
BOOM
BOOM
BOOM

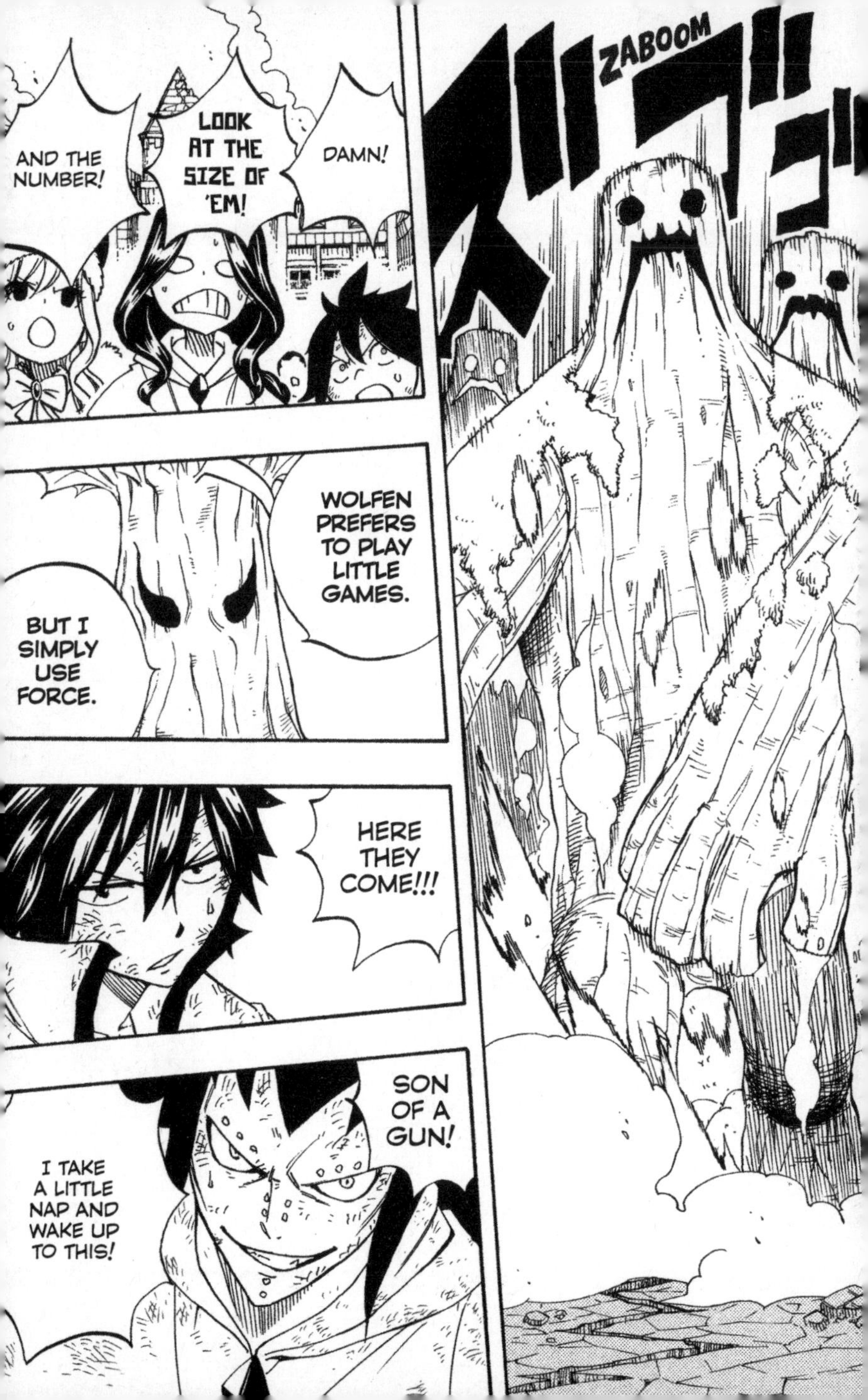
ZABOOM
DAMN!
LOOK AT THE SIZE OF 'EM!
AND THE NUMBER!
WOLFEN PREFERS TO PLAY LITTLE GAMES.
BUT I SIMPLY USE FORCE.
HERE THEY COME!!!
SON OF A GUN!
I TAKE A LITTLE NAP AND WAKE UP TO THIS!

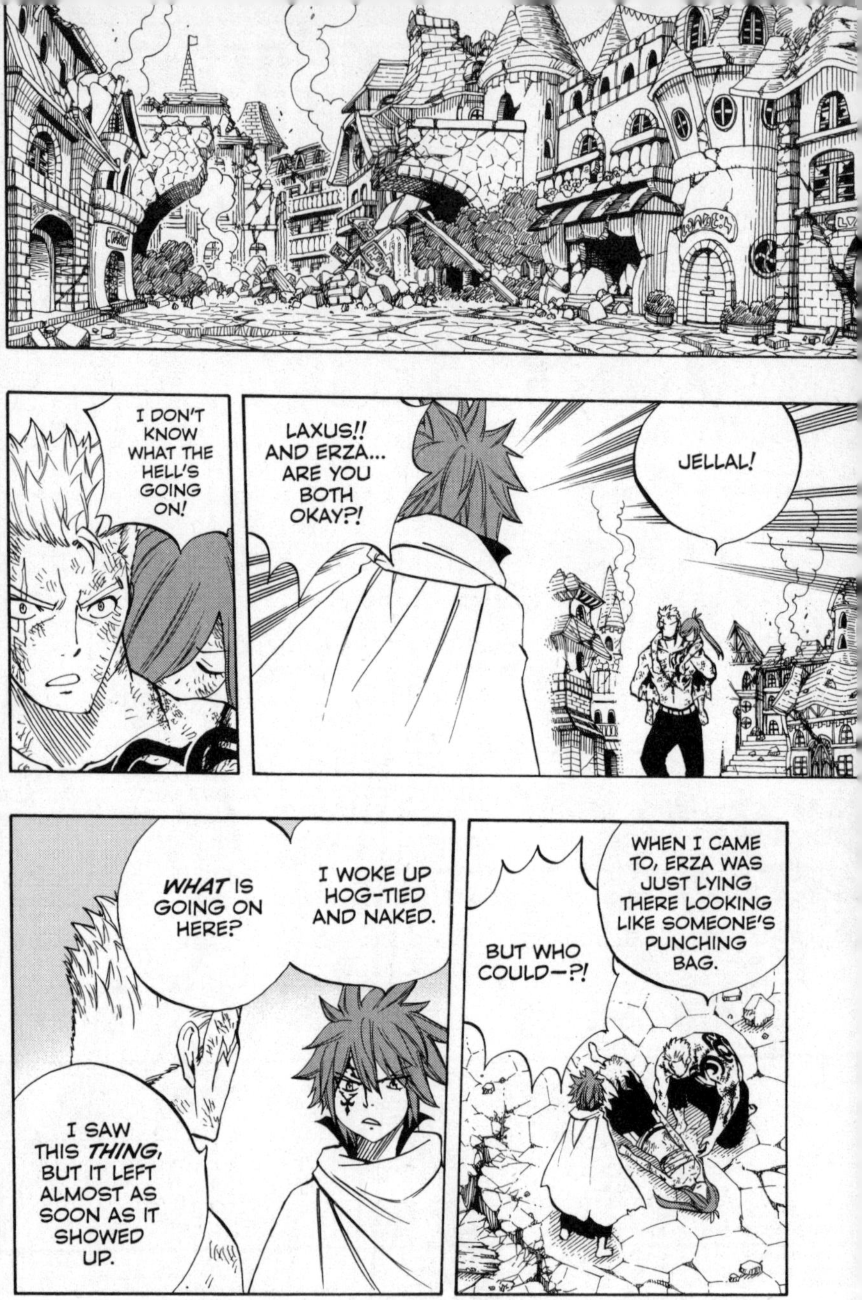
JELLAL!
LAXUS!! AND ERZA... ARE YOU BOTH OKAY?!
I DON'T KNOW WHAT THE HELL'S GOING ON!
WHEN I CAME TO, ERZA WAS JUST LYING THERE LOOKING LIKE SOMEONE'S PUNCHING BAG.
BUT WHO COULD—?!
I WOKE UP HOG-TIED AND NAKED.
WHAT IS GOING ON HERE?
I SAW THIS *THING*, BUT IT LEFT ALMOST AS SOON AS IT SHOWED UP.

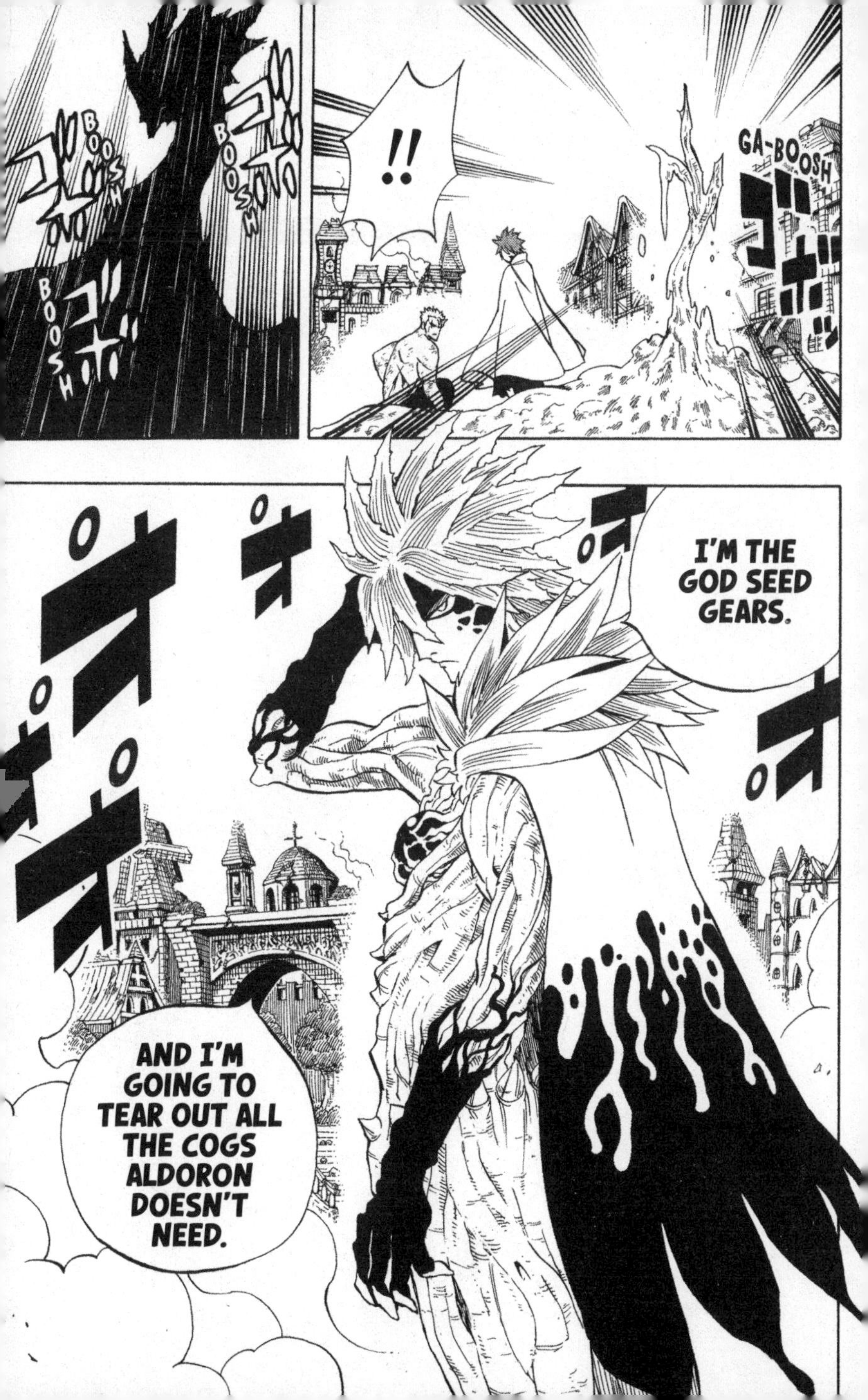
GA-BOOSH
!!
BOOSH
BOOSH
BOOSH
I'M THE GOD SEED GEARS.
AND I'M GOING TO TEAR OUT ALL THE COGS ALDORON DOESN'T NEED.

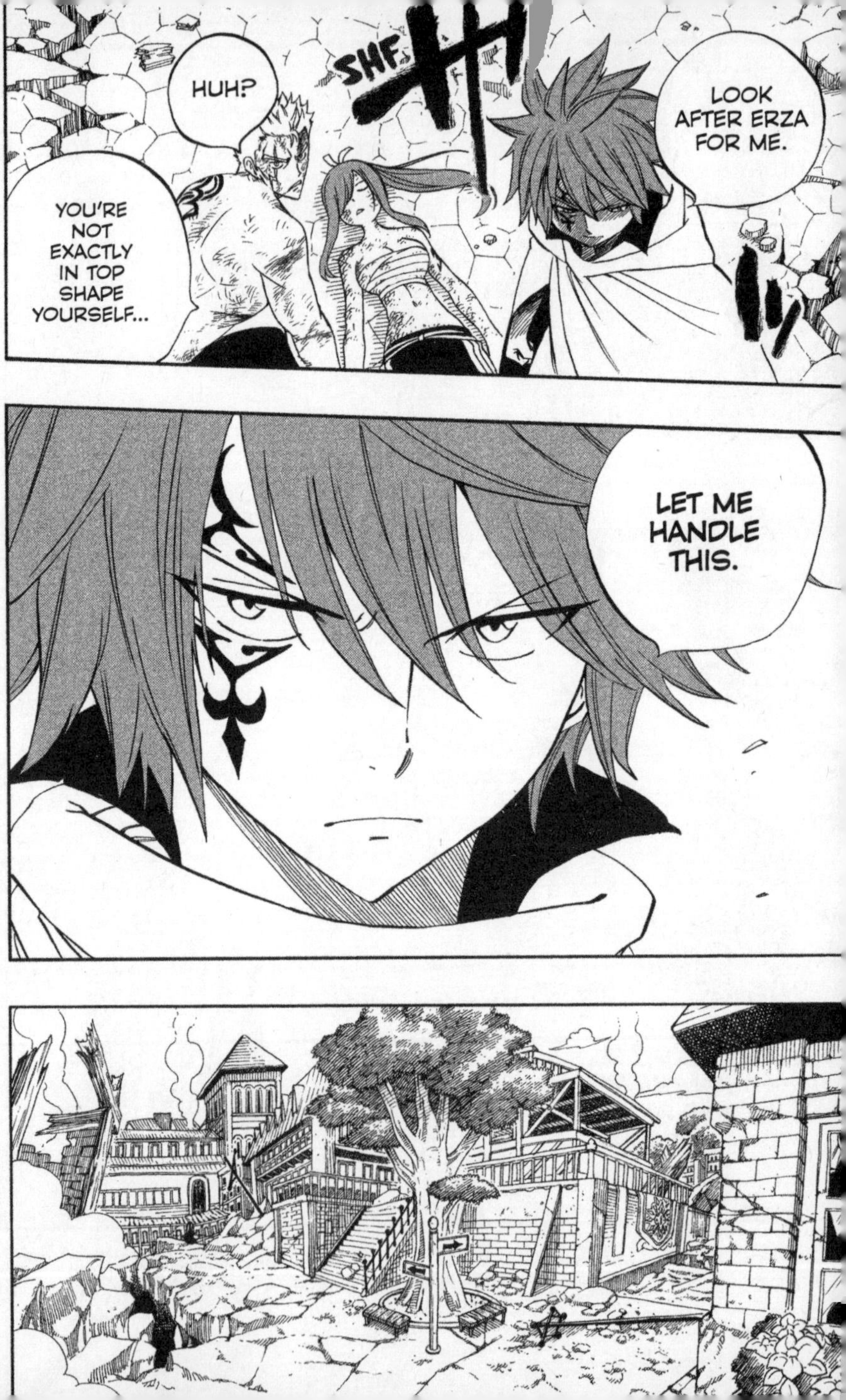
LOOK AFTER ERZA FOR ME.
SHF
HUH?
YOU'RE NOT EXACTLY IN TOP SHAPE YOURSELF...
LET ME HANDLE THIS.

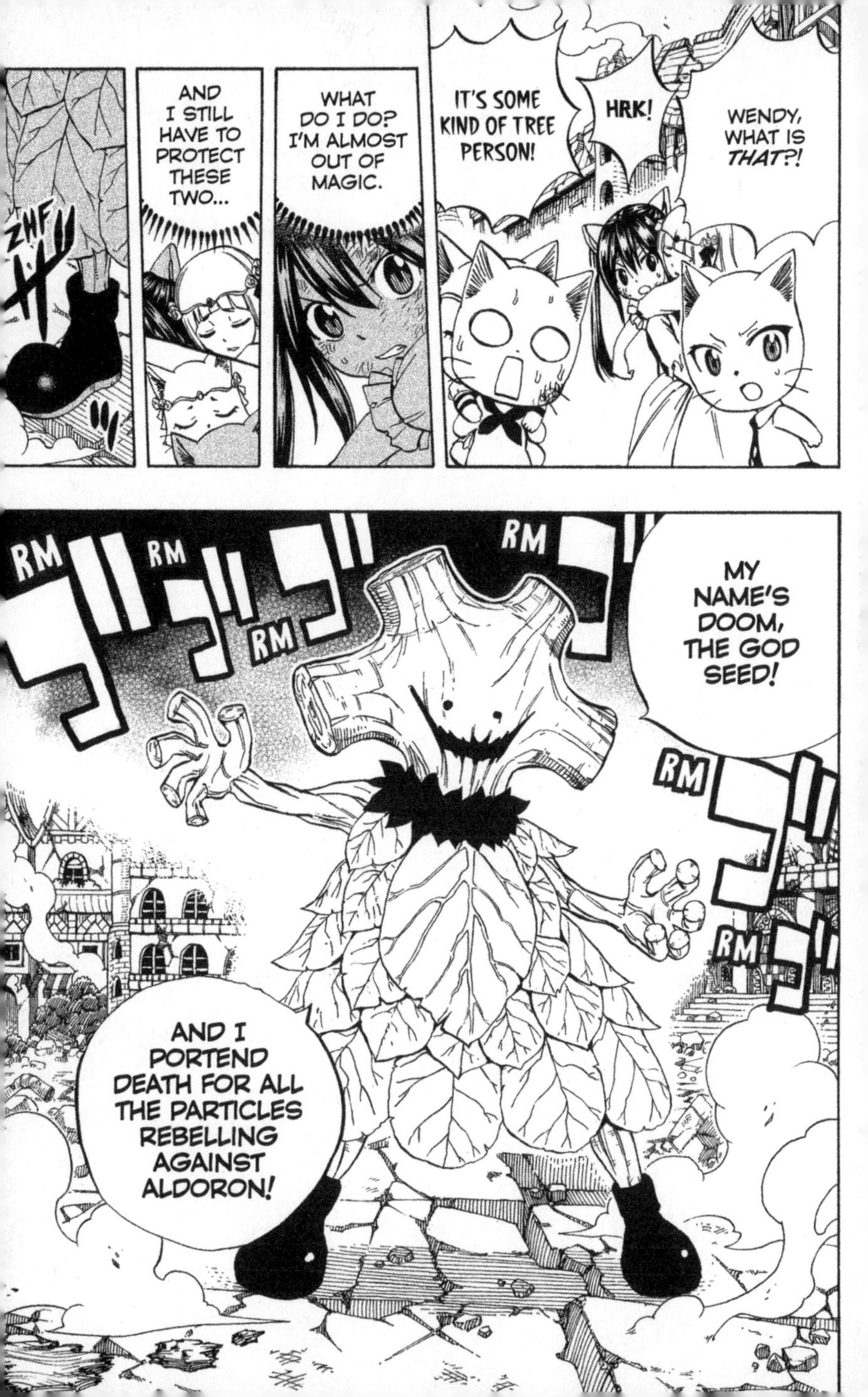

WENDY, WHAT IS *THAT*?!
HRK!
IT'S SOME KIND OF TREE PERSON!
WHAT DO I DO? I'M ALMOST OUT OF MAGIC.
AND I STILL HAVE TO PROTECT THESE TWO...
ZHF
RM
MY NAME'S DOOM, THE GOD SEED!
RM
RM
RM
RM
RM
RM
AND I PORTEND DEATH FOR ALL THE PARTICLES REBELLING AGAINST ALDORON!

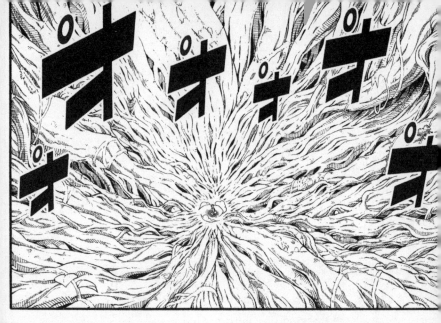

IS THIS ALDORON'S STOMACH?

WHERE AM I?

!!

WITHIN THE FIVE ORBS RESIDED FIVE GUARDIAN SPIRITS.

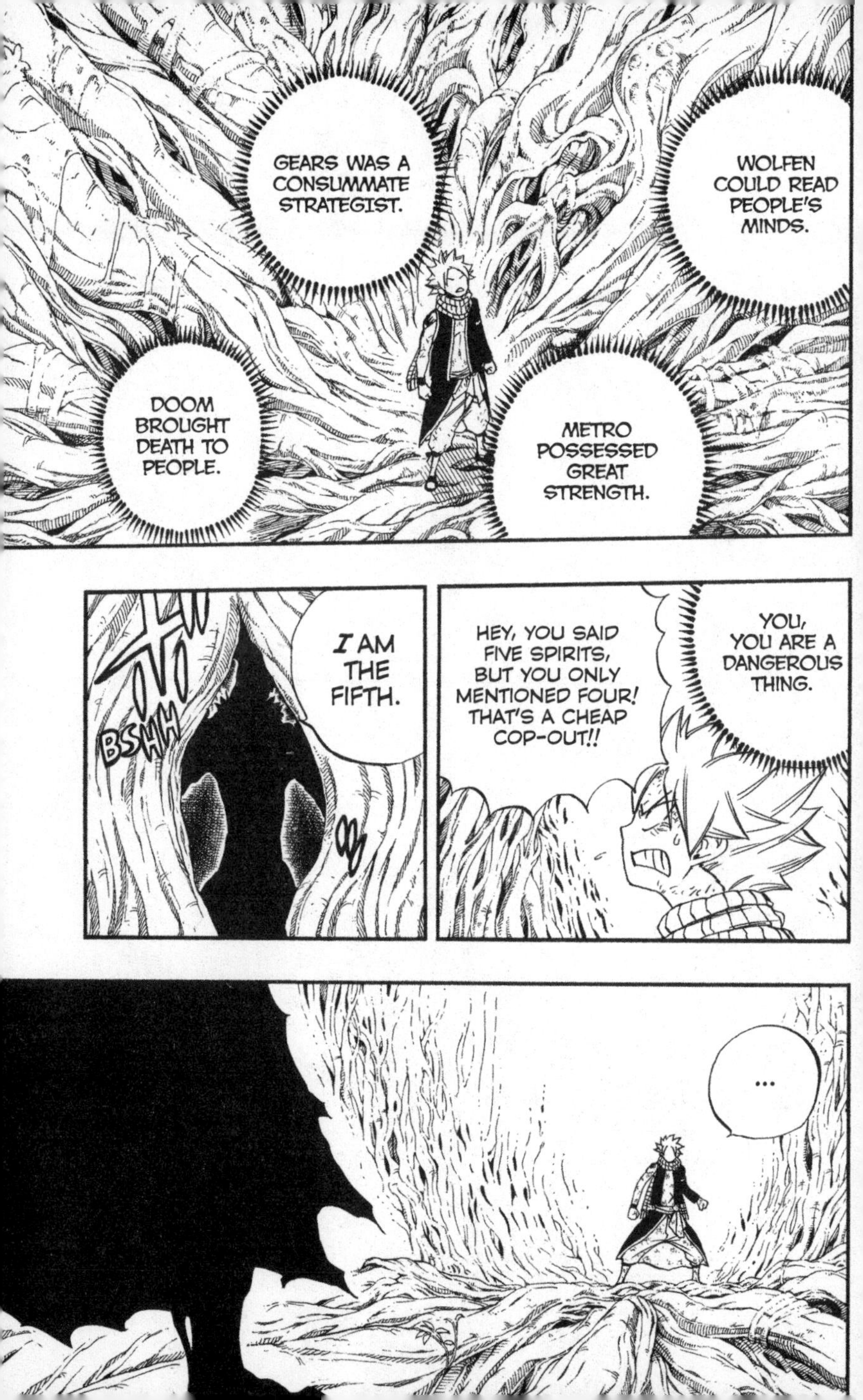
WOLFEN COULD READ PEOPLE'S MINDS.
GEARS WAS A CONSUMMATE STRATEGIST.
METRO POSSESSED GREAT STRENGTH.
DOOM BROUGHT DEATH TO PEOPLE.
YOU, YOU ARE A DANGEROUS THING.
HEY, YOU SAID FIVE SPIRITS, BUT YOU ONLY MENTIONED FOUR! THAT'S A CHEAP COP-OUT!!
I AM THE FIFTH.
BSHH
...

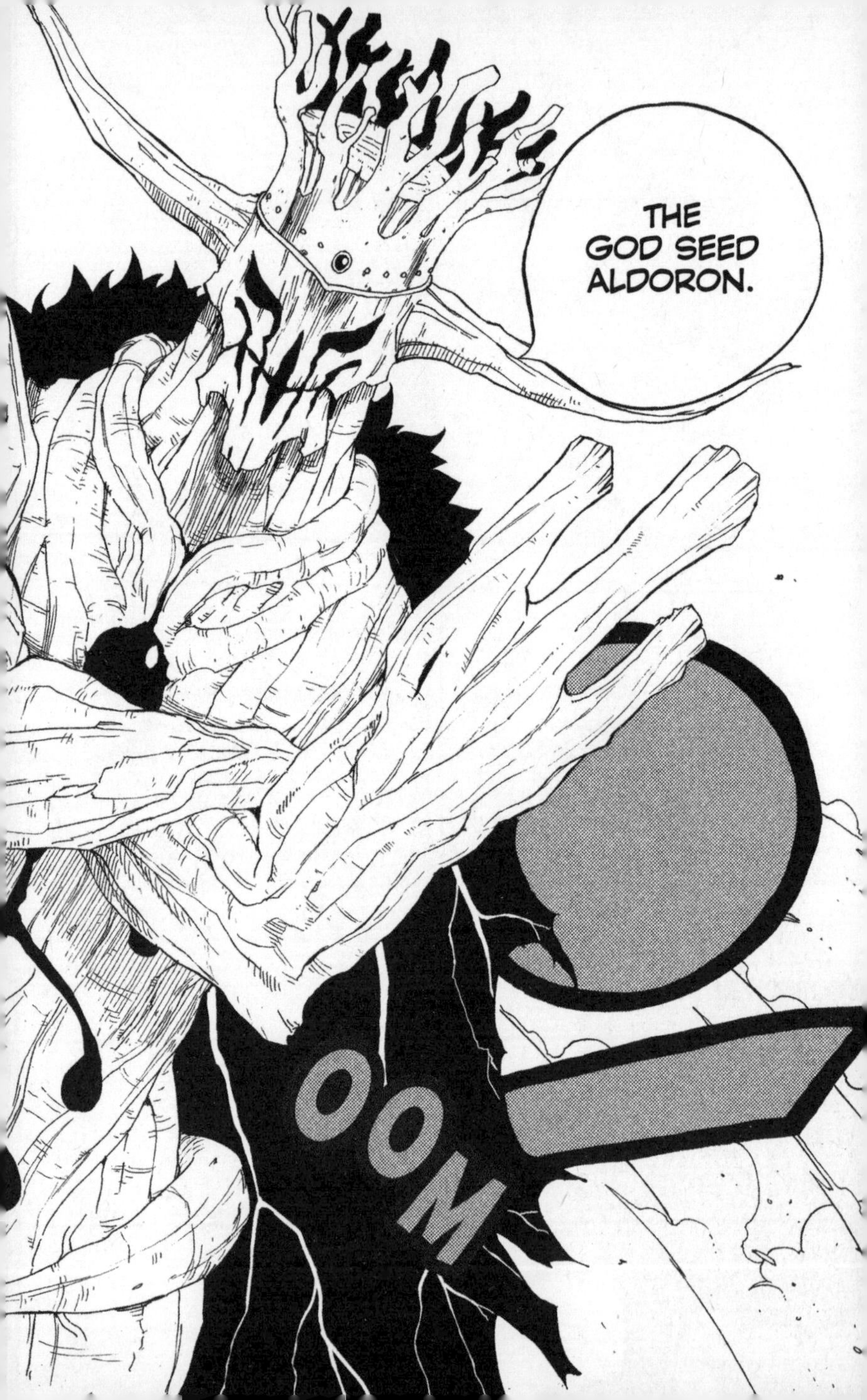
THE GOD SEED ALDORON.
OOM

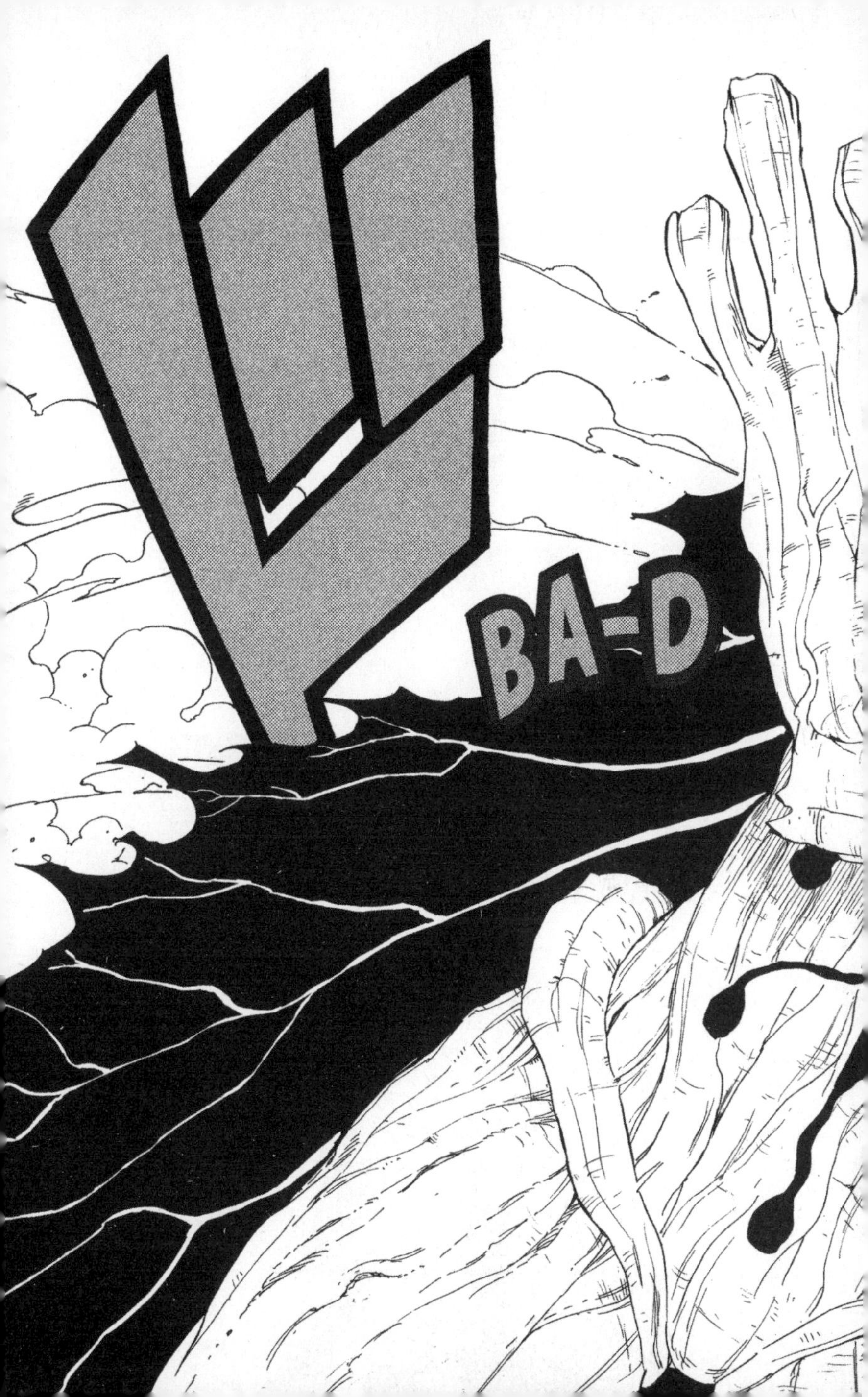
BA-D

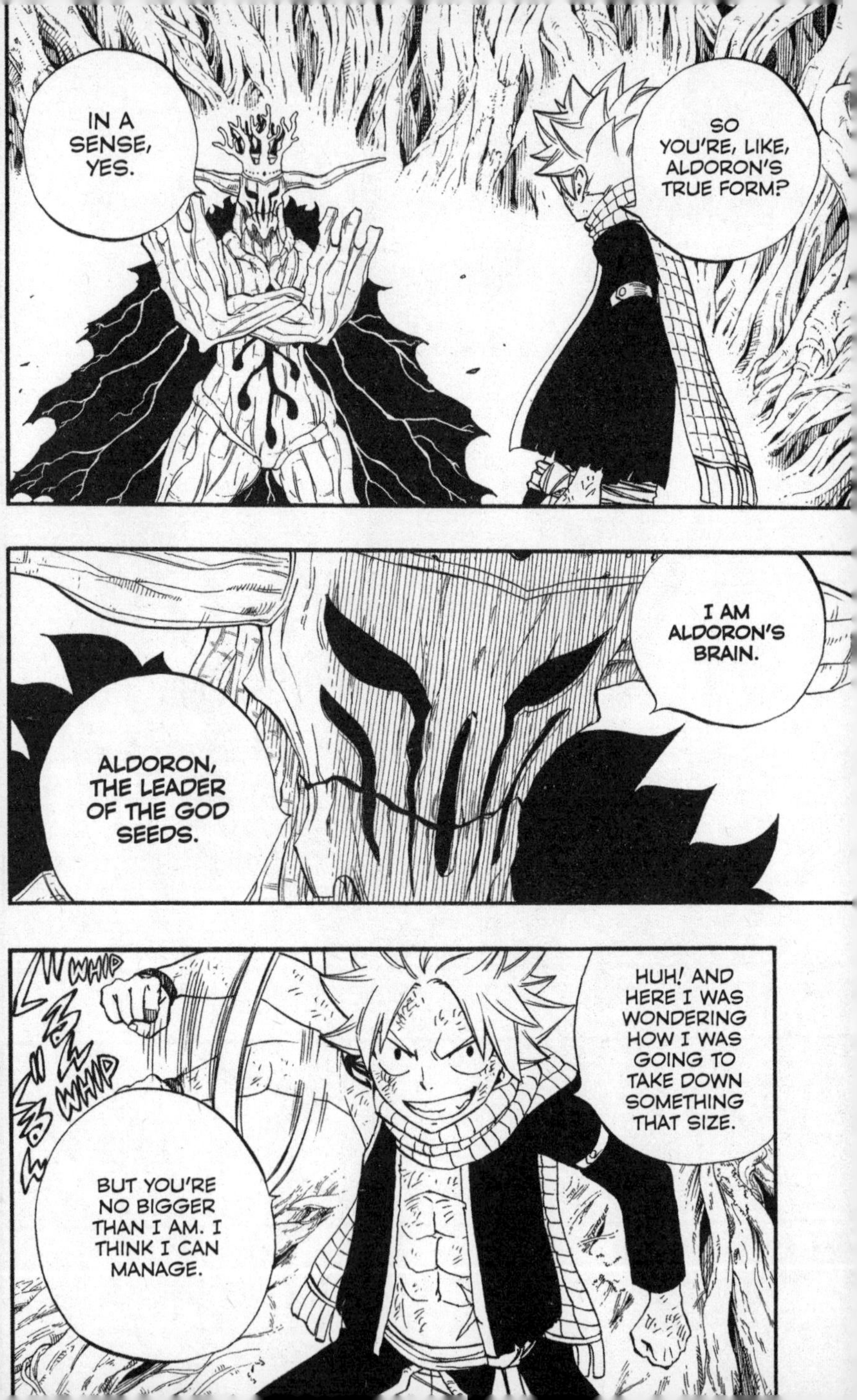
SO YOU'RE, LIKE, ALDORON'S TRUE FORM?
IN A SENSE, YES.
I AM ALDORON'S BRAIN.
ALDORON, THE LEADER OF THE GOD SEEDS.
HUH! AND HERE I WAS WONDERING HOW I WAS GOING TO TAKE DOWN SOMETHING THAT SIZE.
WHIP
WHIP
BUT YOU'RE NO BIGGER THAN I AM. I THINK I CAN MANAGE.

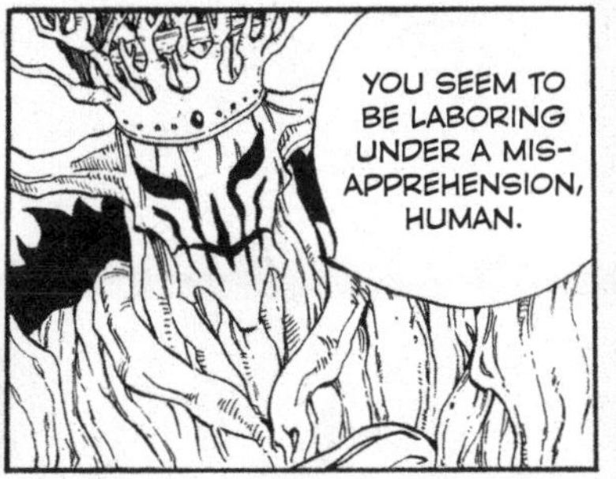
YOU SEEM TO BE LABORING UNDER A MIS-APPREHENSION, HUMAN.

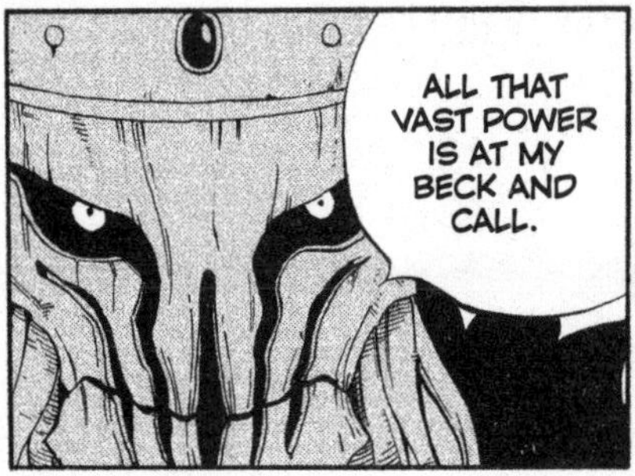
ALL THAT VAST POWER IS AT MY BECK AND CALL.

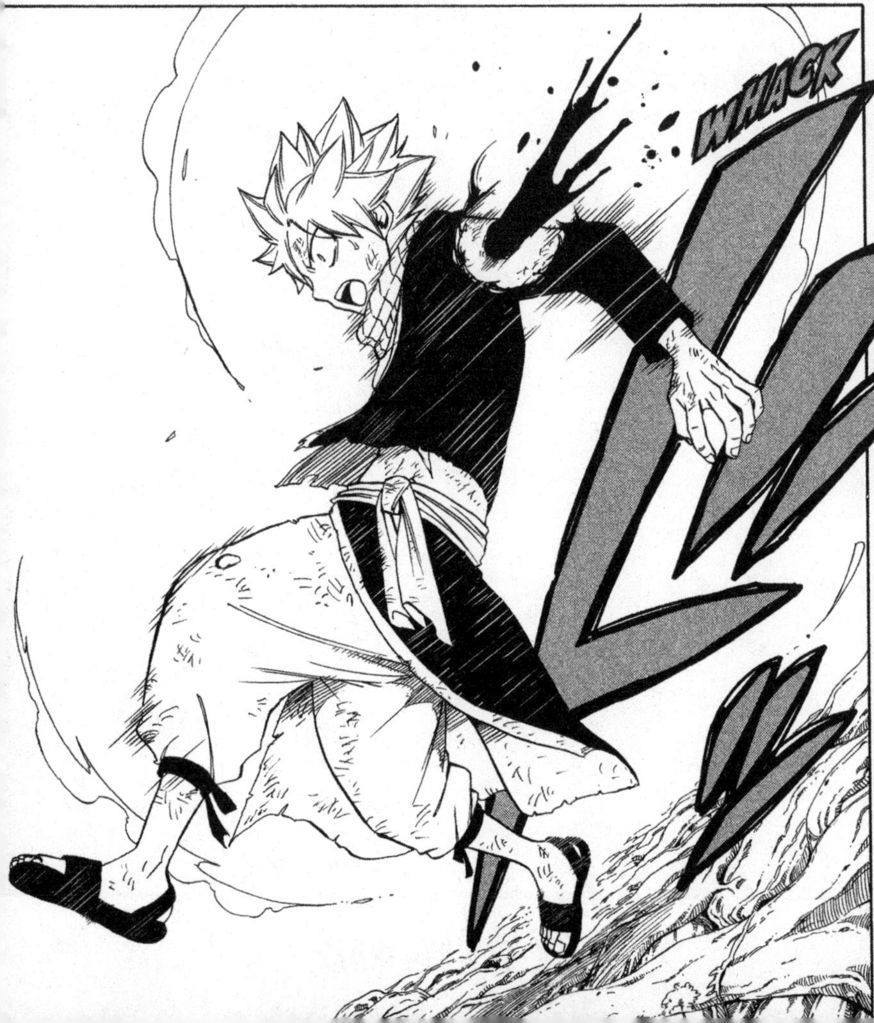
WHACK

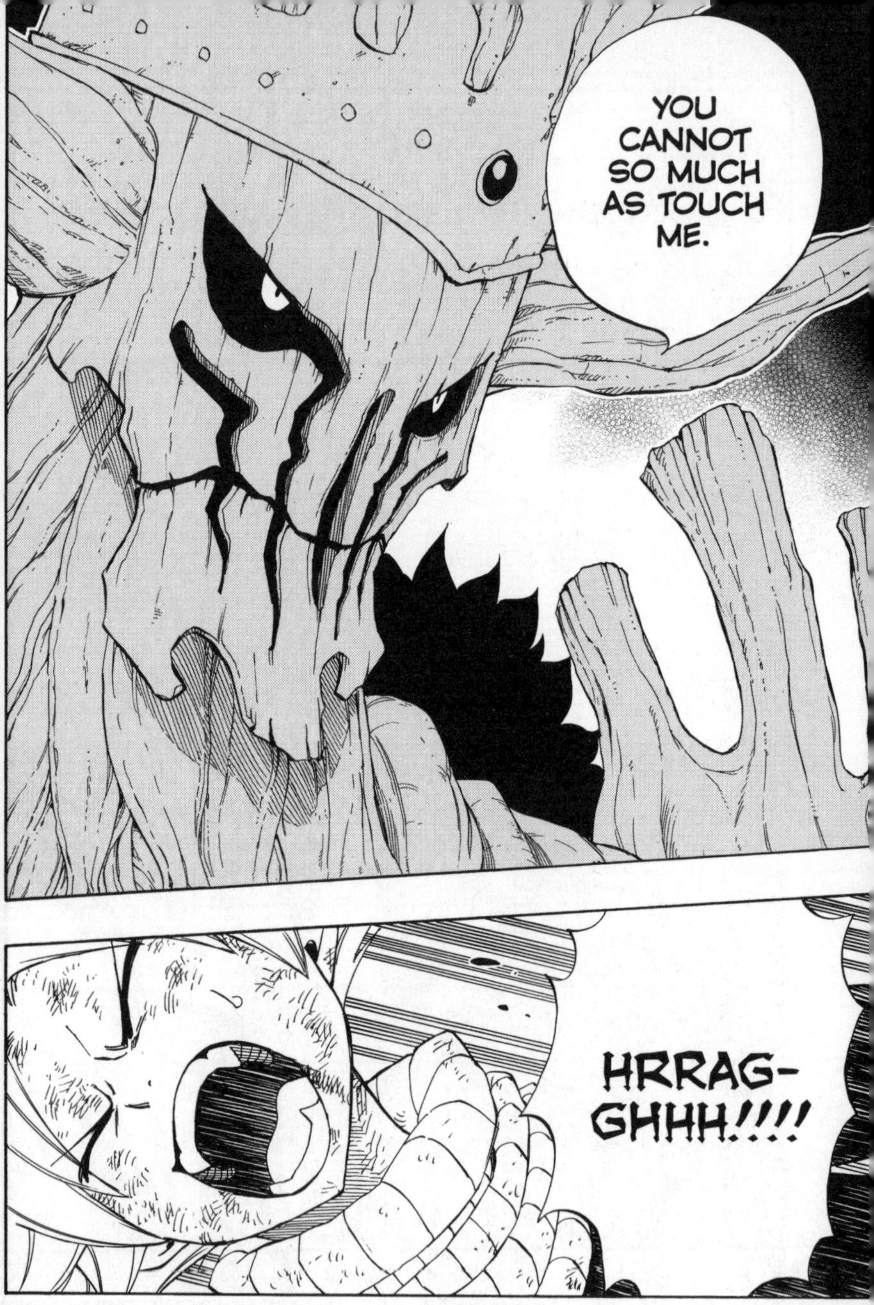
YOU CANNOT SO MUCH AS TOUCH ME.
HRRAG-GHHH!!!!

TO BE CONTINUED

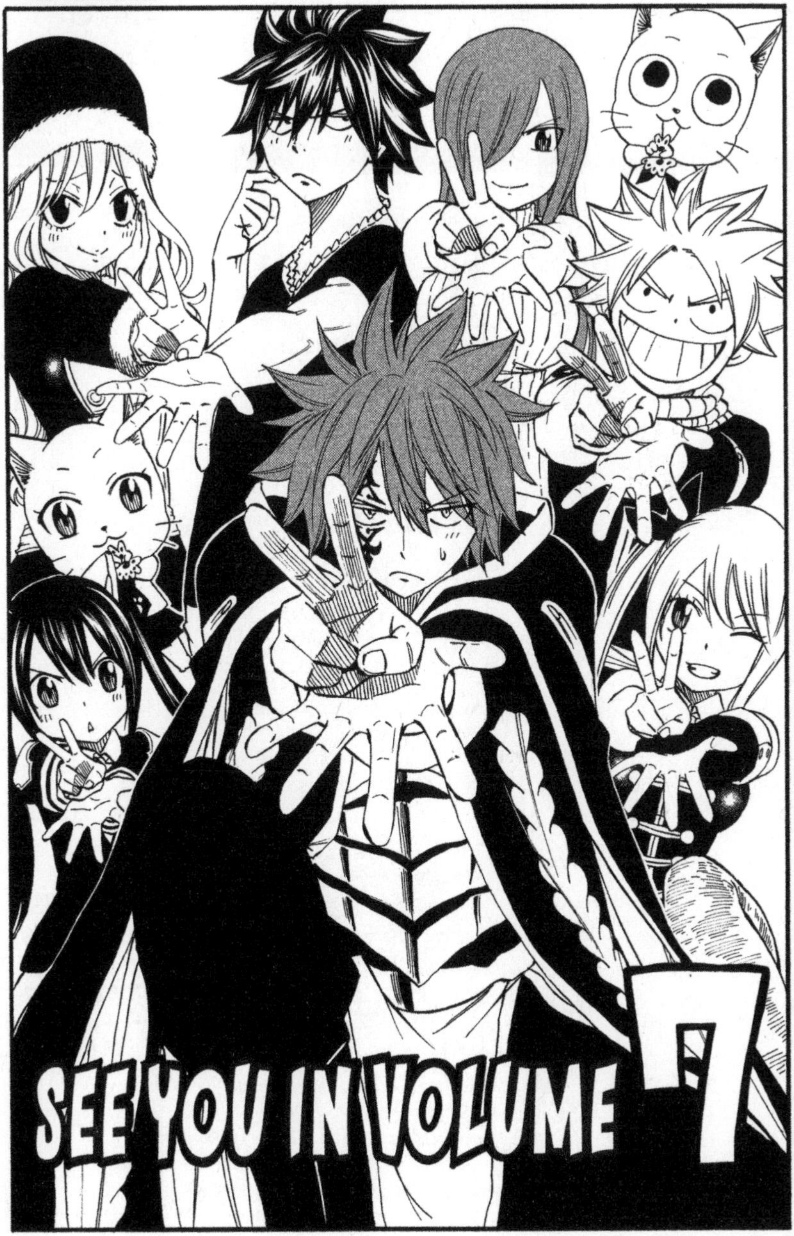
SEE YOU IN VOLUME 7

A Kodansha Comics Trade Paperback Original
FAIRY TAIL: 100 Years Quest 6 copyright © 2020 Hiro Mashima/Atsuo Ueda
English translation copyright © 2020 Hiro Mashima/Atsuo Ueda

Published in the United States by Kodansha Comics, an imprint of
Kodansha USA Publishing, LLC, New York.

Publication rights for this English edition arranged through
Kodansha Ltd., Tokyo.

First published in Japan in 2020 by Kodansha Ltd., Tokyo.

ISBN 978-1-64651-039-9

Original cover design by Hisao Ogawa (Blue in Green)

Printed in **Mexico**.

www.kodansha.**us**

9 8 7 6 5 4 3
Translation: Kevin Steinbach
Lettering: Phil Christie
Editing: David Yoo
Kodansha Comics edition cover design by Phil Balsman

Publisher: Kiichiro Sugawara

Director of publishing services: Ben Applegate
Associate director of operations: Stephen Pakula
Publishing services managing editor: Noelle Webster
Assistant production manager: Emi Lotto, Angela Zurlo